Encyclopedia of German Resistance to the Nazi Movement

Wolfgang Benz
and Walter H. Pehle, Editors

Germans of many persuasions resisted Nazi rule for many different reasons, but until recently political considerations often determined who were regarded as genuine resisters and who were not. The *Encyclopedia of German Resistance to the Nazi Movement* does justice to all facets of the opposition to Hitler and his regime. Approximately seven thousand individuals known by name come under the broad notion of resistance governing this volume. The encyclopedia is divided into three copiously cross-referenced parts, moving from general overviews to highly specific short entries.

In Part One, ten long essays survey the main groups of resisters and opponents of the Nazi regime, including Communists, socialists, Jews, Christians, Jehovah's Witnesses, the military, women, young people, and emigrés. Part Two contains shorter articles on specific topics, groups, and events, ranging from the Confessing Church and the Jewish Chug Chaluzi to military sabotage, desertion, everyday disobedience, and assassination attempts. Part Three consists of 550 brief biographies of the main opponents of National Socialism mentioned.

Encyclopedia of German Resistance to the Nazi Movement

Encyclopedia of German Resistance to the Nazi Movement

Edited by Wolfgang Benz
and Walter H. Pehle

Translated by
Lance W. Garmer

CONTINUUM · NEW YORK

1997

The Continuum Publishing Company
370 Lexington Avenue
New York, NY 10017

Originally published in German under the title *Lexikon des Deutschen Widerstandes* © 1994 by S. Fischer Verlag GmbH, Frankfurt am Main

English translation copyright ©1997 by The Continuum Publishing Company

Printed in the United States of America

Library of Congress Cataloging-in-Publication Data

Lexikon des deutschen Widerstandes. English
   Encyclopedia of German resistance to the Nazi movement / edited by Wolfgang Benz and Walter H. Pehle ; translated by Lance W. Garner.
      p.   cm.
   Includes bibliographical references and index.
   ISBN 0-8264-0945-8
   1. Anti-nazi movement—German—Encyclopedias.   2. Germany—Politics and government—1933–1945—Encyclopedias.   3. National socialism—Encyclopedias.   I. Benz, Wolfgang.   II. Pehle, Walter H., 1941-   III. Title.
DD256.5.L51313   1996
943.086′03—dc20   96–20003

Contents

Preface

Germans resisted National Socialist rule out of political or religious conviction, due to insight into the ruinous nature of the regime, out of horror and shame about the crimes that were committed in the name of the state, out of decency and compassion with the victims, and for other reasons. The memory of the resistance had a secure place in the political landscape of the Federal Republic of Germany (FRG) and of the German Democratic Republic (GDR). Of course, citizens of both German states, which had been founded on the ruins of the German Reich and were burdened with the National Socialist legacy, had quite different views of the resistance.

In the West, commemoration of opposition by conservative members of the military, bureaucratic, and political elites against the Nazi regime was recognized quite early on as a source of identity for postwar society. For this reason, memory of the resistance by the men involved in the July 20, 1944, assassination attempt on Hitler, by the Kreisau Circle, by the Goerdeler Group, by the White Rose, by opposition within the military, and by others was canonized, inveighed at memorial ceremonies, and kept present in political education.

At least during the first couple decades of the FRG, resistance by Communists and leftist intellectual antifascists, the quiet opposition of simple people of social democratic or Catholic conviction, and the intransigence of Jehovah's Witnesses vis-à-vis the regime were barely appreciated, indeed denied. A prominent Social Democrat experienced this as late as the 1970s when he wanted to give the official speech commemorating the anniversary of the July 20, 1944, assassination attempt on Hitler. Herbert Wehner was to deliver the speech, yet, because he had still been a Communist while in the resistance against Nazism, his legitimacy to appear as an opponent of the criminal regime with equal standing alongside officers, bureaucrats, and diplomats of the established resistance was contested. Public controversy recurred when the question arose over whether the men of the National Committee "Free Germany" (NKFD) were to be counted as part of the resistance and whether they might thus have a place of memorial at the main monument in Berlin.

In the GDR, dealing with the Nazi past was marked by a heroization of the Communist resistance, a heroization that was manifest in national places of remembrance and memorial, in historical exhibits and museums, in monuments, and in the dedication of streets and squares. The ritualized concept of antifascism united the German Communist Party (KPD) and individual Communist resistance groups together in a single image in which there had been only a single force opposing National Socialism, that is, the Communist-dominated workers' movement that culminated in the German Socialist Unity Party (SED). The resistance was portrayed in such a way that it became an antifascist mythos, a vehicle for the GDR's self-image as well as a means of remaining apart from the FRG.

The *Encyclopedia of German Resistance to the Nazi Movement* attempts to do justice to all facets of the resistance against Hitler's state, to the Communist group gathered around Anton Saefkow and Franz Jacob as well as to the men gathered around Edgar Jung who came from the reactionary, German nationalist bourgeoisie and rightfully felt that they were partially responsible for Hitler's having gained power, yet who came to the late realization of that responsibility — a realization for which they, like so many opponents within the workers' movement, paid with their lives. Articles are devoted to all of the main organizations and groups of the resistance (from the Anti-Nazi German People's Front to the Uhrig-Römer Group, from the Edelweiss Pirates to the Freedom Action of Bavaria, from the Jewish group Chug Chaluzi to the Catholic Rösch Circle); to important events, such as the July 20, 1944, assassination attempt against Hitler and the assassination attempt at the Bürgerbräu cellar by the lone wolf Georg Elser; to the problems surrounding previously unsuccessful attacks on Hitler; and to the monarchist resistance.

In view of the approximately seven thousand resistance fighters and other persons who are known by name and come under the broad notion of resistance within this encyclopedia, it is not necessary to explain why all opponents of National Socialism are not honored individually.

At first sight, therefore, the names of the "deserters" Wolfgang Abendroth, Alfred Andersch, and Gerhard Zwerenz might be missed, especially since these persons, due to their role as "moral authorities" in postwar society, were regarded by posterity as embodiments of the spirit of resistance against Hitler. The reasons for their actions are honored in the appropriate topical articles.

In part 1, detailed essays offer a broad overview of events. In part 2, these essays are supplemented by articles about specific topics, such as dissidence, everyday disobedience, military sabotage, desertion, and assistance and solidarity. Part 3, which is comprised of short biographies of the opponents of National Socialism mentioned in the book, also serves as an index of names.

It hardly needs to be said that this encyclopedia is based on a broad notion of resistance that must include every form of disobedience and opposition, from quiet obstruction to the attempted murder of a tyrant. The editors' and authors' goal was to do justice to all forces that opposed National Socialist ideology and rule. If, in addition, this reference book could contribute to an overcoming of historical views that are beholden to contrary political goals, and if this book could thereby serve to bring about a reconciliation, then an additional goal would have been reached.

WOLFGANG BENZ
WALTER H. PEHLE

Part I

General Overview

Resistance against National Socialism before 1933

Wolfgang Benz

The National Socialist German Workers' Party (NSDAP) arose in Munich after the end of World War I as a small splinter group of the *völkisch,* radical-right protest movement. Its successes remained limited to a local level until, in 1922–23, it assumed the leadership of the militant "patriotic battle and defense organizations" in Bavaria. The group worked to put an end to the Reich government in Berlin by operating in Munich as a storm unit of a "national revolution." After the failure of the putsch in the fall of 1923, Hitler's movement sank into insignificance. Hitler, who had written his programmatic ideological book *Mein Kampf* during his short imprisonment in Landsberg, nevertheless used the years from 1924 to 1928 to rebuild and to consolidate party organization and to test techniques of agitation and mass manipulation. The NSDAP used parliamentary elections only for propaganda purposes and as a barometer of success. The Reichstag election of 1928 garnered the party 2.6 percent of the votes and twelve mandates.

The rise of the radical political sect to a mass party occurred after the collapse of Müller's Reich government in the spring of 1930. With the end of the Grand Coalition, the Weimar Republic was no longer a parliamentarily governed state; the conservative governments under Brüning, Papen, and Schleicher were supported only on the authority of Hindenburg, the Reich president. The Depression created the background for the further radicalization of public life. In the Reichstag elections of September 1930, the NSDAP received 18.3 percent of the votes and, with 107 mandates, became the second most powerful party. In July 1932, it improved its standing to 37.3 percent of the votes and 230 mandates. It was the most powerful party, but it had thereby also passed its zenith. When elections were again held in November 1932, the NSDAP received 33.1 percent of the votes and 196 mandates. This was still threatening enough for its opponents in the bourgeois-democratic camp and for the workers' parties.

There was resistance to Hitler's antidemocratic, racist, and national-socialist party from the beginning. At the end of the Weimar Republic, such resistance became stronger due to the increasingly unrestrained agitation and growing terror of the Storm Unit (SA), Hitler's civil war army. Yet many voters and members of the bourgeois-democratic parties (such as the Center Party, the German People's Party, and the Bavarian People's Party) were undoubtedly not entirely aware of the menacing danger of National Socialism.

In his poem "Deutschland erwache" (Germany, awake), Kurt Tucholsky asked in 1930, "Germany, don't you see that the Nazi is braiding a funeral wreath for you?" Two years later, he wrote the vicious satire "Hitler und Goethe," in which a school essay serves as a format to show radical rightists' simplemindedness and National Socialist gobbledygook. The comparison, of course, is to Goethe's disadvantage ("In contrast, Hitler is the opponent of the materialistic world order and will do away with it as well as the lost war, unemployment, and the bad weather when he takes power"). At the end of 1931, when Hitler seemed to have reached the threshold of power, Carl von Ossietzky, the other star of the journal *Weltbühne* (World stage), penned his verdict of National Socialism:

> The same dire predicament that makes everyone weak is Hitler's strength. At least National Socialism provides the last hope of those who are starving: cannibalism. In the end, people can still eat one another. That is the terrible attraction of this doctrine of salvation. It is consistent not only with the growing barbaric instincts of an age of progressive misery, but most of all with mental stubbornness and the political ignorance of the sinking petty bourgeoisie who are marching behind Hitler.

An editorial note at the end of the final issue of *Weltbühne* — the tenth issue of its twenty-ninth year, March 7, 1933 — reports that the editor of the publication, Carl von Ossietzky, had been arrested "after the events of February 27." The journal also stated that it could no longer take a position with respect to the election results of March 5, 1933 (which brought the NSDAP 43.9 percent of the votes and its German nationalist allies 8 percent), but that a new chapter in the history of the German republic had begun: "We can indeed now say that we have always raised our voice in warning and that we did not shy away from calling down upon ourselves the cries of incessant grumblers for whom nothing can be done right. As painful as the realization is, we say that our criticism, our warnings, were more than justified."

The earliest and most decisive resistance against Hitler and his National Socialist movement came from intellectuals, artists, and literati. Their weapons were irony and satire, derision and mockery, and finally the pathos of despair. Because of their artistic status, the antifascist graphic works and pictures of George Grosz are legendary, and the photographic collages by John Heartfield are no less so. Both were members of the German Communist Party (KPD) and regarded themselves as fighters in the class struggle and against reactionism and fascism in the Weimar Republic. John Heartfield's media were the political poster and *Arbeiter-Illustrierten-Zeitung* (Worker's illustrated news). Together with Grosz, Heartfield also worked for what was the most important literary and artistic forum for revolutionary leftists until 1933, the Malik Publishing House of his brother Wieland Herzfelde. It was there that Ernst Ottwalt's *Deutschland erwache!* (Germany, awake!), which was hardly heeded because of its unorthodox Marxist viewpoint, appeared in 1932.

In 1923, Ernst Toller, imprisoned in a fortress where he paid for his cooperation with the 1919 Munich soviet council, wrote the comedy *Der entfesselte Wotan* (Wotan unbound), in which Adolf Hitler figures as an obsessed barber. The piece, which had its premiere in Berlin in 1926, was unsuccessful. After the Munich putsch fiasco, people no longer took Hitler seriously or did not yet take him seriously again. Toller's anticipation of the career of the führer-to-be was visionary. Paul Kampffmeyer's work *Faschismus in Deutschland* (Fascism in Germany) appeared very early as well, in 1923.

In his novel portraying contemporary times, *Erfolg: Drei Jahre Geschichte einer Provinz* (Success: Three years in the history of a province), which was published in 1930, Lion Feuchtwanger painted a minutely detailed picture of the time's political landscape in Bavaria. In the book, Hitler, as Rupert Kutzner, the leader of the "true Germans," is portrayed as being no less ridiculous than dangerous. Hitler's rise, the attempted putsch of 1923, the breast-beating of the 1924 trial, and supporters' enthusiasm and approval appear as a regrettable and repellent conglomeration of nationalistic bravado, disorientation, and longing for a sound world, as preached by a street comedy actor whose gestures are rehearsed and who, driven by ambition and a sense of his own mission, is a cowardly braggart: "Talking was the meaning of his existence." Yet the murder of the servant girl Amalie Sandhuber, who, as a supposed traitor, becomes a victim of a National Socialist political assassination, is also a part of Feuchtwanger's picture.

The academic Emil Julius Gumbel, who began work as an unsalaried university lecturer on statistics at the University of Heidelberg in 1923 and was known as a pacifist and contentious journalist, dealt with radical-rightist murderers from the advent of the Weimar Republic. As a member of the German League for Human Rights, a resolute republican, and a champion of reconciliation with France, he wrote about extreme rightist underground organizations, about the Black Reichswehr, and repeatedly about the number of "political assassinations." In 1931, in cooperation with the League for Human Rights, he put together a pamphlet entitled "Lasst Köpfe rollen: Faschistische Morde 1924–1931"

(Off with their heads: Fascist murders from 1924 to 1931). The title was a quote from Nazi propaganda. In twenty-three pages, the pamphlet lists and describes sixty-three murders committed by the National Socialists up to 1931. Gumbel's conclusion was that "these numbers run approximately parallel to the growth of the National Socialist movement, very slowly from 1924 until 1929, then all of a sudden quickly. In these bloody acts, fascism reveals its true face. It shows the German people the methods of which it will avail itself should it only come to power."

Gumbel, who had long since incurred the displeasure of the bourgeois right, became a victim of his resistance even before the transfer of power to the NSDAP. After many riots by the extreme rightist student movement, a disciplinary proceeding was held against him because of a pacifist statement he had made in the summer of 1932, and his permission to teach was rescinded on August 5. Gumbel became one of the first emigrés.

Things went even worse for the philosopher Theodor Lessing, who, as a vocal leftist, pacifist, and fighter against rightist extremism, essentially lost his position as university lecturer at the Technical College of Hannover as early as 1926 due to his criticism of Hindenburg. In the spring of 1933, Lessing fled into exile in Prague. At the end of August, he was murdered there by National Socialists.

Pacifists were marked as opponents by Hitler's supporters from the beginning and thus were numerous on the lists of people whose citizenship was revoked when the National Socialists came to power. A number of these pacifists had fought on the barricades of journalism against Hitler's movement, as in the cases of Kurt Hiller, Berthold Jacob, and Helmut von Gerlach. Constanze Hallgarten stood in the middle of the "pacifist scandal" in Munich in 1932 when, at a large demonstration of women who were rallying for peace, she put marauding Nazis in their place. Just a short time later, she, like most representatives of German pacifism, was fleeing Hitler as an emigré.

Many forms of resistance against National Socialist ideology came from the bourgeois, liberal left wing as well. The most prominent representative was no doubt Theodor Heuss, who — like Reinhold Maier, a fellow member of their party's cadre — became silent after the "seizure of power" and remained in "inner emigration" after the fateful approval of the Enabling Act in March 1933. Heuss spoke out early against the NSDAP's anti-Semitism. In a speech before the Reichstag as a representative of the State Party in May 1932, he locked horns with Göring and criticized National Socialist ideas about foreign policy. His book *Hitlers Weg: Eine historisch-politische Studie über den Nationalsozialismus* (Hitler's way: A historical and political study of National Socialism) was published at the beginning of 1932. It was the first of eight printings, and the book was translated into Swedish, Dutch, and Italian. Heuss wanted to make a decidedly distanced, dispassionate contribution to the discussion about National Socialism and wanted to discuss argumentatively rather than polemically the historical and psychological preconditions of Hitler's movement. To be sure, Heuss the liberal political journalist lacked the imagination to conceive of the brutality and bloodthirstiness by means of which the NSDAP's program and more were eventually to be made a reality. Nevertheless, his book contains sentences such as, "The destruction of Jewish cemeteries must deeply affect a community in which, contrary to all of the babble about the individualistic, dissipating power of things Jewish, the family signifies a lively connection to the past as well. It besoils us all. We bear a stain ever since such cowardly and irreverent things have become possible in Germany."

The National Socialists were more irritated by another opponent, the liberal journalist Konrad Heiden, than by Heuss. In 1932, Heiden published a book, *Geschichte des Nationalsozialismus: Die Karriere einer Idee* (The history of National Socialism: The career of an idea), that was effective as a well-researched and impartially analytic polemic. The author, a former correspondent and editor of the *Frankfurter Zeitung* (Frankfurt times) and a contributor to the *Vossische Zeitung*, emigrated in April 1933. With the book *Geburt des Dritten Reiches* (Birth of the Third Reich [1934]) and his writings "Hitler rast" (Hitler is mad [1934]) and "Sind die Nazis Sozialisten?" (Are the Nazis socialists? [1934]), he continued his resistance against National Socialism in the Saarland. Heiden was also the author of the first large and critical biography of Hitler, which, written in the spirit of resistance, was published in two volumes in Zurich in 1936–37, with English, American, and French editions appearing simultaneously.

Ernst Niekisch, a former Social Democrat and the hub of an elite opposition movement with national-conservative and national-Bolshevist elements, also published his admonition *Hitler: Ein deutsches Verhängnis* (Hitler: A German misfortune) in the critical year 1932. Niekisch, whose journal *Widerstand: Blätter für national-revolutionäre Politik* (Resistance: Notes for national-revolutionary politics) had been outlawed since 1934, was sentenced to life imprisonment in 1937. The Red Army liberated him in 1945.

At the head of the liberal *Berliner Tageblatt* (Berlin daily), Theodor Wolff was among staunch defenders of the Weimar Republic. The paper's style was to argue intellectually by means of innuendo and irony. It was below the editorial staff's level to deal with the NSDAP's bellicose anti-Semitism. Its positions, however, were unmistakably defined. On June 8, 1930, Theodor Wolff wrote about National Socialism and National Socialists:

No crafted phrase, no vague ideology can conceal the fact that, with their screaming for revolutionary violence and their racial bating, they are inciting crudeness, stupidity, and the basest motives of the mob and are pushing for criminal explosions. If one could do a study, one would find among these wandering prophets of National Socialism, who are pampered by old wives and patronized by uneducated industrialists, not a few brains of pathologic interest, and the billowing steam that comes out of them extends over a mass that reacts to any narcotic. The befuddled, who understand nothing about theoretical issues, grab for an actual revolver and start shooting.

Theodor Wolff, who tried in vain to win over Thomas Mann as an arbiter of reason and agitator against Hitler during the final months of the Weimar Republic (the writer, still adverse to such things, was to have stood up as a speaker of a "Republican cartel"), became an emigré in the spring of 1933. His flight from Hitler ended in 1943 in Nice, where he was handed over to the Gestapo by the Italian occupation police.

At the May 10, 1933, book burning staged by the regime as an "action against the non-German spirit," Theodor Wolff, together with Georg Bernhard, the other great liberal journalistic opponent of the NSDAP, had been damned by name in one of the "fire speeches." A student yelled about being "against foreign journalism of democratic-Jewish making [and] for conscientious cooperation in working to build the nation," and the writings of Wolff and Bernhard then landed on the pyre.

The last of the "fire speeches" was devoted to especially hated journalists, who had to pay terribly for their early resistance: one, in exile in Sweden, saw no exit other than suicide; the other was run down to the point of physical ruin in concentration camps. "Against audacity and impudence, for respect and regard for the immortal spirit of the German *Volk!* Flames, consume as well the writings of Tucholsky and Ossietzky!"

This verdict was also intended for journalists such as Franz Pfempfert, whose journal *Die Aktion* (The task) put up indefatigable resistance until 1932, or Leopold Schwarzschild and his *Das Tage-Buch* (The diary). *Die neue Rundschau* (The new review), Fritz Küster's *Das andere Deutschland* (The other Germany), Erich Schairer's *Sonntags-Zeitung* (Sunday times), and the *Welt am Montag* (World on Monday), which was headed by Helmut von Gerlach until 1931, also distinguished themselves no less in the fight against National Socialism.

Among conservative opponents of National Socialism, the Munich journalist Fritz Michael Gerlich was one of the most prolific. A member of the pan-Germanic movement during World War I and later a fervent opponent of Marxism and communism, the influential journalist began fighting against Hitler and his followers in 1923. With the support of Catholic circles, he began publishing the journal *Der Gerade Weg* (The straight path) in 1930. The journal, supported by its own news agency, published memoranda from the National Socialist movement with the intention of exposing its criminal character. Gerlich was arrested by the SA in March 1933, was repeatedly mistreated, and finally was a victim of the murder spree of June 30, 1934. In July 1932, he published the assessment that "National Socialism...means enmity with neighboring nations, rule by violence at home, civil war, ethnic war. National Socialism means lies, hate, fratricide and boundless danger!"

Public opposition to the NSDAP, which was grappling for power, ended as a matter of necessity on January 30, 1933, with foreign or inner emigration, that is, with flight from Germany or quiet retreat into the apolitical. It was hardly ever possible to save republican-democratic structures from the NSDAP's grasp on power and to transform them into resistance activities. However, one instance of this is the *Strassmann Group, which had its roots in the activity of a political circle of friends in Hamburg. This was the "October 3rd Club," formed in 1924 by seven young people — uncompromising democrats and republicans who allied themselves with the left wing of the German Social Democratic Party (SPD) and the German Democratic Party (DDP). Two members were Gustav Dahrendorf and Theodor Haubach, who later became prominent in the resistance within the *Goerdeler and *Kreisau Circles. Ernst Strassmann, a lawyer, and Hans Robinsohn, an economist and businessman, played important roles in the Hamburg DDP.

The founding of the club on October 3, 1924 — the name was not a programmatic reference to a particular historical or political date — occurred due to vexation with the political atmosphere and the "quiet and legal development of law" in the Weimar Republic. The Kapp-Lüttwitz Putsch of 1920, the murder of Walther Rathenau in 1922, the Hitler Putsch of 1923, as well as a Hamburg milieu and political romanticism had given impetus to the organization of the circle of friends. The idea of turning Hamburg into a republican bulwark that would likewise offer haven to a democratic Reich government fleeing from putsch instigators also played some role.

According to the view of the club founders, "republican-democratic structures" had remained intact after the Kapp Putsch, "but a real republic that could be attacked from the right no longer existed." The club — which defined itself as a workers' group of republican, actively democratic young people who were active in their parties and who, as a circle of friends, wanted to have an effect on those parties — had elitist characteristics and was also not without a conspiratorial tinge. In

1926, the club had its most spectacular success when it blocked an empowerment law to Article 48 of the Reich constitution that had been planned by the Reich Ministry of the Interior. The draft law had made its way to the club through discreet channels, and several members subjected it to fundamental criticism in a memorandum. The draft law and the memorandum were presented by the October Club at a press conference in Berlin. All news agencies and the major newspapers were present and reported it. The outcry was considerable, and the Reich Ministry of the Interior had to deny that it knew anything about it. The law, which would have given the military authorities greater powers, was not passed.

The club, which had just under one hundred members at its peak, could not withstand the frictions of its members' partisan commitments for long. In 1928, dispute over the panzer cruiser A divided club members as well. Party discipline and ideology brought several members into unresolvable conflicts. Papen's coup d'état of July 20, 1932, which was the beginning of the visible end of the Weimar Republic, then again gave reason to question resistance activities whose goal was the destruction of the republic. As radical democrats and liberals, Ernst Strassmann and Hans Robinsohn did not come around to the party line of the DDP, nor were they prepared to adapt themselves to circumstances after January 30, 1933. By the spring of 1934, the Berlin Regional Court judge and the Hamburg businessman came to terms with one another. With civil courage and pugnacity, they were determined to continue against National Socialism the resistance that had begun in 1919 against the first republic's tendency toward restoration.

As a writer and stage actor, Erich Mühsam, an idealistic anarchist aloof from partisan political attachments, called upon the SPD and KPD for a common fight against Hitler. In his journal *Fanal* (Beacon), which he had founded in 1926 as a forum for the fight against the politics and legal system of a republic that was drifting toward the right, he called for a united front of all antifascist forces: "The only power that would be able to hinder Hitler's seizure of power is the combined will of German workers who have not been disarrayed by National Socialism." As a warning to the SPD and the KPD in 1929, Mühsam followed up this appeal, which was as anticipatory as it was fruitless, with a vision that became a reality in 1933. He wrote that a terrible time would come "when the dance of the Third Reich begins, when the dissolution of all workers' coalitions is decreed by a Hitler, a Frick, or someone else, when summary shootings, pogroms, lootings, and mass arrests represent the law in Germany."

During the night of the Reichstag fire, Mühsam was arrested and, after months of mistreatment, was murdered in Oranienburg concentration camp.

The rise of National Socialism was also resisted by legal means. Without being a member of a party, Hans Achim Litten, a young lawyer in Berlin, became active as a counselor within the German Red Aid for workers who were brought to court for political reasons. Litten resisted National Socialism by acquiring mandates against it. In the "Felseneck Case," 150 SA men had attacked a small private garden and left two dead. He reconstructed the course of events and brought indictments of at least five National Socialists. In November 1930, the notorious Berlin SA Unit 33 had attacked a workers' bar, the Edenpalast, and seriously injured four men. Litten represented them as a coplaintiff and had Hitler, as the accountable head of the NSDAP, brought to the witness stand, where he vigorously put him on the defensive. Litten intended to show that the SA's acts of violence were not excesses of its lower ranks and that violence as a means for the attainment of the party leadership's political goals was not only sanctioned but planned. Litten succeeded in forcing Hitler to distance himself publicly from Goebbels, the Berlin gauleiter. It was a spectacular case in Litten's legal activity but was by no means the only one of its sort.

The National Socialists took terrible revenge for the embarrassing cross-examination of Hitler. During the night of February 28, 1933, Litten was arrested. For the following five years until his death in Dachau, he was in prisons and concentration camps.

Before Hitler's NSDAP assumed power, the driving forces of resistance to it within the workers' movement were the movement's ideological counterposition as well as partisan political competition (see *Socialist Resistance and *Communist Resistance). Of course, the forces of the SPD and KPD were to a large extent tied up within the confines of their own positions: that is, the SPD kept guard against the left, and the KPD fought against the Social Democrats, whom they denounced as "social fascists." The leftist groups between these two (see *International Socialist Combat League, *New Beginning, and *German Socialist Workers' Party) were constant opponents of the NSDAP, yet their numerical strength was minimal. The KPD's intransigent opposition to the parliamentary democratic system necessarily included Social Democrats. Social Democrats, on the other hand, were hindered from effective resistance activities (such as general strikes) due to the strictly legal course of action that they chose and due to constitutional breaches perpetrated by the government, such as Papen's July 20, 1932, coup d'état against Prussia.

The electoral success of the National Socialists in the fall of 1930 led to the resuscitation of the militant political organization Reichsbanner Schwarz Rot Gold (Reichsbanner Black Red Gold), which had been founded in 1924 for the self-protection of democratic leftists. Officially nonpartisan, the organization was controlled almost entirely by the SPD, which provided nearly four-fifths of the approximately three million members who fought for control of the streets against the SA, the Stahlhelm, and other civilian armies. Otto Hörsing, the mayor of Magdeburg, was its founder and federal chairman until 1932; he was succeeded by Karl Höltermann, a Social Democratic journalist and World War I volunteer who was born in 1894. The "Defensive Formations" (Schufo) of the actual "unit" of the Reichsbanner were comprised of members, upwards of four hundred thousand strong, who had been active in the civil war–like clashes during the final phase of the Weimar Republic and had engaged in its defense against extremists from the right and left.

After Papen's coup d'état in July 1932, the Reichsbanner became increasingly complacent. Against a rightist bourgeois coalition with Hitler, the Iron Front was founded in December 1931 as a "bulwark of human bodies" against the threat of fascism. Led by Höltermann, the forces of the SPD, the Free Trade Unions, the Reichsbanner, and workers' athletic leagues were to unite in a republican alliance. However, only organizations of the liberal leftist State Party (DDP) joined. Detachments of the Schufo formed the core of the Iron Front. Although fundamentally in opposition to the NSDAP, political Catholicism, with its "popular front," maintained its distance from the Iron Front. Legal wrangling and indecision within the leadership thwarted actions by the Reichsbanner and the Iron Front against Hitler's assumption of power. However, resistance activities were repeatedly called for until the spring of 1933.

Within the SPD, a group of young intellectual Reichstag representatives were critical of the party leadership and actively engaged in fighting for the republic. They were called the Militant Socialists. Among them were Carlo Mierendorff, Theodor Haubach, and Kurt Schumacher. By attacking Goebbels and the NSDAP in a speech before the Reichstag on February 23, 1932, the young Schumacher stepped forward from the back rows of the junior members of the Reichstag. Even as the leader of the Württemberg Veterans' Association, he had drawn the anger of the National Socialists. He had to spend nearly the entire duration of the National Socialists' rule in a concentration camp. In the Reichstag in February 1932, he told the NSDAP that he refused "to fight on this level of moral and intellectual depravity and raunchiness. . . . The National Socialists' entire agitation is a constant appeal to man's cowardice."

Bibliography

Belke, Ingrid. "Publizisten warnen vor Hitler: Frühe Analysen des National-sozialismus." In *Conditio Judaica: Judentum, Antisemitismus und deutsch-sprachige Literatur vom Ersten Weltkrieg bis 1933/1938*. Edited by Hans Otto Horch and Horst Denkler. Tübingen, 1993.

Holl, Karl, and Wolfram Wette, eds. *Pazifismus in der Weimarer Republik: Beiträge zur historischen Friedensforschung.* Paderborn, 1981.

Mommsen, Hans. *Die verspielte Freiheit: Der Weg der Republik von Weimar in den Untergang, 1918 bis 1933.* Berlin, 1989.

Rohe, Karl. *Das Reichsbanner Schwarz Rot Gold: Ein Beitrag zur Geschichte und Struktur der politischen Kampfverbände zur Zeit der Weimarer Republik.* Düsseldorf, 1966.

Serke, Jürgen. *Die verbrannten Dichter: Berichte, Texte, Bilder einer Zeit.* Weinheim/Basel, 1977.

Winkler, Heinrich August. *Weimar 1918–1933: Die Geschichte der ersten deutschen Demokratie.* Munich, 1993.

Communist Resistance

Beatrix Herlemann

Toward the end of the Weimar Republic, the German Communist Party (KPD) became the third strongest party. In the Reichstag elections in November 1932, it garnered nearly six million votes, or 16.9 percent of votes cast; in the same election the SPD received 20.7 percent, and the NSDAP tallied 33.1 percent. At the end of 1932, the KPD's registered members numbered approximately 360,000. Roughly 250,000 of its primarily unemployed members — in April 1932, 85 percent of all members were without an income — still paid their party dues. The party also claimed a large number of sympathizers in numerous subsidiary and affiliated organizations. As a section of the Communist International, the party had pursued an ultra-leftist policy since 1929, a policy that the SPD viewed as its primary opponent and the "twin brother of fascism" (the so-called "socialist-fascist thesis"), with whom there could be no cooperation. In spite of the sharpest political differences, the NSDAP and KPD had a sporadic affinity that resulted from this irreconcilable opposition, the most spectacular case being the 1931 plebiscite against the Social Democratic–led Prussian government.

However, due to the great number of dangers in a situation that was increasingly resembling a civil war, the party leadership prepared for a period in which the party would be banned and for the requisite underground activity. The leaders' ideas were marked by their own memories of the short period in 1923–24 during which the party was banned after the unsuccessful attempt to revolt in Hamburg, by the experiences of those who had been persecuted under Bismarck's Socialist Law, and by the example of the Bolshevists who had been hard pressed by the czarist Ochrana. The expected ban was seen as a sign of a growingly revolutionary situation that the party would, if necessary, transform into a victory even from the underground.

As a consequence of their plan for the continuation of the party as an underground mass organization, leaders on the various levels, from precinct to local chapter, had been rehearsing for the actual event since the end of the 1920s. They rehearsed conversion to groups consisting of three people; made arrangements for hiding mimeographs, paper, and membership files; encouraged functionaries to find hiding places; and entrusted their military unit with appropriate special tasks. At this time, though, an overcentralization that was already crippling party life, combined with strong tendencies toward bureaucratization and a somewhat excessive and pointless activism, made this organizational plan one of many. In addition, an unquestioned general certainty of victory and the belief in their own strength made for a relativization of the danger.

Indeed, hardly anyone in the entire organized workers' movement seriously believed until January 1933 that the strong, disciplined German workers' movement, admired in the entire world for its social successes, could have the same fate as, say, their Italian comrades, who had been oppressed for years by Mussolini. Thus, all the greater was the shock in the spring of 1933 when a barbaric campaign of terror befell leadership cadres as well as simple members, ruthlessly excluded the party from public life, and imprisoned the chairman, Ernst Thälmann, in the first days of March.

Still, neither the leadership nor wide segments within the membership saw an uncontested defeat in the debacle that they had suffered. Rather, they agreed with the Social Democrats, trade unions, and even bourgeois parties in their assessment that Hitler, like his predecessors, would be in power for only a short interlude. In contrast to the others, though, they decided to oppose him energetically in order to stake a claim on what would come after him.

First, however, gaps made by the mass arrests after the Reichstag fire and by the Storm Unit (SA) Kommandos' campaign of revenge had to be filled in, and interrupted contacts between the leadership in Berlin with regions in Silesia, Saxony, and central Germany had to be reestablished — a task that could be done only with difficulty in the face of the daily losses sustained from the beginning of the underground struggle. In June, for example, only one-half of the roughly forty participants who had attended the already underground meeting of the central committee in the Sporthaus Ziegenhals near Berlin on February 7, 1933 (at which Ernst Thälmann elaborated the new strategy that included all forms of resistance from demonstrations and constantly spreading strikes up to a general strike), were still free. Seventeen of twenty-eight regional leaders had been arrested, as well as at least one-third of the eighty-one Reichstag representatives and sixty-three Prussian state representatives who had been elected on March 5, 1933. At the beginning of July, Fritz Heckert, the German representative of Comintern, had to acknowledge that the party had already lost substantial parts of its midlevel functionaries during the first weeks of March, insofar as some eleven thousand Communists had been arrested. Yet this number must be seen as too low, since, according to Gestapo reports, roughly eight thousand Communists had been imprisoned during March and April in the Ruhr district alone.

Under these circumstances, the politburo decided to set up three of its members — Wilhelm Pieck, Franz Dahlem, and Wilhelm Florin — in Paris in order to take care of tasks that could no longer be dealt with in Germany. The remaining four members — Walter Ulbricht, John Schehr, Hermann Schubert, and Fritz Schulte — stayed in Berlin to manage matters domestically.

Insofar as anything could be done, the traditional tripartite structure (with political, organizational, and agitational components) was maintained at all levels, from the factory and city district level, to the subregional level, and up to the regional level. Eight new supraregions had been created in December 1932. In concert with the politburo, so-called superior advisers were each supposed to lead several regions. The regular payment of party dues with receipt stickers was maintained, a practice that became a curse for many a member.

The political struggle was waged primarily with propagandistic writings. Countless flyers about current events, small-format newspapers continuing in the style of outlawed local, regional, and national papers, factory newspapers, and leaflets were produced and distributed under the greatest dangers and at constantly changing sites. *Die Rote Fahne* (The red banner) and other key papers still appeared from 1933 until 1935. Isolated actions such as chantings in the backyards of houses in Berlin, hoisting red banners on chimneys and water towers, or cutting the main electric cable at one of Hitler's speeches in Stuttgart were supposed to attest to the party's survival, and secret May Day celebrations in the smallest of circles in remote places were supposed to encourage members to hold out.

At no time did anyone think seriously about an armed uprising, despite what repeated National Socialist news reports about discoveries of Communist weapons caches in the spring of 1933 would suggest. "Propaganda as a weapon"; enlightenment about National Socialist actions, terror, demagoguery, murder, and torture in the hellish concentration camps of the SA; enlightenment about the elimination of all hard-won rights and social gains of the working class; and practical instructions on how to resist and on how to behave during interrogation and in court — these were the means with which the heavily decimated party sought to fight the National Socialist regime from the underground. More and more often, printed materials were smuggled over borders, the production and distribution of these materials being carried out in bases that had been set up in regions of Czechoslovakia, Switzerland, the Saar, the Netherlands, and Denmark that lay close to the border. It was from there that the now-famous *Braunbuch über Reichstagsbrand und Hitlerterror* (Brown book about the Reichstag fire and Hitler's terror), as well as the eyewitness report *Mörderlager Dachau* (Murderers' camp Dachau), written by Hans Beimler after his successful escape from

Dachau, came to Germany in great number, disguised as Reclam editions (Reclam is a German publishing house) mixed with works by
Schiller and Goethe.

The border bases became relay stations for underground activists
seeking advice as well as for refugees who were being tracked by the
Gestapo. When there was an acute threat in an area, the nearest directorate often did not have time to make a decision about whether
individuals should emigrate or hide in the country, though the party had
stipulated that the directorates should control such decisions. According
to the leadership, an antifascist fighter was to go abroad only when it
was no longer possible for him or her to stay within the country. Party
strategists refused "to recognize as sufficient reason for emigration the
fact that someone did not like things in the Third Reich." And a person who was recognized as a refugee and modestly cared for by the
Red Aid in the exile country was also subject to the party's emigration offices, which had sprung up in nearly every country that had a
border with Germany. Since, according to Comintern, the right of asylum in the Soviet Union "was not a type of personal life insurance,"
but rather, as the *Rundschau über Politik, Wirtschaft und Arbeiterbewegung* (Review of politics, economics, and the workers' movement)
unequivocally announced in April 1935, served to restore the persecuted
fighters bodily and mentally in such a way "that they could again hold
their own on the front of the class struggle," emigrés were examined in
the Soviet Union and elsewhere for their redeployment in the German
underground.

In accordance with the motto "Emigration as battle station," those
persons who were in too great a danger and who had emigrated had to
assist the resistance back in Germany. They served as couriers, helped
in the examination of arriving refugees, gathered news from deep within
Germany, and brought contraband by the hundreds of pounds over the
borders via transport columns. This helped fill the gaps in the underground groups' production of printed materials, gaps that had been
created by the continued arrests. This type of work had been decimated
because it was precisely the production and distribution of underground
printed materials that had given the Gestapo sufficient information for
the discovery of entire groups and networks. Between 1933 and 1936,
mass legal proceedings before provincial courts in the entire Third Reich
sent thousands of Communists to prisons and penitentiaries for years
for the production, publication, failed registration, and channeling of
prohibited writings.

Although underground work doubtlessly strengthened the activists'
consciousness and will to hold out, and thereby simultaneously fostered identity and organization, the desired goal was nevertheless not
reached. Mass circulation of printed materials did not have a broad

effect. The wide-scale dissemination of flyers in houses, streets, and squares, tossed from bicycles or from garret windows of public buildings, brought notice yet did not provide for the growth of a Communist opposition movement. Under the particular conditions of the Third Reich, the nearly irreconcilable contradiction between clandestine work and open agitation became the fate of almost every resistance group and relentlessly decimated the Communist resistance.

Thus, the party leadership endured an extremely painful, sacrificial learning process during the first years of National Socialist rule. In retrospect, a successful activist was one who was able to carry out three months of relatively effective underground work before being captured or murdered. Increasingly on their own, the underground activists learned that the practices of earlier periods when the party was banned were just as useless under a murderous, megalomaniac regime as the retention of organizational structures had been during times when the party was legal. More and more, doubt set in abroad about the significance and meaning of the printed materials, which were distributed under such great dangers. The electoral results in the Saar; the absence of any reaction whatsoever to the liquidation of the SA leadership; the reduction of unemployment (albeit as a result of growing rearmament); the inconsequential breach of the Versailles Treaty through the introduction of universal conscription in March 1935; and the entry of German troops into the demilitarized Rhineland zone the following year — all these made it clear even to the most die-hard Communists that the National Socialist regime had consolidated itself, had been accepted by the greatest part of the population, and had not by any means encountered repudiation from the governments of leading nations.

In contrast, the Communist underground was in complete isolation after continuing retreat. The party's youth, military, and sports organizations, which had also begun to resist in 1933, were almost entirely crushed during the next two years: of the approximately 425 leading members initially in the central and regional directorates, more than one-half were in prisons and concentration camps; 125 spent their days in exile; 41 had turned their backs on the party; and 24 had been murdered. Individual regional directorates, such as the one in Hamburg, had to be replaced — up to seven times — after repeated Gestapo raids. The last central domestic directorate in Berlin was broken up in March 1935 after not even three weeks of existence, and two of its members — Adolf Rembte and Robert Stamm — were sentenced to death and executed like dozens before them. In this situation, the party substructure drew conclusions in the face of its leadership and gave up the offensive tactics that had been superseded by developments. It regeared itself to simple survival with the establishment of contacts within immediate vicinities and the exchange of ideas in the smallest of circles.

A process of rethinking that gradually set in within Comintern leadership during 1934 finally led to an official strategic and tactical change of course at the Seventh World Congress of the Communist International in August 1935. Realistically viewing its own weakness, the Communist International switched from making slanderous charges of "social fascism" to offering an alliance. The new popular front policy signaled a readiness to cooperate with the socialistic and bourgeois-democratic forces in all countries that were threatened or already ruled by fascism. With the clandestinely operating "Trojan horse policy," the mass influence that had been lost was supposed to have been regained. In implementing the new, realistic line, the subsequent German party conference near Moscow (code-named "Brussels Conference"), only a small proportion of whose delegates came from the German underground, the much larger part coming from emigration, agreed on a revision of the old centralistic organizational structure, which hardly continued to exist anyhow, in favor of the smallest independent entities.

The massive transfer of printed materials was ended. According to the party leadership, the social conflicts in factories — involving low wages, increasing overtime, compulsory fees, and inadequate social services — offered enough ways to refute Nazi propaganda and to win over discontented workers. Existing border bases in the countries around Germany were converted to divisional administration centers that maintained contacts with the inner-German party basis via briefers who regularly traveled to Germany. These emissaries had merely advisory functions and otherwise limited themselves to collecting information.

According to the leadership's directives, the remaining underground activists were to decide on their own about the manner and extent of their activity. However, they subsequently decided that the suggested tactic of ostensible cooperation in National Socialist organizations could hardly be realized. Most Communists' affiliations were known, and they were subject to special observation at the workplace; their room for action in covert workers' struggles was thus minimal. The same was true of the assumption of sudden activity in National Socialist organizations such as the German Workers' Front, the National Socialist People's Welfare, and the Hitler Youth. Further, in joining these groups they subjected themselves to the danger of being shunned as turncoats by colleagues and old comrades. And the Social Democrats as well, who were now supposed to be won over in droves, did not think much of this tactic. True, many of them considered the division of the workers' movement as ominous and a union as desirable; for most, however, this was conceivable only in a rather long process of gradual convergence brought about by growing trust. Thus, there were only isolated instances, such as in Berlin, Hildesheim, and Calbe/Saale, of agreements concerning mutual aid services, the exchange of printed materials, and the like.

Cooperative efforts among emigrés initially turned out to be substantially more promising. The *Committee for the Preparation of a German People's Front in Paris brought together top Social Democratic and Communist functionaries, representatives of socialist splinter groups, and the bourgeois intelligentsia under the chairmanship of Heinrich Mann; its purpose was to establish a binding program for an opposition united against Hitler. Yet the initiative failed for a number of reasons: the methods of Walter Ulbricht, who pushed out Willi Münzenberg, the cosponsor of the committee who had come into Comintern's line of fire; Stalinist purges whose effects reached to western Europe; and the persecution of *Trotskyites and defamations of individual committee members.

Comintern's return to its old front positions became noticeable, since the popular front policy, indebted to Soviet security interests, could not check German plans for aggression. The German party leaders had to recognize that the new methods also did not enable their domestic German basis to create and to make use of an effective antiwar mood within the population. In addition, militant Communist Party members at home and abroad enlisted in the International Brigade at the outbreak of the Spanish Civil War, as the opportunity to counter fascism with arms presented itself for the first time. Of the approximately five thousand German brigade members, nearly nine-tenths were probably Communists, having come primarily from emigration. Two thousand of them lost their lives in Spain.

In contrast, the "heroic phase" of Communist resistance in Germany had come to its end in 1935. Supporters still living in freedom were no longer willing to risk their lives for a goal that, under the circumstances, was recognized as hopeless, even if the executive committee of the Communist International in Moscow again requested of the German party leadership in February 1937 that it counter defeatism with respect to large-scale work within its membership and even if the Paris foreign secretary's office subsequently made efforts to revitalize activities at home, thereby again strongly attracting emigrés. Women were regarded as less endangered during a possible war and were thus employed in the preparations of individual divisional directorates for underground return to Germany. The party conference (the "Bern Conference") held near Paris in January 1939 — again almost entirely without delegates from the domestic German resistance, as only two of the forty to fifty briefers who traveled to Germany in several-week intervals were present — thus yielded a generally negative result: the policy of the united workers' block and the popular front did not get beyond preliminary matters.

Work with the youth lay fallow, and cadre instruction was extremely deficient.

This woeful state of affairs led to a rather undisguised retrograde orientation to the methods that had been discarded in 1935 as too risky and too ineffective. Yet, instead of vitalization, a strong disconcertment and paralysis among Communists who had emigrated or stayed in Germany followed the German-Soviet Nonaggression Treaty in August 1939. Even though the Paris foreign secretary's office of the Communist Party spoke of an "act of peace," the opposite effects of the attack on Poland and that country's partition by the new pact partners could not be overlooked. Emigrés in western Europe also felt the consequences of the outbreak of war in the form of mass internments. Thus, no one there could accept the advice of the leadership of Comintern and of the KPD in Moscow concerning the new tasks under the conditions of the war. Only the director of the Divisional Directorate Center, which had been moved from Prague to Stockholm, reported on the status of the organization in Berlin. And although the Soviet Comintern representatives had already repeatedly expressed doubt about the viability, indeed about the existence, of a German underground organization, and the German politburo was entirely aware of the weakness of its own basis, a document, the "Political Platform of the KPD," was approved that, measured against the situation in Germany, proposed completely unrealistic and thus unmanageable tasks, such as the formation of a central directorate with regional directorates in industrial areas, the publication of *Die Rote Fahne,* the initiation of intelligence activities in fascist mass organizations, and the recruitment of sympathizers from the various strata of society.

The regional directorates formed in 1936 were dissolved in favor of a foreign directorate that was to be newly formed and that, operating in Stockholm, was supposed to bring about the return of top cadres (such as members of the regional directorates, briefers, and so on) to Germany so that the foreign directorate could itself finally return. Along with two leaders of the Divisional Directorate Center, Herbert Wehner, who had been living in Soviet exile since 1936, was named a member of the overall management team of the domestic German resistance that had been planned in Moscow. The "Political Platform" had given them an unrealistic maxim for action, a maxim that had taken for granted far-reaching changes in class structures and new conditions for the struggle in Germany, supposedly brought about by the "Soviet-German Friendship Pact." Demands for the restitution of political and social rights were supposed to be fought for particularly under the more severe security conditions of the war, and a battle to push back the Gestapo and the SS was supposed to be waged after successful wide-scale work and deep entrenchment within broad circles of the populace, thereby enabling a transition to semilegal activity in order finally to fight for complete legality.

The remnants of the former underground network — reconstructed in secrecy mostly by functionaries who had returned to their old places of activity after long-term prison stays — were initially hesitant at the outbreak of the war. They did indeed inform briefers, who arrived from Scandinavia and who were known to them from before, about the status of their organization, and they assisted in the underground production of the *Berliner Volkszeitung* (Berlin people's news) that was published in November 1939 and of several issues of *Die Rote Fahne* that appeared between 1940 and 1941. Yet they were hardly noticed by the Gestapo, even when four of the briefers were arrested. In 1940–41, the leaders of the loosely associated groups in Berlin — Robert Uhrig and John Sieg (see *Uhrig-Römer Group) — extended their contacts to other regional organizations that had been formed on the initiative of several functionaries who had been released from prison in 1939–40, such as the organization in Hamburg under *Bernhard Bästlein, Franz Jacob (see *Saefkow-Jacob Group), and Robert Abshagen or the one in Munich under former Freikorps leader Josef Römer. They were also successful in reaching out beyond the Communist circle in cooperation with the circle surrounding a first lieutenant in the Ministry of Aviation, Harro Schulze-Boysen, and a senior government adviser in the Reich Ministry of Economics, Arvid Harnack (see *Red Orchestra), a circle heterogeneously comprised of artists, intellectuals, high officials, and military personnel. Like several groups operating on their own in the Reich, they stepped up their activities after the attack on the Soviet Union, again published flyers and newspapers, increasingly recruited foreign forced laborers into their activities as consignees and potential allies, and concentrated all their powers on ending the war as quickly as possible, thereby supporting whenever possible the Soviet Union — honored as the "fatherland of all proletarians" since the founding of the KPD — in its difficult defense against the German aggressors.

Independently and barely in contact with these domestic groups, a single group of functionaries succeeded in establishing itself within Germany according to the directives of the exile leadership in Moscow after rather extensive preparations during the beginning of 1942. Wilhelm Knöchel, a central committee member since 1935 and battle-tried in the German underground as well as in western European emigration, had worked toward his return since 1940 in conjunction with Herbert Wehner in Stockholm. Yet while Wehner and the other two men who had been expected to assume the central direction in Germany were arrested in Scandinavia, Knöchel, operating in Berlin and supported by several collaborators who had already come to Germany from the Netherlands, began to form his own organization in western Germany, the former area controlled by Divisional Directorate West, of which Knöchel had been a member since 1936 (see *Knöchel Organization). In the first issue (February 1942) of the monthly published by him, *Der Friedenskämpfer* (The freedom fighter), he adopted a strictly nonpartisan position. In this as well as in the following issues up to December, the KPD was not once mentioned, nor was it represented as the leader of the movement that sought to gather together all "anti-Hitler and anti-militaristic groups," as had been postulated in the writings of the other Communist groups during the war. The *Friedenskämpfer* presented itself exclusively as the engine of a peace movement for the preservation of the German people in the face of ruin through a military defeat that was predicted as certain.

Not quite one month after Knöchel's arrival in Berlin, the Gestapo broke up the Uhrig Organization with mass arrests. After a generally unsuccessful arson attack on the rabble-rousing exhibition "The Soviet Paradise," it crushed at the end of May a group of young, predominantly Communist-oriented Jews surrounding *Herbert Baum who were in contact with members of the Uhrig Organization. Then, in September/October, the Schulze-Boysen/Harnack Circle (Red Orchestra) collapsed with all of its various connections, including the Communist cadres recruited by John Sieg. Their connections with Hamburg, once discovered by the Gestapo, brought an end to the organization there in October.

Anton Saefkow and Franz Jacob, who were part of the leadership in Berlin and Hamburg (see *Saefkow-Jacob Group) and were able to evade arrest, later attempted again to reestablish the network and to extend it over all of Germany. Their comrades from long years of imprisonment helped them establish cooperation with the groups surrounding *Georg Schumann in Saxony, *Theodor Neubauer in Thuringia, and *Hermann Danz and *Martin Schwantes in Magdeburg-Anhalt. They all developed considerable activities directed toward affecting the public. Supported by contacts in factories, they pushed for work slowdowns in order to reduce war production, attempted munitions sabotage (albeit for the most part unsuccessfully), again published materials against Nazi rule and military madness, and agreed in their political writings on a political organization of Germany after Hitler. In so doing, the majority of them maintained old ideas of the "dictatorship of the proletariat" and of a socialist Germany that was supposed to stand on equal terms next to the Soviet Union, the world's first socialist state. On this and other points, their ideas diverged from those of the party leadership, which, while not forgetting the leading role of the Soviet Union, spoke via Radio Moscow of a democratic Germany given birth to by all antifascist forces.

Domestic German resistance groups of the party did indeed listen to their leadership, yet they now acted on their own. The bitter experiences of the 1930s with a failed policy that bore no small part of the responsibility for the greatest defeat of the German workers' movement and for the thousands of victims within their own ranks after 1933, as well as the success of a new beginning wrought by their own hands, enabled the forces of the resistance to become more self-confident and thus more independent. As the exile leadership's final connection with the German underground was torn asunder with the arrest of the *Knöchel Organization at the beginning of 1943, the regional organizations that were tenaciously stretched out in Berlin, Saxony, Thuringia, and Magdeburg-Anhalt asserted themselves until July 1944, only to be smashed nearly to the last man after Saefkow's and Jacob's first contact with Julius Leber and Adolf Reichwein, who were members of the Social Democratic circle of anti-Hitler conspirators. An undercover informant had been among the unsuspecting Communists. The Communist underground, which through its broad activities provided the most leads for the Gestapo, had been more subject to such informants than other resistance groups since 1933.

The mass arrests in the summer of 1944 marked the end of Communist attempts to eliminate Hitler's regime from within. At the same time, they deprived the workers' movement of some of its best representatives — people who, even under the hardest conditions, had uncompromisingly and courageously never ceased fighting a criminal regime. Even if they themselves did not speak up for a democratic alternative, and even if their accomplishments and associated sacrifices were denied success, their engagement alone nevertheless refutes the thesis of the collective guilt of the German people.

Bibliography

Duhnke, Horst. *Die KDP von 1933 bis 1945.* Cologne, 1971.

Herlemann, Beatrix. *Die Emigration als Kampfposten: Die Anleitung des kommunistischen Widerstandes in Deutschland aus Frankreich, Belgien und den Niederlanden.* Königstein/Taunus, 1982.

———. *Auf verlorenem Posten: Kommunistischer Widerstand im Zweiten Weltkrieg: Die Knöchel-Organisation.* Bonn, 1986.

Peukert, Detlev. *Die KPD im Widerstand: Verfolgung und Untergrundarbeit an Rhein und Ruhr 1933–1945.* Wuppertal, 1980.

Stroech, Jürgen. *Die illegale Presse: Eine Waffe im Kampf gegen den deutschen Faschismus. Ein Beitrag zur Geschichte und Bibliographie der illegalen antifaschistischen Presse 1933–1945.* Leipzig, 1979.

Socialist Resistance

Hartmut Mehringer _____

The term "socialist resistance" encompasses the resistance of the non-Communist workers' movement against National Socialism and therefore of the Social Democratic Party and the Free Trade Unions as well of the so-called leftist center groups. Among these on the socialist side are the *German Socialist Workers' Party (SAPD or SAP), the *International Socialist Combat League (ISK), *New Beginning, the *Red Militants (who were active primarily in northern and central Germany), as well as the *German Communist Party/Opposition (KPDO or KPO), the Left Opposition of the German Communist Party (see *Trotskyites), and anarcho-syndicalistic groups (see *Anarcho-Syndicalists).

The SPD, Free Trade Unions, and leftist-socialist center groups represent three entirely different types of organizations within the German workers' movement and consequently reacted entirely differently to the threat that was posed by the National Socialist assumption of power on January 30, 1933, a threat that became manifest in all German states during the course of subsequent weeks.

The process of the National Socialist seizure of power — from the naming of Hitler as Reich chancellor on January 30, 1933, to the outlawing (that is, self-dissolution) of the parties at the end of June and beginning of July — took place partially via individual steps that were taken consciously and deliberately and partially via chance opportunities that the National Socialist leadership zealously exploited, such as the Reichstag fire during the night of Monday/Tuesday before Lent in 1933. Corresponding to this and feeding off of it was a process of increasing dissolution and organizational disintegration on the Social Democratic side. After the election campaign preceding the March 5, 1933, Reichstag elections, the National Socialist leadership's repressive and prohibitive measures vis-à-vis social democracy took the form of prohibitions against the freedom of the press and of assembly. These measures, which were characteristic of the leadership's pseudological modus operandi, were initially directed not against the SPD as a party but rather against its secondary manifestations — the Reichsbanner as a Social Democratic defense organization and the diversely stratified network of workers' organizations. Next to the National Socialists' attempt to maintain the appearance of the legality of their accession to power, there presumably also stood an overestimation, typical of National Socialism, of (pseudo-) military organizations as well as the probably instinctive awareness that the actual coherence of the workers' movement lay less in its political parties than in its leisure-time, educational, sports, youth, self-defense, and self-help organizations.

Despite the attempt of their leadership to maintain their organizational integrity even under the new circumstances by means of accommodation and integration in the "national unity front," the Free Trade Unions were dissolved throughout the entire Reich, and their coffers were confiscated on May 2, 1933. Since this attempt to circumvent the threat of being outlawed by means of a formal tactic of accommodation was in vain, the SPD's attempt to pursue a double strategy of continuing its activity in the Reichstag while simultaneously setting up a center abroad (that is, Sopade, the exile executive committee in Prague) and making other preparations for underground activity was bound to fail. On May 10, 1933, the SPD's coffers were confiscated — insofar as the party could not save them abroad — and, on June 22, 1933, the party was forbidden from any further political activity; the tabling of Social Democratic mandates at all parliamentary levels was decreed; and massive protective custody measures against Social Democratic functionaries were ordered. The regime had prepared for the final attack against the SPD and the entire Weimar party system; in the following weeks, the last remnants of trade union life within the workers' movement were finally dissolved, and their finances were confiscated.

Leftist center groups had predicted substantially more realistically that there would be no legal means of survival for socialist organizations under the National Socialist regime and thus, to some degree, made concrete preparations for their own prohibition before the National Socialist accession to power. Some of them, such as the German Socialist Workers' Party and the International Socialist Combat League (ISK), even formally dissolved themselves in order to circumvent anticipated police surveillance and persecution. As a result, they remained largely unscathed by the wave of mass arrests in the spring of 1933. They were helped by the relatively small number of people in their ranks, which numbered several hundred active members at most; only the German Socialist Workers' Party, with over seventeen thousand members in 1933, attained anything like the character of a mass party. The great majority of the leftist center groups represented themselves as elite organizations with highly qualified cadres — albeit with correspondingly ambitious claims to political leadership — who still had commensurate experience and training from the Weimar period. In addition, they were hardly known to the police due to the small number of their ranks, the relatively late date of their founding, their previous manner of operating, and the manner of their entrance onto the scene, which had frequently been made under a covert cloak even before 1933.

Their preparatory measures, even if differently conceived and not always implemented in an equally rigid manner, were initially based on an only seemingly uncomplicated and conspiratorially invulnerable system of groups of five or three persons as an organizational basis. In order to reduce as much as possible the danger of infiltration after arrests by the Gestapo, only one member in a group was to have contact with a neighboring unit at the next highest level of the organization — a system that failed often enough due to the fact that the active members of the workers' movement personally also knew one another all too well from their common political activity during the time of the Weimar Republic and due to the fact that borders between covert groups had been artificially erected. Membership lists and organization files were destroyed, hidden, or stored safely abroad, where nearly all of the organizations named, as well as the two large workers' parties, built centers and bases in exile, secured apartments where plans could be made, produced falsified documents (or at least provided for the possibility of their production), developed secret codes and invisible inks, and organized courier systems.

Corresponding to their character and self-image as cadre organizations, the leftist center groups had conducted no large-scale membership recruitment before 1933 and thus — also for reasons of safety while engaging in covert work — refrained from large-scale activities such as circulating huge amounts of flyers and reading materials. They placed their emphasis overwhelmingly on the maintenance of contacts and organizational integrity, on the training of cadres, and on an annual, in part highly developed system for reporting to centers abroad in order thereby to break the National Socialist regime's monopoly on news and information; they justifiably saw this tactic as one of their strongest weapons. New Beginning was most prominent in this respect because, having conducted different and more thorough analyses of fascism, it had made more realistic estimations than the SPD and the KPD generally had in 1933 with regard to the regime's duration, its potential for persecution, and the consequences for the underground workers' movement. As a result, its goal involved not so much the dissemination of underground propaganda as the doctrinal education and training of cadres for the collapse of Hitler's rule, after which the cadres, held in reserve, would be able to assume the leading role in the mass revolutionary movement that was predicted, although the collapse of Hitler's rule, according to their analysis, still lay in the distant future and could be realistically expected only after another world war.

In 1933, social democracy and its organizational periphery dissolved into roughly three or four large groups. The first group was constituted of those many members who resigned or withdrew from active politics into the realm of private survival. A great number of these tried to keep their political sympathies and *Weltanschauung* more or less secret and often maintained loose contacts with former associates in neighborhoods, in clubs, and at the workplace. Social democratic surroundings in the workers' suburbs and housing developments of the larger cities also offered protection for such contact. Numerically, this was without doubt the largest group — by far — within this category.

Belonging to this category were also those types of social democratic organizations and associations that apparently existed in the myriad form of informal symposia and pub gatherings, loosely planned discussion circles that met regularly, news groups, cliques, and circles of friends; knowledge of only the smallest number of these activities, which often took place in stores and restaurants run by former Social Democrats, was documented or handed down to posterity.

The capability for resistance that this form of social democratic activity offered did indeed weaken markedly when, in the mid-1930s, full employment and increasing demands for production and working hours left less time for meetings that had previously benefited from unemployment and temporary employment and that been held in an individual's own area of town. This capability was compromised even more by the effects of the drafting of able-bodied men into the military, the geographic shuffling of the population due to the war, and so on. Even by the mid-1930s, the latently oppositional attitude of such still-existing groups that were united in their sympathies was often reduced to the exchange of opinions and recollections at pub tables frequented by pensioners and invalids. Nevertheless, one must attest to the remarkable consistency and tenability that this gave to the resistive capability of the Social Democrats. Their substance consisted mostly in the more instinctive rather than conscious attempt to maintain, in concert with former associates, well-worn political and moral norms and an integrity that, despite the destruction of their organizational structures by the National Socialist regime, had developed in part over the course of generations. This tenacity outlived the more than twelve years of National Socialist rule at least in part and was one of the essential preconditions for the incredibly rapid reconstruction of the SPD's organization immediately after the end of the war.

Formerly highly placed party, trade union, and guild functionaries constituted a second group. Even beyond their own geographic regions, they maintained loose, privately made contacts with their longtime friends and colleagues; when necessary, these contacts could be set into motion beyond the local level, as was shown by the *July 20, 1944, assassination attempt on Hitler.

A third, numerically strong group consisted of socialist "illegals" in a stricter sense of the word; in the years following 1933, they became the true representatives of socialist underground work. Many of them did not come from the party organization of the SPD but rather from its periphery organizations, especially its youth groups, such as the Reichsbanner, the Socialist Workers' Youth, the Friends of Youth, and workers' clubs.

Finally, the emigrated party and trade union functionaries were the fourth, and relatively small, group. In neighboring countries, they established border secretariats and posts (such as Sopade and its ring of border secretariats surrounding the German Reich), foreign executive committees, and various support mechanisms for illegals in the Reich, providing the latter with printed materials and news and receiving from them reports and information from Germany. Into the war years, this "party emigration" received a constant influx of members from socialist resistance organizations who were threatened by arrest.

In making these categorizations, one must always keep in mind that these groups were not actually strictly differentiated from one another but were connected with one another to varying degrees; further, one must remember that there were numerous minglings and hybrid forms among them on the local level, particularly during the initial years of National Socialist rule (1933–1935/36), which, from the standpoint of the workers' movement, constituted the period of mass resistance. In a realistic assessment of the situation, the SPD and its organizational periphery had for their part neither the intention nor the opportunity to establish centrally coordinated activity in the underground, and they also did not intend to "transfer" the "organization" outside the law. For that reason, local party sections, the divisions of secondary and suborganizations, as well as groups of the outlawed (that is, politically co-opted) workers' clubs were initially entirely on their own. An especially common reaction of such groups to the new set of circumstances was the attempt by their most active members simply to continue to meet after the police had disbanded their organizations and to go on with normal organization and club life; these attempts were usually undertaken quite spontaneously and without further ado. It is true that these attempts were all too often marked by dilettantism, by a naive underestimation of the enemy and his political means of power and surveillance, and by a lack of experience in covert activity. Nevertheless, a number of highly active underground groups arose from such organizations, especially from former youth organizations, whenever they succeeded in establishing connections with Sopade in Prague or border secretariats and in obtaining underground literature from them.

The groups that can be called "resistance groups" in the classic sense of the term — and that to a certain extent formed the tip of the iceberg in this far-reaching, many-layered, and differentiated substratus of Social Democratic opposition, nonconformity, enlightenment, and refusal to accommodate — could hold themselves together only for a limited time. For the most part, they arose between autumn 1933 and spring 1934 after establishing contacts with Sopade and the border secretariats on the other side of the German border; their geographic strongholds, aside from Berlin, which was the hub for foreign contacts, were naturally in the industrial regions of Upper Silesia, Saxony, the Rhine-Main-Neckar area, the Ruhr district, the Lower Rhine, the North Sea, and the large ports on the Baltic Sea coast. With the border secretariats in Mies, Eger, Neuern, and St. Gallen as their source, such organizations were also formed in the large southern German cities of Nuremberg, Munich, Augsburg, and Stuttgart and quickly sprang up in neighboring midsized cities due to personal acquaintances within the party. The possibility of their access to and distribution of printed materials, which were provided by Sopade, formed the core of their activity; of course, these materials were distributed primarily to known and reliable associates and were not publicly disseminated. In doing this, these organizations were mostly concerned with information and enlightenment and not with public mass agitation, which was rightly seen as suicidal; as an activist from that time accurately said in retrospect, "It was not supposed to turn into a mass movement, but to be a shot in the arm for people who were already committed."

Because of their generally defensive forms of activity, these groups were initially tracked down by the Gestapo far more slowly than comparable Communist underground groups. Their heyday was in 1934; hardly any resistance groups of this type survived the following year. Almost without exception, they fell victim to the Gestapo's close surveillance and were convicted by the National Socialist justice system up to 1937, sometimes in mammoth court proceedings involving dozens or hundreds of defendants.

A number of other Social Democratic groups displayed a clearly higher covert ability and degree of organization. Like the leftist center groups, they had considerable reservations about Sopade, which, in their eyes, was the direct successor of the old party leadership and which they saw as being responsible for the party's uncontested defeat and failure at the hands of National Socialism. With respect to their self-image, organizational structure, and critical appraisal (that is, their rejection of Sopade's literature), they bear strong resemblance to the leftist center groups. In this context, one must especially mention the *Socialist Front of Hannover surrounding Werner Blumenberg, which had an unusually large number of members and collaborators, disseminated the underground organ *Sozialistische Blätter* (Socialist notes) in great numbers, and was able to function for a long time due to its highly developed organizational structure and its mooring in Hannover's Social Democratic milieu. Not until the late summer of 1936 did the Gestapo succeed in planting an undercover agent in the organization and in finally crushing it for the most part. Approximately 250 of its members were convicted.

There were similarly structured, if hardly as sizable, groups in a whole series of large cities. One should mention the Rote Stosstrupp (Red Shock Troop) in Berlin (which the Gestapo had smashed at the end of 1933), the Winzen Group in Dortmund (which, as a relatively esoteric and exclusive discussion circle, was not mopped up by the Gestapo until 1940), and underground groups in Leipzig and other central German cities that continued to function into wartime.

The longer such groups strictly cut themselves off from the outside and maintained covert security measures in their dealings with one another, the longer they generally were able to exist — yet the less they were able to have any broad effect. The attempt to have an outward effect or to establish transregional contacts almost without exception led to the infiltration of these underground organizations by the Gestapo.

In their resistance against National Socialism, the leftist center groups played a role that significantly outweighed their actual numerical percentage of the workers' movement. This resulted primarily because they were initially not well known to the police, were structured as highly qualified cadre organizations, and renounced massive outward agitation.

The German Socialist Workers' Party (SAPD or SAP), in strength the most significant of the leftist center groups, had its hub in Berlin and central Germany yet also presided over regional organizations and bases in large cities in Silesia, northern Germany, southern and southwestern Germany, the Rhine-Ruhr area, and Frankfurt am Main. This group played a significant role insofar as it served during the initial years of National Socialist rule as a refuge point for endangered members who were then channeled to the safer Saar region.

The composition of the underground Reich directorate surrounding Walter Fabian frequently changed due to the threat of arrest and the emigration of its members, yet it continued to exist up to the mid-1930s. Its members who emigrated usually hooked up with the SAP's foreign executive committee surrounding Jacob Walcher and Paul Frölich, who, operating in Paris, sought until the end of the war to support and coordinate the underground SAP groups. Although, according to an internal status report from that time, four to five thousand SAP underground agents were working in the Reich during the mid-1930s, the Gestapo from that point on succeeded in making decisive breaches. In 1937, the SAP still had three functioning area organizations (in Berlin, Mannheim, and the Hamburg area), their existence being documented up to 1939. Even if they all finally fell victim to the Gestapo, remnants of these organizations no doubt continued to exist into the war or even until the war's end.

The International Socialist Combat League (ISK), a small but tight group under Willi Eichler, also had a presence within the entire Reich after 1933 in the form of local bases. After nearly two years of meticulous and ambitious work, the ISK's underground organization throughout the Reich comprised six regional units that were in close contact with the executive committee in exile under Willi Eichler in Paris. The most important centers of underground activity were five vegetarian restaurants owned by the organization as well as a bread store that served as inconspicuous bases for the publication and distribution of illegal printed materials and whose profits were also able to cover most of the organization's financial needs. The *Neue Politische Briefe* (New political letters), also dubbed the "Reinhart Briefe" (Reinhart was Eichler's alias), appeared monthly from October 1933 until the end of 1937; copies were smuggled in from abroad and, abstaining from self-serving propaganda, were marked especially by their high informational value and their decidedly objective style.

The destruction of the ISK began at the end of 1936. After making individual arrests, the Gestapo obtained clues about the ISK's organizational setup throughout the Reich and then established an office that succeeded in arresting the main domestic functionary, Julius Philippson, in the summer of 1937. Afterward, there were more than one hundred arrests throughout the entire Reich at the end of 1937 and beginning of 1938, and, in the late summer of 1938, the southern German groups of the ISK were the final victims of the wave of arrests. Individual pockets of the organization in the Rhine-Ruhr area were able to survive the war and were still able to play a certain role at the end of the war.

The *Red Militants organization surrounding Arthur Goldstein, Alexander Schwab, and Karl Schröder comprised a number of groups in Berlin, Saxony, and the Rhine-Ruhr area in 1933, having approximately four hundred members who came primarily from socialist educational programs. Having arisen from the Social Sciences Union of Berlin, the Red Militants were a circle of debaters who were marked especially by ideas of deliberative democracy and had clandestine organizational forms. The conscious renunciation of extensive propaganda activity offered effective protection from police persecution. Not until 1936 did the Gestapo run across the group, and then mostly by chance. By the early summer of 1937, approximately 150 members were arrested, and the organization was thereby nearly entirely broken up.

Finally, one must mention as a special group the Leninist Organization surrounding Walter Loewenheim that, in accordance with its party platform, went by the name New Beginning as of 1933. In this party platform, entitled "New Beginning," which was published by Loewenheim under the pseudonym Miles in September 1933 by Sopade's Graphia Publishing House in Karlsbad, the organization staked its claim for leadership of the outlawed workers' movement. The brochure had resounding success because it accurately dealt with and brought to a head questions of political direction, the mood of the times, and especially the criticism that socialists living underground in the Reich and in emigration had of the leadership of the old workers' parties. That Sopade, under pressure from the Socialist Workers' International, published in its own press this harshest of attacks on the policy and reformist principles of the executive committee of the Weimar SPD, upon whose mandate Sopade relied, attests to the pressure under which it then stood to legitimize itself.

The leadership crisis that affected the organization in the mid-1930s no doubt contributed to the Gestapo's success in infiltrating the Berlin organization and in largely breaking it up by means of a wave of arrests during the autumn of 1935 and the spring of 1936. Nevertheless, cadres who were spared arrest — one must mention Fritz Erler above all — continued their work and tried to establish new networks.

Via the foreign directorate, they were able to establish close contact with Otto Brass and Hermann Brill in the so-called *German People's Front, which was comprised of older SPD, KPD, and trade union members. The group thus formed was called the Ten-Point Group. Its ten-point program aimed primarily at unity within the workers' movement and played an important role in the debate about legitimation of the popular and unity fronts, a debate conducted in exile. In conjunction with the arrest of the Ten-Point Group, the New Beginning organization in Berlin was also finally broken up in the autumn of 1938. However, the New Beginning organization in southern Bavaria, surrounding Bebo Wager in Augsburg and Hermann Frieb in Munich and aided by Waldemar von Knoeringen, was able to expand into the Tyrol and Vienna (where it was associated with Johann Otto Haas) after the Anschluss of Austria. It did not fall victim to the Gestapo until 1942.

After the Free Trade Unions were outlawed on May 2, 1933, a specifically trade unionist resistance also sprang up. Trade union groups, just like political parties and workers' organizations, sought means to ensure the survival of their organizations. Already in 1933, a leadership circle surrounding former leading trade union functionaries, such as Heinrich Schliestedt, Hans Gottfurcht, and others, arose and was later joined by Wilhelm Leuschner after his release from a concentration camp. They attempted to gather information about the situation in factories and to extend themselves outside of Germany in conjunction with the German trade unions' representative office abroad, which was established in Reichenberg in the Republic of Czechoslovakia in 1934 and cooperated with the International Trade Union Alliance and especially with the International Transport Workers' Federation (ITF) under Edo Fimmen; they also tried to establish and maintain contacts among local outlawed trade union groups. Given the groups they cooperated with, it is no accident that their activities occurred especially in occupations involving transportation, such as among railway workers, sailors, and river-boat workers. According to its own statistics, the railway workers' underground organization alone had 137 bases and more than 1,300 functionaries in the spring of 1936 who were engaged in resistance work. However, the organization was almost entirely destroyed by mass arrests in 1937.

Members of the socialist resistance were also associated with the July 20, 1944, assassination attempt on Hitler, with Julius Leber, Wilhelm Leuschner, Theodor Haubach, and Carlo Mierendorff leading the way. Leber, Leuschner, and Haubach were executed, and Mierendorff was the victim of an air attack while he was incarcerated.

Bibliography

Edinger, Lewis, and J. Edinger. *Sozialdemokratie und Nationalsozialismus.* Hannover/Frankfurt am Main, 1960.

Grasmann, Peter. *Sozialdemokraten gegen Hitler 1933–1945.* Munich, 1968.

Klotzbach, Kurt. *Gegen den Nationalsozialismus: Widerstand und Verfolgung in Dortmund 1930–1945: Eine historisch-politische Studie.* Hannover, 1969.

Mehringer, Hartmut. "Die bayerische Sozialdemokratie bis zum Ende des NS-Regimes: Vorgeschichte, Verfolgung und Widerstand." In *Bayern in der NS-Zeit.* Volume 5, *Die Parteien KPD, SPD und BVP in Verfolgung und Widerstand.* Edited by Martin Broszat and Hartmut Mehringer. Munich/Vienna, 1983.

Pelger, Hans, and Helmut Esters. *Gewerkschafter im Widerstand.* With a review of the historical research by Alexandra Schlingenspiepen. Bonn, 1983.

Steinberg, Hans-Josef. *Widerstand und Verfolgung in Essen 1933–1945.* Hannover, 1969.

Widerstand und Exil der deutschen Arbeiterbewegung 1933–1945. Bonn, 1982.

Bourgeois (National-Conservative) Resistance

Hans Mommsen

The notion of bourgeois resistance encompasses those groups in the German opposition against Hitler who are not counted as part of the Communist or socialist workers' resistance. This is misleading insofar as the movement involving the July 20, 1944, assassination attempt on Hitler, which is attributed to the bourgeois resistance, included not a small number of Social Democrats and trade unionists and did not see itself as bourgeois but rather sought to overcome class barriers. The typological distinction can be seen much more in the fact that this part of the opposition did not develop by hooking up with the organized workers' movement, which had been pushed into the underground, but rather arose on the initiative of critics of the regime who were at first isolated.

Despite the overwhelmingly bourgeois character of the opposition groups that comprised the movement involved in the July 20, 1944, assassination attempt on Hitler, they can be delineated only inadequately by sociological criteria. Although consisting overwhelmingly of members of the bourgeois upper class, most of them sought contacts with the proletariat and frequently included socialists and trade unionists. In contrast, the groups that made up the movement involved in the July 20, 1944, assassination attempt were distinguished from the leftist resistance by the specific profile of their political goals and ideas, a profile that justifies one in subsuming them under the concept "national-conservative," which should be seen as an umbrella notion for positions that differed in their particulars. Moreover, members of the educated elite played an important role in the leftist opposition, such as in the German Communist Party (KPD), the *Red Orchestra, and the group *New Beginning.

The movement involved in the July 20, 1944, assassination attempt consisted predominantly of persons who belonged to the upper class, were university educated, and were generally in government service or entered it later. Oppositionists active from the very beginning, such as Ewald von Kleist-Schmenzin, Baron von und zu Guttenberg, and Helmuth James von Moltke, were exceptions. As a rule, national-conservative resistance was comprised of personalities who had, at least in part, initially given National Socialist policy their blessing and had been loyal to the regime, had they not, like the trade unionists, been politically disenfranchised by the regime or, like the representatives of the workers' movement, been openly oppressed.

The later conspirators progressed through several degrees of alienation from the regime until they decided to commit high treason actively. In the phase up to 1938, they hoped to strengthen the moderate groups of the NSDAP and to roll back corruption, despotism, and the dissolution of the constitutional state. From 1938 to 1941 — the actual time varied from individual to individual — they believed that they would be able to effect the necessary changes through a restructuring of the government and to force Hitler to resign or to make him a lame duck. After 1941, there arose the belief that the situation required the removal of the regime and a new order from the ground up.

The members of the group called "Other Germany" represented a counterelite to the National Socialist leadership. This group was composed of high officials, diplomats, trade union functionaries, officers, and scientists, most of whom had held and continued to hold top positions within the system. Despite their varying political origins, they agreed on a series of goals. On the one hand, they reacted angrily to the regime's increasingly criminal methods — the Kristallnacht in November 1938, in particular, served as a rallying point — and demanded a return to the norms of a constitutional state. On the other hand, they rejected, albeit to varying degrees, a return to the liberal-parliamentary system of the Weimar Republic, whose deficiencies, in their view, had paved Hitler's way to power. For the future political and social shape of the Reich, they saw a "third way" between Western capitalistic individualism and eastern European socialistic collectivism. They thought predominantly in terms of the state, even if they had in view European cooperation for overcoming the consequences of World War II. Left-wing national conservatives in the resistance also assumed that the Reich would remain "the supreme leading authority," whereby there would be federative variants, from pan-German and central European plans to ones about a new Reich.

The Enlightenment tradition represented by liberalism was firmly rejected by the conspirators, who, in this respect, were beholden to the conservative and neoconservative tendencies of the Weimar period. Among the older generation, the influence of the Prussian state tradition predominated, while younger people followed neoconservative trends of thought more avidly. The experience of National Socialist tyranny and despotism challenged them to work toward a thoroughly new order that, by solving social and constitutional questions, would do away with the reasons that led to the rule, in Ludwig Beck's words, of "brown Bolshevism."

The formation of the national-conservative resistance can be traced to the autumn of 1938, when an oppositional group surrounding retired General Erwin von Witzleben and the chief of the General Staff, Brigadier General Ludwig Beck, who had resigned in protest, established connections with the Foreign Office, respected dignitaries, and the retired mayor of Leipzig, Carl Goerdeler, in order to block, by means of a putsch if necessary, Hitler's intention to solve the Czechoslovakian question by military means. As a result of British prime minister Neville Chamberlain's readiness to compromise — against which emissaries of the growing opposition had advised in vain — the prerequisite for a coup went by the boards, yet the nucleus of the opposition continued to exist and considered overthrowing Hitler in the event that the war were to continue after the successful campaign against Poland.

The victory over France deprived these premature plans of their basis both domestically and abroad and forced a reconstruction of the opposition, which could no longer limit itself to a restructuring of the government through the elimination of Hitler but now worked toward toppling the entire system. In the reformation of the resistance beginning in 1940, civilians played a more important leading role than the military, which, like Brigadier General Franz Halder, had largely withdrawn. Among them, there was, first, the circle around Carl Goerdeler, who, next to the rightist conservatives Ulrich von Hassell, Johannes Popitz, Jens Jessen, and Carl Langbehn, was joined by Christian and independent trade union functionaries under the leadership of Jakob Kaiser and Wilhelm Leuschner. Through the contacts that these people had with former trade unionists, Goerdeler hoped to garner greater political representation for dignitaries, who had been only loosely associated up to that point, so that they could conduct negotiations with foreign countries. On the initiative of Goerdeler, who was constantly gathering like-minded individuals around himself, the first systematic thoughts about the future shape of the state and the composition of a transitional government were fleshed out. This seemed necessary in order to guard on the home front against the military's political intentions.

The second center of civilian resistance was the *Kreisau Circle, which was formed by Count Helmuth James von Moltke and Count Peter Yorck zu Wartenburg (the Gestapo later named the group after Moltke's family estate of Kreisau in the Lower Silesian county of Schweidnitz). The Kreisau Circle established contacts with other oppositionist circles, such as the resistance group within the *Counterintelligence Office (Abwehr), the *Solf and Sperr Circles, and Munich Jesuits. Although meetings of the Kreisau Circle were no longer held after Moltke's arrest in January 1944, the majority of its members, despite Moltke's reservations, selected Count Claus Schenk von Stauffenberg to carry out the assassination of Hitler. Goerdeler and Leuschner worked closely together with the military opposition, which had been reanimated by Henning von Tresckow and Stauffenberg. Since the beginning of 1943, a core of conspirators had been forming in Bendlerstrasse, among whom were Julius Leber, Adam von Trott zu Solz, and Fritz-Dietlof von der Schulenburg from the civilian ranks, whereas Goerdeler had moved rather to the periphery with respect to the preparations for the coup, as von Hassell and Popitz had done before him, their contact with Himmler having been met with reservation.

Both centers of the civilian resistance were marked by their refraining from adopting covert tactics in their organizations. True, Moltke used fictitious names in his correspondence, as did Hassell in his diaries, but any sort of organizational connection was avoided by insiders. The number of persons with whom Goerdeler spoke in order to recruit them for the plot was considerable, but discussions about future plans were limited to very few people. Among them were primarily Beck, Witzleben, and the former trade union leaders. Members of the Kreisau Circle also refrained from formal membership, although Moltke tried to commit the parties concerned to common principles in order to establish a firm consensus of sentiment. Next to a rather tight circle that met regularly, he and Yorck drew upon various experts to answer whatever questions arose as well as upon representatives of the churches and the workers' movement. Moltke tried to formulate a concrete program for the new order toward which they were working, a program that also concerned, next to questions pertaining to the constitution and economic and social policy, the legal system and the relationship between church and state.

Originally, Goerdeler, von Hassell, and Popitz had worked on the assumption that it would be possible to bring about the necessary change of government while largely maintaining existing institutions, including the German Labor Front, and to eliminate the regime's most dangerous exponents, Heinrich Himmler and Joseph Goebbels. If necessary, Hitler was to be replaced by Hermann Göring, who was regarded as a moderate. The early plans for the constitution, in the drafting of which von Hassell and Popitz had played a decisive role, were based on the assumption of the establishment of an authoritarian system of government having corporative features and providing only limited participatory democratic rights.

Whereas Goerdeler had initially held on to the illusion of forcing Hitler to resign through a common démarche by army leaders, there arose in the opposition group surrounding Beck, Witzleben, General Olbricht, von Hassell, and Popitz the belief that it was necessary to eliminate Hitler by assassination, which Goerdeler, fearing a return of the "stab in the back" legend, hoped to be able to avoid. In conjunction with this, Goerdeler believed that a comprehensive program and personal commitments for the planned transitional government were necessary for civilian support of the military-led national government. This also seemed necessary in order to provide the coup with the required legitimacy at home and abroad.

The Kreisau Circle, which began to coalesce after 1940, had at first assumed that it would be necessary to wait for the National Socialist regime to collapse by itself. In the overall historical-philosophical view of the circle's members, National Socialism stood at the apex of a secular social and intellectual crisis in European society that had begun during the age of the Reformation and had led to the progressive loss of the personal ties of the individual, to the advent of the anonymous bureaucratic institution of the state, and to nearly total secularization. Consequently, the circle's members intended to make preparations for the coming day that, with the demise of the regime, would bring the anticipated secular sea change and usher in a fundamental social new beginning without their having to lift a finger to topple the regime. Nevertheless, the Kreisau Circle had worked out definite guidelines in case of a collapse. They modified their position only after being struck by the escalating crimes of the regime and the destructive effects of the war, which led them to fear an internal "Bolshevization" of the German people and the complete destruction of the Western tradition. Many of them then became actively involved in preparations for a coup.

Although Goerdeler felt a certain rivalry toward the members of the Kreisau Circle, and Moltke polemically attacked Goerdeler's half-hearted "Kerenski methods" and called for a genuine revolution, and von Hassell and Popitz, with their restorative views, rejected Goerdeler's national-liberal ideas as "reactionary," there was in practice a remarkable convergence in both sides' views. This was in good part due to the mediation of the socialists and trade unionists and also to the influence of the ideas of related groups, including the *Freiburg Circles. Because of this convergence, one can sketch an idealized picture of the constitutional and social order toward which the national-conservative resistance was striving.

The conspirators agreed that a "revolution from above" should take place through a declaration of martial law, although there remained considerable differences regarding the extent and orientation of the revolution. With the exception of some of the socialists, who sought to construct an underground communication network in some areas, the national-conservative opposition fundamentally rejected setting up a covert organization within the country and believed that the men who assumed the leadership of the new government would, by virtue of their personal authority, find sufficient support among the people.

In the course of the general rethinking of policy that had become apparent since the beginning of 1943, persons closer to Stauffenberg began to wonder whether it would not be more reasonable to entrust the cabinet leadership to a socialist such as Leuschner or Leber instead of to Goerdeler in order to ensure the support of the proletariat. Leber did not share Goerdeler's belief that the new government would find sufficient support from the former trade unions.

The members of the Kreisau Circle thus came to see the path of a "revolution from above" as an option of last resort because they believed that the new sociopolitical order toward which they were striving could be realized only from below on the basis of "small communities" that were united in a spirit of neighborliness and like-mindedness and because they relied on the initiative of individuals. Consequently, they wanted to keep away from supraregional political parties as much as possible and to limit their influence to the forging of political will. Goerdeler's program, which provided for a three-party system if necessary, left just as little room for political parties.

The social and constitutional plans of the national-conservative resistance were developed for the most part in a vacuum, as it were, and rested on the utopian assumption that the tabula rasa created by the National Socialist regime in domestic policy, that is, the outlawing of the KPD, would continue to exist. The founding of the *National Committee "Free Germany" in July 1943 made the national-conservative conspirators realize that they would have to take into account the rival KPD, whose influence they had up to that point largely ignored. It was quite illusory to want to stabilize the situation by strengthening the "left wing" of the provisional government and accepting, as Moltke's supporters had urged, "Communists not bound to Moscow."

Through the efforts of Carlo Mierendorff, however, there were ideas for conjuring up a nonpartisan democratic people's movement that was supposed to function as a collection "of all surviving and viable social and democratic forces" and to anchor the government in the masses. Goerdeler considered a state-led mass organization that would be founded after the coup, whereas the members of the Kreisau Circle saw in the creation of a nonpartisan people's movement the chance to extricate policy from its partisan rut and to increase the participation of the middle class. The Goerdeler Circle's demand that this people's movement have a Christian orientation led to a break with the socialist wing under Julius Leber, which was already taking into consideration the claims to representation made by the exiled German Social Democratic Party (SPD) and the KPD's strengthened position.

On the other hand, there was progressive agreement with respect to more specific constitutional questions. However, certain concessions by the Kreisau Circle were to be in effect only during the transition period; among those concessions was the recognition of the German Trade Union's program, a program that, developed by Leuschner, was incompatible with the Kreisau Circle's favored plan of a partnership between employers and workers. The constitutional plans developed in Kreisau and presented by Goerdeler sought to eliminate plebiscitary influences. They allowed direct elections only at the local level and provided for a stratified system of representation that was based entirely on delegation from subordinate representative bodies and that thereby introduced a strong oligarchic element. By means of a multivote system, limitations on passive voting (the members of the Kreisau Circle wanted to exclude women) and indirect voting, qualified dignitaries were supposed to be favored and expertise was supposed to supplant demagoguery. It was hoped that these provisions, playing off against one another in practice, would strengthen the personal element in politics and yield an organic division of the "atomized" political corpus.

Toward this end, constitutional plans sought to avoid a return to the massing of power at the top of the commonwealth. In both plans, the principle of self-government was expressly given its due, yet this had the effect that the federal status of the states remained indefinite, and an unfilled gap existed between the demand for decentralization and the de facto strengthening of the executive branch of the federal government. For, in both plans, the privileging of the head of state — be he the representative of the Reich in Goerdeler's view or the administrator of the Reich in the view of the members of the Kreisau Circle — vis-à-vis the central parliament, which could oust the Reich chancellor only by a two-thirds majority and whose power to act was further limited by an upper house that was based on a corporative scheme, went beyond an extensive modification of the parliamentary principle and granted an unusual amount of power to the Reich government appointed by the head of state.

Of course, no one intended these plans to have such drastic results, which derived in part from an incorrect interpretation of the Weimar constitutional crisis. This was apparently due to the fact that professional politicians, toward whom there was a clear mistrust in the constitutional plans, were not sufficiently involved in the drafting of those plans. This is true of the overregulation of the conditions for candidacy and the indirect election process, which de facto opened the door for manipulation by small, resolute groups. Moreover, the centralization of decisions involving economic policy could hardly be reconciled with the pledge to decentralization and the federative principle.

With modifications, the ideas that the national-conservative resistance had regarding the constitution closely followed the changes of the Weimar constitution that parties on the right and neoconservative intellectuals had propagated since the 1920s and, in part, harked back to the constitutional law of the early nineteenth century. They stood in stark contrast to the principle of parliamentarism and to party pluralism and were derived from the vision of an order that was free of conflict and a politics that, as a rule, was oriented toward the common good — a vision that had inspired German political thought. At the same time, they drew from corporative ideas that did not seem to have been discredited by developments up to that point.

The conservative criticism of civilization during the Weimar years formed the background of the German opposition's constitutional plans, which, understandably, were not quite fully developed. The common point of departure of the intended political and social reforms was the watchword "massification," which refers to a process that was held responsible for the surge of materialistic attitudes, the commercialization and standardization of culture, mass consumption, and the "tabloid press." In various formulations, the representatives of the opposition decried the loss of the feeling for quality and of religious commitments among the masses and thereby revealed the strong elitist characteristic of their thought, which also came to the fore among socialists, as in the case of Theodor Haubach.

The massive NSDAP rallies and the frenetic cheering by whipped-up multitudes of people seemed to confirm fears of the destructive effects of the "age of the masses," National Socialism being seen as its incarnation. In contrast, the national-conservative conspirators proclaimed a program of, in Gerhard Ritter's words, a "de-massification of the masses." They wanted to replace social leveling with a stratified social order that allowed the individual to reflect on the personal and moral foundations of Christian existence.

The socially critical attitude of the national-conservative opposition fit in with variously hued attempts to find a solution for the social problem, which the opposition held responsible for the social crisis that had favored the rise of National Socialism. The Jesuit priest Alfred Delp, who played a decisive role in Kreisau, called for the realization of a "personal socialism" that included, above and beyond the restoration of religious security, the guarantee of the proletariat's social existence.

Despite varying degrees of criticism of liberal capitalism — whereas Goerdeler assumed a position of laissez-faire, Moltke and Trott regarded themselves as socialists — the private ownership of the means of production was not at all put into question. However, even Goerdeler agreed on the nationalization of raw materials industries, an idea that was accepted only with reservation by the economists of the Freiburg Circle. Insofar as there were anticapitalist ideas in the opposition, they were, as a rule, accompanied by decidedly socially paternalistic views. These views had their strongest supporter in Fritz-Dietlof von der Schulenburg, who wanted to replace the national social-security system with a system of public assistance provided by manorial estates. Oswald Spengler's idea of "Prussian socialism" had a pervasive influence.

Suggestions for social structural reform were directed altogether against modern large industry, forbade the formation of clusters of industrial regions, idealized the middle-class economic structure of Württemberg, and attacked rampantly growing large city centers and massive working-class housing districts. The enmity toward large cities expressed in these suggestions was countered by an idealization of an agrarian lifestyle, which culminated in the demand to maintain a viable peasant class, since that class formed the basis of the social organism. This was in accord with the idealization, long prevalent in conservative thought, of agrarian Lebensraum. A few individuals felt that large estates performed the function of a "healthy" counterbalance to industry.

The social-reform plans reflect the strong influence of the youth movement and — not least — of the workers' movement and its desire to bring about a balance between labor and capital on the level of the workplace. Despite the advice of leading representatives of orthodox liberalism, the planners' economic ideas abstracted to a large degree from the realities of large industry; through the utopia of a "commonwealth divorced from class" (in Goerdeler's words), they contributed just as little to a solution of social conflicts as did National Socialist social policy, elements of which they wanted to appropriate.

Not only the National Socialists but also their opponents were under the spell of the experience of the November Revolution. Fear of a "social revolution from below" strengthened them in their fight against the regime that, in their view, would only end in a "second November 9, 1918," and thereby lead to an internal and external Bolshevization. Thus, the bourgeois upper class's interest in ensuring its endangered social status also stood behind the ideas for reform. On the other hand, the opposition's thinking was not beholden to a policy of maintaining property and was marked by a readiness to surrender antiquated privileges.

On the one hand, the political vision of most of the conspirators remained indebted to the idea of a "German way" (or, as Delp put it, a "third way") and shunned the adoption of Western constitutional models without succeeding in finding truly viable alternative solutions. On the other hand, they overcame the predominance of a cynicism vis-à-vis the pragmatics of power, a cynicism that would have led de facto to inaction. The opposition's suggestions for reform were no doubt full of utopian features, yet a certain measure of utopian thought apparently provided the necessary precondition for the opposition's determination to resist. The goals of the national-conservative resistance also reflect the political alternatives to fascist dictatorship that existed in Germany. They did not exactly anticipate the return to a liberal-parliamentary type of constitution, which was not definitively realized until 1948 in the Parliamentary Council — against the protest of leading representatives of the Kreisau Circle.

The representatives of the opposition did not foresee the manner of the complete collapse of the National Socialist system of rule as occurred during the spring of 1945. As a rule, to act under the conditions of the existing political system meant to bear a heavy load, quite aside from the fact that the strict dichotomy between National Socialism and the "Other Germany," as it was portrayed by early postwar journalism, was a fiction. There no doubt was an ideological affinity, varying in degree from individual to individual, between National Socialism and the national-conservative resistance, and this was the case not only within the military opposition. This was shown by the ambivalent attitude toward the persecution of the Jews, however little the opposition approved of the regime's criminal methods. Moreover, only very few conspirators, such as Helmuth James von Moltke or Joachim Oster, were able to free themselves of the illusion that the Reich would be able to hold on to its foreign policy successes after the regime's collapse and maintain German hegemony in central Europe.

On the other hand, one must call special attention to the perseverance and personal engagement that the men and women involved in the July 20, 1944, assassination attempt on Hitler displayed against the continuation of the war and Hitler's criminal policies, a display that was made despite ever-dwindling chances of success and the risk of their being subjected to accusations of treason. Beyond all political interests and ideologies, there stood the morally grounded conviction that it was necessary to act against the regime's inhumanity in order, as Helmuth James von Moltke described the opposition's central goal with characteristic eloquence, "to restore the image of humankind in the hearts of our citizens."

Bibliography

Hoffmann, Peter. *Widerstand, Staatsstreich, Attentat: Der Kampf der Opposition gegen Hitler*. Munich, 1985.

Mommsen, Hans. "Gesellschaftsbild und Verfassungspläne des deutschen Widerstands." In *Widerstand im Dritten Reich: Probleme, Ereignisse, Gestalten*. Edited by Hermann Graml. Frankfurt am Main, 1984.

Ritter, Gerhard. *The German Resistance: Carl Goerdeler's Struggle against Tyranny*. New York, 1958.

Schmädecke, Jürgen, and Peter Steinbach, eds. *Der Widerstand gegen den Nationalsozialismus: Die deutsche Gesellschaft und der Widerstand gegen Hitler*. Munich, 1986.

Opposition by Churches and Christians

Günther van Norden _____

The National Socialists' accession to power with the help of the old, conservative elites during the first half of 1933 was not a call to any sort of political protest or resistance for either the Protestant or the Catholic Church. On the contrary: at least after March 1933, both institutions viewed with growing sympathy the gradual transition of the pluralistic parliamentary democracy into what they thought and hoped would be a Christian and authoritarian oligarchy.

In the case of Protestantism, which bore a Lutheran mark, the reasons for this were largely derived from its history. It stood in the four-hundred-year-old tradition of "throne and altar," a generally happy relationship between a government hospitable to the church and a church hospitable to the government, which made the obedience of subjects, as demanded in Romans 13, a pleasant matter of course. For the most part, it viewed the so-called Second Reich, the Hohenzollerns' Protestant empire, as a merciful gift from God that was to be defended from all enemies within and without. Having developed in this way, the Protestant mentality perceived the collapse of the monarchical government through the "revolution" of 1918 as a barely fathomable judgment by God and treated the new parliamentary democracy as the "child of the revolution" with nothing less than distance. Even if the church described itself as standing above political parties, its members were largely in the camp of the conservative parties: political Protestantism of the Weimar period was represented mainly in the German National People's Party. As the self-surrender of the Weimar Republic drew to a close in 1933, the overwhelming majority of the Protestant milieu saw its hopes fulfilled: the Second Reich appeared to arise again in the form of a Christian-authoritarian state under the leadership of conservative elites in alliance with the representatives of a Third Reich. With the solemn religious state ceremony in the historic Garrison Church in Potsdam on March 21, 1933, the God-given continuity of German history seemed to have been restored.

A plethora of statements friendly to the church made by the Reich government and the National Socialist German Workers' Party (NSDAP) seemed to confirm all hopes. The fact that democratic institutions were done away with and opponents of the regime were threatened with concentration camps, prisons, and prohibitions to work in their professions gave no reason for protest, since authority "does not bear the sword in vain" (Romans 13:4) and used it — so it was said — to punish and fight the atheistic-materialistic enemies of the German people.

The reasons the Catholic Church and political Catholicism said yes to the new regime were not, as in the case of Protestantism, derived from history but rather derived more from the structure of Catholicism. In the "holy Protestant Reich of the Germans," it, like the workers' movement, was among the enemies of the Reich, and the *Kulturkampf* had had a strong effect on it: it had been a struggle against the ruling powers. Thus, Catholicism could not identify with the Second Reich as existentially as Protestantism and, for the most part, went through the transition to parliamentary democracy relatively smoothly. The representative of political Catholicism, the Center Party, was even one of the pillars of the Weimar state from the very beginning to the end. Nevertheless, no substantial help in defending the republic came from it.

This was no doubt due to the fact that, during the final years of the Weimar Republic, the Center Party had drawn closer to the conservative camp and thus had lost its readiness to fight for pluralistic democracy. Connected with this trend was the reality that organizational elements of Catholicism, that is, its hierarchical-authoritarian aspect and radical rejection of liberal and materialistic ideas, also had a political effect. There clearly are affinities to the "national rightists" in this.

Because of its history, German Catholicism perhaps had the chance, in an alliance of the Center Party and social democracy, to ward off the National Socialists. It also recognized the dangers presented by the National Socialists much more clearly than Protestantism. Thus, even in 1930, it unequivocally warned of National Socialism through church prohibitions and made clear the incommensurability of National Socialism and church doctrine. It defended this position up to March 1933. But when the Reich chancellor, in his speech concerning the Enabling Act, promised all the things that a Weimar government had never clearly promised — to make the church a fundament in the life of the state once again — and as the welcome association between German National Socialism and church-friendly Italian fascism seemed to be so clear, the Center Party, albeit hesitantly, gave up its resistance, agreed to the Enabling Act, and thereby dug a grave for itself and democracy.

A few days later, on March 28, 1933, the German bishops rescinded their prohibitions and warnings and thereby opened the way to National Socialism for Catholics. This concession to the new political circumstances was considered to be tactically wise in order for the church to remain a loyal dialogue partner of the state, and, in a remarkable pastoral letter, the bishops could thus expressly point to substantive common features between the new thinking and the church. The Vatican followed suit on July 20, 1933, by concluding a concordat with the new regime that, on the one hand, granted international respectability to the regime and, on the other hand, simultaneously promised existential security for the Catholic Church in Germany — after political Catholicism was crushed.

One must be aware of this initial situation, since only then can the later opposition of the churches and Christians be correctly appreciated.

First, we will look at political and theological protest by groups and individuals in 1933. In the tumult of Protestant enthusiasm for the fatherland, there were only a few, quantitatively small groups that looked with extreme skepticism upon the National Socialists, the primary allies of the conservatives. These were members of the Religious Socialists (such as Emil Fuchs), the Liberal Protestants (such as Martin Rade and Hermann Mulert), some defenders of dialectical theology, and several very different representatives from the Lutheran corner (such as Hermann Sasse and Dietrich Bonhoeffer).

The first two groups were motivated primarily by political ideology and had always affirmed Weimar democracy, having been for the most part active in the German Social Democratic Party (SPD) and the German Democratic Party (DDP). The small group from the larger circle of dialectical theology surrounding Karl Barth was indeed close to the SPD but, like the Lutherans, was primarily theologically motivated. During the first half of 1933, its opposition was directed against the rise of dictatorship and its inhuman ideology. It was an opposition of words, of rational arguments with the goal of informing and warning in order perhaps to slow the trend — and was just as powerless as completely unrepresentative of German Protestantism in 1933. These groups must nevertheless be named because they show that it was possible from the very beginning to see things as other people later saw them.

In Catholicism, too, there were still a few groups and individuals who sought to offer resistance in the form of contradiction after the church's expressions of loyalty, such as the circle surrounding the *Rhein-Mainische Volkszeitung* (Rhine-Main people's news) (one of these being Walter Dirks), segments of the Catholic Workers' Movement (Otto Müller, Jakob Kaiser), and individual priests (such as Karl Klinkhammer).

Clerical protest from institutions arose out of the desire for theological and ethical autonomy, in defense against control by the state, and in the attempt to escape the process of social *Gleichschaltung.** This

---

*The term *Gleichschaltung*, variously translated as coordination, synchronization, or literally as "putting in the same gear," was first used by Justice Minister Franz Gürtner,

protest took the form not only of nonconformity and passive resistance but also of organized, actively oppositional acts not in the private sphere but among the German public. This was accomplished in three areas.

Opposition in the defense of clerical organizations can be seen as early as 1933. It was manifest in the Protestant church's attempt to keep the institution's structure free of the National Socialists' attempts to coordinate it, this attempt being apparent in the election of Bodelschwingh as Reich bishop and in the maintenance of separate administrative branches. Catholic bishops protested primarily against the persecution of Catholic clubs and the denunciation of Catholic denominational schools.

This protest by church leaderships was indeed directed against certain interests of the National Socialist authorities, but not against the state; on the contrary, this protest was repeatedly accompanied with the affirmation that the protest basically served the state. Church leaders watched the National Socialists' actions in the political and social spheres with sympathy, as can be seen in the November 12, 1933, pastoral letter by the Bavarian bishops, which speaks of saving the German people from "the horror of Bolshevism." Resistance by church leaders, as vehement as it was exclusive, was confined to matters of the church. There was a strict division between the sphere of the church, in which the state was not to become involved, and the sphere of the state, in which the church was not to become involved. Only where the state overstepped this boundary did it meet with church opposition.

People did not see that this naive separation was a fiction from the very beginning. On the one hand, the churches as large elements in society were so closely tied up sociologically, economically, and intellectually in the social structures whose milieus they had helped form that they had no or hardly any distance from political events and the expressions those events found in views of the world (anti-Communism, for example). On the other hand, their protest against National Socialism's claim to totalitarianism was itself opposition against a key element of National Socialist policy.

---

who used it in the formulation of a new law called the Temporary Law for Coordination (*Gleichschaltung*) of the States with the Reich (March 31, 1933). The Nazis subsequently used the term *Gleichschaltung* to describe the process by which German institutions must be coordinated to conform to the principles of National Socialism. German also contains the term *Gleichrichter*, which refers to a device that allows electric current to flow in only one direction, thus changing alternating into direct current. Similarly, the führer, representing the will of the German people, was said to direct the flow of policy through the institutions of state and party down to the people. All aspects of German life not already in the Nazi path must be redirected (coordinated) to do so. (Sources: Christian Zentner and Friedemann Budürftig, eds., *Das Grosse Lexikon des Dritten Reiches* [Munich, 1985], 216; Helmut Krausnick, "Stages of Coordination," in *The Path to Dictatorship, 1918–1933* [New York, 1966], 133—52; and Klaus P. Fischer, *Nazi Germany: A New History* [New York, 1995], 278–84, 642).

At this point, it becomes especially clear how very poor the churches' opportunities for protest were at the beginning of the Third Reich. Because of their own theological traditions (such as their interpretation of the commandment of subservience to authority in Romans 13 and the doctrine of the two kingdoms) and politico-ideological biases (such as anti-Communism), it was not possible for them to look past their own domains. Because of its more consistent stance, the Catholic Church was able to assert its position more successfully within its domain than was the Protestant church.

This opposition in defense of church doctrine stood in the foreground as of 1934–35. Among Protestants, it first became manifest in the struggle against the introduction of the Aryan paragraph into the church's legislative matters; Martin Niemöller's call for the formation of the Emergency League of Clergymen in 1933 is an example of this. The *Confessing Church, which arose in opposition to the Reich's official German-Christian Church, did not protest against the exclusion of Jews from national life but rather objected to the denominational breach that it saw in the ecclesiastical Aryan paragraph. Here it becomes clear that the Confessing Church, which opposed the German-Christian Church, also stood firmly in the tradition of a Lutheran doctrine of two kingdoms and just as firmly in the conservative-bourgeois Protestant tradition with its adopted paradigms, including, for example, anti-Judaism. For this reason, resistance by the Confessing Church with respect to issues pertaining to the state, and thus with respect to illegal measures taken by the state, was entirely impossible at first.

A change correcting both of these deeply rooted strains in tradition came about only very gradually. One can see this change in two instances: (1) the Barmen theological declaration of 1933, which expressed the Confessing Church's protest against the National Socialist state's claim to totality; and (2) sermons delivered in 1935 against National Socialism's "racist-*völkisch* worldview." In these protests, the state met resistance from a church that had always emphasized its loyalty to the state and that continued to do so, yet that, because of its beliefs, also drew the line vis-à-vis this state and the system of views that it promulgated. This was a political issue, although the Confessing Church did not want it to be, and the state viewed it as such.

Analogous to these actions by Protestants, the Catholic Church — in a bishops' pastoral letter of August 20, 1935, which was read from the pulpits — also protested against the massive attack by the politically sponsored "new paganism." For the bishops, it was clear that "Catholics do not instigate revolts and engage in violent resistance." Yet it was also clear that Catholics were to resist the propaganda of the new paganism, the secularization of public life, and the de-Christianization of youth. Since the Reich minister of the interior had shortly before (in July

1935) declared the "secularization of public life" to be a watchword of National Socialism's struggle, the bishops' call to the faithful was, with all due respect to "the state," a call to opposition against all party and state attempts to destroy Catholic sexual morality, the Catholic creed, and Catholic organizations.

The dilemma in which the churches found themselves becomes clear here and characterizes the difficulty and rift in ecclesiastical protest: to honor the state in accordance with Romans 13, yet at the same time to be required to resist elements of its "ideology."

When the Nuremberg Laws heightened discrimination against German Jews on September 15, 1935, the churches did not offer a word of protest. From this, it becomes clear that they were still fighting almost exclusively for their own existence during this phase. In hindsight, this shows the weakness of their opposition, which was limited by theological traditions and politico-ideological constraints.

What has been said of opposition with respect to the two previous matters is also true of the churches' defense of law and humanity, albeit with two differences. Beginning in 1935–36, the defense of law and humanity shifted from the public sphere primarily to the sphere of internal writings by church leaders to the führer. One reason for this was that church leaders saw themselves subject to growing pressure from the Gestapo; another reason was that church leaders guaranteed themselves greater resonance if they did not attack the government leadership in public. In addition, the issue was no longer solely the maintenance of their own institutions and teachings, but rather the maintenance of *humanum extra muros ecclesiae* (the human outside the walls of the church).

There were varying positions in both churches with respect to the question of how protest was to be realized. Among Protestants, differences culminated in 1938 when Karl Barth stated in his letter to the Prague professor Hromadka that every Czech soldier who fought against German aggression was also doing this for the church of Jesus Christ. Indeed, Bonhoeffer had already said in 1933 that the church not only should help persons suffering under the yoke of oppression but, in extreme cases, should also throw off that yoke. Yet should that be done not only by using the weapons of the church — the spoken word, passive disobedience, martyrdom — but also by calling for struggle, for tyrannicide, by a theology of revolution?

Even the Confessing Church's "radical" group could not agree to this type of resistance. It rejected Barth's statement as intolerable. Yet this rejection did not prevent "moderate" leaders of the Confessing Church at the state level from distancing themselves from this group "for religious and patriotic reasons," since they did not want to come under suspicion should their respectful dissent against authority be misunderstood as resistance — perhaps even as political resistance.

The chairman of the Catholic bishops' conference, Cardinal Adolf Bertram, reacted similarly to attempts to extend dissent further into the public domain. In view of the March 1937 papal encyclical *Mit brennender Sorge* (With burning concern), the bishop of Berlin, Count Konrad von Preysing, called for a more effective idea of defense for the episcopate ("The Public Sphere and Mass Reaction"), especially since the encyclical's wide circulation in Germany had had a liberating effect among Catholic churchgoers. Yet Cardinal Bertram, like Protestant bishops, shrank from any church protest actions that could have heightened tensions with the state.

One must mention Protestant protest against illegal measures taken by the state, such as the manipulation of the Reichstag election, the establishment of concentration camps, as well as the ideological demand for "Jew-hatred"; an example of such protest was the March 28, 1936, statement "to the führer and Reich chancellor" by the "provisional church leadership," that is, the leadership of the Confessing Church's radical wing. This expression of dissent — the harshest up to that point — was not a battle cry directed at the criminal state; yet it was an instance of opposition against concrete injustice in an area where the church was not immediately concerned — the arena of national politics — and it sought to hinder further injustice. In a public proclamation read in churches, the provisional church leadership warned the faithful that they were required to render obedience to the ruling authority as long as that authority did not demand what was against the will of God and that they were required to resist when they were called upon to do anything contrary to the gospel. This public call for Christians to resist authority — and thus the führer — when God so demanded was a remarkable act at a time when unconditional and fervent obedience to the führer was the highest duty and virtue. With respect to the Catholic Church, one must mention the protest of the Rottenburg bishop Johannes Baptista Sproll, who refused to participate in the Reichstag election of April 1938.

In the fall of 1938 (during Kristallnacht), German Jewry saw itself subject to the National Socialist regime's renewed, brutal aggression. There was no unified protest by the Catholic Church and Protestant Confessing Church — to say nothing of the official Protestant church leadership. But, in a few instances, there was public opposition (such as by the cathedral provost Bernhard Lichtenberg and the pastor Friedrich Winter) and assistance (such as by the pastors Heinrich Grüber and Werner Sylten, the curate Katharina Staritz, Dr. Margarethe Sommer, and Gertrud Luckner).

Within the ecclesiastical opposition, there were indeed some parallels between Protestants and Catholics — in their motives, methods, and goals — but there was little coordination. At the end of 1941, however, there was a coordinated action: on December 9, state bishop Theophil Wurm protested in a letter to the führer against the intolerable and disgraceful oppression of the church. Wurm acted on behalf of the Protestant church leaders' conference, to which about half of all state-level Protestant church leaders belonged. He mentioned the measures taken to eliminate the mentally ill and the growing severity in the treatment of the Jews. And on December 10, Cardinal Bertram of Breslau, acting on behalf of the German bishops' conference, protested in a letter to the Reich government against the oppression of the Catholic Church and the violation of "eternal" laws. In this letter, too, the disrespect of personal freedom through violent acts by the Gestapo and the killing of innocent sick people were denounced. Prior to these statements, documents such as these had been accompanied by proclamations of loyalty, but such proclamations now became weaker, and the language vis-à-vis the ruling authorities became more urgent and clearer. Already in the summer of 1941, the Bishop of Münster, Count von Galen, had protested publicly against acts of murder. This protest by the churches presumably led to the limiting of so-called euthanasia at the end of 1941. This means that the goal of the protest, that is, the elimination of a particular injustice, was able in this case to be reached for the most part through the common protest of representatives of institutions that were still resolute.

The churches did not offer similarly clear opposition to the persecution of the Jews. Thus, the question of whether they would also have had success on that issue must remain open.

The sharpest protest against the extermination of the Jews came from German Protestantism in the form of the secretly circulated "Letter of the Laity of Munich" of 1943, in which the church was called upon to resist to the utmost the state's attempt to annihilate Jewry. During the same year, the Prussian Confessing Church, in an exegesis of the commandment "Thou shalt not kill," spoke up in admonition by noting that the annihilation of humans for racist reasons could not be grounded on appeals to the ruling authority's sword of justice.

In its pastoral letter during that same year, the Catholic Church also emphasized the significance of the Ten Commandments as the "law of life of all peoples" and as the foundation of human rights. The church stated that the killing of innocent life — that is, of defenseless persons who were mentally impaired or ill, of "incurable invalids," of the "genetically handicapped," of unarmed prisoners and POWs, and of humans of foreign race and origin — was an attack against God.

The churches' institutional protest grew analogously with the increase of National Socialist terror. Not in the sense that this protest was initially a more passive resistance and later a more active and political one. Nor in the sense that it initially attacked only sectors of the system in a piecemeal fashion and later fought it generally as such. Nor in the sense that it was initially active more in the private sector and later more in the public sector. One can not here apply the model of an incremental gradation from nonconformity to dissent and protest up to organized political resistance that can perhaps be applied to other areas of resistance. Rather, ecclesiastical opposition at all times during the Third Reich manifested itself simultaneously as nonconformity in certain areas and conformity in others, as dissent in certain areas and accommodation in others, and as organized protest alongside a fundamental loyalty to the state. The simultaneity of apparently incompatible phenomena, which was an essential criterion of the Third Reich, was also a facet of the church's resistance.

Yet one can discern a development in this insofar as dissent was initially (1933–34) primarily in the service of the institutions' self-defense and then, beginning in 1934–35, was primarily in the defense of church doctrine, whereby such dissent remained firmly embedded in an unquestioned loyalty to the state. In a third phase beginning in 1936, dissent extended to the political sphere, as at least some people recognized that the churches' vigilance should not be limited to the ecclesiastical sphere, but rather had to be present wherever human rights were violated. With the increase in National Socialist aggression, ethical motives for opposition also grew.

On the other hand, the modus operandi remained largely unquestioned. It is true that the churches' commitment to loyalty to the state decreased and their tone became harsher as they increasingly saw the state as a criminal regime, but their opposition remained confined to public and private protest speech and dissent. There was no place for political means such as conspiracy and the use of force — obvious criteria of political resistance. The churches' goals also differed from those of the political resistance movement: at issue was not the toppling of the "evil" authorities, let alone revolution, but rather the maintenance of the churches' own positions and norms and, finally, the partial remediation of concrete injustice outside the sphere of the churches.

Our references here to ecclesiastical-theological protest and the political resistance of individuals, congregations, and churchgoers does not encompass the more politically motivated protest actions of ecclesiastical organizations and clubs or the more theologically motivated protestations of individual pastors as could still be seen in 1933. Nor are we referring to the statements and measures of ecclesiastically legitimated and authorized executive boards, synods, or bishops. Rather, we are referring here to the protest of Christians who not only put up resistance as individuals but were held up and heartened by the solidarity

of their congregations, that is, of their ecclesiastical milieus. Thus, at issue in most cases here is not individual, but congregational, opposition,
that is, resistance of the milieu. One can discern two aspects of this:
ecclesiastical-theological protest and theologically grounded political
resistance.

During the years after 1933, conflict with the party and the state was
primarily brought about on ecclesiastical-theological grounds: this involved the reading and dissemination of proclamations from the pulpit
that were considered to be unfavorable to the state as well as oppositional statements delivered in sermons and other contexts, examples of
this having been given by Martin Niemöller and Paul Schneider, Bernhard Lichtenberg and Heinrich Feurstein, and Hermann and Helmut
Hesse. The defense of Christian youth work was also a pressing motive,
as seen in the efforts of Joseph Rossaint, Albert Riesterer, Franz Weinmann, and Horst Thurmann. Other clerics and nuns exposed murder
in hospitals and nursing homes or tried to stop it; they, too, were sent
to concentration camps. There were 387 Austrian and German Catholic
priests and 35 Protestant pastors in the clerics' block at Dachau alone
who had to suffer for their ecclesiastical dissent.

Especially among Catholics, a key motive was the maintenance and
defense of traditional customs. It was these customs in particular that
occasioned considerable popular resistance within a wide spectrum of
the faithful, an example being the debate over the presence of crucifixes
in schools. Party and state authorities usually reacted cautiously to such
defiant statements by the populace and frequently acquiesced. This also
clearly shows that the churches — usually the Catholic Church — had
considerable influence over their members, an influence that they could
assert when they wanted.

It is difficult to make specific claims about the point at which this
opposition, manifested in the form of protest and intransigence, became political resistance. Nevertheless, one can see that, particularly
within the fraternally organized, "radical" Confessing Church and in
segments of the Catholic Church, which looked more and more criti-
cally upon Breslau Cardinal Bertram's cautious course, the distance from
the National Socialist regime increasingly turned into dissent and led to
political opposition. Thus, in March 1936, for example, several Catholic and Protestant clerics refused to vote. The refusal of pastors to
swear an oath in 1938 was just as significant as the refusal of individual
Protestants and Catholics to serve in the military.

In most cases, the motivation for this opposition was certainly
ecclesiastical-theological, yet the regime always saw itself as being under
political and ideological attack. The justifications for the issuing of arrest warrants show this: "statements hostile to the state," "incitement of
youth," "violation of the law against malicious gossip," "refusal to give

the Hitler salute," "prayer for the Jews," "actions injurious to the military," "agitation against the NSDAP," and so on. Yet it seems dubious to subsume these and other expressions of opposition under the notion of political "resistance," since they were neither politically motivated nor had a political goal.

As an opposition with bourgeois features arose in various circles during the course of the war, Christians were on hand as well. They not only stood by "those suffering under the yoke of oppression" and denounced the injustice but cooperated in the resistance with all the consequences associated with being involved in conspiracy. On the basis of numerous international connections, they informed their foreign contacts about the German resistance movement and its plans and worked on memoranda concerning the future democratic shape of Germany; here, one must mention Dietrich Bonhoeffer and Max Josef Metzger.

The *Kreisau Circle was particularly informed by Christian ideas. Count Helmuth James von Moltke, Adam von Trott zu Solz, and Henning von Tresckow justified their participation in the resistance by their Christian faith. The Jesuit priests Rösch, Delp, and König (see *Rösch Circle) cooperated in this. Augustin Rösch established contacts with the episcopate, and Alfred Delp established links with Catholic workers' leaders such as Bernhard Letterhaus, Nikolaus Gross, and Otto Müller. These people worked in concert toward the overthrow of the system. Delp, in particular, introduced social components (for example, the trade union question and the idea of factory employees' trade unions) into the considerations of the members of the Kreisau Circle. He also acted as middleman to the *Goerdeler Circle.

A group of persons surrounding the Catholic workers' leader Jakob Kaiser and the Berlin attorney Josef Wirmer was part of this circle. With the help of his old connections to the Center Party, Kaiser, in particular, organized a network of resistance centers in Germany. Together with close contacts with the Social Democratic trade unionist Wilhelm Leuschner, the conservative Goerdeler Circle found a broader social basis.

In Freiburg, the Freiburg Council (see *Freiburg Circles) was the circle of political resistance most strongly influenced by members and sympathizers of the Confessing Church. The national-conservative group surrounding the professors Gerhard Ritter, Constantin von Dietze, and Adolf Lampe worked out memoranda that were to have served as the basis for the new order in Germany after its liberation. The first memorandum was written in the fall of 1938 after Kristallnacht and bore the title "Church and World: A Necessary Reflection on the Tasks of Christians and the Church in Our Time." In 1942, Dietrich Bonhoeffer initiated the drafting of an article, "Political Order of the Community: An Essay concerning the Self-Reflection of the Christian Conscience during the Political Troubles of Our Time," which presented fundamentals of a program and on which noted men of the Confessing Church also ` worked.

In sum, one must say that, in view of the regime's crimes, neither the Catholic nor the Protestant church had the power to incite their faithful to political resistance, that is, to "tyrannicide." Individual Christians, either alone or aided by their groups, took this path. They had recognized that they were face-to-face with a criminal state in the form of the National Socialist dictatorship, a state that they had to oppose — including by force.

Next to these stood other dissenters who sought to fight concrete injustice with the word (protest) or refusal to comply. This also often led to arrest and sometimes to death. This dissent is all the more significant because it shows that another possibility of Christian existence presented itself vis-à-vis the silence or jubilation of the churches' leaders and members.

Bibliography

Conway, John S. *The Nazi Persecution of the Churches, 1933–1945.* London, 1968.

Denzler, Georg, and Volker Fabricius. *Christen und Nationalsozialisten.* Frankfurt am Main, 1993.

Gotto, Klaus, and Konrad Repgen, eds. *Kirche, Katholiken und National-* ` *sozialismus.* Mainz, 1980.

Müller, Klaus-Jürgen, ed. *Der deutsche Widerstand 1933–1945.* 2d ed. Paderborn, 1990. See especially Gunther van Norden, "Widerstand im deutschen Protestantismus 1933–1945"; and Heinz Hürten, "Selbstbehauptung und Widerstand der katholischen Kirche."

Nowak, Kurt. "Kirchenkampf und Widerstand im 'Dritten Reich': Erwägungen zu einem historiographischen Prinzipienproblem." *Wissenschaftliche Zeitschrift der Karl-Marx-Universität Leipzig.* Gesellschafts- und sprachwissenschaftliche Reihe 6 (1981).

Schmädeke, Jürgen, and Peter Steinbach, eds. *Der Widerstand gegen den Nationalsozialismus: Die deutsche Gesellschaft und der Widerstand gegen Hitler.* 2d ed. Munich, 1982. See especially "Dritter Teil: Kirchen und Konfessionen zwischen Kooperation und Teilwiderstand."

Scholder, Klaus. *The Churches and the Third Reich.* Vol. 1, *Preliminary History and the Time of Illusions, 1918–1934;* vol. 2, *The Year of Disillusionment, 1934–Barmen and Rome.* London and Philadelphia, 1988.

Military Resistance

Hermann Graml

Out of the German Imperial Reich and its states, which were also constituted on monarchical lines, the social and constitutional change at the end of World War I created republican and parliamentarily governed state entities in which the democratic left, social democracy, was able to play an influential role for the first time. The Treaty of Versailles, which the subsequent Weimar Republic was forced to accept after the military defeat and the political collapse of Wilhelmine Germany in 1919, initially shackled the German attempt to gain hegemony in Europe and to assume the position of a world power. Through the Versailles treaty, the armed might of the German Reich was reduced to an army that was only one hundred thousand men strong and that was forbidden to have heavy artillery, tanks, and planes; the navy was limited to a total number of fifteen thousand men and could maintain neither large battleships nor submarines. In order to preclude a gradual increase in size through the training of reservists, the treaty further forbade Germany universal conscription and imposed upon the armed forces, which were now called the Reichswehr, the character of a professional army composed of long-term volunteers.

The political consequences of these military clauses in the treaty — all products of an exaggerated, misleading need for security on the part of the victorious powers, albeit a need that, especially in the case of France, was understandable after four years of war — were severe and far-reaching. In fact, the treaty weakened the armed forces to such a degree that they were not even up to fighting a war against one of Germany's smaller neighbors and were not even able to fulfill a defensive function. Thus, an expansionist tendency arose in the Reichswehr that was cultivated by all in its ranks, not only by those of good conscience, and that, being ascribed supreme importance, was furthermore thought to be called for in the national interest. So the Reichswehr thought itself justified in giving its sympathies to any political movement in Germany that proclaimed uncompromising struggle against Versailles and particularly to those movements that promised to shake off the treaty's military limitations, regardless of whatever dubious aspects those movements might otherwise have.

The demand for a professional army was even more significant. In view of the divide between the army, on the one hand, and liberal, democratic, and socialist forces in society, on the other hand — a divide that existed in Wilhelmine Germany due to the close connection between officers' and noncommissioned officers' corps and an illiberal monarchy hostile to democracy — the ban on universal conscription had the effect that the Weimar Republic by necessity initially recruited its armed forces almost entirely from the Wilhelmine army. Another effect was that, in following years as well, the Reichswehr was able without interruption to obtain future officers, noncommissioned officers, and troops primarily from those circles that had already been providing them: the nobility, the upper middle class, groups from the bourgeois middle class who stood on the political right, and the rural folk. The Reichswehr thus became and remained a refuge of political convictions that had been characteristic of, and still dominated, Wilhelmine Germany's social elite and bourgeois and peasant classes that were hospitable to the military. The convictions included monarchism, nationalism, and flat rejection of liberalism, democracy, parliamentarism, and socialism — and not only socialism's Communist variant but its democratic-parliamentary ones as well.

Consequently, the members of the Reichswehr by no means served the Weimar state, a parliamentarily governed republic with a strong and influential social democracy. Rather, they simply served *in* the state of Weimar. Oriented toward an "extratemporal idea of the state" and viewing themselves as the safeguards of the "true Germany," they hoped for the quick dissolution of the Weimar Republic through the restoration of the monarchy or, should this no longer be possible after the prince's discredited abdication at the war's end, through the creation of a powerful nationalistic state characterized by rightist views on domestic policy.

Thus, it was only logical that the Reichswehr reacted to Hitler's being named Reich chancellor on January 30, 1933, and to the National Socialist movement's subsequent conquest of political power with feelings that ranged from cautiously positive anticipation to enthusiastic approval; skepticism was seldom heard. Here were a man and a political force that had taken power and promised to fulfill all of the Reichswehr's hopes: from rearmament (which meant better career opportunities), to the restoration of Germany's status as a great power, to a new domestic order under the auspices of right-wing authoritarianism. The Reichswehr and its leadership thus had no reservations about helping Hitler construct the National Socialist regime in three ways.

First, the Reichswehr maintained well-wishing neutrality while the political left, including social democracy, was eliminated and persecuted, while the parliamentary system was completely liquidated, and while a one-party state was established. Already at the end of February 1933, the chief of staff in the Reich Ministry of War, Colonel von Reichenau, said in a meeting of commanders, "One must know that we are amidst a revolution. The rot in the state must go, and that can happen only through terror. The party will attack Marxism mercilessly. The task of the Wehrmacht is this: be at the ready. No help in case the hunted seek safety in the armed forces." And on June 1, 1933, Reich minister of war von Blomberg said, "It will be good if this [National Socialist] movement soon achieves the totality that it is striving for." Second, the Reichswehr, as a result of such leanings, gave its support to Hitler in his conflict with the SA (Storm Unit), especially since the SA's ambition of becoming the National Socialist people's army directly challenged the army. Without the Reichswehr's logistical support, Hitler's murderous action against the SA leadership on June 30, 1934, would not have been possible. Third, immediately after this, the leadership of the armed forces covered up the fact that, after the death of Reich president von Hindenburg on August 2, 1934, Hitler had assumed Hindenburg's office and thereby become commander in chief of the Reichswehr. Blomberg immediately went so far as to introduce a new oath and to have the armed forces swear this oath to Hitler personally instead of to "*Volk* and Fatherland," as had previously been the case.

The murder of the SA leaders and other alleged or actual opponents of the regime — including two former generals of the Reichswehr, Kurt von Schleicher and Ferdinand von Bredow, Schleicher having even been minister of war and Reich chancellor — did indeed cause much unease and, here and there, horror as well. While being interrogated by the Gestapo, Hans Oster, who had been a major in the Counterintelligence Office of the Ministry of the Reichswehr at the time of the murders, spoke even in 1944 of the horror that the "methods of a gang of robbers" had caused in him. The destruction of the constitutional state by the Gestapo and by a progressive politicization of the justice system, apparent everywhere, also provoked criticism and nervousness; the regime's brutal anti-Semitism and hostility toward the churches also had a negative effect. Yet no one turned against Hitler and the führer-state. Even people who, like Oster, were already quite critical did not develop an opposition of any substantial import until the end of 1937 or beginning of 1938.

The end of 1937 and beginning of 1938 saw the coalescence of the first circles of officers who began to believe in the necessity of neutralizing Hitler and reconstructing the political system as well. The reasons for this lay in part in one of Hitler's domestic policy maneuvers and in part in the transition of National Socialist foreign policy to its first expansionist phase. When Minister of War von Blomberg, faithful to the führer, had to resign on February 4, 1938, because his second marriage was, as later became known, to a woman of ill-repute, Hitler, in a vicious intrigue involving a charge of homosexuality, used the opportunity to sack the commander in chief of the army, General von Fritsch, who had also become troublesome. At the same time, various other conservative generals were given their walking papers. Hitler assumed command of the Ministry of War, which had been renamed the High Command of the Armed Forces, and, while he had hitherto been rather the nominal commander in chief of the armed forces, he now exercised direct and actual supreme command with the help of a small staff under General Keitel. He thereby came a big step closer to having coordinated the Wehrmacht. In contrast, the goal of the politically conservative military establishment seemed to have been pushed out of reach. That goal had been to make the commander in chief of the army (namely, the chief of the General Staff) the führer's closest expert adviser on military-political and, to a certain extent, foreign policy matters as well, an action that also promised to restore the social and political dominance that the military establishment had had in Wilhelmine Germany and Prussia.

Outraged over the intrigue against Fritsch and crestfallen over the army's serious political defeat, several officers who had watched the regime's policies toward the churches, the legal system, and the Jews with growing criticism decided to put an end to the alliance between conservative groups and the National Socialist movement that had brought Hitler to power and to oppose these altogether menacing developments. Two such officers were Admiral Canaris, the director of the Counterintelligence Office, and First Lieutenant Oster, who had become director of the Main Office at Counterintelligence and functioned as the admiral's chief of staff. General Beck, chief of the General Staff at Army High Command, also reacted angrily over the events surrounding Fritsch. A few months before, he had become aware of the minutes that Colonel Hossbach, Hitler's army adjutant, had taken down at a meeting on November 5, 1937. According to these minutes, the führer had made it known to the Reich foreign minister and the heads of the Wehrmacht that he intended to solve the problem of German "living space" by war in 1943–45 at the latest and that he would take the first steps toward this — that is, the annexation of Austria and Czechoslovakia — in 1938 if possible. Confronted with the reality of National Socialist imperialism, Beck subjected Hitler's plans to a written criticism so biting and deep that it appeared to be an announcement of an impending revocation of obedience.

The opposition of Beck and within the circle of the *Counterintelligence Office (Abwehr) assumed more definite form during the course of 1938, when Hitler, having been enabled to annex Austria in March by a more or less fortuitous development, was preparing a campaign against Czechoslovakia by instigating a planned German-Czech crisis, which threatened to bring Germany to war with France and Great Britain as well. Beck at first tried to influence the course of developments by sending imploring memoranda to Fritsch's successor, General von Brauchitsch, and, through him, to Hitler. When the fruitlessness of such efforts became clear, Beck considered a collective act of insubordination on the part of the generals — that is, a strike. In a statement in which he called upon Brauchitsch to organize such a step by the generals, the chief of the General Staff wrote, "One's obedience as a solider has its limit where one's knowledge, conscience, and responsibility forbid one from carrying out an order." History, he said, would "burden these leaders with murder if they do not act in accordance with their professional and political knowledge and conscience." However, the commander in chief of the army rejected Beck's ideas; there was no action by the generals; and Beck resigned from his post in August 1938.

In view of the impossibility of winning over a majority of the General Staff for a collective action against Hitler, Beck and his successor, General Halder, came up with the idea of stopping Hitler with a putsch by a small group of reliable officers. A coup d'état no longer seemed impossible since (1) the views and actions of Beck and Halder had won over officers such as Erwin von Witzleben, the commanding general in Army Corps Area III (Berlin), and Count Brockdorff-Ahlefeldt, the commander of the Potsdam Garrison; (2) Hans Oster was able to recruit a large number of determined officers from the Counterintelligence Office to work for Hitler's imprisonment; and (3) the military establishment had in the meantime made contact with the civilian resistance surrounding the *Goerdeler Circle and Hassell. In contrast to members of the Counterintelligence Office's shock troops, whose leader, First Lieutenant Heinz, intended to shoot Hitler upon arrest, Beck and Halder did not consider assassination. Rather, the older officers held to the idea that their putsch would not topple — let alone kill — Hitler, but would simply force him to give up his warlike policies. There was undoubtedly some contradiction in the fact that Beck began to see a reform of the political system in Germany as the goal of a coup d'état although the prevention of a major European war was the central motive of Beck and the other officers and although this motive had pushed the earlier desire for an improvement in the Army High Command's position *qua* institution into the background. He wanted the putsch to be accomplished not only under the motto "Maintain the peace!" but also under mottoes such as "Peace with the church!" "Freedom of expression!" and "Restore law in the Reich!" It remained unclear, however, how such a demolition of the National Socialist regime could be reconciled with keeping the führer.

Contradictions of this type and various organizational problems involving a putsch remained unsolved until the 1938 Munich Conference and the Munich Pact (September 29 and 30) pulled the ground from under any coup d'état in the opinion of civil and military organizers. British and French appeasement policy had kept Hitler from marching on Prague and led to the incomplete triumph at Munich, yet, on the other hand, with the Anschluss of the Sudeten region to Germany it delivered a great success. A European war had been avoided. Officers such as Beck, Witzleben, Canaris, and Oster did not retract their fundamental rejection of the National Socialist Weltanschauung and regime, yet they saw themselves defeated and resigned for a while, especially since Hitler annexed the rest of Bohemia and Moravia without bloodshed in March 1939 and was allowed to force Slovakia to his bidding as a dependent satellite state.

In January 1939, a young officer of the General Staff, Count Claus Schenk von Stauffenberg — who had not heard of the plans during the fall of the previous year but who himself had developed radically oppositional ideas especially due to heightened persecution of the Jews as it had become manifest during Kristallnacht in November 1938 — had a conversation with a friend about the possibility of a coup. Stauffenberg said that, given Hitler's latest successes, things looked bad and that, aside from Beck, who was no longer in active service, there were only a few officers who could be counted on at that time.

Resignation had become so deeply ingrained that the passivity continued when the German-Polish conflict, already in the air between the fall of 1938 and March 1939, became apparent to the public in the spring of 1939 and when high-level military officers could see that Hitler, unafraid of intervention by France and Great Britain, had decided on a fall campaign against Poland. Also playing a role was the fact that conservative critics of the regime in the officer corps had anti-Polish sentiments and saw the reacquisition of territories that had been lost to Poland after World War I — under the motto "Restoration of the borders of 1914" — as an important goal of German policy.

The German-Soviet Pact of August 23, 1939, had a different effect. Several oppositional officers viewed Hitler's agreement with Stalin, which was to spare Germany from a seriously dangerous two-front war, as a success of the führer similar to the one that the conference at Munich had brought during the previous year; they fell even deeper into apathy. On the other hand, other officers, not least among them the resistance circle in the Counterintelligence Office, saw the pact as the beginning of the regime's further drift toward the left and again began to search for ways to arrange a coup; such ways, though, were initially not at hand.

The situation did not change until the German army defeated Poland during a short campaign in September. Hitler transferred the bulk of armed forces to the western border immediately after the end of the campaign and declared his firm intention to attack France and Great Britain, which had entered the war on September 3, 1939, and thereby to violate the neutrality of Holland, Belgium, and Luxembourg. After the experiences of the Polish campaign, though, practically all military leaders were convinced that the German armed forces were not yet up to a large-scale offensive against the Western powers and that only defeat awaited them at the end of a bloody war of attrition. On October 11, General von Leeb, commander of Army Group C, made such fears known in a note that he sent to von Brauchitsch. Furthermore, many high officers were of the opinion that the violation of Belgian and Dutch neutrality could have a most disadvantageous effect throughout the world, particularly in stirring up the United States, and that the peace treaty coming after an inevitable German defeat would only be all the more severe. Parallel to plans for western Europe, the organs of the National Socialist state, in accordance with Hitler's will, also set up a system of terror in Poland. Quite aside from the complete disenfranchisement of rights for the Polish population and the beginning of a merciless exploitation of the country, countless Poles were driven from their homes, and thousands upon thousands of members of the leading classes of the Polish people were butchered on command. There were also several large-scale and numerous small-scale massacres of Jews. The result was a formidable crisis between troops stationed in Poland and their commanders, on the one hand, and the SS and the police, on the other hand. General Blaskowitz, the head of the occupation army, wrote to von Brauchitsch, "The attitude of the troops toward the SS and the police wavers between horror and hate. Every soldier feels disgusted and repelled by these crimes."

In this situation, the oppositional officers, driven by the same set of professional, political, and moral motives that had been key for activities planned during the fall of 1938, again saw the necessity of and the chance for active resistance. On October 18, General Wagner, the quartermaster general, briefed the chief of the General Staff, Halder, about the atrocities in Poland, and Halder, deeply convinced that an offensive in western Europe would fail, charged First Lieutenant Helmuth Groscurth, a liaison officer of the Wehrmacht High Command's Counterintelligence Office at Army High Command, with the planning of a coup d'état by the General Staff. In addition, Halder requested that Colonel Oster, who was still the director of the Counterintelligence Office's Central Division, "bring the preparations of 1938 up to a level befitting the current situation." Part of these preparations were that officers in the opposition — their core being the same groups that had wanted to act during the previous year — would have to reestablish contact with civilian resistance circles via Beck and Goerdeler. In addition, Halder sent General Carl-Heinrich von Stülpnagel, chief quarter master I at Army High Command, to the leaders of the army groups and armies in the west in order to gain their support for a putsch. Groscurth went on the same trip, causing "great excitement" among high-level staffs on the western front with Blaskowitz's reports of atrocities in Poland and noting in his diary, "We riled up the most important segments of the western front. Hopefully with success!"

But the period of hope did not last long. When Hitler, in a conference with von Brauchitsch on November 5, 1939, coarsely lashed out against the senior general himself, the Army High Command in Zossen, and the entire General Staff for their rejection of an attack in the west and threatened "to root out the spirit of Zossen," Halder broke off preparations for a putsch, believing that Hitler had let him know that the conspiratorial activities within the officer corps were not a secret to Hitler. In truth, information about such activities could become known only through the officers' civilian cohorts, and, even then, that information was vague; then as later, the officers' collegiality and camaraderie reliably covered up "treasonous" discussions, and this remained true even when one or more of the participants in the discussions decided not to participate in the conspiracy. In any event, Halder gave the order to destroy all traces of the conspiracy and then persistently resisted pressure by younger officers and civilian opponents of the regime to continue preparations for the coup. Groscurth, who was not in agreement with this, was first transferred to the reserve at Army High Command and then to the Seventy-fifth Infantry Division. Without the core within Army High Command, those officers who were prepared to put up resistance were rendered powerless. They had hardly anywhere or nowhere else to turn, especially since, with few exceptions, the commanders and the members of leadership staffs of the army groups and armies that had marched to the west had refused to participate in a putsch.

Colonel Oster was so disappointed with the behavior of Army High Command and the General Staff that he went so far as to inform The Hague of the dates of the western offensive (which was repeatedly postponed) via the Dutch military attaché in Berlin, Colonel Sas, in the hope of bringing about an early failure of the attack; with the same intention, he sought to warn Denmark and Norway of the German attack. He hoped that, after such a failure, it would indeed be possible to win over the leaders of the armed forces for an action against Hitler and the National Socialist regime. The resistance circle within the Counterintelligence Office presumably made a serious as well as partially successful attempt — with Beck's approval — to establish contact with the British government via Pope Pius XII with the help Dr. Josef Müller, a Catholic attorney from Munich, and to prepare for peace negotiations.

The conquest of Denmark, Norway, and western Europe by the German armed forces rendered this moot and created an entirely new situation. Hitler's prestige rose to dizzying heights within the officer corps, and the mass of officers now accepted not only the authority of the führer but also his goals and those of the National Socialist movement, whether those goals involved a continuation of the war against Great Britain or the attack on Russia during the summer of 1941. The march to the east was accepted not only as a struggle for "living space" but also as a struggle against "Jewish Bolshevism." This made possible the army's deep complicity in the crimes of the regime.

On the other hand, it is remarkable that nearly all officers who had been against Hitler and the regime up to this point remained unimpressed by the triumphs of the Third Reich — aside from moments of uncertainty after the victory in France — and by no means gave up the idea of a coup. They knew that all the successes had changed nothing with respect to the hopelessness of Germany's strategic position and that these successes had only postponed the inevitable defeat at the end of the war. They had also come to realize that Hitler and the National Socialist movement would never create a humane political system in Germany and would bring nothing to the now-occupied countries except a sterile domination exerted through a terror that constantly intensified hate toward Germany and the Germans.

Although a coup could no longer be an immediate goal due to the idol worship of Hitler, centers of oppositional sentiments arose next to the Counterintelligence Office circle (which was crushed in April 1943) within three high-level staffs between the summer of 1940 and the winter of 1941–42. The first of these developed around the commander of the Home Army in the General Army Office, which was directed by General Friedrich Olbricht; the second arose around the military commander in occupied France, General Carl-Heinrich von Stülpnagel, who had assumed that post in February 1942 and had been among the important figures who had made plans for a coup in 1938 and in the fall of 1939; and the third group developed within Army Group Middle in Russia, whose senior operations officer, Henning von Tresckow, systematically gathered opponents of Hitler and of the National Socialist regime around himself.

In these three centers, which gradually established contact with one another, there were again thoughts at the end of 1941 and beginning of 1942 about whether a coup should and could be attempted soon. Professional, political, and moral motives again came together. The conflicts concerning the leadership of operations in Russia that constantly erupted from the summer until the beginning of winter had badly shaken the relationship between Hitler and the General Staff, and the winter crisis itself had shown that the idea of a Blitzkrieg against the Soviet Union had definitely failed; in addition, the Japanese attack on Pearl Harbor had brought the United States into the war. On the domestic front, the totalitarian features of the National Socialist dictatorship had become more pronounced than ever. After Hitler's speech before the Reichstag on April 26, 1942, for example (a speech in which Hitler stated that, as the "supreme judge," he stood above "formal law"), Count Stauffenberg, now a major in the Organization Department of Army High Command, said to General von Loeper that "all legality is now abandoned." Most of all, though, the officers in the opposition saw the necessity of a putsch after the attempt to eliminate the European Jews had begun. Initiated during the summer of 1941 with the mass murders perpetrated by the Einsatzgruppen in the Soviet Union, the "final solution to the Jewish question" assumed its European dimension at the end of 1941 and the start of 1942 with the beginning of operations in several annihilation camps: Chelmno, Auschwitz-Birkenau, and Belzec. Several times in discussions during the course of the spring and summer of 1942, Count Stauffenberg said, "They are shooting Jews en masse. The crimes cannot go on."

However, oppositional members of the military were forced to see that they were able to find only a few partners among officers of the General Staff and officers of the troops at the front. Hardly anything changed in this regard even after the turning point in the war marked by the defeat at Stalingrad and the subsequent downfall of the army fighting in North Africa. Most of all, no army group leader could be found to play the role of the leading figure in the revolt. Stauffenberg failed in trying to recruit Field Marshal von Manstein (January 26, 1943), as had both Colonel von Gersdorff (August 8, 1943), who had been sent by Tresckow, and Tresckow himself (November 25, 1943). Attempts to recruit the commander in chief in the West, Field Marshal von Runstedt, also failed during the summer of 1943; Tresckow's attempts to win over Field Marshal von Kluge, commander in chief of Army Group Middle, produced only dubious results, and Field Marshal Rommel, as commander in chief of Army Group B in France, did not enter the resistance until July 1944.

It became even clearer to the conspirators that any coup that might avoid chaos — that might lead to a somewhat orderly transition to a new political beginning — presumed the assassination of Hitler. Stauffenberg was already convinced in the spring of 1942 that Hitler had to be killed. It might afterward be possible to grab power in Berlin through a putsch and to draw the entire army — released from its oath and tied to its traditional reins of command — over to the side of the putschists. In addition, the oppositional officers hardly thought beyond the short period of a military dictatorship that would be necessary after a putsch; they essentially left the discussion concerning the domestic order of a

Germany liberated from Hitler and National Socialism to civilian resistance groups, with which they were in contact through Beck and Count Moltke of the *Kreisau Circle.

Yet as one assassination attempt after the other failed or had to be postponed due to various reasons (see *Assassination Attempts against Hitler) and as month after month passed without a putsch, the constant worsening of Germany's military situation necessarily brought about a decrease in motivation to orchestrate a coup and save the Reich. The principal focus became simply ending the war — a war that was claiming hetacombs of victims by the day. Of course, this focus was for a time accompanied by the political hope that a Germany that had shaken off National Socialist rule by itself would receive better conditions for peace from the Allies. Yet such hopes became ever dimmer from week to week, and, in April 1944, Stauffenberg professed that the Reich could no longer be saved. After the successful landing of the Allies in France in June 1944, it was finally clear that an assassination and a coup could no longer serve short-term political goals. Nevertheless, the participating officers believed that something had to be done. Aside from putting an end to the suffering that the war brought, the important issue was now, as Tresckow said, that "the German resistance movement [make a] decisive move before the world and before history." Stauffenberg and Colonel Mertz von Quirnheim, chief of staff with General Olbricht, made statements to the same effect in the days before the assassination attempt of July 20, 1944. In view of the action's probable failure, there was also another motive, which was expressed by Count Nikolaus Üxküll, an uncle of Stauffenberg: "I can take my leave from the pack of gangsters only through death."

Bibliography

Graml, Hermann. *Die deutsche Militäropposition vom Sommer 1940 bis zum Frühjahr 1943*. Volume 2 of *Die Vollmacht des Gewissens*. Edited by the European Publication Association. Frankfurt, 1965.

Groscurth, Helmuth. *Tagebücher eines Abwehroffiziers 1938–1940*. Edited by Helmut Krausnick and Harold Deutsch with the cooperation of Hildegard von Kotze. Stuttgart, 1970.

Hoffmann, Peter. *Stauffenberg: A Family History, 1905–1944*. Cambridge, 1992.

Krausnick, Helmut. "Vorgeschichte und Beginn des militärischen Widerstandes gegen Hitler." In *Die Vollmacht des Gewissens*. Edited by the European Publication Association. Munich, 1965.

Office of Research in Military History, ed. *Aufstand des Gewissens: Der militärische Widerstand gegen Hitler und das NS-Regime*. Herford/Bonn, 1987. Published under the auspices of the Federal Defense Ministry.

Youth Opposition

Jürgen Zarusky

The policies of subjugation and "coordination" (see the footnote on p. 47 above) affected youth organizations when National Socialism took power. Within just a few months, nearly all these organizations, with the exception of ecclesiastical ones, were either outlawed or absorbed by the Hitler Youth. But this process did not stop with the elimination of competing organizations. The National Socialist regime and its Reich Youth Leader Baldur von Schirach strove for the Hitler Youth's total control over fraternization among youth outside of school and home. The December 1936 law pertaining to the Hitler Youth made it the state youth organization, and the second decree pertaining to this law, enacted in March 1939, made service in the Hitler Youth compulsory, with those who refused to serve being subject to criminal punishment.

This totalitarian attack by the National Socialist regime upon youth, as well as its dictatorial character generally, ignited a variety of oppositional activities among youth. These activities were propelled by an extremely wide spectrum of motives, and the methods of action were wide-ranging — from the youth movement's continuation of outlawed forms of culture within the Hitler Youth to decisive political resistance against the National Socialist regime.

The activities of leftist youth organizations, which had been driven into the underground, were part of the initial political resistance. The German Communist Youth Organization (KJVD) had fifty-five thousand members in 1932 and was a relatively small organization not only in comparison with other youth organizations but also in comparison with other secondary organizations within the German Communist Party. Yet it assumed considerable significance within early Communist resistance, which was marked by expectations of an imminent crisis within the regime and a subsequent revolutionary change. The idea of a "new heroic age of socialism" especially addressed the willingness of youth to become engaged and to make sacrifices. Some daring and spectacular forms of action bore the mark of a youthful desire to play pranks, and yet they also involved high risk and serious political intention. These acts included instantaneous demonstrations in public squares and throwing flyers from the upper floors of department stores, as practiced in Berlin in 1933 and at the beginning of 1934 under the direction of Erich Honecker in Essen as well.

In the expectation of an imminent revolution, the Communist resistance focused primarily on the reconstruction and expansion of the party organization until approximately 1934–35. This line of action set the tone for the KJVD. The attempt to restore broken connections between the remaining individual organizations and the dissemination of their own writings, especially the newspaper *Junge Garde* (Young guard), which was published outside of Germany after the end of 1933, constituted the essential fields of activity within the Communist youth resistance. Next to engaging in agitation in factories and labor service camps, they wanted to win over fellow combatants from the social democratic Socialist Workers' Youth (SAJ) and from among Catholic youth as part of a unified-front policy. The Hitler Youth was also supposed to be undermined from within. These goals were achieved only to a minimal extent.

There was intensive cooperation with Catholic youth in only one case. The Düsseldorf chaplain Joseph Rossaint and the leader of the Catholic Storm Troops, Frank Steber, had contacts with leading members of the KJVD until 1935, which made it possible for them, among other things, to speak in front of rather large groups of Catholic youths. After these activities were uncovered in 1936, Rossaint, Steber, and others were tried for high treason before the People's Court in April 1937, which National Socialist propaganda exploited as proof of a general Catholic-Communist plot.

In general, though, the KJVD remained largely isolated — in part because of its unrealistic propaganda. In addition, the KJVD's offensive tactics led to frequent arrests of its activists, whose presence and influence in proletarian surroundings became less common due to the decrease in unemployment and the abatement of expectations of imminent revolution. Furthermore, KJVD activists increasingly had to fill the gaps that the Gestapo's persecutions had created in the apparatus of the German Communist Party (KPD). The arrest of a considerable portion of leading KJVD functionaries was one reason the appointment of a new central committee became necessary. This occurred at a Reich-level conference attended by approximately thirty KJVD members in Moscow in December 1934. Even though Soviet functionaries intoned their praises of the KJVD, pronouncing that it, rather than the party, had brought such a conference into being, this was less a beginning than a conclusion. One cannot speak of independent activity on the part of the KJVD after the middle of the 1930s.

Communist youth resistance continued into the war years only in the case of a few isolated groups, such as those surrounding Heinz Kapelle or *Hanno Günther in Berlin. Another exception was the

Berlin group surrounding former KJVD member *Herbert Baum, in which Communist ideas and the self-assertion of young Jews achieved a synthesis.

In the milieu of adult Social Democrats, the prevalent reaction to the National Socialists' assumption of power was not offensive resistance but rather retreat into the company of persons who shared their ideas and who did not become publicly active. This is also true of those youths who were oriented toward social democracy. Many members of the SAJ continued to maintain their former contacts covertly. For example, SAJ or Friends of Nature groups established themselves as hiking clubs that even sported their old SAJ hiking clothes when they thought they were no longer being watched. One instance of this is the Falkenhorst group of the Nuremberg chapter of the Friends of Nature. Some underground groups simply ceased their initial offensive resistance activities after encounters with the National Socialist apparatus of repression.

However, among segments of youth oriented toward social democracy, a radicalization did develop. Under the influence of the covertly active organization *New Beginning, the Berlin chapter of the SAJ in February 1933 decided — against the will of the party leadership — to resist with illegal methods. Another group in Berlin, the Red Shock Troop, formed from a group of Social Democratic students; this group operated independently of party leadership and was able to publish sixteen issues of the newspaper bearing the group's name. In Hamburg-Eimsbüttel, the SAJ under Friedrich Börth was able to draw support from approximately 150 of its former 400 members until the middle of 1934. Through the SAJ Central Office in Berlin, which was camouflaged as the Fritz List Sporting and Hiking Goods Store, it was possible to obtain underground written materials from the party's exiled leadership in Prague. These materials, however, were circulated primarily in insider circles. A youth group of the Central Employees' Union in Frankfurt was marked by particular militancy: it not only published its own newspaper, *Junger Kämpfer* (Young fighter), but even organized paramilitary exercises.

Resistance groups comprised of young people who were oriented toward social democracy and socialism were essentially broken up by the Gestapo by the mid-1930s; this is also true of the Socialist Youth Organization of the Socialist Workers' Party. After the National Socialist dictatorship prevented the organization's political activity, those groups were just as unable as the KJVD to hold themselves aloft in a specifically youth-oriented milieu that, if it had been used wisely, could have functioned to guarantee the groups' continued integrity.

If the underground activities of the socialist youth organizations were clearly directed toward toppling the regime, confessional youth groups were primarily concerned with defending their domain of activity. An example of this is the Catholic Young Men's Association (KJMV), which was led by prelate Ludwig Wolker and, with four hundred thousand members, was the most important of these organizations. The association clearly opted for the Center Party in a proclamation concerning the March 1933 elections and sharply criticized Hitler's government, but it then fell in line with the strategy of the Catholic Church, which, in the course of the negotiations on the Reich concordat that was concluded on July 20, 1933, was prepared to sacrifice political Catholicism for a guarantee of the Catholic Church's status. The concordat negotiations counteracted von Schirach's attempt to eliminate Catholic youth organizations. According to Article 31 of the treaty, the activities of those Catholic organizations and clubs that served only religious, purely cultural, and charitable purposes were to be protected. However, the regime circumvented and to a certain degree often openly violated this condition through a number of measures, such as by narrowly interpreting what constituted such church activities, by putting pressure on government officials to withdraw their children from Catholic organizations, and by forbidding people to have simultaneous membership in confessional and National Socialist organizations under threat of professional sanctions.

There were violent attacks by the Hitler Youth on Catholic youth groups, especially during the early phase of the regime. Under these circumstances, mere membership in such an organization demanded a considerable amount of civil courage. However, as when National Socialism was on the rise in the Weimar Republic, the Catholic milieu showed significant stability. By the middle of 1934, for example, the KJMV had lost only one-fourth of its members. The sport clubs of the German Youth Force, in contrast, had great losses, since Catholic organizations were forbidden from having any organized sports activities whatsoever.

An important basis of the integrity of the Catholic youth was that they reacted to the various repressions with a specific form of militancy. As a rule, attacks were immediately answered by protests from church authorities. Within a few days, a call issued in the middle of 1934 against propaganda attacks by the Hitler Youth gained ten thousand signatures in the diocese of Münster. At the same time, the group called Defense against Anti-Christian Propaganda circulated sermon materials on the topic "Concerning the Good Right of Catholic Youth." This effort helped foster processions, pilgrimages, and other church festivals that expressed Catholic youths' will for self-assertion. Thus, the Catholic Storm Troop undertook a pilgrimage to Rome on Easter 1935 in a convoy of fifty busses. In Rome, they demonstrated in St. Peter's Square during the blessing *urbi et orbi* and, at a papal audience, received encouraging words from Pope Pius XI.

The journal *Junge Front* (Young front), which later had to be renamed *Michael* and was able to appear until 1936, was the most
important mouthpiece of Catholic youth. It was frequently circulated in
front of the entrances to churches by young newsmongers called "front-
line sentinels" and managed to increase its circulation from eighty-five
thousand in July 1933 to two hundred thousand in July 1934. It reflects
Catholics' increased reception of elements from the allied youth. The
considerable activities by Catholic youth, though, should not distract
one from the fact that youth were ultimately in a defensive position.
This led to their increasing orientation toward, in Barbara Schellenberger's words, a "growth within," toward the solidification of religious
education and faith.

The regime increased its pressure beginning in the middle of 1935.
In July 1935, the Gestapo forbade Catholic youth any activity that was
not of a purely religious and ecclesiastical nature, such as group hiking and camping. More and more Catholic youth organizations were
outlawed on a regional level beginning in 1937, which led to the complete dissolution of activity by Catholic youth organizations by 1939.
Work by Catholic youth was afterward possible only within the confines of congregational pastoral duties, even though individual groups
continued to work underground. Fred Josef, who directed underground
groups of Catholic scouts in Würzburg, was sent to Auschwitz in 1942
as a "half-Jew," and he was killed at the concentration camp at the
beginning of 1944.

In Protestant youth organizations, there was enthusiasm in 1933 for
the new national beginning. Due to an agreement between the German Christian Reich bishop Müller and Reich Youth Leader Baldur von
Schirach, the Evangelical Youth Work, which was the federation of Protestant youth organizations, was incorporated into the Hitler Youth in
December 1933. This was done over the heads of the persons whom it
concerned and caused many, albeit ineffectual, protests. The members of
evangelical youth organizations thereby became members of the Hitler
Youth (with certain specific rights for religious activity). Several evangelical youth organizations, such as the League of German Biblical Circles
under Udo Smidt, dissolved themselves in order to avoid being incorporated into the Hitler Youth. In contrast to Catholic youth, evangelical
youth for the most part failed to fight for the maintenance of their youth
organizations.

Similar to Catholic youth work, on the other hand, evangelical youth
work, which was also carried out primarily within the confines of
congregational pastoral duties, displayed a type of "growth within," especially after the *Confessing Church arose out of the dispute with the
National Socialist German Christians; having its own Reich Chamber of
Youth as of 1935, the Confessing Church had influence on significant

segments of the evangelical youth. In this respect, the most important publication was *Junge Kirche* (Young church), which was published by Hanns Lilje. Attempts to make room for independent youth activities within the confines of congregational youth work met with increasingly aggressive reactions by the National Socialist regime. As in the case of Catholic youth, evangelical youth was forbidden from engaging in anything other than purely ecclesiastical and religious activity as of 1935. Nevertheless, meetings of several thousand participants took place up to 1937, and leisure-time gatherings for Bible study, which ended up being excursions and trips as well, continued to be held on a rather large scale until 1939. Especially during the initial years after the Evangelical Youth Work was incorporated into the Hitler Youth, individual groups composed of disbanded organizations illegally continued their activities on their own.

However, these persecutions, some of which were extensive, should not obscure the fact that opposition by youth who were active in the churches was limited to maintaining their freedom to act within the churches. In view of such a background, political resistance against the National Socialist regime appeared detrimental to their aims, and the thought of such resistance was beyond the mental horizon of the overwhelming majority of Christian youth. Thus, despite all "inner rejection" of the Third Reich, activities such as Rossaint's or the wartime distribution of flyers hostile to the regime by Catholic youths from Würzburg remained the exception.

Large segments of organized youth who continued the tradition of the German Youth Movement, which had arisen at the turn of the century, also made an attempt to assert themselves in conformity with the system, but this attempt quickly failed. On March 30, 1933, the majority of the most important organizations united in the Greater German Alliance, with the retired vice admiral Carl Dietrich von Trotha being named as their leader for life. In an internal circular, the nationwide leadership stated that it was fighting "against being incorporated into the National Socialist movement and for the Alliance's freedom to exist." However, Baldur von Schirach outlawed the Greater German Alliance on June 17, 1933, the day on which he was named youth leader of the German Reich. The Hitler Youth did not allow the organizations to be incorporated into itself; entry into the Hitler Youth was possible only on an individual basis. Even organizations that had not united with the Greater German Alliance were outlawed. The *völkisch* Artamans were one exception. This organization, to which Himmler and Höss, the future commandant at Auschwitz, had belonged, propagated the idea of establishing settlements and became the core of the Hitler Youth Land Service in 1934.

Eberhard Koebel (nicknamed "tusk"), the charismatic leader of the German Boys' Club of November 1 (generally referred to as "d.j. 1.11."), took a different path. Although he had joined the German Communist Party on April 20, 1932, he called upon his followers after the National Socialists gained power to join the German Young Folk, which was comprised of ten- to fourteen-year-olds in the Hitler Youth. However, he did not do this without at the same time emphasizing the bond among members of the German Boys' Club — a bond that was based on common intellectual roots and that, as it were, established a secret society. Members of the club were supposed to represent a sort of cultural elite within the Hitler Youth that was intended to promote the ideals of autonomy and initiative formulated, but not explicitly elaborated, by Koebel in his programmatic writings. In one very prominent case, this strategy of infiltration did indeed produce far-reaching results that Koebel certainly did not intend at the time: Hans Scholl first encountered the ideas of the German Boys' Club while he was in the Hitler Youth, and the history of the *White Rose cannot be understood without a knowledge of the organizational ideas of several of the club's most important members and benefactors. Koebel himself was arrested at the beginning of 1934, was released after two suicide attempts, and, in June, went into exile, from where he maintained contact with his followers.

Since the Hitler Youth was a numerically not very significant organization before the National Socialists gained power, insofar as it was involved primarily in the political struggle, the rapid growth that it experienced beginning in 1933 could not have been kept under control had it not drawn on the pedagogic potential of youth leaders from the incorporated organizations. This not infrequently led to clublike groups, as self-contained Hitler Youth units, continuing their former activities. Thus, in 1934 and 1935 there was a comprehensive "cleansing" of clublike elements from within the Hitler Youth and especially from within the German Young Folk. This cleansing was primarily a struggle against a world of symbols whose political dimension becomes apparent only if one keeps in mind the power that a group's symbols can have for young people in the process of discovering their identity. The latent explosiveness of youthful wishes for autonomy — as expressed, for example, in the writings from the Günther Wolff publishing company in Plauen, which were very popular in club circles — was branded in National Socialist terminology as "cultural Bolshevism." Consequently, the purchase of songbooks and other publications from this publishing company was forbidden in the Hitler Youth, and Günther Wolff himself was subjected to extensive repressions.

The removal of clublike elements from the Hitler Youth did not entail the complete eradication of all clubs. Rather, this removal to a certain extent strengthened clublike groups that continued underground, as can be seen from, among other things, repeated Gestapo orders to forbid them. The most important of these groups were the German Boys' Club and the Neroth Hikers. Frequently — and this was especially true of the Neroth Hikers — the National Socialist regime's persecutory apparatus went against these groups under the charge that they had a homosexual orientation. The German Boys' Club was labeled "Eastern" and "Bolshevist" because of the longing for Russia that was common in its ranks, although such a longing should by no means be equated with a political identification with the Soviet Union. In 1936, the Gestapo set up an office that was charged specifically with fighting so-called clublike intrigues. Here too, the primary issue was the monopoly of the Hitler Youth on social life and not the fighting of political opponents per se. Sights were set on youth groups that went on independent trips, on persons who spent the night whenever possible in the Lappish "Kohten" tents that Koebel had introduced to the youth movement, on persons who wore the German Boys' Club blazer designed by Koebel, and on persons who, in concerts given by Don Cossacks, all too conspicuously called upon the choir to sing the especially beloved "Platoff Song."

In a series of cases, a somewhat militant political resistance grew out of the underground clublike milieu, a process that not infrequently fostered a gradual transition toward the national-revolutionary camp. At the end of 1936, the former German Boys' Club member Helmut Hirsch planned a bomb attack on the grounds of the Reich Party Day celebration in Nuremberg but was arrested before the plan was carried out. Of Jewish origin himself, he had gotten his motivation for this action from Otto Strasser's *Black Front; he had come into contact with Strasser in Prague, where he studied, and wanted to protest against the increasing persecution of the Jews. In the spring of 1936, he had written an article for Strasser's journal *Deutsche Revolution* in which organized youth was portrayed as a political opposition against National Socialism. In March 1937, Hirsch was sentenced to death by the People's Court and was executed three months later.

The Black Young Men's Club was also in contact with the Black Front and recruited members from former youth organizations and from the Hitler Youth, searching for people in those groups who had socially revolutionary ideas. The club, however, was crushed during the initial phase of the Third Reich.

Important impulses for political engagement by former youth organizations came from emigrés Karl Otto Paetel in Paris and Theo Hespers and Hans Ebeling in the Netherlands. Paetel and Ebeling had arrived at national-revolutionary positions via the German Youth Movement; both had played important roles in this regard in the Weimar Republic. Hespers, who came from the Catholic youth movement, had joined the leftist-Catholic Vitus Heller Movement. Working in exile, Ebeling tried to continue to lead youth groups that he had directed on the Lower Rhine and to spur on the formation of militant cells that were supposed to come into action as soon as the National Socialist regime entered a threatening crisis. Together with Hespers, he published a series of publications beginning in 1937, including from 1937 to 1940 the journal *Kameradschaft* (Camaraderie), which was smuggled into Germany. Ebeling and Hespers also founded the German Youth Front in Brussels in 1937, which was supposed to function as the umbrella movement for youth with oppositional leanings. The circle surrounding *Kameradschaft* saw the National Socialist regime steering inevitably toward a war and propagated the notion that, in this case, it was one's duty to work toward Germany's military defeat. Hespers was arrested by the Gestapo after the Netherlands was occupied and was sentenced to death by the People's Court in the fall of 1943.

In Paris, Karl Otto Paetel published the *Schriften der jungen Nation* (Writings of the young nation) and attempted to contact former youth organization members who went to France and to stir them to political activity. Among Paetel's followers in Germany was the future West German ambassador to Rumania and Algeria, Michael Jovy, who was sentenced to eight years in prison by the People's Court in 1941.

In spite of impressive examples of opposition by former Youth Movement members, such active political engagement was the case only with the minority. The overwhelming majority of underground groups consisting of former Youth Movement members did not break from the traditional political abstinence of the Youth Movement.

While it does seem that the regime was successful in largely pushing the former Youth Movement underground by the end of the 1930s, quiet by no means descended upon the "youth front." On the contrary: a series of documents from the Reich Youth leadership and the Gestapo attests to the disquiet that the increase of so-called wild cliques caused on that front. The term "wild cliques" covered groups hostile to the Hitler Youth and youth gangs involved in crime, where the distinctions are vague in some cases.

One of the most significant manifestations of the phenomenon of "wild cliques" was the *Leipzig Hound Packs, which appeared primarily in workers' districts beginning about 1937. These were spontaneous meetings of youths of both sexes who came from certain districts, wore the same clothes (boys usually wore short Lederhosen and girls dark shirts with checkered shirts or blouses), and greeted one another with the Russian Youth Pioneers' bellowing call. They met almost daily on particular street corners or in certain bars and went on independent trips on weekends. Under the influence of Communist youths, some of them actually did work toward forming a political counterorganization to the Hitler Youth. They frequently listened to Radio Moscow. They all decisively rejected the Hitler Youth and, not infrequently, fistfights with the Hitler Youth broke out, sometimes having the character of turf battles. In 1938, the Leipzig Hound Packs had about fifteen hundred members. In January 1940, some of the political leaders of the Leipzig Hound Packs were sentenced by the People's Court and the State Court of Dresden to many years of imprisonment.

The Rhineland was a center of clique formation. The "wild" groups of working-class youths who arose there called themselves Navajos, Kittelbach Pirates, or *Edelweiss Pirates. Aside from their short pants and loudly checked shirts, the most common accessories of the group were the edelweiss insignia on their lapels and their death's-head rings. Independent excursions, the adoption of songs from the Youth Movement, opposition against the Hitler Youth (which not infrequently vented itself in brawls), and the communal group life of boys and girls were just as typical of the Edelweiss Pirates as of the Hound Packs. Although both groups sometimes referred to themselves as "organized youth" and both were sometimes placed in this category by National Socialist authorities, there was no immediate contact with underground organizations such as the German Boys' Club. If the youth organizations and the German Youth Movement as a whole were phenomena of the bourgeoisie, then the Leipzig Hound Packs and the Edelweiss Pirates were working-class phenomena. Nor were the sexes separated, as was common in the German Youth Movement. Indeed, the fact that young people in these diverse groups — in contrast to the Hitler Youth — could meet members of the opposite sex without effort might well have made a not insignificant contribution to the groups' attractiveness.

In contrast to the Leipzig Hound Packs, the Edelweiss Pirates had no contact with circles of political opposition. Among some groups of Edelweiss Pirates, however, the emotional opposition against all things National Socialist, having arisen out of a rejection of the Hitler Youth's system of coercion, led to forms of political resistance. Thus, Edelweiss Pirates made contact with the underground German Communist Party in Düsseldorf in 1942 and helped party members distribute leaflets and posters. Also in Düsseldorf, in the district of Gerresheim, one group put up anti-Nazi slogans in a railway underpass. And in the bombed-out ruins of the working-class district of Ehrenfeld in Cologne in 1944, there was a group comprised of Edelweiss Pirates, German deserters, and escaped foreign workers who maintained loose contact with the German Communist Party and carried out more than two dozen assassinations of National Socialist functionaries. Thirteen members of the group, including three Edelweiss Pirates who had not yet reached the age of majority, were publicly hanged by the Gestapo on November 10, 1944.

Among bourgeois youth living in large cities, and especially in Hamburg, there arose another new youth subculture at the end of the 1930s:

the Swing Youth. The Swingers, so called because of their preference for the danceable forms of swing jazz, had a decidedly civil and Anglophile appearance. Typical features were long hair, checkered jackets out of whose side pockets a foreign newspaper was supposed to protrude when possible, and umbrellas slung on arms. In addition, they greeted one another with English nicknames. The Swingers' leisure-time ideal was "to hang out" and "to hit it" (that is, to sit around in bars and to dance wildly and uninhibitedly to swing music). These habits, mocking the officially propagated soldierly ideal and demonstratively careless, sent SS Reichsführer Heinrich Himmler into a blind rage. In a letter written in January 1942 to Reinhard Heydrich, the chief of the Security Police and of the Security Service, Himmler demanded that all ringleaders of the Swing Youth be sent to concentration camps. In fact, arrests had already produced the results that Himmler wanted by October 1940.

The Swingers mark a paradigm change in youth culture: they replaced youth excursions, which the Hitler Youth had adopted and which were also popular among the Edelweiss Pirates, with a big-city lifestyle that focused on pleasurable consumption. At the same time, the Parisian Zazous and the Viennese Shufflers had similar tendencies, although these groups were not composed of the *jeunesse dorée,* but rather of working-class youths. The Swingers showed no interest in political activities.

A number of youth groups that arose during the war represented an antithesis to the Swingers, who were concerned only with their own youth subculture; these groups (see *Juvenile "Gangs of Four") were motivated to political resistance because of their experiences with the National Socialist regime. From the late summer of 1941 until February 1942, the Hamburg administrative apprentice Helmuth Hübener converted news reports by the BBC and other "enemy broadcasters" into leaflets that he distributed together with three friends. The seventeen-year-old was sentenced to death by the People's Court on August 11, 1942, and was decapitated two and one-half months later in Berlin-Plötzensee. Walter Klingenbeck, a Catholic mechanic in Munich, suffered the same fate, having formed his opinions on the basis of "enemy broadcasters" and National Socialist policy toward the church. Together with two friends in 1941, he had put up the V-for-victory sign on more than forty buildings as a symbol of the victory of the Western powers and prepared to set up his own radio station for anti-Nazi propaganda. Klingenbeck was arrested in January 1942 and, after receiving a death sentence from the People's Court on September 24, was executed in the summer of 1943. The group surrounding the seventeen-year-old Viennese high school student Josef Landgraf was organized on similar lines; in the fall of 1941, it also converted BBC news reports into several leaflets and thereby adopted the V-campaign propagated by

London. Landgraf too was sentenced to death, although he was later pardoned. The social background of all three groups was primarily petty bourgeois. They did not have a program that went beyond opposition to National Socialism, yet they all had a strong affinity for Germany's democratic war opponents and a basic Christian orientation. In this and other ways, they are similar to the resistance of the White Rose, which was moored in the youth resistance in many aspects but went far beyond the intellectual and organizational limits set by juvenile milieus.

Bibliography

Breyvogel, Wilfried. *Piraten, Swings und Junge Garde: Jugendwiderstand im Nationalsozialismus.* Bonn, 1991.

Hellfeld, Matthias von. *Bündische Jugend und Hitlerjugend: Zur Geschichte von Anpassung und Widerstand 1930–1939.* Cologne, 1987.

Klönne, Arno. *Jugend im Dritten Reich: Die Hitler-Jugend und ihre Gegner.* Düsseldorf/Cologne, 1982.

Koch, H. N. *The Hitler Youth: Origins and Development, 1922–45.* New York, 1975.

Laqueur, Walter. *Young Germany: A History of the German Youth Movement.* London, 1962.

Peukert, Detlev. *Die Edelweiss-Piraten: Protestbewegungen jugendlicher Arbeiter im Dritten Reich: Eine Dokumentation.* 2d ed. Cologne, 1983.

Schellenberger, Barbara. *Katholische Jugend und Drittes Reich: Die Geschichte des Katholischen Jungmännerverbandes 1933–1939.* Mainz, 1975.

Resistance by the Persecuted

Barbara Distel

"Not like sheep to the slaughter" is how Hermann Langbein, himself a survivor of the camps at Dachau, Auschwitz, and Neuengamme and a tireless chronicler of the history of the concentration camps since his liberation, described resistance in the National Socialist concentration camps. To this day, his is the most comprehensive attempt to recount actions of resistance and solidarity among prisoners of the "SS state." Historical research in the Federal Republic of Germany (FRG) did not treat aspects of the history of the National Socialist concentration camps until they arose in the context of questions that were raised during the 1960s in German court cases involving National Socialist crimes. To this day, findings by the West German justice authorities concerning the annihilation installations of Belzec, Sobibor, and Treblinka form the most important basis of knowledge about the history of these camps and the prisoners' revolts that occurred there. Because hardly any information concerning events within the concentration camps, such as retribution for resistance activities, can be found in surviving National Socialist documents, this chapter of history is almost exclusively conveyed by the memories of surviving witnesses. However, a wider reception of these recollections did not occur in the FRG until the 1960s.

In the German Democratic Republic (GDR), on the other hand, the resistance of the workers' movement against National Socialism became a central topic of teaching, study, and political education, albeit nearly exclusively from the viewpoint of Communist Party history. Former concentration camps located in East Germany, which were turned into places of memorial earlier than in the West, also served primarily to convey the history of Communist prisoners and their resistance. Victimized groups such as the Gypsies as well as the history of the annihilation of the European Jews neither came to the attention of a broader public nor were the subject of relatively large-scale research plans. For this reason, a large proportion of surviving resistance fighters often felt misunderstood and falsely interpreted in East and West Germany soon after their liberation.

Now, many decades after the first concentration camps were set up for political opponents of the regime, what can be summarily said about the resistance of persons who were persecuted, about the resistance of individuals in the face of massive death and dying? What can be said about that resistance in the face of today's certain knowledge of the murder of millions, in the face of the historical fact that it was only Allied armies that brought about the collapse of the system of camps set up for endless expansion and that stopped the murdering that continued until the end? From today's vantage point, how can one do justice to those who acted in the extreme situation of the concentration camps without unduly heroizing them or discrediting them carte blanche as helpless, inept victims, lackeys, or criminals?

In order to answer these questions, one must start from the advent of the concentration camps, which appears in retrospect to be relatively harmless, and then acquire a picture of an entire decade's development toward a gigantic network of murder and slave labor. In the "universe of the concentration camps," the conditions for prisoners' solidarity and resistance activities changed with the system over the course of the years.

The concentration camps became an instrument of terror that cannot be compared with any other state correctional or penal system and that was very quickly withdrawn from any sort of supervision by the justice system. After being sent to the concentration camps, prisoners had no legal protection whatsoever and no possibilities whatsoever to defend themselves against attacks and violence. The duration of their imprisonment was unknown, and they were defenselessly subject to the whims of SS guards. At any time, any of them could be the victim of horrible tortures, be driven to suicide, or be murdered. For this reason, one must understand the concept of "resistance" more broadly than is commonly the case.

There was no chance for an armed "resistance fighter" in the concentration camps; any open rebellion meant the prisoner's immediate death. Isolated revolts in the annihilation camps were desperate attempts by prisoners to determine at least the type of death that awaited them. For the prisoners of the "SS state," anything that was directed against the plans of the camp leadership — from the moral support of a prisoner who threatened to lose hope, to the distribution of news, to the organized smuggling of food or medicine — was resistance against the SS's boundless power over its victims. The term "self-assertion" probably best describes the prisoners' attitude toward themselves and their strategy vis-à-vis their oppressors.

In March 1933, Communist Party functionaries and activists became the first prisoners at Dachau, which became the "model camp" for later camps. These prisoners' behavior and strategies were based on the experiences that they had had in political battles before 1933 and during the time of their being outlawed after January 30, 1933. As members of a rigidly organized party made up of cadres, they tried from the beginning to strengthen their cohesiveness with one another and to stand together against the SS guards. Their attitude toward the Social Democrats, who were sent to concentration camps in greater numbers after their party was outlawed in June 1933, was much the same as the Communist Party's stance prior to 1933: standoffish to hostile. The attitude of Social Democratic prisoners toward their Communist co-prisoners was, with some exceptions, also mistrustful. They accused one another of having had the wrong policy toward the National Socialists. Younger functionaries of both parties were especially disappointed and embittered that the leftist parties had not joined together against the Nazis. The two largest groups of political prisoners were not able to join in unified action against the SS guards until they had spent a rather long period of imprisonment together. From the beginning, however, attempts by the SS to incite Communist prisoners to acts of violence against prominent Social Democratic functionaries failed. These functionaries were often badly mistreated when they arrived at a camp and then immediately had the help and support of their Communist companions in misfortune.

The most important instrument for all attempts to bring about improvements for prisoners, to protect endangered inmates, or to help the sick was the so-called prisoners' self-administration. This entity, which was set up by the SS and whose organizational structure nearly corresponded to the SS hierarchy, tended to the entire functioning and maintenance of the camp. The camp was structured according to a rigid hierarchy, from the "camp elder," who was given the responsibility of being the prisoners' speaker and representative to the SS, to the "barrack-room elder," who was responsible for a "barrack-room" within a prisoners' barracks: for the distribution of beds, cleanliness, the distribution of rations, and so on. Work details were supervised and led by foremen, so-called Kapos. At Dachau, Communist prisoners tried from the beginning to gain all-important positions, which they succeeded in doing over the course of a long time. The solidarity of individual groups was at first based on common place or region of origin; often, political friends who had previously worked together illegally met again behind barbed wire.

The so-called prisoner functionaries constituted the very top of the hierarchy of the inmates' community, which became increasingly more differentiated, especially during the war years. From the beginning, however, when no one yet considered the mass murder of the European Jews imaginable, Jewish prisoners were at the bottom rung and had to suffer most. The first Jewish inmates came to Dachau as political opponents of the Nazis. In 1935, after the decree of the Nuremberg Laws, Jews were sent to the camps for other reasons, for example, under the charge of having committed the newly created crime of "racial defilement." They were kept separate from the other inmates and repeatedly had to endure collective punitive measures as well.

Heinz Eschen, a Communist student of Jewish origin who had been sent to Dachau in 1933, became the Kapo of the Jewish block in Dachau and acquired an almost legendary reputation among his fellow inmates as a protector of Jewish inmates. Through acceptance of the SS's military presence, tireless work, and courageous intercession on the behalf of other inmates, he enjoyed a certain respect even among the SS men. Heinz Eschen organized talks, recitations, and discussions in order to keep the morale of the isolated prisoners from sinking completely when, following foreign press reports about Dachau in 1937, Jewish prisoners were not allowed to leave their barracks for several weeks, the barracks windows were covered over, and the doors were locked. Heinz Eschen was killed in 1938 after being terribly tortured.

Aside from the political inmates, the *Jehovah's Witnesses — who, under the rubric of being "serious Bible students," were sent to the concentration camps because they refused military service for religious reasons — were considered to be upright and mostly incorruptible.

With the arrival of criminal prisoners, who were automatically sent in rather large numbers to concentration camps after they had served their time in prisons or penitentiaries, the struggle of groups of inmates among one another for influence and positions of power within the inmates' hierarchy began. Political prisoners were required to wear a red chevron on their clothing, while recidivist criminal prisoners had to wear a green chevron, and "red against green" was the rule in all concentration camps. In all camps, the degree to which one or the other group could prevail within the inmates' hierarchy determined until the end the possibilities for saving individuals or for succeeding in obtaining from the SS improvements of the prisoners' living conditions.

The concentration camp system was solidified and consolidated during the second half of the 1930s. Dachau was the only camp founded in 1933 that was maintained; all other earlier concentration camps were dissolved. Additional concentration camps were set up beginning in 1936: Sachsenhausen near Berlin in 1936; Buchenwald near Weimar in 1937; Flossenbürg in the Upper Palatinate and Mauthausen near Linz in Austria in 1938; and finally Ravensbrück near Fürstenberg on the Havel as a women's concentration camp in 1939. As at the other camps, the prisoners' self-government at Ravensbrück was determined by struggles for power and influence, although women acted much more practically than men in organizing day-to-day assistance. Their particular vulnerability was their children, whom they brought with them to the camp during the war or bore there and for whom little could be done in the extreme situation of the concentration camp.

It was primarily inmates with the green chevron who were used to build the new camps, which led to their often holding the most important positions within the inmates' hierarchy from the beginning; at the

Mauthausen camp, this hierarchization meant that there was no possibility of organized solidarity among the inmates until the spring of
1944. With exceptions, the criminal inmates were feared and avoided
by the other prisoners as the "extended arm of the SS." They worked as
informers for the SS, and not a few of them became the torturers and
murderers of their fellow prisoners.

At Buchenwald, where the illegal resistance movement is best documented, political and criminal inmate functionaries fought one another
to the end. "During my entire imprisonment, one of my heaviest psychological burdens was that I had been thrown into the same pot as criminal
elements," wrote the Social Democrat Walter Poller, who was a medical
secretary in Buchenwald until his release in 1940. According to him,
there were SS men in the concentration camps who viewed the political
prisoners as being superior to the criminal ones, and he sees this as one
reason it was possible for political prisoners to assume more and more
prisoners' functions in Buchenwald. In Buchenwald, the Communists
played the most important role in the prisoner's self-administration and
in the illegal resistance organization. Eugen Kogon, a non-Communist
chronicler of the camps, wrote of them: "The Communists' service to
the KZ prisoners can hardly be estimated highly enough. In some cases,
camp inmates literally are indebted to them for everyone's rescue, even
if their motivations seldom sprang from pure unselfishness, but rather
usually from the group's survival instinct, in whose positive results an
entire camp then sometimes shared."

In the spring of 1938, the first non-German prisoners arrived in the
concentration camps: they were Austrians, although they were registered
as Germans. After the pogrom of November 9, 1938, approximately
thirty thousand Jewish men from Germany and Austria were sent to the
concentration camps, more than ten thousand of them to Dachau. It was
the first large-scale action in which thousands were dragged off and mistreated and in which there were hundreds of deaths. Benedikt Kautsky
wrote of Buchenwald: "The accommodation of the new arrivals mocked
any description.... The inmates were mistreated and plundered by both
the SS and supervisory Aryan inmates from criminal circles.... Then I
learned for the first time what solidarity among inmates meant: at risk
to their own lives, the Aryan political inmates who worked in a supervisory capacity smuggled bandages and medicine to the Jewish blocks,
where Jewish doctors provided at least provisionary treatment."

During the course of the war years, the structure and living conditions of the prisoners' community changed fundamentally. First, the
Dachau camp was evacuated from September 1939 to March 1940 so
that an SS division could be trained there. The inmates were sent to
camps at Buchenwald, Flossenbürg, and Mauthausen, where they were
subject to the criminal Kapos and for the first time had to endure,

in the quarries, the consequences of the concept of "annihilation by work." They were especially dependent upon one another for help and support during this time, and, as they returned to Dachau in reduced numbers and in completely exhausted condition during the spring of 1940, this first terrible winter of the war had permanently strengthened the group's solidarity. Subsequently, large numbers of inmates arrived from the countries that had been attacked by the German Wehrmacht: Czechs and Poles at first, and, after the expansion of the war, representatives of all countries against which Germany had waged war. Among these prisoners were representatives of the political and cultural elites as well as simple people who had taken up arms against the occupation of their countries.

The concentration camp at Auschwitz was opened in June 1940 and initially received only Polish prisoners. Thirty German criminal prisoners from Sachsenhausen, who received the numbers 1 to 30, were appointed as prisoner functionaries in Auschwitz. The Polish prisoners very quickly organized an underground movement that, in contrast to the camps located in Germany, could count on the help and support of the population living nearby and that was directed not by Communists but by Polish officers. There were repeated successes in organizing escapes, and very soon there was detailed information in Poland about the conditions in the Auschwitz camp. With the help of civilian workers, food stuffs, clothes, and medicine were smuggled into the camp. The German camp administration fought against any resistance activity with the most brutal methods, and most of the officers of the underground organization were shot in the camp. Construction of Auschwitz II just a couple miles away in Birkenau began in October 1941; in the following years, this camp became the largest installation for the murder of European Jews and other groups of victims.

In 1941, the conduct of the war by the German Wehrmacht as well as the methods of oppression and murder became radicalized. The first mass murders of the sick and the handicapped with poison gas were carried out not in the concentration camps but in killing installations that were set up in hospitals. In the summer of 1941, a medical commission from Berlin selected the as yet unsuspecting sick inmates from Dachau as victims, and, in the winter of 1941, transports to the sanitarium at Castle Hartheim near Linz began, where a total of more than three thousand inmates from Dachau were murdered with poison gas. It very quickly became clear to those who remained that the "transport of invalids" did not lead, as was said, to a sanitarium but rather to death. No one else volunteered, but it was impossible for the prisoners' self-administration to hinder or to sabotage these transports. In some cases, it was possible to hide prisoners with obvious physical ailments in the infirmary for a while, but, from then on, every prisoner who arrived at the camp handicapped or physically badly weakened stood under the threat of being murdered immediately.

In the summer of 1941, after the Germans' march into France, members of the International Brigades who had fought in the Spanish Civil War and who had been interned in France were deported to Germany. Austrians who had fought in the Spanish Civil War were sent as an independent group to the camp at Dachau, where from the beginning they enjoyed high regard among the prisoners because of their struggle against the fascist Franco regime and where some of them quickly rose to key positions in the prisoners' self-administration. The "Red Spaniards," who arrived having already had long years of experience in sticking together under the most difficult living conditions, proved themselves as capable and reliable organizers of covert work in all camps.

Beginning in October 1941, thousands of Soviet prisoners of war, having been selected from POW camps by special units of the Security Police, were brought to concentration camps to be murdered. These prisoners arrived at the camps in a physical condition whose seriousness had been hitherto unimaginable and produced among the other prisoners a wave of sympathy and willingness to help. The implications of the German-Soviet Nonaggression Treaty that had earlier divided the leftist groups of inmates had also made underground cooperation between Communists and Social Democrats difficult, but now there was recognition that fellow inmates were not the real foes. Thus, there are reports from many camps that the Soviet inmates, at first kept isolated from the other prisoners, were secretly supplied with food and medical assistance. After a few months, not all Soviet POWs were shot. Then, forced laborers arrived in the concentration camps as the second large group of Soviet inmates. These were people who had earlier been taken to work in Germany and who, in the eyes of those who wielded power, had deserved punishment. Among them were many children and teenagers, who especially aroused the sympathy of the "old" concentration camp prisoners and some of whom, under the care of older inmates, were able to be placed in light work details.

In 1942, as the German planners built the installations and created the conditions necessary for the murder of millions in gas chambers and the burning of the dead in large crematoria, German prisoners in camps located on Reich territory more and more became a minority. Inmates' communities became multinational groups in which there were numerous conflicts of nationality. There arose a differentiated scheme of values according to which the individual groups were classified. After the German and Austrian groups, northern and western Europeans were in the upper range, unless they had arrived tagged *"Nacht und Nebel"* (night and fog) and were thus subject to severer conditions of imprisonment in accordance with an order given by the chief of the High Command of the Armed Forces, Keitel, on December 12, 1941, under which persons who committed offenses against the German occupation forces could be killed or secretly snatched during the "night and fog." Among eastern Europeans, on the other hand, the Czechs, many of whom had a mastery of the German language, were in a more favorable position than the Poles or the Russians. The Yugoslavians, most of whom had fought as partisans against the Germans, enjoyed high regard among the inmates.

Every national group developed its specific forms of resistance and of staying together. People tried to help newly arrived compatriots through the shocking experience of being sent to the camp by providing information and encouragement and by giving them instructions on how to act toward the SS and the criminal Kapos. Prominent compatriots such as well-known politicians or important clerics, who were also symbols of injured national identity for the other inmates, enjoyed particular attention and devotion. In this way, the father of a member of the exiled Czech government could be hidden in the infirmary at the Dachau camp with the help of Czech inmates; at age eighty-five, he died shortly after being liberated.

In all camps, some work details, such as the clerk's office, the political division (that is, the camp Gestapo), the kitchen, the labor department, and the infirmary, offered the most possibilities for helping others and acquiring information about the plans and actions of the SS. All inmates in those details held key positions, and the extent to which they placed themselves in personal danger for the interests of the inmates' community depended on their willingness to act and their courage. Solidarity and agreements with one's own group of friends, with whom one weighed the dangers and chances of illegal actions, were also always of decisive importance. Most of all, contacts and arrangements with individual SS persons had to be agreed upon so that there would be no impression of collaboration. Eugon Kogon, who, as first medical clerk of Buchenwald, gained great influence on an SS physician through whose help he was able to accomplish much, speaks of an "elastic bulkhead" that existed between the inmates and the SS and that was not allowed to be lifted.

Beginning in 1942, the expansion of the subcamps and the work details was set into high gear primarily for the armaments industry. Resistance against the production of German weapons became a primary concern for the prisoners, who thereby hoped to be able to influence the course of the war. Since even suspicion of "sabotage" was sufficient to bring a death sentence, absolute secrecy was even more necessary in this field than elsewhere. From reports by survivors, one can conclude that there were attempts in many places at least to draw out work and, if possible, to do shoddy work. All prisoners were supposed to be deterred from any attempt at sabotage by public executions on the roll-call square.

As the number of inmates became greater, the inmates' self-administration became more indispensable for the SS camp administration, and thus the room for individual actions by the prisoners became greater. Karl Wagner, the camp elder of the Dachau subcamp Allach, publicly refused to whip another inmate and was then not immediately shot, as everyone expected, but punished only with bunker confinement. In order to maintain the prisoners' capacity for work, certain improvements were introduced in 1943, such as additional rations and, for prisoners' groups in the upper range of the value scheme, permission to receive packages containing food. At the same time, political inmates attempted to place their confidence men in the important positions at the subcamps.

With the gradual worsening of the situation on the German front, the prisoners' hope of holding out until the end of the war grew, and members of the SS also began to think about an "afterward." The circulation of news about the military situation and the march of the Allies became an essential task for building morale. There are reports from all camps of the existence of hidden radio receivers by which people secretly listened to Allied broadcasts.

Morgues and wards for contagious diseases in infirmaries, which were avoided everywhere by members of the SS, served as meeting points for planning conspiracies and intrigues. In many concentration camps, cultural activities, such as theater and concert events, discussions about literature and philosophy, or study groups concerning a wide range of topics, also became an instrument of resistance against the destruction of the inmates' individuality. Listening to music, one could forget one's surroundings for a short time; attempts to educate oneself further meant that one still believed in a personal future outside the camp. In the Dachau camp, to which more than two thousand clerics were sent, the underground practice of religion also played an important role in the struggle against spiritual oppression.

On the other hand, living conditions dramatically worsened for the majority of prisoners during the final years of the war. There were an ever larger number of prisoners who, completely insufficiently nourished and clothed and without medical treatment, had to perform the heaviest physical work under catastrophic living conditions. The survival expectancy, which was estimated in the Auschwitz camp to be an average of three months for prisoners who were not gassed immediately after their arrival but selected for work, decreased in the other camps as well. The discrepancy in the living conditions of prisoners whose physical strength became fully exhausted within the shortest time and who almost certainly were either murdered, fell victim to an epidemic, or died of physical exhaustion and those prisoners who had work in an enclosed space and were not immediately threatened constantly grew. For that reason, inmates' help and solidarity reached mostly only those who were already in a better position and had contacts with other compatriots or political friends. With the help of a confidence man in the Labor Utilization Office, an individual could be relieved of quarry work and placed in the kitchen for a while. However, the prisoners could do nothing against the murderous setup of quarry work per se.

At the same time, millions of Jews from nearly all European countries were deported to Poland and, aside from a small number of younger ones who were sent to work, immediately murdered there. They were deceived about the destination of their deportation until the end. Isolated attempts to revolt on the short path between selection and the gas chambers, attempts about which there is scanty evidence, were not able to stop the murder machine.

During the last phase in the history of the concentration camps — from the summer of 1944 until the spring of 1945 — the actions of the inmates were guided by their hope for the end and their fear of being murdered at the last minute. A large number of German political prisoners were drafted into *Parole Units and sent to the front. In all camps, cooperation developed between individual national groups, which tried in underground committees of inmates to develop strategies until the arrival of the Allies and to prepare for an armed uprising if necessary. At many places, weapons and ammunition parts were smuggled from armaments plants into the camps for this purpose and hidden there. Prisoners of war secretly instructed inmates in the use of weapons. In the camp at Buchenwald, German political inmate functionaries of various political persuasions united to form a popular front committee that developed political perspectives for a postwar Germany.

The evacuation of the concentration camps in the face of the advancing Allied armies, which began in July 1944 with the evacuation of the camp at Majdanek, canceled preparations in many camps for the end. In Auschwitz, there had been an international resistance group already in 1943, the Battle Group Auschwitz, that was in constant contact with the Polish underground movement. Medicine was smuggled into the camp; escapes by particularly endangered prisoners were organized; and information about the mass gassings was passed on out of the camp. Several plans for rebellion had also been prepared, none of which, though, was realized, either because partisan groups in the vicinity did not yet consider themselves to be in a position to offer help from without or because the plans became known to the SS ahead of time. There were also contacts with members of the Sonderkommando, who, strictly isolated from the other prisoners, were forced to work in the crematoria and were also gassed at regular intervals. By providing explosives, the Battle Group

Auschwitz assisted the revolt of the Auschwitz Sonderkommando, which broke out on October 4, 1944, and which no prisoner survived. The gradual evacuation of inmates from Auschwitz between October 1944 and January 1945 tore the Battle Group Auschwitz apart and ended resistance activity there.

There had already been armed revolts in the Bialystok Ghetto and in the annihilation camp at Treblinka in August 1943. A revolt in Sobibor followed in October 1943. They were quickly put down and, aside from the successful escape of a few inmates, were unable to achieve any success due to the extreme circumstances of imprisonment.

The situation in the camps located in Germany became increasingly insufferable up to the spring of 1945 due to the continuous arrival of new transports of sick and exhausted prisoners from other camps that could no longer be supplied. The evacuation of prisoners then began in Germany as well; due to the approaching liberators, these evacuations could not be continued, yet thousands fell victim to them even a few days before liberation. In Buchenwald, Dachau, and Mauthausen, which was the last camp to be liberated (May 5, 1945), the underground committees were able to guarantee the Allies' bloodless takeover of the camps and afterward to organize necessary care with food and medical help and the subsequent return of the survivors to their homelands.

The resistance of those persecuted in the concentration camps was not marked by spectacular deeds. A young, still physically strong prisoner who volunteered to work as a nurse in a typhus ward in order to stand by his dying comrade, and who thereby placed himself in mortal danger not because of coercion but because of inner duty, did not think of the fame of posterity. Yet with undiminished, pressing importance, his action confronts us with fundamental questions about humans beings' possibilities for making decisions.

Bibliography

Dunin-Wasowicz, Krzysztof. *Resistance in the Nazi Concentration Camps 1933–1945.* Warsaw, 1982.

Kogon, Eugen. *Der SS-Staat: Das System der deutschen Konzentrationslager.* Stockholm, 1947 (numerous reprints).

———. *The Theory and Practice of Hell: The German Concentration Camps and the System behind Them.* New York, 1958.

Langbein, Hermann. *Against All Hope: Resistance in the Nazi Concentration Camps, 1938–1945.* New York, 1994.

Pingel, Falk. *Häftlinge unter SS-Herrschaft: Widerstand, Selbstbehauptung und Vernichtung im Konzentrationslager.* Hamburg, 1978.

Sofsky, Wolfgang. *Die Ordnung des Terrors: Das Konzentrationslager.* Frankfurt am Main, 1993.

"Solidarität und Widerstand." *Dachauer Hefte* 7 (1991).

Exile and Resistance

Patrik von zur Mühlen ⸻

"Exile" and "resistance" can be complementary concepts if they refer to two possibilities of political activity that presented themselves to opponents of the Third Reich after Hitler's seizure of power, insofar as one excludes as a third possibility the resigned retreat into private life, into "inner immigration." One can narrow the spectrum of activity by those who were persecuted by the National Socialist regime if one combines the concepts in a different manner: exile or resistance. This would certainly juxtapose safe exile in another land and active struggle against the Hitler dictatorship in such a way as though exile would have meant the renunciation of further political activities.

This might have been the case for some emigrés who avoided persecution by fleeing abroad, since far more than 90 percent of those who left Germany were Jews, victims of the racist persecution. Often completely apolitical, some of them would have accepted the Third Reich if its anti-Semitic policies and propaganda had not driven them out of the country. One would be able to say that, in this form, the question *Exile or resistance?* admitted only a single answer: exile.

Active opponents of the Third Reich would have seen and answered this question differently. Members of (primarily leftist) parties that had been outlawed, members of trade unions, representatives of political public life (including those of bourgeois, liberal, conservative, and Christian origin), writers critical of the regime, scientists and intellectuals as well as dissident artists saw in exile the chance to continue their activities abroad with an eye toward Germany, these activities having been interrupted or suppressed as a result of the "seizure of power" by the National Socialist German Workers' Party (NSDAP).

The Jewish — primarily apolitical — exodus took place over several years until it was stopped in October 1941 due to already existing plans for the Holocaust. There was no continuous exodus of political emigrés. Almost all those who fled due to political reasons had done so in 1933, in many cases even during the first months of that year. Only a few people followed them in subsequent years. Many were no longer able to flee because they had since been incarcerated in prisons or camps, whereas others had come to terms with the new conditions at the price of their good political behavior.

Many who left Germany as victims of racist persecution broke from their homeland for good, especially since National Socialist propaganda had for years denied Jews their Germanness. Political refugees maintained their "gaze at Germany" much more strongly. They hoped to be able to return to Germany as soon as possible after a much-desired and much-anticipated collapse of the National Socialist dictatorship. In many cases, this also determined their choice of an exile country. They emigrated to neighboring countries where they were as close as possible to the German border and to events and where they could also actively intervene more easily in what was happening.

At this point, we run into the problem of geography, which was to become significant for exile and resistance and for the combination of the two. Of course, there were also chance factors that determined to which country the refugees fled: geographical proximity, personal contacts, travel connections, and knowledge of languages. Nevertheless, certain centers of German refugees formed for reasons that were not at all accidental. In this respect, one must mention France first and Czechoslovakia second. Other states either accepted fewer refugees or caused them bureaucratic difficulties in every regard, especially since dictatorial conditions had been established in some of them as well (Poland, Austria, Hungary, Yugoslavia). France and Czechoslovakia, on the other hand, had long since had liberal laws of asylum and guaranteed bourgeois freedoms as preconditions for political activity.

France — particularly Paris — became the most important center of German emigration until 1938–39. For the meanwhile, approximately three thousand Social Democrats and around fifty-five hundred Communists settled there, as did representatives of other leftist parties and organizations from Germany (see *German Socialist Workers' Party, *German Communist Party/Opposition, and *Anarcho-Syndicalists). The presence of politically prominent persons in Paris — from Rudolf Breitscheid, a Social Democrat, to Willi Münzenberg, a Communist — was important. A considerable portion of exiled German or German-speaking writers found haven in France: Heinrich and Klaus Mann, Lion Feuchtwanger, Franz Werfel, and others. In Paris, exile publishing houses settled (Éditions du Carrefours); German-language daily newspapers (*Pariser Tageblatt*) and other periodicals were published; and clubs, circles, cafés, and other establishments, run almost exclusively by and for emigrés from Germany, were formed.

In Czechoslovakia, the political presence of German-speaking emigrés was numerically not quite so great, but it nevertheless was quite impressive. The prevalence of the German language in the Republic of Czechoslovakia as well as the republic's liberal laws of asylum made it easier for refugees from Germany to stay in the country. The executive committee of the German Social Democratic Party (SPD) settled in

Prague under the name Sopade and worked there with the support of Sudeten German Social Democrats until it relocated to Paris for a short time and from there to London in 1940 due to political developments. *Neuer Vorwärts* (New forward) was published in Prague and Paris until 1940. The German Communist Party (KPD) had one of its most important exile centers in Prague — only those in Moscow and Paris were more important. Even the *Black Front, a dissident Nazi movement, operated primarily on Czechoslovakian soil under its so-called führer, Otto Strasser. A third important center of "exile and resistance" was the Saar region, which was governed by the League of Nations until it was reincorporated into the German Reich in 1935.

Political resistance involves opposing a dictatorial regime with words, writings, and deeds; contesting the regime's legitimacy; informing the people; supporting endangered persons; fighting the efficiency of the regime's apparatus — especially its organs of repression; and shaking its base of power by sabotage and other measures. The collapse of the regime is then the ultimate and highest goal toward which most variants of political resistance strive. Yet that means that oppositional activities must be carried out to a large degree within the country itself. In this regard, exile can perform only a complementary, supporting function, which does not preclude the possibility that, in extreme cases, resistance can still be offered only from abroad.

For the resistance against National Socialism, the important exile countries were primarily operational areas for activities in Germany. In them, one could print flyers more easily (and in relative safety), gather reports, direct information to the world public, and prepare various actions. Violent acts by the Gestapo — involving the planting of informants and agents in political committees and groups and the kidnapping or murdering of opponents of National Socialism — prove that this security was not absolute even abroad. Financial machinations in the editorial offices of some exile periodicals, intrigues in some emigré committees, the abduction (and later execution) of political refugees — up to the assassination of the well-known oppositional philosopher Theodor Lessing — give clear evidence of this.

The contact of resistance groups operating from exile with the inner-German resistance was almost always the weak point of activities hostile to the regime. On the one hand, proclamations against the Third Reich and anti-Nazi political information were noticed mostly only by emigrés themselves and at best by some members of the interested public in the host countries; on the other hand, such proclamations and information could be taken into Germany only with the greatest difficulty. The borders around Germany were guarded, ships and international trains checked, mail censored. One could transport flyers and other political writings to Germany only through underground, covert means.

For these purposes, Sopade established sixteen so-called border secretariats around Germany. They were manned by reliable, well-paid party
functionaries who were well acquainted with areas neighboring Germany and who built up their own network of confidence men there.
Political writings were smuggled to Germany from abroad through these
channels; conversely, functionaries of the outlawed SPD gathered information and sent it abroad via the same channels such that Sopade, as
we can conclude from its *Deutschland-Berichte* (Reports on Germany),
was quite well informed about conditions in Germany. The International
Transport Workers' Federation (ITP) also provided invaluable services
in this regard, as it allowed propaganda material to be smuggled by
member sailors on foreign ships. The warning and rescue of endangered
persons were also organized from abroad.

The modus operandi of the Communists was similar, as they utilized
"backpack caravans" to a much greater extent and thus also had to
chalk up the greatest losses through arrests. Geography played a not insignificant role in this regard. Favored smuggling trails were the wooded
areas of the Palatinate Forest, the Erzgebirge, and the Bavarian Forest,
through which illegal printed materials were smuggled to Germany from
the Saar region, France, and Czechoslovakia. Within Germany, covert
resistance groups received the material and saw that it was distributed
further.

Smaller parties and groupings, such as the German Socialist Workers' Party (SAP), the German Communist Party/Opposition (KPO), the
Anarcho-Syndicalists, the Strasser Movement (see *Black Front), as well
as Christian and conservative opposition groups, worked in a similar
fashion, albeit with some differences. The Jesuit priest Friedrich Muckermann, for example, supplied opposition circles close to the church in
the Rhineland and in Westphalia with writings critical of the regime.
The extent of these transports of material to Germany, it must be admitted, remained minimal. In addition, all contacts between the resistance
within and outside of Germany were endangered by strict observation
by the Gestapo, by infiltration, or by the unreliability of the resistance's
own people. Moreover, the Third Reich's ever-improving surveillance
apparatus led to the gradual smashing of the resistance's infrastructures
during the mid-1930s and to their general dissolution at the beginning
of the war in 1939.

In addition to these conspiratorial forms of resistance, there were
some political actions that had a rather demonstrative character. In this
regard, one must consider primarily the popular front activities of German exile parties. It is well known that, during the entire National
Socialist period, opponents of Hitler were not able to form a German
exile government that could have served as an alternative for the world
public and especially the German people. In some exile countries, there

were indeed committees that made claims to speak for the German emigrés and that strove to assume the role of a mouthpiece vis-à-vis the public of a given host country. But an internationally recognized, democratic countergovernment to the Hitler regime such as those that existed for occupied countries during the war never came to be. There were various reasons for this, not the least of which was that the host countries did not take these attempts seriously or simply did not want such a countergovernment within their borders.

Even a nonpartisan alliance, broadened by renowned emigrés from German intellectual life, did not come about in exile. The so-called popular front negotiations in the Hotel Lutetia in Paris, in which representatives from the SPD, KPD, SAP, and other parties and groups participated under the crucial assistance of Heinrich Mann, dragged on from 1935 until the end of the war without producing concrete results. The negotiations failed due in part to unbreachable differences of opinion among the participants, yet the main reason was the Communists' claim to authority, which was pursued by numerous unpleasant tactical maneuvers (see *Committee for the Preparation of a German People's Front).

A turning point in the relationship between exile and resistance occurred with the outbreak of the Spanish Civil War. At that time, there was the prevalent idea — today no longer tenable — among leftists that Franco wanted to topple the legal republican government of Spain as a puppet of and under the auspices of Hitler. The view ignored the predominantly Spanish roots of the civil war. Nevertheless, the strong military and technical support that Hitler and Mussolini gave to the Spanish rebels was and is undeniable. The view that Franco was Hitler's Iberian viceroy led people to regard the struggle against Franco as a war of proxy against the National Socialist government on Spanish soil.

Thus the Spanish Civil War was a strong lure for a sizable number of German political emigrés. The belief that it was possible to fight the National Socialist regime on the other side of the Pyrenees actively and not just with slogans and resolutions might have been one of the reasons these German emigrés went to Spain to fight during the initial period. Emigrés streamed into Spain from numerous countries of exile in order to hook up there with the International Brigades or other units in the fight against Franco. Despite a ban and strict border control, approximately one-third of the roughly five thousand German fighters in the Spanish Civil War succeeded in going to Spain from Germany. Approximately two-thirds were Communists; roughly 15 percent were Social Democrats and members of smaller parties and groups. It is assumed that between fifteen hundred and two thousand of them were killed.

Thus, those fighters who had interpreted the war as a proxy war against the National Socialist regime must have seen the defeat of the

Spanish republic in the spring of 1939 as a victory for Hitler. The consequences were catastrophic for the mood of Germans in exile. Not only did events give the impression of helplessness and of the invincibility of fascist powers, but internal squabbles among the various wings of German emigrés produced serious irritations. The Communist Party's persecution of non-Communists in Spain, the simultaneous purges in the Soviet Union, and the failure of the popular front negotiations in France led to renowned Communist intellectuals — such as Willi Münzenberg and the writers Arthur Koestler, Gustav Regler, and Manès Sperber — breaking from their party and ordinary party members retreating from activity. Finally, the German-Soviet Nonaggression Treaty (the Hitler-Stalin Pact) led to profound disappointment among all emigrés. Up to that point, the Soviet Union had been respected by non-Communists at least as an ally against the Third Reich. For some, the question now arose as to whom they should regard as the more dangerous opponent.

The political crisis in the resistance in exile also had its sources in the conditions of exile in the individual countries. An important country of exile was lost with the destruction of Czechoslovakia in the fall of 1938 and the occupation of "remaining Czechoslovakia" half a year later. In view of the increasingly threatening foreign policy situation and also as a result of internal legal developments, France imposed restrictions on German emigrés that compromised the emigrés' political activities more and more. Other countries of exile in Europe followed this example. When World War II then began with the Wehrmacht's march into Poland on September 1, 1939, thoughtful opponents of National Socialism had to admit to themselves that their efforts to fight against the Third Reich in exile had not had any effect.

Nevertheless, the sharp caesura of the beginning of the war did not lead to an end of antifascist activities abroad, though such activities had become far more restricted and difficult. Contact with Germany had become almost impossible due to the conditions of war. An additional consequence of the new situation was that political groups in exile could no longer appear or hardly continue to appear as independently functioning powers. In Switzerland, they were forbidden to engage in any political work for fear of possible German reprisals. In Sweden, restrictions did not go so far, yet, for similar reasons, emigrés were largely deprived of their latitude for action. Thus, one could fight against the National Socialist regime only in concert with the forces of a given country of exile and within the bounds set by it.

In countries occupied by Germany, this meant cooperation with the respective resistance. In Norway, such activities were exemplified by the work of Willy Brandt. There were also examples of such activities in the Netherlands, Belgium, Luxembourg, and Czechoslovakia and isolated examples in other countries as well. Yet this cooperation assumed a notable dimension only in France. Beginning in 1941, several hundred Germans were active there in the unit Travail Anti-Allemand of the Communist-dominated Front National de la Libération (FNL). Their work consisted of assisting in all matters in which a knowledge of German and Germany was required: espionage for the Résistance, the establishment of contacts, the dissemination of antifascist propaganda among German soldiers, and similar activities. Some — mostly Communist — Germans also fought in the French partisan organization Francs-Tireurs et Partisans Français. Smaller groups of persons of different political persuasions also worked in Gaullist and other resistance organizations. In the fall of 1944, the Communist-led "Free Germany" Committee for the West formed in the French underground, having been patterned on the *National Committee "Free Germany," which had previously been established in Moscow; after the liberation of France, it was recognized as a part of the French Résistance.

There were similar forms of struggle against the Third Reich in cooperation with its war enemies in the Soviet Union. Even during the 1930s, the activities of the almost exclusively Communist German emigrés there had been under the auspices of Comintern, that is, of the Soviet regime. The KPD had its center in Moscow and from there directed the work of its units in Germany and in European exile countries. The secret organization *Red Orchestra sent military information to Moscow via radio from Berlin and from various European countries. The receiver and commissioner of the reports was the Soviet Union, that is, an enemy power. Members of the Red Orchestra acted entirely out of political conviction and in opposition to the Third Reich. In this, the resistance moved in the direction of foreign espionage in an area of fuzzy delineations.

During the so-called eastern campaign, German emigrés fought in the Red Army or worked for the Soviets by distributing propaganda among German POWs. After the defeat at Stalingrad, the Soviets in the summer of 1943 established the National Committee "Free Germany" with German emigrés and Wehrmacht officers who had been taken prisoner. De facto control was in the hands of KPD functionaries and their Soviet "advisers," while prominent German generals were placed in nominal posts. This fact, as well as the committee's programmatic statements and external characteristics, implied a German-national stance in order to guard against the possible charge of treason and enemy coercion. The transition from resistance to activity in the interest of an enemy power is even fuzzier here than in the case of the Red Orchestra, and it is more problematic to count the committee clearly among German opposition groups. If one does not take into account the KPD functionaries in key positions, it was a group that operated for the most part not in exile but rather in POW camps.

Great Britain was one of the few European countries in which German political exile organizations were able to continue to work to a certain extent even during the war. The SPD's executive committee, Sopade, was able to move its seat to London in good time before the occupation of Paris. Other leftist parties and groups had retreated to England as well. Of course, their freedom to act was narrowly limited as a result of the war situation and British dictates. Political activities like those in the 1930s, such as fighting the National Socialist regime by means of information and the formation and support of resistance organizations, were not possible. Nevertheless, German emigrés were politically active in Great Britain. Through their contacts with the Labour Party, some of them assisted in the area of policy consultation, especially with respect to the shaping of postwar Germany. Emigrés worked in British radio propaganda, in the care and political education of German POWs, and in other areas. Although this work was done solely on behalf of the host country, it nevertheless also corresponded to the emigrés' convictions and was, at least in their subjective view, a small contribution to the resistance.

The relation between exile and resistance was also problematic in overseas countries. Contact with events in Germany was so difficult there that an immediate influence on things in the homeland was impossible both before and after the beginning of the war. Nevertheless, it would be wrong to divorce German emigrés' political activities in North and Latin America entirely from the topic of resistance. As was the case in the German fighters' engagement in the Spanish Civil War, German exiles in the Americas — primarily in Latin America — engaged in a "representative struggle" against the Third Reich. In Latin America, the target of this representative struggle was the presence of National Socialism within Latin American nations themselves. It is well known that ex-patriot Germans and people of German descent in Latin American countries were influenced to a large degree by National Socialism and that their journals, schools, organizations, and church congregations had been in part "coordinated" with its principles. Nazi organizations formed branches overseas and conducted or supported espionage or other activities for the Third Reich. In some countries, they also attacked refugees from Germany (primarily Jews) or attempted to influence the indigenous population in the spirit of National Socialism.

As early as the 1930s, committees and political associations of emigrés who expressly defined themselves as part of a worldwide resistance against National Socialism had been formed against these activities, for self-protection, and for the purpose of self-help in cases of social need. The first political organization of this type was the committee The Other Germany, which was formed in Argentina in 1937 and which soon set up branches in other Latin American countries of exile. The Free Germany Movement was formed in Mexico in 1941–42 from already existing rudiments of organizations. In 1943, both committees created supraregional umbrella organizations with branches in all important Latin American metropolises where significant numbers of German refugees were staying. The Free Germany Movement bore similarities to the National Committee "Free Germany" not only in name; like the latter, it was led by Communists, although it, too, elected prominent non-Communists — in this case, Heinrich Mann — to honorary posts.

These committees were not of real political significance. Only a dwindling, tiny portion of the mostly apolitical emigrés was interested in them. Lack of money as well as political dictates of the host countries hindered their work. Essentially, they could perform only intelligence work among people who did not need it. Due to the war and the great distance, they were able to have no influence on Germany whatsoever. So they directed their attention largely to theoretical topics such as the shape of Germany after the war. They developed ideas for a new political order in their homeland and in Europe and, on behalf of these ideas, made demands that were primarily rhetorical — not a single government recognized the groups as discussion partners.

The situation was similar in the United States, which, in terms of the number of emigrés admitted, was the most important country of exile. As in other countries in North and Latin America, the distance from Europe prohibited any immediate influence on events in Germany. In the case of the United States, one can only repeat what has already been said of Great Britain and the Soviet Union: one could fight the National Socialist regime only in concert with the government of the host country and within the confines of the host country's political and military plan. In the United States, some German emigrés made themselves available as specialists on Germany, as advisers on the shape of policy toward postwar Germany, and as advisers to the military and to key state committees. Thus, one can speak of resistance against the Third Reich in exile only in a very loose sense.

Nevertheless, an additional aspect should be mentioned especially in conjunction with the United States. The United States, as hardly any other country, took in a circle of intellectually important refugees: scientists, writers, and artists. They brought with them knowledge and experience from their areas of expertise that had been outlawed or disparaged as "degenerate" in their homeland. The theory of relativity, sociology and psychoanalysis, the architecture of the Bauhaus, twelve-tone music, and expressionist or abstract painting were of course no resistance. At the beginning, we characterized as resistance only activity that, through practical action, questioned the omnipotence of an authoritarian regime: counterpropaganda, worldwide enlightenment, the rescue of threatened persons, acts of sabotage against the apparatus of repression, up to armed forms of struggle that were supposed to facilitate or to cause the toppling of the regime.

The rescue of German democratic and progressive cultural riches does not, in a strict sense, meet these criterion. Yet this phenomenon should not be entirely divorced from the topic of resistance. It is well known that the resistance within Germany and in exile did not succeed in toppling Hitler or in shortening the period of National Socialist rule. The weakness of opponents of National Socialism, the passivity of the German population, the political blindness of large segments of the populace, and unfortunate coincidences kept the regime in power until it was defeated militarily.

The lack of success of the German resistance with respect to its final goal does not, however, imply its senselessness. In spite of all of its weakness, resistance in exile was not in vain. In exile, it at least disputed the National Socialist dictatorship's omnipotence insofar as it maintained a democratic ideological tradition and saved from the Third Reich the progressive cultural legacy that Hitler had wanted to destroy. In an impressive manner, it also showed the Third Reich that its "long arm" had limits, and it showed the world public that, in exile, there was a different, a democratic, Germany.

Bibliography

Edinger, Lewis J. *Sozialdemokratie und Nationalsozialismus: Der Parteivorstand der SPD von 1933–1945.* Hannover/Frankfurt am Main, 1960.

Langkau-Alex, Ursula. *Volksfront für Deutschland.* Volume 1: *Vorgeschichte und Gründung des "Ausschusses zur Vorbereitung einer deutschen Volksfront," 1933–1936.* Frankfurt am Main, 1977.

Mühlen, Patrik von zur. *Spanien war ihre Hoffnung: Die deutsche Linke im Spanischen Bürgerkrieg 1936 bis 1939.* Berlin/Bonn, 1985.

Pech, Karlheinz. *An der Seite der Résistance: Zum Kampf der Bewegung "Freies Deutschland" für den Westen in Frankreich, 1943–1945.* Frankfurt am Main, 1974.

Pohle, Fritz. *Das mexikanische Exil: Ein Beitrag zur Geschichte der politisch-kulturellen Emigration aus Deutschland, 1937–1946.* Stuttgart, 1986.

Scheurig, Bodo. *"Freies Deutschland": Das Nationalkomitee und der Bund Deutscher Offiziere in der Sowjetunion 1943–1945.* Munich, 1961. New edition Cologne, 1984.

Women between Dissent and Resistance

Christl Wickert

Quite regardless of the social class or political milieu from which they came, women as critics and opponents of National Socialism are often taken into account only in their capacity as the wives, sisters, or mothers of men who were active against the National Socialist state. An independent resistance by women has hitherto been scarcely appreciated by researchers. There have indeed been various speculations about their roles in the German resistance and their contribution, but the political and military manifestation of the resistance has been viewed as the particular domain of men. By looking at things in this manner, however, researchers have restricted their view too much to documented cases: it was indeed almost exclusively men who appeared to the public and thereby also to the eyes of the persecutors as members of the outlawed parties or of the military — in accordance with the social assignment of roles, women made their contribution on the other side of this public sphere. Yet it was not therefore less important for the success of the opposition.

Because resistance activities by women are seen only as a subordinate part of resistance by men, the question of gender-specific characteristics has been excluded or remains at the periphery — that is, women have not been viewed as acting on their own as women; their actions have been viewed as only a kind of subcategory of men's actions. Recent research is indeed finally taking into account the social context of people who were opponents of the National Socialist regime or who were seen as such. However, even with this development, the influence of gender on attitudes and actions continues to remain at the periphery of consideration. In such research, women who had been delivered into the National Socialists' system of persecution are frequently praised for their particular survival skills: they were often better at forming secret communication networks and judicious in dividing up scant food supplies and in caring for their bodies and clothes.

Resistance and disloyalty by women seem to be documented only in memoirs; they are dominated by Communist women, who, next to Jewish women and "Gypsy" women, were most severely persecuted. While historical women's studies have also dealt with the role, function, and situation of women during the National Socialist period, the question of women's activity in the resistance has nevertheless hardly been investigated. In the English edition of her book *Mothers in the Fatherland,* Claudia Koonz tries for the first time to look at the entire spectrum of women's activity, from National Socialist women who wanted to break away from the 1920s paradigm of the "new woman," to conservative women in their helplessness and opportunism, to religiously oriented women with their contradictory attitude, and to the victims, primarily Jewish women. Yet she treats women in the resistance only peripherally, although they were responsible for a large part of the help for Jews who sought to survive in their hiding places.

I repeatedly asked men and women witnesses from the National Socialist period about the motivation and impetus for their critical, often oppositionist attitudes and actions between 1933 and 1945. What woman, in view of her responsibility for her family and children, could afford to live a life even half in illegality, let alone entirely in the underground? What became of the children if she was constantly fleeing from the Gestapo? What if she were arrested and convicted? How much time remained for activities against the regime next to housework? There were only a few things that could be integrated into one's day-to-day life: to disguise an action for distributing leaflets as a shopping spree, to transport materials in baby carriages, to find housing for Jews and resistance fighters who had gone underground, to collect food and money for the families of persons who had been imprisoned, to disregard National Socialist events of the most various sorts, to complain — especially during the war — about the greater difficulties of everyday existence, such as rising costs, overly harsh demands on labor, bomb damage, and so on.

According to existing research, women were less endangered than men during the initial period of the Third Reich. In the course of the consolidation of the National Socialist regime, however, they increasingly came into the view of the Gestapo apparatus and prosecuting authorities and thus felt the progressive perfecting of the "instruments of the disciplinary state." The first, initially provisionary women's concentration camp was set up in Moringen at the end of 1933. In 1938, the women were moved to Castle Lichtenburg, where there was more space, until the women's concentration camp at Ravensbrück was opened in 1939, where a total of 132,000 women were to have been imprisoned by 1945. As of 1941, there were also women's sections in other concentration camps, such as in Auschwitz-Birkenau and Gross-Rosen.

Women who had not been politically active prior to 1933 were apparently not endangered until 1935. Beginning in 1936, as resistance by political parties had been largely eliminated, one can notice a broadening of the police's concept of opponents as "enemies of the state" in a politically narrow sense to one of "antisocial parasites," which culminated in the Antisocial Parasite Decree of September 1939. Persecution by the Gestapo thereby extended to everyday activities as well.

That the first death sentence against a women (Liselotte Hermann) was not carried out until 1938 can be explained by the fact that the National Socialists initially feared repercussions on the "movement's battle morale" if women were persecuted too obviously and relentlessly. Changes can be seen after the beginning of the war. Not only did the People's Court pronounce more death sentences in absolute numbers, but the proportion of women among persons convicted also rose.

There were various forms of oppositional activity by women and men in the Third Reich. Often, it was not quite goal-oriented resistance targeted at the regime but rather dissent and disloyalty as a result of (spontaneous) dissatisfaction. With regard to the question of the form and extent to which women were involved in resistance activities, the following considerations hold true.

1. A considerable, hardly quantifiable proportion of resistance activities, for various reasons, has not been discovered by researchers and indeed has often not even been sought by them. A possible reason for this is that the active persons were women, who usually operated outside of the public sphere that was observed by the persecutors. The work of resistance fighters would have been impossible without this frequently undiscovered and undocumented support by women relatives, secretaries, associates, and so on.

2. With its increasing permeation of day-to-day existence and private life, the Gestapo apparatus, especially during the war years, was more and more inclined to deny or to ignore the differing manners of behavior of women and men. It is therefore necessary in studying the sources to look between the lines for clues to differences in the treatment of persecuted men and women.

3. The ruptures in the life of a given person, which were especially deep under the circumstances of National Socialism, can be discerned more clearly in the biographies of women than in those of men.

4. Women and men interacted more cooperatively with one another in the ranks of the opponents and victims of National Socialism than, for example, in the political parties of the Weimar Republic; memoirs give this impression. In time of great danger, women played an important role in the network of confidence and material assistance, especially with respect to the solidarity of the various resistance groups among one another.

5. Police and court files as well as discussions with survivors show how strongly the actions of women were oriented toward their husbands, lovers, fathers, and brothers. This aspect has hardly been the

subject of discussion in memoirs, however, because women authors were inclined to idealize in the face of the emancipation movement.

•

Social disobedience as the most elementary form of oppositional behavior was usually an immediate reaction to the National Socialist regime's prerogative to integrate all areas of life into its racial and martial policies. War policy not only resulted in the need for more labor but also tried — in contrast to the superficial ideology of hearth and home — to draw in women politically. The grip of National Socialism on all areas of life extended into day-to-day family life, such that all infractions or even mere protests against laws pertaining to family life now suddenly became resistance activities, indeed, even when this was not the conscious intention of the persons concerned. This is true, for example, in cases involving "malicious gossip," "radio crimes," "racial defilement," and association with foreign workers and prisoners of war, and it is also true of youth opposition and labor conflicts (including those of men and women foreign workers). The gender-specific perspective makes it clear that women were less conformatist in their behavior than men and frequently fought spontaneously against demands for their work deployment.

Labor conflicts became significant at the beginning of the war, when women were increasingly used in the armaments industry; beginning in 1940, they were required to work. Their workday was lengthened to ten hours; they received at most only one-half of men's wages for comparable jobs. The Reich trustees of labor seldom called in the Gestapo in labor disputes. That is why, for example, only 4.2 percent (or 3,040) of surviving documents from Gestapo headquarters in Düsseldorf pertain to labor disputes; women were involved in those reported disputes only 13.4 percent of the time (or 407 documents).

Women's violations of labor laws of the Third Reich were manifestations of women's having been doubly burdened by demands of family and state: in case of conflict, women chose their family responsibilities. Those who were charged complained about the heavy work and, in one-half of the cases, emphasized this by referring to abdominal and menstrual pains. The Gestapo generally let things go with a warning; in case of a repeat offense, though, the women were sent to a labor education camp for one or two months. Most foreign workers from eastern Europe who had been brought to Germany were not so fortunate, as they could cite no family responsibilities for their "faulty behavior." Jewish women were immediately sent to concentration camps.

Factories such as Krupp in Essen, where production important for the war was kept up by Germans who were required to work, by women foreign workers, and by prisoners of war, paid strict attention to separating these three groups of workers. Yet violations were repeatedly reported to the Reich trustees of labor. These usually involved acts of assistance (for example, giving sandwiches to workers and prisoners of war) but often also involved love affairs or sexual contacts between Germans and foreigners, which fell under the so-called racial defilement law. Although the proportion of women in these "offenses" was disproportionately high, one cannot speak of a typical woman's crime. If the suspicion of "racial defilement" was confirmed in the case of a German woman, Gestapo officials asked about all details in their hearings; they apparently wanted to have confirmation of their prejudices about the abnormal sexuality of the "racially inferior." Such hearings frequently provoked resistance by those who were charged; yet the women, most of whom came from the lower classes, were generally not a match for the Gestapo officials who conducted the hearings.

After the Youth Service Decree of 1936 had ordered that, at age ten, all boys enter the Hitler Youth and all girls enter the Girls' Youth League and that all girls enter the German Girls' League at age fourteen, only a few people were able to avoid this third educational authority next to home and school. In an attempt to gain autonomy and to arrange independent leisure time, groups such as the Swingers in Hamburg and the *Edelweiss Pirates in the Rhineland formed in large cities; young Catholics continued to meet in congregational groups; and people who had previously been organized in the Young Friends of Nature continued to make excursions. Parents, but mostly mothers, certainly knew about such activities of their children.

If youths became conspicuous, the Gestapo took notice of them, but out of the persecution and criminalization of isolated cases there suddenly arose the formation of political resistance that then did indeed produce an attitude of political opposition. Even if participation by girls became known to the Gestapo, they were rarely persecuted (we have evidence of this in, for example, the records of Gestapo headquarters in Düsseldorf). Girls usually succeeded in portraying their participation as coincidental or in portraying themselves as having been persuaded by boys. They pretended to be harmless and innocent and thereby got off.

The Gestapo counted as "opposition" all violations of the innumerable laws, all of which a civilian could not possibly have known. Most cases involved suspicions that were not confirmed. Nevertheless, the charged or denounced person was on the record in any case, even if he or she had not been interrogated at all. If proceedings involving a certain crime became common, then this was noted in the monthly canvass of opinion that was sent to the Gestapo office in Berlin. During the war, the Gestapo paid particular attention to the mood of women, who, as mothers and workers in factories important for the war, were subject to a double burden. Most proceedings were initiated due to "malicious gossip" or, albeit far less common, to listening to "enemy broadcasters." Violations of the radio guidelines of November 18, 1932, and of the Radio Laws of September 1, 1939, as well as offenses against the decree pertaining to malicious gossip (Emergency Decree of November 21, 1933) or against the Malicious Gossip Law of December 20, 1934, were viewed and prosecuted by the National Socialists as acts of resistance.

By normal standards, violations involving malicious gossip were not even acts of civil disobedience but rather, in Hüttenberger's words, "harmless, individual statements critical of the regime" pertaining to the banalities of day-to-day life. Often spontaneous, they occurred in the private sphere (at home), in semipublic places (for example, in the neighborhood), and in local public places (in stores, at bars, in the workplace). In the store or at the workplace, women gave open vent to their irritation with economic and social problems, idiocies of National Socialist propaganda, the bombing, and the absurdities of reports concerning the war. Men also did this at the workplace or — usually under the influence of alcohol — in bars. Women wore their hearts on their sleeves, as they had to bear the burden of day-to-day life. The proportion of women in cases involving malicious gossip was approximately 20 percent. "Little people" were especially frequently charged with malicious gossip, which implies not so much the existence of disproportionately great displeasure among the lower classes as their willingness to inform on one another. Fifty percent of women who were charged were turned in by other women. In addition, accused persons were in many cases members of National Socialist organizations and could often point to a good party record as well. In these cases, oppositional activity seems to have been not so much on the side of the person accused as on that of the informer, who tried to wound the hated party member. Sixty percent of informers came from the neighborhood and from circles of friends and colleagues. One might well suspect that interpersonal conflicts were carried out and unsettled accounts were resolved with the help of a denunciation.

Foreign radio broadcasts undercut National Socialism's news propaganda, and the illegal reception of these broadcasts could have been altogether oppositionally, even politically, motivated, yet it was not necessarily so. In such cases, the proportion of women was approximately 14 percent and was thus higher than in cases involving concrete accusations of political resistance (which was from 5 to 10 percent), yet lower than in cases involving ideological dissent (which was from 20 to 25 percent).

After radio broadcasts were "coordinated" with the principles of National Socialism in 1933, the possibility of receiving foreign news reports was a particular thorn in the side of the Reich Ministry of Propaganda. Yet initial concerns surrounded the proliferation of the relatively weak

"people's receivers," and the establishment of companies for the production of radio equipment was forbidden on November 25, 1936. Not
until the beginning of the war was it forbidden under threat of prison or
even the death sentence to listen to and to pass on news from abroad.
Until then, most people before the state courts who stood accused of
making plans for treason could only have been said to have listened to
Radio Moscow. Men, who were usually more familiar with radio tech-
nology than women, listened to foreign broadcasts in their homes with
their wives. If women were caught selling radios, they were also threatened with indictment and conviction. The number of "radio crimes"
increased during the course of the war, and the proportion of women
in this "crime" also rose, as they depended on information about the
actual development of the war in order to learn something about the
situation of their family members at the front.

In their fear of changes in opinion as a result of the war's effect on
day-to-day life, the National Socialists interpreted listening to enemy
broadcasts, which was indeed a manifestation of deep mistrust toward
Nazi news reporting, as politically motivated resistance.

•

Ideological dissent expressed itself in the activity of members of religious
groups — Jehovah's Witnesses, Catholics, Protestants, and religious
Jews; in the activity of religiously motivated, individual women fighters; as well as in the recalcitrance of intellectuals and women artists
who, in the words of Richard Löwenthal, were concerned with "maintaining the humane and humanistic tradition of our civilization" and
who therefore rejected National Socialist ideology. Such dissent did not
necessarily have to culminate in activities or statements against the National Socialist state. With religiously motivated inner strength, women
and men initially defended themselves against National Socialism's attacks on private and religious life in order to protect their respective
communities.

In 1933, the new Reich chancellor's intention to transform Catholicism and Protestantism into a "Germanic" religion did not seem to
have quite come to the attention of many members of the two large
churches or to that of their leaders. The attempt of the two large German churches to find their place in National Socialist Germany acquired
particular explosive power because church leaders tried to use women's
organizations as a "dead pledge" in their negotiations — that is, in
Koonz's words, the churches offered "government representatives influence over women in exchange for the church's maintenance of autonomy
in other areas."

National Socialist family policy forced a particular conflict of conscience upon Catholic women, a conflict that church officialdom only

made worse by its rather wait-and-see attitude: for Catholics, repro-
duction is subject to the will of God alone. Yet Hitler subjugated it
to the interests of *Volk* and kin; in this regard, "racial regeneration"
was a sin.

Emma Horion is an example of women who became caught up within
the relation of the church to National Socialism. Horion, who was from
Düsseldorf, became chairwoman of the regional branch of the Catholic
German Women's League in 1923. Without interruption, she continued
her work with girls and women after 1933 and paid little heed to the
ideas of National Socialist policy toward women. She remained unboth-
ered during the 1930s but attracted the Gestapo's attention beginning
in 1940. There was a thorough hearing on February 10, 1941: Emma
Horion had participated in sending utensils for the Mass to Catholic
priests in the field. Another summons came in April of the same year
because after the destruction of her parish church she had offered the
congregation the use of her apartment for the celebration of Mass. On
April 6, she had to confirm in writing that, in accordance with the respective law of December 7, 1934, activities of an ecclesiastical nature
would not take place in her private home. In addition, she was forced
to countersign the outlawing of the Catholic German Women's League
in Düsseldorf.

There is no further evidence of activities by Catholic women in
Düsseldorf until the end of the National Socialist period. Nevertheless,
Emma Horion remained faithful to her convictions and continued to live
according to her religious beliefs. Like most Catholic women and men,
though, she no longer actively resisted the system and its presumptions.

The *Confessing Church arose in 1934 as a federation of individual
congregations, churches, and ministers against attempts by the National
Socialists, with the help of Reich Bishop Müller and the German Christians, to "coordinate" the evangelical church with the principles of
National Socialism. The Confessing Church was organized on a democratic basis and directed by "fraternal councils." There was no place
for women. Yet the Confessing Church's practical implementation of
"ecclesiastical resistance" would not have been conceivable without the
women curates who were allowed to assume even ministerial positions
during the war, without the women ministers who cared for the congregations of their men who had been drafted into military service,
without the women assistants in congregations, and without the women
secretaries and active women congregation members.

The coordinator of the Confessing Church in the Ruhr area, the Essen minister Heinrich Held of the congregation in Rüttenscheid, was
able to produce and distribute large quantities of information and
leaflets, for example, only with the help of his right hand, the fearless
Irene Thiessies. On a printing machine next to the stage of the Ernst

Moritz Arndt House, she made copies of printed materials that she then distributed with a driver in the Ruhr area.

State persecution of the International Bible Students' Association (IBV), which was softened for a short time in 1934 due to international pressure, forced its members underground without notice. In order to emphasize the Witnesses' exclusion from society, the National Socialists, with their "actions against covert teachings," equated the endangerment of the state at the hands of Jehovah's Witnesses with the supposed endangerment posed by Jews and Communists. The Witnesses were regarded as resolute disavowers of the worldly state who felt committed only to their God Jehovah, and they knowingly accepted concentration camp imprisonment and the death sentence for it. On the other hand, sources show many examples of people, especially women, who renounced their faith in order to escape these consequences.

In studying Gestapo and court files on the Jehovah's Witnesses, one notices that, aside from the socially unstable milieu from which most of them came and which was marked by unemployment and isolation, a comparatively high number of women were targeted even from quite early on — women constituted at least two-fifths of Witnesses persecuted.

Beginning in 1936, Jehovah's Witnesses were increasingly deprived in custody hearings of their right to raise their children. Up until that point, women had often been released immediately after arrest, in consideration of their children. Housing provisions for children then opened the way for the imprisonment of their mothers as well. If Jehovah's Witnesses did not agree to leave their religious community by the end of their sentence at the latest, then they were threatened with a labor education or concentration camp.

The first mass arrests of Witnesses occurred in 1935–36 in the Rhine and Ruhr areas. Many families and married couples were affected by this. Husbands were generally punished considerably more severely, whereas some women were not even indicted. Yet they were on record from that point on. Next to their private missionary activities, women took on tasks of coordination and distribution in order to maintain contacts between groups when their men remained imprisoned for rather long periods of time. This meant that they could expect no further mercy from the Gestapo or from the courts if they were arrested again.

National Socialism across the board proclaimed the Jews as its main enemies and as the principal opponents of society. If they became documented — be it due to "malicious gossip," labor conflicts, or in conjunction with resistance activities — they as a rule received worse treatment and harsher punishment than non-Jews; in the end, they were threatened by annihilation. Only a few Jews tried to look for a new life abroad as early as 1933. The majority retreated into private life in the hope that the harassments would soon pass. Along with the men, mothers and wives sought to keep as many unpleasantries as possible away from family life in spite of the limitations and underhanded dealings brought on by the more than four hundred laws and decrees that excluded Jews from public life over the course of the period.

One can speak of a "massive flight" of Jews only after the pogrom of November 1938. The proportion of single women among the emigrés is surprisingly small; women seldom decided to take this step alone. Yet, again and again, there were people who helped Jewish neighbors survive: by helping Jews when they were fleeing, by offering them hiding places, food, and attention — all instances typical of family care. Women played a traditional role in this as well. They did this not without danger to themselves, as shown by the example of two sisters-in-law from Düsseldorf, Johanna and Maria F., who were Dutch citizens by marriage. In agreement with her brother-in-law and sister-in-law, the widow Johanna F. tried to help a Polish Jew, disguised as her husband, flee to Holland. The fifty-three-year-old Johanna F. was sentenced to four months in prison for violating passport laws and was pardoned on September 9, 1939; after serving her six months in prison, the fifty-two-year-old Maria F. spent an additional five months in protective custody.

The total number of illegal border crossings is not known; in any case, such crossings saved the lives of many people. By October 23, 1941, approximately three hundred thousand Jews, or roughly two-thirds of all Jews who had been living in the German Reich in 1933, had emigrated legally.

•

The political struggle of oppositional parties and other political organizations was directed explicitly at the National Socialist dictatorship. Participants came from groups with well-developed identities and traditions. They chose various paths of resistance in order to preserve their cohesion. The charge, levied at the beginning of this discussion, that research has excluded a gender-specific perspective is especially true of the portrayal of the political resistance.

Women in the German Social Democratic Party (SPD) have hitherto been treated by researchers in a step-motherly manner. Remnants of the executive committee and of the party organization were able to remain active until May 22, 1933, despite the severe restrictions imposed after the Reichstag fire. Several Social Democratic women parliamentarians, such as Toni Pfülf, criticized the party leadership for remaining on a strictly legal course after January 30, 1933, and even after the arrests and for pushing for the faction's participation in the Reichstag session of March 23, 1933, at which a vote was taken on the Enabling Act.

Toni Pfülf warned that, even if the party voted with a resolute no, the party's participation legitimized a government that had not been formed in conformity with the constitution. Shortly afterward, Pfülf took her own life — and she was not the only one who chose death in her despair. With few exceptions, women Social Democrats remained untouched by the wave of arrests in 1933 or, as in the case of Clara Bohm-Schuch, did not remain in protective custody for very long. This is the reason there is hardly any mention of Social Democratic women in Gestapo and court files. They retreated into family life; in large cities such as Berlin, they maintained contact in small groups. They took walks in Grunewald. The funeral of Clara Bohm-Schuch in May 1936, whose death was attributed to the treatment she received while in protective custody, became a demonstration against National Socialism. More than one hundred people took part in her funeral procession.

Women were responsible for typing and making copies of SPD documents. The Berliner Ella Kay reports proudly of her assistance in a leaflet action at Kaufhaus des Westens (Department Store of the West) during the Olympic Games in the summer of 1936.

The "thunderstorm action" after the July 20, 1944, assassination attempt on Hitler sent many women Social Democrats into protective custody and concentration camps, even when it could not be shown that they had engaged in active resistance against National Socialism.

The German Communist Party (KPD) was effectively outlawed on February 28, 1933. While it took part in elections to the Reichstag on March 5, 1933, and garnered 12.3 percent of the votes, its activities were already illegal. Uncertainty still prevails about the role of women in the KDP despite excellent individual studies, but they were no doubt of central importance for the party's underground work. Yet in her recollections, Maria Wachter, who was from Düsseldorf, emphatically distances herself from the idea that "women were accorded a specific role." If, for example, women transported leaflets in baby carriages or accompanied men in operations involving leaflets in order to give the appearance that they were a couple in the event that Gestapo agents should turn up, then, according to Maria Wachter, this was for purely tactical reasons.

The more firmly the National Socialist regime became established, the more important it was for underground work to maintain a day-to-day existence that looked normal from the outside. Party organizations that, by 1936 at the latest, had had to make due without interregional contacts henceforth consisted of circles of friends who gave news to and helped one another, listened to Radio Moscow, and engaged in individual actions.

Within circles of family and friends, nothing could be organized without wives, daughters, sisters, and lovers. Women played a decisive role

in providing shelter and maintaining relay stations in attempts to revive broken contacts. The Gestapo also knew this: young women were
frequently summoned to hearings who themselves had never been politically prominent but who had once had a relationship with a Communist
then being sought. A denunciation was sometimes sufficient to deliver a
young girl into the grinding machine of the Gestapo. Women for whom
no membership and no party activities could be demonstrated were
registered under the suspicion of "Communism." The proportion of
women in these situations was higher than in the area of demonstrable
Communist resistance.

The number of female trade unionists registered by the Gestapo is
minuscule: in Düsseldorf and Essen, there were exactly eleven.

In summary, literature pertaining to the resistance has estimated that
approximately 15 percent of known resistance fighters were women,
and this estimate is confirmed by random samples of Gestapo files in
Düsseldorf (14.5 percent) and in Essen (14.1 percent). Active political
resistance was primarily the business of men; the proportion of women
in this was less than 10 percent. Varying according to religious affiliation, 20 percent to 25 percent of ideological dissent involved women.
Social disobedience, that is, the fight against the National Socialists' attempt to regulate all facets of everyday life, was also a woman's business
to a clearly greater degree. This is demonstrated by the relatively high
proportion of women involved in violations of laws concerning malicious gossip (19 to 21 percent) and in forbidden contacts with foreign
workers and prisoners of war (15 percent in Düsseldorf and 22 percent
in Essen).

With its all-encompassing attempt to integrate all citizens into the
society of the *Volk,* the National Socialist system and its apparatus of
repression partially eradicated the difference between the behavior of
men and women who tried to avoid this attack. On the other hand,
it is certain that many accused women were able to convince people
at Gestapo hearings that they had not been aware of the full consequences of their actions. Compassion was the primary motive when
women made contact with Jews, foreign workers, and prisoners of war
and helped them.

In considering ideological dissent and politically motivated opposition against National Socialism, it becomes clear that a few women took
over the activities of men after the waves of arrests and the dishevelment
of life; this would not normally have been possible for them. If the Gestapo discovered them, it regarded them as extremely dangerous. They
were then threatened by especially harsh ordeals, and they could not
count on the relatively merciful treatment that was often accorded to
other women because of their family responsibilities.

In the face of danger and persecution, however, the majority of women accepted their age-old role as necessary for the survival and success of the resistance without ever having the chance or even the personal wish to go beyond the gender-specific allocation of specific tasks.

Bibliography

Eiber, Ludwig. "Frauen in der Kriegsindustrie." In *Bayern in der NS-Zeit: Herrschaft und Gesellschaft im Konflikt,* edited by Martin Broszat et al., vol. 3, pp. 569 ff. Munich/Vienna, 1981.

"Frauen — Verfolgung und Widerstand." *Dachauer Hefte* 3 (1987).

Koonz, Claudia. *Mothers in the Fatherland: Women, the Family, and Nazi Politics.* New York, 1987.

Mallmann, Klaus-Michael, and Gerhard Paul. "Resistenz oder loyale Widerwilligkeit? Anmerkungenen zu einem umstrittenen Begriff." *Zeitschrift für Geschichtswissenschaft* 41, no. 2 (1993): 99ff.

Meding, Dorothee von. *Mit dem Mut des Herzens: Die Frauen des 20. Juli.* Berlin, 1992.

Reese, Dagmar, and Carola Sachse. "Frauenforschung zum Nationalsozialismus. Eine Bilanz." In *Töchter-Fragen: NS Frauen-Geschichte,* edited by L. Gravenhorts and C. Tatschmurate, 73ff. Freiburg, 1990.

Strobl, Ingrid. *"Sag nie, du gehst den letzten Weg": Frauen im bewaffneten Widerstand gegen Faschismus und deutsche Besatzung.* Frankfurt am Main, 1989.

Part II

Encyclopedia

Academic Legion. *See* Resistance against National Socialism before 1933.

The Action (*Die Aktion*). *See* Resistance against National Socialism before 1933.

Against the Current (*Gegen den Strom*). *See* German Communist Party/Opposition (KPDO or KPO).

Die Aktion **(The Action).** *See* Resistance against National Socialism before 1933.

Alliance of German Officers. *See* National Committee "Free Germany."

Anarcho-Syndicalists. The anarcho-syndicalist organizations hold a special position among leftist splinter groups insofar as they are not splinters of the German Communist Party (KPD) or the German Social Democratic Party (SPD) from the final years of the Weimar Republic but rather trace their beginnings back to the revolution of 1918–1919 and to the years of the Antisocialist Law. Thus, the anarcho-syndicalists formed an autonomous strand of the workers' movement in the Imperial Reich and the Weimar Republic from the beginning, and their fundamentally extra- and antiparliamentarian orientation made questions of conspiracy and illegal political work basic, constitutive conditions of their political existence from the beginning.

Founded in 1919, the Free Workers' Union of Germany (FAUD) consciously continued the traditions of anarcho-syndicalist trade union activity from the decades prior to 1914. It distanced itself from the legalistically oriented political workers' movement (KPD and SPD), rejected the influence of political parties and organizations on political processes, and was organized on the local level according to occupational branches. The so-called business office in Berlin and the journal *Der Syndikalist* (later called *Arbeiter-Echo* [Workers' echo]) were also important supraregional organs. The heyday of the FAUD and other anarcho-syndicalist organizations and groups was during the first five years of the Weimar Republic; in particular, one should mention the German Communist Workers' Party (KAPD), from which the *Red Militants evolved; the General Workers' Union of Germany, which was founded in 1920; and the General Workers' Union Unity Organization, which was formed in 1921. Membership and political influence later decreased significantly. At the end of the Weimar Republic, the FAUD still numbered between six thousand and ten thousand members and, aside from Berlin, had its organizational bases primarily in central and western Germany.

The internal development of the anarcho-syndicalist groups was marked by infighting. In the resistance, it was primarily the FAUD that played a role. It, however, formally disbanded in February 1933 in order to evade its prohibition, which was decreed at the beginning of March. Leadership of the continued underground organization was initially assumed by Gerhard Wartenberg in Berlin, who was succeeded somewhat later by Emil Zehner in Erfurt and his cohorts Karolus Heber and Johannes Zühlke. Four regional centers of the outlawed FAUD very quickly crystalized: along with Berlin and central Germany, there were also regional centers in western and southwestern Germany.

In the Rhine-Ruhr region, a broad network arose with numerous local centers under the leadership of Julius Nolden. An additional affiliated organization formed in the Mannheim/Ludwigshafen area, Darmstadt, and Frankfurt/Offenbach; in the summer of 1934, it began to publish and distribute the hectographic monthly newspaper *Fanal* (Beacon). In Saxony (Leipzig, Bitterfeld, Gotha, Erfurt, Chemnitz, and Dresden), an FAUD organization coalesced under Ferdinand Götze and, later, under Richard Thiede. Rather broad local centers of outlawed FAUD groups existed in Hamburg, Stettin, Königsberg, Breslau, and Ratibor. Although the Gestapo was successful in making rather minor infiltrations into the FAUD organization in southern Germany and in the Rhine-Ruhr region in 1935, the FAUD's domestic organization initially remained intact; its public activities were sharply curtailed by the middle of the 1930s, however.

After the beginning of the Spanish Civil War, the Gestapo markedly intensified its searches for and persecutions of the FAUD, as it feared political assassinations and the message that they would send. In the spring of 1937, it was definitively able to break up and eliminate the organization of the FAUD. In western Germany alone, more than one hundred activists were arrested, in Leipzig approximately forty, and in Berlin about two dozen.

HARTMUT MEHRINGER

Bibliography

Beck, Hans Manfred. *Geschichte des "linken Radikalismus" in Deutschland: Ein Versuch*. Frankfurt am Main, 1976.

Foitzik, Jan. *Zwischen den Fronten: Zur Politik, Organisation und Funktion linker politischer Kleinorganisationen im Widerstand 1933 bis 1939/40*. Bonn, 1986.

Andere Deutschland, Das. *See* Resistance to National Socialism before 1933.

Andere Deutschland, Das (The Other Germany) (group). *See* Exile and Resistance.

Antifascist Committees. *See* National Committee "Free Germany."

Anti-Nazi German People's Front (ADV). In June 1937, the book publisher Rupert Huber and the locksmith Karl Zimmet published their first leaflets in Munich. One was directed against support for the Spanish putschist Franco, the other against terror and preparations for war. Huber and Zimmet were members of the Catholic Christian Social Reich Party; Zimmet had previously been a member of the German Communist Party (KPD) for a while. Their other publications from May until August 1939 called upon people to act against the National Socialist regime and its predictable war. Immediately after the German attack on the Soviet Union, both again stepped forward and published twelve leaflets from the end of June 1941 until November 1943. One condemned the campaign of plunder in eastern Europe, and the other spoke up for understanding with the Russian people. In the final leaflet, they recalled the German defeat of 1918 and evoked the revolution that was to open up the path to other peoples. This leaflet was signed "Anti-Nazi German People's Front."

In the meantime, Zimmet had intensified his long acquaintance with the mechanic Hans Hutzelmann and his wife, Emma, who was a bookkeeper; both of them were also members of the Christian Social Reich Party, and had gotten to know the Communist locksmith Georg Jahres. Jahres stirred up a broad group of opponents of Hitler and the war. In order to arrive at a consensus among themselves, the group produced two writings in the fall of 1943, "The Alarm Clock: Information Service of the ADV" and "Points of Guidance and Reference." These writings stated that "the ADV is fighting for the elimination of Nazi rule and all the calamity that it has caused. In order to fulfill this task, the ADV must become a powerful popular movement." At this time, the circle drew other oppositionists around itself, especially from industrial factories in Munich.

In June 1943, Emma Hutzelmann made contact with the *Fraternal Cooperation of Prisoners of War (BSV) through a Soviet forced laborer at her place of work. This organization had been founded in March 1943 by Soviet officers in a POW camp in Munich. Beginning in July 1943, the Hutzelmanns maintained constant contact with one of its functionaries, First Lieutenant Ivan Korbukov. The drafted Czech chemist Karel Mervart helped as an interpreter and intermediary. Through this connection, the ADV assisted the BSV with food, clothing, and identification documents; gave information about the military situation; built a shortwave receiver; and acquired weapons and ammunitions that were to be used in a rising by the imprisoned Red Army men when Allied troops approached.

Due to reports by informants, arrests of BSV members began in November 1943 (already on September 4, ninety-two of them had been shot in Dachau); arrests of ADV members began on January 6, 1944. Jahres died while being interrogated. On December 8, 1944, the People's Court sentenced Huber, Hutzelmann, and Mervart to death, and they were executed in Brandenburg prison on January 15, 1945; others were sentenced to several years in prison. Emma Hutzelmann was able to hide but died during an airraid on November 27, 1944. Zimmet pretended to be mentally ill and escaped punishment.

KLAUS DROBISCH

Bibliography

Bretschneider, Heike. *Der Widerstand gegen den Nationalsozialismus in München 1933–1945.* Munich, 1968.
Brodskij, Josif A. *Im Kampf gegen den Faschismus: Sowjetische Widerstandskämpfer in Hitlerdeutschland 1941–1945.* Berlin, 1975.

Arbeiter-Illustrierte-Zeitung **(Workers' Illustrated News).** *See* Resistance against National Socialism before 1933.

Assassination Attempts against Hitler. While the danger of being the victim of an assassination was rather small for the chancellors of the Imperial Reich and the Weimar Republic, it increased significantly after Hitler assumed the post. Of the assassination threats made nearly every week from March 1933 until the end of that year, the police considered ten to be dangerous. Most of these serious or merely feigned assassination threats during the initial years after the Nazis came to power were probably made by Communists and Social Democrats, insofar as they had a political motivation. Police information seldom led to the identification of possible perpetrators. In one case, the Communist ship carpenter Kurt Lutter of Königsberg, along with political friends in March 1933, had planned a bomb attack against the Reich chancellor, who was expected at an election campaign rally, but due to a lack of evidence, Lutter was released by the court.

After the so-called Röhm Putsch, the police expected acts of revenge especially from Otto Strasser's *Black Front. With the help of the Black Front, the Jewish student Helmut Hirsch, who had emigrated to Prague, went from Stuttgart to Nuremberg in December 1936 in order to carry out a bomb attack against the vulgar anti-Semite Julius Streicher or Hitler. Before the explosives were delivered, Hirsch was arrested by the Gestapo. He was sentenced to death by the People's Court and executed on June 4, 1937, in Berlin-Plötzensee. The Black Front was involved in planning bomb attacks against Hitler in 1937 and 1938 as well.

Yet assassination plans did not assume a concrete form until the arrival of Maurice Bavaud, a student from Lausanne who was an anti-Communist theologian without a connection to German circles of opposition. With dogged perseverance, he planned to shoot Hitler during a memorial service in Munich on November 9, 1938. Because security measures prevented him from carrying out his plan, he attempted in subsequent days to shoot Hitler while pretending to give him a letter. Yet he had raised suspicion by repeatedly turning up at the Obersalzberg and in the Brown House in Munich. Bavaud was arrested and sentenced to death by the People's Court on December 18, 1939; he was finally executed in May 1941.

Within the circle of conspirators surrounding Carl Goerdeler, Generals Beck and von Witzleben, Fritz-Dietlof von der Schulenburg, and others, a hard core of counterintelligence officers surrounding Hans Oster and Major Friedrich Wilhelm Heinz were convinced that only Hitler's death could guarantee an intended coup d'état. They planned a shock troop action against the Reich chancellery for around September 20, 1938, intending to shoot down Hitler during the action. Yet their plan became pointless in view of the Munich Pact.

In October and November 1939, military circles around Chief of the General Staff Halder believed that it was still possible to avoid the outbreak of war against the Western powers through a putsch. Hitler was supposed to be eliminated by a bomb attack carried out by the legation counselor in the Foreign Office, Erich Kordt. Heightened security measures after the *Bürgerbräu Assassination Attempt and difficulties in acquiring explosives caused the project to fail. On the Communist side, Retired Captain Dr. Beppo Römer, a former Freikorps leader, explored possibilities of an assassination of Hitler from 1939 until his arrest in 1942. Römer behaved in a conspicuous manner and, after his arrest and conviction in September 1942, was executed together with Nikolaus von Halem, who had commissioned him to carry out the assassination, and a group of persons who worked covertly for the Communist resistance.

After the beginning of the Russian campaign, the staff of Army Group Center around its first officer Henning von Tresckow became a new hub of military resistance. After many failed plans, a visit by Hitler at the army group on March 13, 1943, in Smolensk was supposed to offer the opportunity to shoot him. When this went astray out of concern for officers who were not participating, Tresckow had a bomb smuggled onto the plane used for Hitler's return trip, yet the bomb's detonator failed to work. Carrying a bomb, Colonel von Gersdorff, an intelligence officer of the army group, was able to enter an exhibition of war plunder at the Berlin Arsenal where Hitler was expected on March 21, 1944. His plan to blow himself up with Hitler failed because Hitler did not stick to his agenda and left in a hurry. At the beginning of 1944, Captain Axel von dem Bussche and Lieutenant Ewald von Kleist showed the same readiness, planning independently of each other to kill Hitler and themselves at a presentation of new uniforms. Both plans failed due to external circumstances that prevented Hitler from appearing. The attempt by Cavalry Captain von Breitenbuch — a staff officer with General Field Marshal Busch — to shoot Hitler during a conference at the Berghof on March 11, 1944, could not be carried out because staff officers were not invited to the conference. Finally, Colonel von Stauffenberg held off from carrying out bomb attacks against Hitler on July 6 and 11 prior to the *July 20, 1944, assassination attempt because Goering and Himmler had not appeared at the conferences for which the attacks were planned.

HERMANN WEISS

Bibliography

Hoffmann, Peter. *Widerstand, Staatsstreich, Attentat: Der Kampf der Opposition gegen Hitler.* Munich, 1985.

Assistance and Solidarity. Individuals as well as entire families owe their lives to the resistance from "below" or to the "silent rebellion," that is, to nonorganized assistance in the private sphere that was offered to the politically, religiously, or racially persecuted by persons who stood close to them. Those persons demonstrated their solidarity as well as their political stance against the National Socialist regime by helping Communists, Social Democrats, and especially Jews to escape, by offering them a hiding place, or by simply slipping them food ration cards. As Leo Baeck remarked, "Helping the Jews was sometimes the only way that a German was able to express his opposition against the Nazis."

After being forbidden to emigrate in October 1941, Jews could only flee or go underground in order to avoid certain deportation. Acts of assistance — help in fleeing, offers of hiding places in cellars, apartments, warehouses, arbors, barns, and many other places — were often spontaneous; friends and neighbors, but also acquaintances and even strangers, offered help. Others organized the secret route over the border to Switzerland or the route through France and Spain and on to Lisbon, one of the last free ports. Illegal border crossings succeeded either due to paid smugglers or because obliging peasants pointed out the way to Switzerland. Varian Fry, an American, gambled his life in order to channel primarily persecuted artists from Germany over the Pyrenees. Some refugees succeeded in finding a way to freedom abroad only because they had already lived for a while in hiding.

Many "U-boats," as the people living underground were sometimes called, had spontaneously decided to go underground; others had long planned their "flight," gathered false documents, saved up supplies of food in various hiding places, and discussed the situation with their future helpers. In most cases, "Aryan" relatives, relatives living in "mixed marriages," or former domestic servants were the first "station." Many of those who had initially offered help and who had taken in individuals and sometimes families with small children only gradually became aware of the danger to which they had exposed themselves and their families. For persons who offered hiding places, being discovered usually meant being sent to a concentration camp. Conditions that became cramped due to the presence of additional people, interpersonal tensions that developed from these conditions, as well as the watch for any threat of danger often made life unbearable for helpers and persons who had gone underground. Alternative hiding places and new helpers were sought, and the "U-boats" were handed over from one person to another.

In reconstructing this scenario, we see that there was a whole network of bases and helpers, primarily in Berlin, who at the time knew almost nothing of one another; each person knew at most the next station. In order to avoid being discovered, the hiding places were frequently changed; from the middle of 1942 until the Allies' entry into Germany, some people passed through up to sixty different stations. Men had a harder time than women, since able-bodied men who weren't bearing arms were suspected of having deserted and were often forced to account for their presence. For that reason, men could hardly leave their lodgings without danger, and they posed a greater danger to rescuers.

In spite of all dangers, there were people not only in Germany but also in the countries occupied by the Germans who, for humanitarian, religious, and political reasons, tried to save Jews from deportation to the camps. With few exceptions, assistance in Germany was organized not by groups but by individuals, especially women and retirees. The "unsung heroes," as the helpers are called in the literature, were people from all social strata, many simple workers and craftsmen, but also teachers, professors, diplomats, store and factory owners, and clerics. In the ecclesiastical sphere, it was primarily cloisters and parsonages that offered haven for Jews. Children who had been baptized for the sake of safety were provided for by nuns, the children's actual origin often being known only by the cloister administration. In parsonages, it was primarily the ministers' wives who were entrusted with the task of dealing with daily dangers.

Many of the rescuers were able to help more than one person or one family. One example is Franz Kaufmann (see *Kaufmann Group), and another is Otto Weidt, who employed blind, deaf, and dumb Jews in his broom- and brush-making shop in Berlin and repeatedly saved them from deportation by bribes. Countess Maria von Maltzan, who was active in the Catholic resistance and, together with other people, helped a total of sixty-two people to survive by hiding them, giving them false documents, or escorting them across the border illegally. Pastor Heinrich Grüber, who headed the Grüber Office, which was established in the summer of 1938, initially worked primarily in helping "non-Aryan Christians" to emigrate, but he was also occasionally helpful with false documents.

The small German community of the Religious Society of Friends, comprising 230 members, also actively participated in the rescue of Jews. The respective Catholic and Protestant assistance agencies took care of Jews who had been baptized as Christians. The Quakers, on the other hand, took in "nonconfessional Jews." They organized youth groups, arranged recuperative retreats in their own spa for people who were looking for help, and, in cooperation with English and American Quaker communities, organized possibilities for emigration.

The assistance provided by the inmates of Buchenwald was unique in Germany. They succeeded in hiding many children between the ages of three and fifteen in the camp or in saving them from deportation by falsifying lists and birthdates.

Germans were also active as rescuers abroad. Among many others, the most famous example is Oskar Schindler, who, in his factory in Krakow and later in the Sudetenland, was able to save from certain death more than one thousand Jews who worked for him by bribing the SS and performing similar activities.

Of the approximately ten thousand to twelve thousand Jews who had decided to live a life underground in Germany, most of whom were between the ages of twenty and fifty, an estimated five thousand were concentrated in Berlin; the others found hiding places in other rather large cities, in small cities, or with peasants in the country. According to published estimates, approximately fourteen hundred "U-boats" survived in Berlin; estimates for all of Germany are from thirty-five hundred to four thousand. The number of helpers, from those who falsified documents but never had contact with the people who had gone underground up to those who offered hiding places and jeopardized their own lives, can be estimated only vaguely from sixty thousand to one hundred thousand. Only a very small proportion is known by name, and few were commemorated in the memoirs of the survivors. As of January 1, 1993, 271 Germans had been granted the honorary title of "righteous among the nations of the world" by the Israeli government.

The Israeli parliament passed the law for the creation of a national memorial — Yad Vashem — in Jerusalem on August 19, 1953. After that, a committee for identifying the "righteous among the nations of the world" was established and first met on February 10, 1963. Its task is to research and document — on the basis of evidence and witnesses' statements — the names of those non-Jews who, without benefit to themselves, helped Jews in various countries during World War II. At the end of a lengthy examination conducted by a commission composed of lawyers and members of Yad Vashem, a decision is made whether existing evidence is sufficient to recognize the person in question as "righteous." If the decision is positive, the rescuer receives the honorary title with a document and medal and can plant a tree along the "Avenue of the Righteous" on the "Mountain of Remembrance" in Jerusalem.

As of January 1, 1993, a total of 11,023 persons from thirty nations had been honored. This number by no means includes all who helped. Some saw their assistance as a matter of course and wanted no recognition for it; on the other hand, others could not be identified because survivors no longer remembered their names or had not contacted Yad Vashem. Many remain unknown because the persons who had been saved had already died by the time that Yad Vashem began almost twenty years after the war to conduct its investigations or because the persons who had gone underground were indeed eventually caught and deported by the Gestapo and thus could no longer bear witness.

JULIANE WETZEL

Bibliography

Ginzel, Günther B., ed. *Mut zur Menschlichkeit: Hilfe für Verfolgte während der NS-Zeit.* Cologne, 1993.
Seligmann, Avraham. "An Illegal Way of Life in Nazi Germany." *Yearbook of the Leo Baeck Institute* 37 (1992): 327–61.

"Aufbruch" ("New Beginning"). *See* Uhrig-Römer Group.

Bästlein Group. This was a German Communist Party (KPD) organization whose principal members were Bernhard Bästlein, Franz Jacob, Oskar Reincke, and Robert Abshagen. The group existed in Hamburg and northwestern Germany from 1940 to 1942.

Released from Sachsenhausen concentration camp in April 1939, Abshagen, Hein Bretschneider, and Hans Christoffers remained together not only at Hamburg construction sites but also in political matters. Released from the same camp, Bästlein and Jacob came into contact with Reincke through Abshagen after the spring and fall of 1940 and then formed the head of the resulting organization. Bästlein, a former KPD representative, functioned as political director. Reincke, the KPD subregional director for Flensburg, functioned as organizational manager. Responsible for agitation and propaganda were Jacob, who was a former KPD regional director for Wasserkant and Reichstag assemblyman, and, until the spring of 1942, the insurance salesman Abshagen. They were supported by approximately two hundred KPD functionaries and members and several Social Democrats and politically unaffiliated persons in more than thirty firms in Hamburg, particularly at dock-yards and metal-processing factories, as well as in Bremen, Flensburg, Kiel, Lübeck, and Rostock. In addition, there was good contact with the Berlin organizations under Arvid Harnack and Harro Schulze-Boysen (see *Red Orchestra) and around Robert Uhrig (see *Uhrig-Römer Group) through the Communist editor Wilhelm Guddorf.

Members of the northwestern German organization discussed topical and theoretical problems; aided preparations in Berlin that sometimes led to resistance training; made critical statements at their places of work; supported French, Dutch, and Polish civilian and forced laborers and Soviet POWs; and sometimes sabotaged war production.

They made preparations to produce flyers, gathering military and eco-nomic information that Moscow was to supply via Berlin. When two German Communists from the Soviet Union arrived in Hamburg in July 1942, the organization took them in. The first arrests were made on Oc-tober 15, 1942, due to informants; two days later, Bästlein and Jacob were arrested, followed by approximately one hundred illegals. Jacob escaped to Berlin. Some of those in jail were "furloughed" for a short time after a bombing raid on Hamburg at the end of July 1942, went underground, and continued to plot conspiracies, some of them doing so until April 1945.

From January until October 1944, there were at least fourteen tri-als in Hamburg involving members of the group; at least twenty-two death sentences were handed down, including that against Abshagen on May 2. He was executed on July 10 in Hamburg. In all, more than seventy members of the organization gave their lives. The last ones were murdered on April 21 and 23, 1945, in Neuengamme concen-tration camp. Bästlein escaped from the Berlin-Plötzensee prison after a bombing raid on January 30, 1944. He then joined the leadership of the loosely knit organization under Anton Saefkow and Jacob (see *Saefkow-Jacob Group), which was working together with others in central Germany and still had contact with Hamburg. In Berlin, Bästlein was arrested on May 30; Jacob, Saefkow, and many collaborators in the struggle were arrested on July 4, 1944, and afterward. The People's Court pronounced death sentences against the three on September 5, and they were executed on September 18, 1944, in Brandenburg prison.

KLAUS DROBISCH

Bibliography

Bästlein, Klaus. *"Hitlers Niederlage ist nicht unsere Niederlage, sondern unser Sieg!" Die Bästlein-Organization.* In *Vom Zweifeln und Weitermachen: Fragemente der Hamburger KPD-Geschichte.* Edited by Beate Meyer and Joachim Szodrzynski. Hamburg, 1988.

Puls, Ursula [Ursel Hochmuth]. *Die Bästlein-Jacob-Abshagen-Gruppe.* Berlin, 1959.

Battle Group Auschwitz. *See* Resistance by the Persecuted.

Bavarian Federation for Fatherland and King. *See* Monarchist Resistance in Bavaria.

Beacon (*Fanal*). *See* Anarcho-Syndicalists.

***Berliner Volkszeitung* (Berlin People's News).** *See* Communist Resistance.

Black Chapel. After the Munich Pact of September 1938, Hitler stood at a highpoint of his popularity and power. The British policy of appeasement had disappointed the hopes of the conservative resistance that a foreign policy defeat would create the precondition for a political overthrow of the government in Germany. The German opposition did not back down from its goal of toppling Hitler, but connections between civil and military resistance groups became looser. The military saw no chance of a coup d'état and then, between September 1939 and May 1940, intensified its foreign exploratory probes, especially vis-à-vis Chamberlain's government; since there were not enough resources of power nor sufficient willingness among leading generals for immediate action in Germany itself, they initially attempted to gain assurance that the Western powers would not exploit a coup d'état for an attack on Germany. They wanted to find out whether a non–National Socialist government could count on reasonable peace terms.

The activities of the resistance circles around Admiral Wilhelm Canaris and General Hans Oster (see *Counterintelligence Office [Abwehr]) were monitored by Walter Schellenberg in the Reich Security Main Office on the orders of Reinhard Heydrich. In May 1940, Heydrich chose a portion of the incriminating documents that had been systematically assembled against Canaris and gave it the cover name "Black Chapel," since, according to his investigations, these activities were directly connected with the Vatican. Two matters were at issue here: (1) the guarantee by foreign governments with respect to the plans for a coup d'état (from September 1939 until May 1940); and (2) the beginning of the offensive in the west on May 10, 1940.

In September 1939, Hans Oster had suggested to Canaris that Dr. Josef Müller, a Catholic attorney in Munich, be employed as a first lieutenant in the head counterintelligence office in Munich. At the behest of General Ludwig Beck and Hans Oster, Müller traveled officially to Rome several times between September 1939 and April 1940 in order to hear out Vatican news sources. Müller did indeed make promising contact with the British envoy to the Vatican, Sir Francis d'Arcy Osborne, through the Jesuit priest Robert Leiber, whom he knew and who was a close personal assistant to the pope, as well as through the former chairman of the Center Party, Prelate Ludwig Kaas, and the Flemish general abbot of the Premonstratensers, Hubert Noots. When discussions between Kaas and Osborne became shaky in December 1939 after the *Bürgerbräu Assassination Attempt against Hitler and the incident at Venlo, Pope Pius XII personally acted as an intermediary on four occasions beginning in January 1940. The respectability of the pope was supposed to convince the Western powers of the seriousness of German plans; in addition, Eugenio Pacelli was considered an outstanding expert on political conditions in Germany because of his experience as nuncio in Munich and Berlin from 1917 to 1929.

After the conclusion of the talks in Rome at the end of January 1940, a summary, entitled the "X Report," was written by Hans von Dohnanyi, yet General Halder and the commander in chief of the army, General von Brauchitsch, did not receive the report until April 4, 1940. The draft notes and the "X Report" itself, approximately twelve typewritten pages, have not yet been rediscovered; when the occupation of Denmark and the invasion of Norway began on April 9, 1940, it was too late for the ideas set forth in the "X Report" anyway. The German opposition, which had for so long maintained hopes of a coup d'état, fell into discredit.

This experience then attenuated the effect of the second initiative of providing the Allies in May 1940 with information about the commencement of the western offensive, which had been postponed several times since November 1939. Oster used his long-standing personal contact with the Dutch military attaché in Berlin, Colonel Sas, and Beck called upon Dr. Müller to carry warning about the impending attack, saying that the generals unfortunately could not decide to act, that Hitler would attack, and that the attack was imminent.

In the Vatican, State Secretary Cardinal Maglione informed the nunciatures in Brussels and The Hague about the attack, and Pro State Secretary for Current Events Giovanni Battista Montini, the future Pope Paul VI, warned Osborne and a representative of the French embassy. All radio broadcasts to the respective governments were intercepted and decoded in the German "Research Office" that Göring had set up as a decoding center; at the end of May 1940, Heydrich personally ordered Walter Schellenberg to investigate the divulgence of the western offensive. Canaris initially directed suspicion toward the Dutch mission in Berlin and then had the director of Division III F in the Office of Counterintelligence, Colonel Joachim Rohleder, and Dr. Müller himself search for the leak. Rohleder's investigative material strongly incriminated Müller but was finally discounted by Canaris as the result of an intrigue, and the matter was settled for the meantime. Of course, SS surveillance of the Canaris group, the Black Chapel, was continued. On

July 23, 1944, Admiral Canaris was arrested in Berlin by Schellenberg, the head of the foreign information service in the Reich Security Main Office.

KARL-JOSEPH HUMMEL

Bibliography

Deutsch, Harold C. *The Conspiracy against Hitler in the Twilight War.* Minneapolis, 1968.
Müller, Josef. *Bis zur letzten Konsequenz.* Munich, 1975.

Black Front. In July 1930, Hitler succeeded in forcing Otto Strasser to leave the National Socialist German Workers' Party (NSDAP). Strasser was the younger brother of Gregor Strasser and, since 1928, had been the head of a small national-revolutionary circle within the Berlin NSDAP that was influenced by the ideas of Moeller van den Bruck. As an editor in his brother's Kampf Publishing House, Strasser had diverged from Hitler's "liberal" course and, as a "*völkisch* anarchist," espoused an active "policy of catastrophe" that rejected Hitler as deleterious to the economy. After he left the party, Strasser, along with other members of the Kampf Publishing House, founded the Militant Society of Revolutionary National Socialists in July 1930 in order help "true National Socialism" — a mixture of radically nationalistic, anticapitalistic, and *völkisch* ideas — achieve victory. After several waves of exits from the NSDAP, it was possible for a while in 1931 to raise the number of members in the society through segments of Stennes's Storm Unit (SA), but the number of members never exceeded approximately six thousand.

The Black Front, which Strasser announced in August 1931, was conceived by him as an umbrella organization and unity front of national-revolutionary rightists and national-communistic circles; from the crumbling party system of Weimar, the organization was supposed to gather together all groups that were ready to form a conservative-socialistic "black" front against the "red" front. In addition to segments from the Militant Society, the Black Front recruited additional members only from among the Peasant Movement and extreme right-wing sects such as Fritz Kloppe's Werwolf; in the summer of 1932, disappointed NSDAP members joined as well. The number of members thereby again rose to approximately five thousand for a short time. The Black Front's most important financier at this time was probably the controversial Freikorps leader Captain Ehrhardt.

After the National Socialist takeover of power, the Black Front was outlawed in February 1933; Strasser went to Vienna and, after the arrest of underground leadership groups in Germany and Austria in June 1933, to Prague. There, the Black Front's "Central Foreign Office," with few staff members, tried to encourage the approximately five hundred remaining members in Germany by means of exaggeratedly positive situation reports that were carried in minor publications and in the newspaper *Deutsche Revolution* (which was published from May 1934 until June 1937) and that were "broadcast" with a small shortwave radio. They also tried to keep the underground network alive. Beside planning the assassination attempt that the student Helmut Hirsch was supposed to carry out in 1936 against Hitler or Streicher (see *Assassination Attempts against Hitler), their resistance activity consisted in the distribution of underground information.

In contrast, the Gestapo repeatedly succeeded in turning around Strasser's close associates and in rooting out the Black Front groups in Munich, Cologne, Essen, Breslau, Nuremberg, Berlin, and other cities by 1935–36. Foreign offices in Saarbrücken (run by Fritz Hauch) and Copenhagen (run by Richard Schapke) disappeared after the Saarland and Denmark were drawn into the German sphere of power. With shortwave radios in Brazil and Argentina, the South American office under Bruno Fricke in Buenos Aires maintained a wide information network, which, like the entire Black Front, was practically put out of operation in 1938.

Next to constant financial problems, Strasser's autocratic style of leadership, senseless decisions regarding personnel, and illusory estimation of the situation led time and again to leadership scandals and divisions. Strasser was forced to dissolve the central office in Prague in April 1938. Expelled from Switzerland to France, he fled to Canada in 1940. The attempt to form an antifascist unity front of non-Communist German emigrés in the Free Germany Movement in America failed, not least due to Strasser himself. He officially dissolved the Black Front in 1945.

Hermann Weiss

Bibliography

Moreau, Patrick. *Nationalismus von links: Die "Kampfgemeinschaft Revolutionärer Nationalsozialisten" und die "Schwarze Front" Otto Strassers 1930–1935.* Stuttgart, 1984.

Black Squad. The "Black Squad Youth Troop" formed in Berlin in 1934 from the merger of various youth movement groups; socialist viewpoints were also represented in it, and it participated in a Berlin antifascist youth circle. Various groups of boyscouts, the Communist Red Young Pioneers, and others worked together in this covert circle. The symbol of the boys' group was a large black flag with a red flame and the motto "Despite Everything." Heinz Steurich (nicknamed Jonny) was the leader of the Black Squad. The group from the Wedding district of

Berlin is especially noteworthy because of the existence of a diary that documents the group's history until 1945.

A peculiarity of the clique was its cooperation with groups of the Gymnastics Youth, which it was sometimes able to use as cover. Despite frequent disputes with Hitler Youth patrols — a sort of youth police — and the subsequent arrest of individual members beginning in 1937, the Black Squad went on many excursions, led training sessions for its members, and distributed antifascist flyers. During the 1936 summer Olympic Games, it made contacts with foreign youth organizations and conveyed to them the "picture of a freer and differently behaved youth than that represented by the Hitler Youth."

Paramilitary exercises were held to lend an air of militarism to the group but also to prepare for self-defense. The group distributed forbidden flyers and newspapers in the Reich capital even in the autumn of 1938. During the war, an "army post letter" containing relatively outspoken political language was printed and sent to soldiers. The Black Squad continued to exist until the arrival of the Red Army, which was greeted with the group's flag.

KURT SCHILDE

Bibliography

Klönne, Arno. *Gegen den Strom: Bericht über den Jugendwiderstand im Dritten Reich.* Hannover and Frankfurt am Main, 1958.

Black Young Men's Club. *See* Youth Opposition.

Boberhaus Circle. *See* Kreisau Circle.

Bonhoeffer Circle. *See* Freiburg Circles.

Border Bases. *See* Communist Resistance.

Border Secretariats. *See* Socialist Resistance.

"Buchenwald Manifesto." *See* German People's Front.

Bürgerbräu Assassination Attempt. In commemoration of Hitler's failed putsch of November 8–9, 1923, the "Old Fighters" had regularly gathered in Munich since 1933 for a "memorial day for the fallen of the movement." Aside from a reenactment of the march to the Feldherrnhalle and a pompous ceremony in front of the Temple of Honor on the Königsplatz, the main attraction was a speech by Hitler on the evening of November 8 in the Bürgerbräukeller. Hitler usually began his speech at half past eight in the evening and then spoke until about 10 o'clock. On November 8, 1939, Hitler began his speech a half-hour earlier than usual and ended it at 9:07 in order to leave the room and go to Berlin. At 9:20, a tremendous explosion shook the Bürgerbräukeller. A bomb that had been placed in a column of the room above the podium caused the roof to collapse partially; seven people died in the explosion; one died on the way to the hospital; and more than sixty were badly injured. Hitler himself and his supporters saw the working of "providence" in his escape. On November 9, the *Völkischer Beobachter* proclaimed "the miraculous escape of the führer" with a full-page headline.

While Hitler was still speaking in the Bürgerbräukeller, a thirty-six-year-old cabinetmaker named Johann Georg Elser was arrested in Constance while attempting to cross the Swiss border illegally. Notes concerning the production of munitions, a postcard of the Bürgerbräu-keller's hall, several suspicious pieces of metal, and other things were found on his person. Elser's arrest assumed a more than routine significance as border stations were informed via telegraph around midnight about the assassination attempt in Munich, and the order was given to check persons who were in any way suspicious. The suspect was handed over to the Gestapo in Munich. During the subsequent interrogations, the detainee remained silent or denied having had anything to do with the assassination attempt. Yet the trail of evidence became ever clearer. For example, employees of the Bürgerbräukeller remembered having frequently seen him there, and it had been determined at the site of the explosion that the perpetrator could have worked only while kneeling at the column in which the explosives had been placed. An examination of Elser showed that he had raw, oozing knees. Driven into a corner, the perpetrator finally confessed.

Himmler was not at all content with the result of the investigation. He was looking for collaborators that he and Hitler suspected of working with the British secret service. Hitler's previous opponent within the party, Otto Strasser, was also thought to be a wire-puller. It was simply not supposed to happen that a sole individual could have carried out such a precisely planned attack unhindered. Elser was interrogated in the Reich Main Security Office in Berlin for weeks, but, even under beatings and torture, he gave no names. He could give none because there were none.

On the other hand, people in opposition circles in Germany and abroad were convinced that the assassination attempt had been staged by the National Socialist leadership. It seemed too improbable that a single person could have built the quite complex bomb and then done the considerable work of placing it and that, in view of the supposedly close surveillance of places where Hitler appeared, no one would have noticed any of the activities in the Bürgerbräukeller. Only with help by the Gestapo, people assumed, could it have been possible for Elser to prepare and to carry out his attack. After all, was it not extremely suspicious that Hitler, going against habit, had begun his speech earlier than usual, had seemingly ended it hastily, and then had not mingled with the "Old Fighters" but had immediately left the hall?

After the demise of the National Socialist state, historians were at first nearly unanimously convinced that Elser had acted on order and with the assistance of the Gestapo. Elser himself is said to have told — albeit in completely different versions — two fellow inmates in Sachsenhausen concentration camp and later in Dachau that he had held a leading position in the SA and that the realization of the assassination attempt had been done "on the führer's orders" and with help by the SS. This view, however, has been unequivocally refuted by research. It is possible to show conclusively that Elser planned, prepared, and carried out the act alone.

Georg Elser was born on January 4, 1903, in Hermaringen in the district of Heidenheim. He was a trained cabinetmaker, worked for various firms in Upper Swabia, and became unemployed during the worsening economic crisis in 1930. With difficulty, he held himself above water by means of small unemployment payments and odd jobs. After the National Socialists seized power, he found temporary work as a carpenter and worker's assistant. Elser was described as a quiet, reserved, eccentric person with minimal material needs. He was not politically committed, yet he made one thing clear: he decisively rejected National Socialism and the new regime. The Gestapo's interrogation reports also show that Elser had unequivocally declared himself under questioning to be against the National Socialist regime. He thought that conditions had worsened for the working class after the "national revolution," that wages had gone down and taxes had gone up, and that one could no longer change one's work as one wanted. He felt a person was "no longer master of one's children, and he [could] no longer act so freely in religious matters" because of the Hitler Youth. Because of Hitler's constantly new demands on other countries, Elser was convinced that a war was unavoidable.

In view of the threat of war due to the Sudeten crisis, Elser decided in the fall of 1938 to topple the National Socialist regime by assassination. During that year, he studied the possibility of a bomb attack at the memorial gathering and then discovered that no special precautions were taken in the hall and that the columns behind the podium were best suited as a hiding place for explosives. He immediately began to gather explosives and to experiment with them at home. Elser constructed a device that was supposed to set off the explosives at a precisely determined time by means of a rifle cartridge that was discharged by a timer. Elser moved to Munich in August 1939. He regularly was a guest in the Bürgerbräukeller in the evening; late in the evening, he hid there and waited until the hall was closed. During the course of approximately thirty to thirty-five nights, he hollowed out the column that he had selected, carefully and meticulously, kneeling in the light of a flashlight. The hollowed space was hidden behind a wooden panel that Elser replaced after each night's work. In the morning, he again left the Bürgerbräukeller after the hall was opened. He hid the debris in a handbag and removed it during the afternoon.

Aside from his work during the night, the assassin perfected his time bomb; on November 1, he began to install it in the prepared hollow space. Preparations for the assassination were completed on November 5. After a final inspection during the night of November 8, Elser set his bomb. He had prepared his attack well, and the explosion took place as calculated. The assassin was not able to foresee that his potential victim would leave the scene of the deed shortly before the explosion.

Elser was first sent to Sachsenhausen as a special prisoner of Hitler. Aside from the fact that he was held in closely supervised, constant solitary confinement, he enjoyed privileges at the concentration camp, no doubt because he was to be used as a key witness against the British secret service in a show trial after the war was concluded victoriously. Elser was transferred to Dachau at the end of 1944 or beginning of 1945. When the imminent collapse of the Nazi regime could no longer be doubted by anyone, Elser — the man who had nearly succeeded in 1939 in liberating Germany from Hitler and thereby perhaps also in averting the global catastrophe into which the German dictator led the world — was murdered on April 9, 1945, on orders from "the highest authority."

WOLFRAM SELIG

Bibliography

Albrecht, Ulrike. *Das Attentat: Materialien zur Haidhauser Geschichte 3.* Munich, 1987.

Hoch, Anton, and Lothar Gruchmann. *Georg Elser, Der Attentäter aus dem Volke: Der Anschlag auf Hitler im Münchner Bürgerbräu 1939.* Frankfurt am Main, 1980.

Ortner, Helmut. *Der einsame Attentäter: Der Mann, der Hitler töten wollte.* Göttingen, 1993.

Camaraderie (*Kameradschaft*). *See* Youth Opposition.

Camaraderie League. The Camaraderie League arose within the Bohemian Movement's German-*völkisch,* academic youth movement on the initiative of Walter Heinrich and Heinrich Rutha in 1925. Never having more than two hundred members, it had the character of an elitist secret society, but it had great influence in the Sudeten German Home Front (Konrad Henlein was also a founding member of the league) and tried to gain influence in other non-Marxist parties. It held a moderate position within the Sudeten German movement and was anti–National Socialist. Many of its leading members (such as Walter Heinrich and Walter Brand) were supporters of Othmar Spann and his universalist political theory, which in Austria in 1934 influenced the Dollfuss regime's idea of a Christian state based on class.

The Camaraderie League did not work toward annexing the Sudeten regions to the German Reich, but rather fought for a "Swissification" of Czechoslovakia, a federalization in autonomous cantons. It wanted to overcome thinking in terms of nation-states and especially rejected National Socialist racial theory. After the great election success of the Henlein Movement in May 1935 (which then began to call itself the Sudeten German Party), Henlein leaned more and more toward Hitler as the National Socialists increasingly gained influence. The National Socialists succeeded in gradually pushing out members of the Camaraderie League — who sought support in England for their political goals — from the Sudeten German Party.

Already in 1936, Reinhard Heydrich had a Security Service file made on the circle around Spann in order to document the circle's hostility to the Reich. After the Sudeten region was incorporated into the German Reich, the Camaraderie League's leadership was charged in a court trial in Dresden in 1938–39. In the autumn of 1939, the Gestapo arrested approximately three hundred Sudeten Germans, including many members of the league, under the pretext of homosexual violations. Heydrich frankly admitted that the trials were to serve the sole purpose of eliminating the Sudeten Germans' anti–National Socialist leaders.

Heinrich Rutha, who had already been charged by the Nazis in 1937, committed suicide while in Czech custody. Walter Brand, Walter Becher, and others were sent to concentration camps. Othmar Spann and Walter Heinrich were dismissed from their teaching posts.

HELLMUTH AUERBACH

Bibliography

Schneller, Martin. *Zwischen Romantik und Faschismus: Der Beitrag Othmar Spanns zum Konservativismus in der Weimarer Republik.* Stuttgart, 1970.
Smelser, Ronald M. *Das Sudetenproblem und das Dritte Reich 1933–1938: Von der Volkstumspolitik zur Nationalsozialistischen Außenpolitik.* Munich, 1980.

Catholic Young Men's Association (KJMV). *See* Youth Opposition.

Catholic Youth Movement New Germany. *See* Kreisau Circle; Rösch Circle.

Christian Resistance. *See* Opposition by Churches and Christians.

Chug Chaluzi (Circle of Pioneers). At the end of February 1943, a group of about eleven young Jews who had decided to go underground in Berlin in order to avoid deportation was formed in Berlin around the teacher Jizchak Schwersenz and Edith Wolff, who was the child of a mixed marriage. The youths, who knew one another from various Zionist youth organizations, intentionally chose the name Chug Chaluzi (Circle of Pioneers) in rejection of the umbrella organization of all Zionist youth organizations, Hechaluz (The Pioneer). They intended thereby to emphasize that they wanted to save their lives in order to participate in building up the land of Israel. The decision to live underground was made on February 27, 1943, the day of the "Factory Action," when the Jews of Berlin were taken from their homes and workplaces by complete surprise and sent to collection points.

The initiator of the group, Jizchak Schwersenz, was from the Zionist-religious youth movement and worked as a teacher at the Youth Aliya School, which prepared young people for immigration to Palestine by providing vocational and language training. He had been living underground in Berlin since August 1942. The Chug Chaluzi Group, which was made up of about forty young people until the end of the war, met at regular intervals in order to pray together and to celebrate Jewish holidays, but most of all to study, to maintain contact with one another, and to exchange news. During these meetings, a different overnight accommodation was assigned each member of the group for a particular day of the week such that the youths changed their lodging daily in order to escape anyone's notice. Food ration cards and personal documents were also distributed during these meetings.

In its activities, the group depended on the support of individuals and groups with which Edith Wolff, in particular, had contact (See *Kaufmann Group and persons from the *Confessing Church). Wolff not only helped Chug Chaluzi but also provided food ration cards and personal documents for other persecuted Jews, which led to her arrest in June 1943. When a member of Chug Chaluzi was arrested in September of the same year, the search for escape routes to neighboring countries began. Jizchak Schwersenz was able to flee to Switzerland in February 1944 with the help of a refugee assistance group and with illegal documents. Despite financial support and intensive efforts, he was not able to have other members of the group brought to Switzerland. They remained underground until the end of the war.

MARION NEISS

Bibliography

Schwersenz, Jizchak. *Die versteckte Gruppe: Ein jüdischer Lehrer erinnert sich an Deutschland.* Berlin, 1988.

Circle of Pioneers. *See* Chug Chaluzi (Circle of Pioneers).

Class Struggle (*Klassenkampf*). *See* German Socialist Workers' Party (SAPD or SAP).

Committee for the Preparation of a German People's Front. The Committee for the Preparation of a German People's Front, which existed from 1936 to 1938, was the first (albeit failed) attempt to unite the various camps of German political emigrés in a common struggle against the Third Reich and to give a common, representative voice to the German opposition in exile.

Inspired by Comintern's change of course with regard to the question of a people's front, by the formation of a French people's front, and by the International Congress of Writers for the Defense of Culture, the first attempts to gather together the numerous groups of the splintered German opposition took place in Paris in the summer of 1935. For the first time since 1933, Communists, Social Democrats, Revolutionary Socialists, representatives of the Socialist Workers' Party (SAP), emigré writers, and exponents of the bourgeois opposition came together in a common struggle against Hitler. While the German Communist Party (KPD) and SAP participated in the preparations for the formation of a German People's Front with official representatives, participation by Social Democrats was limited to individual persons in view of continuing doubts held by the Prague executive committee of the German Social Democratic Party (SPD) concerning cooperation with the Communists.

In July 1935, the Preliminary Committee for the Preparation of a German People's Front existed only as a loose circle. It extended invitations to its first meeting on September 26, 1935, in the Paris Hotel Lutetia, which henceforth lent its name to the circle. Beginning in February 1936, the Lutetia Circle was headed by a nine-person task committee, which was made up of three Social Democrats, three Communists, and one member each from the SAP, the bourgeois opposition, and the Catholic opposition; the writer Heinrich Mann was its chairman. A conference attended by more than one hundred people on February 2, 1936, assigned the committee the tasks of working out a political platform for the gathering of all opposition groups and of producing a program for the shaping of a future Germany. Social Democratic members of the committee were the former chairman of the SPD opposition in the Reichstag, Rudolf Breitscheid, and the chief of the SPD in the Saar,

Max Braun; the Communists were represented by Willi Münzenberg and Herbert Wehner.

The debate over the program, which lasted until December 1936, made it very clear how difficult it would be to come to an understanding. The character of the intended new political and social order was most controversial. In contrast to the Communists' ideas of intervening in the status quo of capitalistic ownership only to a limited degree and of proclaiming the democratic republic as the next goal in the struggle of the people's front in order to avoid scaring off potential bourgeois alliance partners, the Social Democrats rejected more specific statements in order to keep open the path to a socialist revolution.

The compromise was the "Call to the German People" of December 21, 1936, which exhausted itself in general appeals (an example being its appeal "against war and autarky, for peace and cooperation"), failed to make a definite statement concerning the question of the future social order, and only cursorily outlined the concrete goals of the people's front. This single programmatic document by the Lutetia Circle was signed by more than seventy people, including the writers Lion Feuchtwanger, Arnold Zweig, Klaus Mann, Ernst Toller, and Ernst Bloch as well as the politicians Walter Ulbricht, Wilhelm Pieck, and Willi Münzenberg from the KPD, Max Braun and Rudolf Breitscheid from the SPD, and the young Willy Brandt as the representative of the SAP.

The Lutetia Circle opposed the terror of the justice system and the preparations for war in Germany with statements of protest and memoranda. It protested against the decisions of the International Olympic Committee to hold the 1936 Olympic Games in Germany and, in flyers in 1937, called upon the German workforce to sabotage the transport of weapons and troops that were being used to support the putschists in Spain. In addition, some members were active in recruiting volunteers for the International Brigades. The statements and appeals of the Committee for the Preparation of a German People's Front were made known in part through *German Information,* a press correspondence published by Max Braun and the Communist Bruno Frei that at times provided more than one hundred foreign editorial offices with news from Germany, as well as through "German Freedom Radio 29.8," which the KPD operated in Spain and made available to the Lutetia Circle for broadcasts to Germany. The Paris people's front experiment inspired other people's and unity front alliances such as the German Labor Committee of the Miner's Independent Trade Union, the Coordination Committee of German Trade Unionists in France, and the Saar People's Front, which was founded in Metz in February 1937.

The high point of the Lutetia Circle's activities was the people's front convention on April 10–11, 1937. At the same time, however, it became apparent that the people's front project had run into a dead-end. No new analytic or programmatic initiatives resulted from the conference. Most of all, there was no discussion concerning the question of how and on what basis the circle could go beyond the preparatory stage and integrate the SPD executive committee in exile (Sopade) as well as exponents of the bourgeois opposition into their work over the long term.

During the summer of 1937, the work of the Lutetia Circle finally came to a stop. The cause of this was the denunciation of SAP functionaries as "Trotskyites" and alleged handymen of the Gestapo by the KPD group, which was now being led by Ulbricht and which conducted its own people's front policy behind the backs of the majority and put pressure on Social Democratic members through so-called circles of friends. Making matters worse was the Parisian Communists' rationalization of the terror trials in Moscow, which gave reason for great doubt about the Communist avowal of democracy. In the fall of 1937, the non-Communists renounced their people's front alliance with the Communists after they had unsuccessfully called upon them to return to joint forms of cooperation. Several attempts to revive the Lutetia Circle in 1938 were unsuccessful. Social Democrats and socialists now oriented their policies primarily toward the project of "socialist concentration," that is, the reunification of socialist leftists with social democracy.

GERHARD PAUL

Bibliography

Langkau-Alex, Ursula. *Volksfront für Deutschland?* Volume 1: *Vorgeschichte und Gründung des "Ausschusses zur Vorbereitung einer deutschen Volksfront" 1933–1936*. Frankfurt am Main, 1977.

Paul, Gerhard. *Max Braun: Eine politische Biographie*. St. Ingbert, 1987.

Community for Peace and Construction. Active from the fall of 1943 until October 1944, this rather unknown resistance group was an unusual alliance of regime opponents. Hans Winkler, an employee in the county court in Luckenwalde, and Werner Scharff, an electrical engineer who was forced to work beginning in 1941 at the assembly points set up by the Gestapo for Berlin Jews, teamed up to work together in the fall of 1943. Winkler's opposition to the regime began when, as a court clerk, he witnessed brutal interrogations in November 1933. Through his longtime Jewish friend Günther Samuel, Winkler was informed of the particulars concerning the persecution of the Jews. When, at the end of 1941, he became acquainted with a married couple that had gone underground and was staying with the Samuels, he decided to help and founded the savings union Large Deposit together with the Samuels at the end of 1941. Its goal was to collect money and food for Jews. Winkler recruited assistants in Luckenwalde as well. After he was unable to stop the Samuel family from being deported in August 1943, Winkler and his family took in sixteen-year-old Eugen Herman-Friede from Berlin, who had been hiding there since January 1943.

Werner Scharff helped those who were waiting for deportation as much as he could. He prepared an underground existence for his wife, his friends, and himself. He went underground on June 10, 1943, but was arrested just one month later and, one month after that, was deported together with a friend, Fancia Grün, from the Berlin assembly point in Grosse Hamburger Strasse to Theresienstadt on August 4, 1943. The Samuel family was in the same transport and told Scharff about the Winklers. Scharff succeeded in escaping from Theresienstadt on September 7, 1943, and he looked for the Winklers shortly thereafter. Motivated by his experiences in the camp, Scharff wanted to save more than his own life. Winkler had also been waiting to fight the National Socialist regime through rather large-scale activities.

Both men thus founded the Community for Peace and Construction, whose approximately thirty members were drawn from the two men's circles of acquaintances and friends. Since a common meeting never took place, they all did not know one another. At the center of their resistance were the production and distribution of three flyers, of which approximately thirty-five hundred copies were made: "For Your Consideration, the Enemy Is Listening In" at the beginning of 1944; "General Mobilization" in April 1944; and "We Explain" in August 1944. They were written as chain letters. Their goal was to mobilize the population and soldiers against the continuation of the war. They called for independent thinking and then for passive as well as active resistance. Since the group was comprised of Jews and non-Jews, the non-Jewish members were at the same time also helpers of the Jews who were living underground. They were provided with lodging, food, and falsified documents.

Another activity was directed against Jewish collaborators who had been recruited by the Gestapo: on stationary that had been pilfered from the county court, the group sentenced Stella Kübler-Isaaksohn, the most notorious informant, to death "in the name of the German people."

The group also sought contact with the well-organized resistance group of the Luckenwald POW camp Stalag IIIa, to which it introduced itself as "the National Committee 'Free Germany.'" No cooperation resulted from these few meetings, however, since Scharff and Winkler were considered to be too careless.

The composition of the group with respect to social and political origin was most heterogeneous. Among its members were Communists, Social Democrats, members of the NSDAP, and nonpolitical persons. Most had a petit bourgeois social background; they were low-level, white-collar employees and self-employed workers. The only exception was Edith Hirschfeldt. Through her sister Lotto Söhnker, she had contacts with film and theater circles, from which she learned of Goebbels's outrage over the flyers.

Scharff, Winkler, and other members of the group were arrested in October 1944. There was a second wave of arrests in December 1944. In four indictments, sixteen non-Jewish members of the group were accused of high treason, treason, and military subversion. The Jewish members of the group were not delivered into the hands of the justice system but became subject to the whims of the Gestapo. Most were able to survive in the Schulstrasse camp, but Werner Scharff was shot without trial in Sachsenhausen concentration camp on March 16, 1945. Because the trial before the People's Court, which was scheduled for April 23, 1945, could not take place due to the end of the war, all of the accused survived. Most of the non-Jewish members who had not been indicted survived in camps to see the end of the war.

BARBARA SCHIEB-SAMIZADEH

Bibliography

Herman-Friede, Eugen. *Für Freudensprünge keine Zeit: Erinnerungen an Illegalität und Aufbegehren 1942–1948.* Berlin, 1991.

"Edith Hirschfeld, Werner Scharff." In *Den Unvergessenen: Opfer des Wahns 1933–1945,* edited by H. Maas and Gustav Radbruch, 11–18. Heidelberg, 1952.

Schieb-Samizadeh, Barbara. "Die Gemeinschaft für Frieden und Aufbau: Eine wenig bekannte Widerstandsgruppe." *Dachauer Hefte* 7 (1991).

Confessing Church. The Confessing Church had its roots in the opposition movement against the church party of the German Christians, which gained much power in many parts of the evangelical church with the support of the NSDAP in 1933 and which, quite consistent with Hitler's thinking, wanted to "coordinate" that church's organization and ideology with the National Socialist regime. At the denominational synod in Wuppertal-Barmen in May 1934, the church opposition represented itself as the rightful evangelical church in Germany; in the Barmen Declaration, the Confessing Church not only rejected the German Christians' heretical theology and ecclesiastical organization but also distanced itself from the National Socialist state; it stated that the church must remain free of all guardianship in teaching, preaching, and outer organization and that the total state was also constrained by God's commandments. According to the declaration, it was therefore the task of the church to call to mind "the responsibility of the governing and the governed."

The Confessing Church did not want to be a resistance organization working toward an overthrow of the government; on the contrary, it repeatedly emphasized its loyalty and its at least partial agreement with the political goals of the National Socialist regime. But its struggle also had a political dimension: with its emphasis on the institutional autonomy of the church and on its right to free and public preaching, it rejected National Socialism's claim to totality. It thereby necessarily came into conflict with the state and the party.

Hitler's planned church policy of integrating the evangelical church into the National Socialist system with the help of the German Christians failed in 1934 due to opposition by the Confessing Church. Even the Reich church minister whom he subsequently personally appointed in the middle of 1935 and who was supposed to restore the unity of the internally torn evangelical church was unsuccessful. His attempt to set up new ecclesiastical governing bodies everywhere in the form of "church committees" met with resistance by the Confessing Church and also led to its division: its larger ("episcopal," "moderate") wing was prepared to cooperate with the church committees under certain circumstances; its smaller ("fraternal," "radical," "thoroughgoing," "determined") wing saw in the minister's policy a theologically untenable intervention by the state in the freedom of the church and rejected any compromise. Without actually wanting to do so, this segment of the Confessing Church thus came into direct confrontation with the National Socialist state. It had to carry the main burden of the "church struggle" and was pushed underground.

On the whole, the Confessing Church thus saw itself challenged not so much by National Socialism itself as by National Socialist church policy. This is why it was also unable to bring itself to question fundamentally the legitimacy of the system or to fight its unjust measures offensively. Yet one must see the Confessing Church's struggle in part as political resistance as well, although these initiatives for political resistance were more the doing of individual committees or personalities than of the Confessing Church as a whole. One should mention, among other things, the public distancings from the "new paganism" that was expressly promoted by the state; these led to the temporary arrest of approximately five hundred ministers in 1935. Martin Niemöller, in particular, became a symbol of the Confessing Church's opposition due to his statements critical of the regime in sermons and lectures; he was arrested for this in July 1937 and was in a concentration camp until the end of the war in 1945. A total of approximately nine hundred evangelical ministers and church-related laypersons were punished to varying degrees for their "confessional resistance," and twelve of them paid with their lives. Compared with the total number of roughly eighteen thousand ministers, this number is small.

An excellent document of resistance by the Confessing Church is a secret memorandum of 1936 to Hitler in which the "fraternal" wing of the Confessing Church condemned statements by individual National Socialist leaders, election fraud, the existence of the concentration camps, the injustice of the Gestapo's methods, and, not least, the state-sponsored anti-Semitism. Representatives of the church spoke here not only in their own defense but for the rights of the disenfranchised — albeit without renouncing their fundamental loyalty. In addition, there were isolated courageous attacks against the "euthanasia" measures and the persecution of the Jews. Seen as a whole, though, the Confessing Church's protests remained minimal in view of the extent of the regime's crimes. The old Prussian Confessing Church synod spoke most clearly in 1943 in its "Exegesis of the Fifth Commandment," in which it branded concepts such as "elimination," "liquidation," and "unworthy life" as a violation of the divine order. Finally, one must mention the civil courage of Bishop Theophil Wurm, who, as speaker for all groups oriented toward the Confessing Church since 1941, protested in numerous petitions to state authorities against the injustice committed by the National Socialists.

Because the Confessing Church saw its struggle primarily in ecclesiastical and theological terms, not in political ones, it was unable to cooperate as a whole in the political resistance movement. Nevertheless, not a few members of the Confessing Church were aware of the plot against Hitler, and some of them became coplotters as well. Among them were Dietrich Bonhoeffer and F. J. Perels, who were executed shortly before the end of the war.

CARSTEN NICOLAISEN

Bibliography

Besier, Gerhard. *Ansätze zum politischen Widerstand in der Bekennenden Kirche.* In *Der Widerstand gegen den Nationalsozialismus.* Edited by Jürgen Schmädeke and Peter Steinbach. Munich, 1986.

Denzler, Georg, and Volker Fabricius. *Christen und Nationalsozialisten.* Frankfurt am Main, 1993.

Meier, Kurt. *Kreuz und Hakenkreuz: Die evangelische Kirche im Dritten Reich.* Munich, 1992.

Norden, Günther van. *Widerstand im deutschen Protestantismus 1933–1945.* In *Der deutsche Widerstand 1933–1945.* Edited by Klaus-Jürgen Müller. Paderborn, 1986.

Conscientious Objection. *See* Military Subversion and Desertion.

Counterintelligence Office (Abwehr). Beginning in 1933, the department that was established in the Ministry of the Reichswehr and in the Reich Ministry of War for counterespionage and foreign reconnaissance developed into an influential office under Staff Captain Patzig and his successor, Rear Admiral (later Admiral) Wilhelm Canaris. This became apparent in its having been upgraded to an "Office Group" in the High Command of the Armed Forces, which was created in 1938, and to "Office of Counterespionage" in 1939, as well as in its being delegated various sabotage and special tasks during wartime after September 1, 1939.

After the Blomberg-Fritsch Affair of February 1938 and with Admiral Canaris's toleration and approval, a significant number of active opponents of the regime who repeatedly forged resistance plans against the National Socialist state were able to gather in the Abwehr under the leadership of the director of the Central Department, Lieutenant Colonel (later Brigadier General) Hans Oster, a resolute opponent of Hitler. Particularly in conjunction with the Sudeten crisis in the fall of 1938 and after the Polish campaign in the fall and winter of 1939–40, the Abwehr, together with the resistance group around the chief of the General Staff, Halder, was one of the most important groups of conspirators against Hitler's war policies. Oster even informed the Western powers about the attack on France and the neutral Benelux countries, which had been planned by Hitler for May 10, 1940. Yet he was unsuccessful in convincing the governments of the Western powers of the seriousness of the information, and the intended effect of bringing about an early defeat of the German offensive was not realized. During the war, Oster and his cohorts Helmuth Groscurth, Count Helmuth James von Moltke, Josef Müller, Hans von Dohnanyi, Hans Bernd Gisevius, and Dietrich Bonhoeffer compiled extensive files about the crimes of the National Socialist leadership that, in the event of an overthrow of the government, they wanted to present to the German public as proof of the criminal nature of the National Socialist regime. These materials also included documents about their own foreign policy contacts, some of which (Müller's secret peace overtures in the Vatican in 1939–40, for example) had been conducted on behalf of Oster and Canaris and could be covered up by them. In the fall of 1942, Canaris, Oster, and von Dohnanyi made it possible for several Jews who were threatened with deportation to leave for safety in Switzerland under the pretext of being "V-people," members of the security force of the SS.

The Counterintelligence Office ceased to be a central link for the German resistance when, in April 1943, von Dohnanyi, Müller, and Bonhoeffer were arrested in conjunction with an investigation of a matter involving foreign currency and Oster was removed from office. Nevertheless, with the help of their coconspirator Dr. Sack, the head judge of the army, it was possible to drag out the legal proceedings against the Abwehr collaborators and to hide their many years of resistance activity from the Gestapo. When Admiral Canaris was finally dismissed in February 1944 and later was placed under house arrest and when a portion of the Abwehr was afterward directly subordinated to the Security Service of the SS in the Reich Security Main Office as a military office ("Amt Mil"), the remaining resisters in the Abwehr could do only a little for the assassination plans for July 20, 1944. Similarly, after Stauffenberg's failed assassination attempt and after Oster's documents were found in the headquarters in Zossen, a number of them were arrested, persecuted by the vengeful National Socialist justice system, and murdered shortly before the end of the war (as in the case of Admiral Canaris, Brigadier General Oster, Hans von Dohnanyi, Dietrich Bonhoeffer, Theodor Strünck, Ludwig Gehre, and others). It is unknown whether the SS and the Gestapo, in coming upon the "Zossen file discovery" in September 1944 and April 1945, also acquired all of Canaris's diary, which would have given detailed information about the resistance activity in the Abwehr and about the effect of military resistance against Hitler.

GERD R. UEBERSCHÄR

Bibliography

Höhne, Heinz. *Canaris: Patriot im Zwielicht.* Munich, 1976.
Thun-Hohenstein, Count Romedio Galeazzo von. *Der Verschwörer: General Oster und die Militäropposition.* Berlin, 1982.

Counts' Circle. *See* Kreisau Circle.

Danz-Schwantes Group (Magdeburg). Hermann Danz was a regional functionary of the German Communist Party (KPD) who came from Thuringia and was transferred from Erfurt to Magdeburg when the KPD was outlawed. Until his own arrest in November 1933, Danz witnessed the arrest of most functionaries who were active in Magdeburg, a stronghold of the German Social Democratic Party (SPD). After a three-year prison sentence, he returned to Magdeburg at the beginning of 1937 and slowly gathered around himself the original underground functionaries, who had gradually been released. Martin Schwantes — a teacher who was released from Sachsenhausen concentration camp at the beginning of 1941 after seven years of imprisonment and who had been an intermediary within the Magdeburg KPD regional administration and a briefer of the central committee until January 1934 — joined the group. As a sales and shipping director of a shoe factory in nearby Gommern, he was able to establish contacts with principal towns in the region while on his business trips without being noticed. At the end of 1942, he made contact with Franz Jacob, whom Schwantes knew from the central committee and who was a member of the supraregional administration that was being formed in Berlin and for which Georg Schumann (see *Schumann Group) in Saxony and Thoedor Neubauer (see *Neubauer Group) in Thuringia worked in 1943.

Schwantes and Danz participated in several of the group's administrative meetings in Berlin. Schwantes, being versed in theory, became a member of the new statewide administration and participated in the preparation of information for cadres that provided additional orientation after the founding of the *National Committee "Free Germany" in July 1943. Schwantes also took part in the drafting of materials in May 1944 ("We Communists and the National Committee 'Free Germany'" and "At the Beginning of the Final Phase of the War").

The political principles and methods formulated in the materials intended to help establish a broad front including Social Democrats and bourgeois opponents of Hitler. The materials were given by Danz and Schwantes to their contacts in Burg, Genthin, Halberstadt, and Stassfurt; to factory cells in large armaments works, especially in Magdeburg (Junkers, Mackensen, R. Wolf, Krupp-Gruson, Zinkhütte, and Polte, which at that time was the largest armaments factory in Europe); and to small groups of nature lovers, physicians, and teachers. They were assisted by their closest associates: Hubert Materlink, who made contacts with foreign workers and POWs; Fritz Rödel, who, prior to 1933, had been a longtime city councilman and editor of the regional organ *Tribüne;* and Johann Schellheimer, who, together with his wife, Cläre, set up illegal contact points and provided typewriters and copy machines.

The Magdeburg group fell victim to the consequences stemming from the arrest of the Berlin administration in July 1944. Although the People's Court remained ignorant of many of their activities, leading cadre members — Danz, Rödel, Schellheimer, and Schwantes — were sentenced to death and executed on February 5, 1945. Hubert Materlink died during the initial interrogations. As a result of the end of the war, twenty-nine members of the group who were in the Magdeburg court prison escaped their already ordered murder.

BEATRIX HERLEMANN

Bibliography

Beiträge zur Geschichte der Stadt und des Bezirkes Magdeburg 2 (1970) and 12 (1980).

Das andere Deutschland **(The Other Germany).** *See* Resistance against National Socialism before 1933.

Das andere Deutschland **(The Other Germany) (group).** *See* Exile and Resistance.

Das freie Wort **(The Free Word).** *See* Hanno-Günther Group/Rütli Group; National Committee "Free Germany."

***Das Tage-Buch* (The Diary).** *See* Resistance against National Socialism before 1933.

"Das Ziel." *See* "The Goal" ("Das Ziel").

Defensive Formations (Schufo). *See* Resistance against National Socialism before 1933; Socialist Front.

Delp Circle. *See* Rösch Circle.

***Der Friedenskämpfer* (The Fighter for Peace).** *See* Communist Resistance; Knöchel Organization.

***Der Gerade Weg* (The Straight Path).** *See* Resistance against National Socialism before 1933.

***Der Verbote* (The Herald).** *See* Lechleiter Group.

Desertion. *See* Everyday Acts of Dissent and Disobedience; Military Subversion and Desertion; Parole Units.

Desertion and Refusal of Military Duty. *See* Jehovah's Witnesses; Military Subversion and Desertion.

***Deutsche Freiheit* (German Freedom).** *See* Saar Battle (Status Quo Movement).

***Deutsche Informationen* (German Information).** *See* Committee for the Preparation of a German People's Front.

***Deutsche Revolution* (German Revolution).** *See* Black Front.

***Deutschland-Berichte* (Reports on Germany).** *See* Exile and Resistance; Foreign Contacts; Socialist Resistance.

The Diary (*Das Tage-Buch*). *See* Resistance against National Socialism before 1933.

***Die Aktion* (The Action).** *See* Resistance against National Socialism before 1933.

***Die Neue Rundschau* (The New Review).** *See* Resistance against National Socialism before 1933.

***Die Rote Fahne* (The Red Banner).** *See* Communist Resistance; Red Orchestra.

Die Sonntags-Zeitung (The Sunday Times). *See* Resistance against National Socialism before 1933.

Ecclesiastical Resistance. *See* Opposition by Churches and Christians.

Edelweiss Pirates. During World War II, the Hitler Youth, Gestapo, and justice system persecuted subcultural groups of youths under the umbrella term "Edelweiss Pirates." Many of these youths did not become oppositional until they were persecuted. It is estimated that there were several thousand youths who were considered to be Edelweiss Pirates. Before the notion of "Edelweiss Pirates" was applied to youth groups existing in the Rhenish-Westphalian industrial area, National Socialist authorities used the term "Kittelbach Pirates," which was traced back to a hiking club of the same name that was founded in Düsseldorf in 1925 and was so named after a small river. This group was initially in line with the Nazis. When they were incorporated into National Socialist organizations in 1933, some members insisted on their own independence and remained in the club, which had since been outlawed. As with the Edelweiss Pirates later, they had the reputation among many youths of being "great guys" and thus became attractive to persons who were discontent with the Hitler Youth. The origin of the term "Edelweiss Pirates" has not been definitively determined. One can surmise that it was coined by the persecuting authorities.

The persecution of the groups and their members' youthful pretensions and boasting were not the only sources of their allure: the presence of girls in the groups also played an important role in the Pirates' great popularity. The Pirates encompassed elements of the Youth Movement along with a proletarian tradition. Their songs and style of dress were adopted by many young people, and a movement of outlawed organized youth were persecuted as Edelweiss Pirates.

One can note a political tendency only in exceptional cases. Among these was an action by five Essen Gallivanters, a local variant of the Edelweiss Pirates. They had painted the slogan "Down with Hitler" on houses in the district of Segeroth and distributed oppositional flyers. One should also view as resistance the activities of the Düsseldorf Edelweiss Pirates, who worked together with the Communist resistance. They received various newspapers and flyers that they then left at their workplaces or on the street. At their otherwise generally social activities — excursions to the surrounding areas of large cities, meetings in parks, and so on — the youths, whose clothing easily distinguished them from the Hitler Youth, clashed with paramilitary patrols of the Hitler Youth. The altercations would for the most part have had the character of large-city turf battles among youths for neighborhoods, streets, and squares, had the Edelweiss Pirates who were arrested at these skirmishes not been handed over to the Gestapo and the National Socialist justice system. The phenomenon of the Edelweiss Pirates manifested youthful nonconformity and protest at various times in different regional variations. Outside of the Rhenish-Westphalian area, there were Edelweiss Pirates in Frankfurt am Main and in Offenbach. There are not yet any studies about many other such youth organizations, such as the Stäuber Gangs in Danzig. The Viennese Shufflers bore similarities to subcultural youth groups in Germany, yet there were also differences. The Shufflers constituted an independent historical phenomenon that was apolitical yet that, with its ostentatious laxity, demonstrated a symbolic contrast to the Hitler Youth. Their manner of behavior is attributable less to political resistance than to youthful disobedience.

The controversy around the Cologne-Ehrenfeld incident (see p. 77) is of special significance. Among the persons hanged on November 10, 1944, without a court trial, were six youths labeled as Edelweiss Pirates, including Bartholomäus Schink, who was only sixteen years old. Schink became stylized as a symbolic figure of the youth resistance struggle. Discussion concerning the question of whether and to what extent one should view these murdered youths as resisters or criminals is still not decided.

Kurt Schilde

Bibliography

Peukert, Detlev. *Die Edelweiß-Piraten: Protestbewegungen jugendlicher Arbeiter im Dritten Reich. Eine Dokumentation.* Cologne, 1983.

Edgar Jung Circle. After studying law for a short time in Lausanne in 1913–14, Edgar J. Jung took part in World War I and returned from it as an antisocialist, antiliberal, and antidemocratic nationalist of staunch conservative convictions. In the Freikorps Epp, he took part in overthrowing soviet rule in Bavaria in 1919, and, after completing his studies and entering an attorney's office in Zweibrücken, he was active in the struggle against Palatinate separatists, which led to his expulsion from the Palatinate by the French occupation forces in 1923. He planned the assassination of the separatist leader Heinz Orbis, which he had prepared with the help of radical right-wing groups such as the Oberland Alliance and the Consul Organization and which was successfully carried out in Speyer on January 8, 1924. In subsequent years, he became one of the journalistic representatives of conservative opposition to the Weimar Republic; his book *The Rule of the Inferior,* a sharp criticism of the liberal and democratic ideas of the French Revolution, was published in 1927 and was reprinted several times. During the final phase of the Weimar Republic, he had contact with leading figures of the right-wing, conservative camp, including pro tempore Reich chancellor Franz von Papen and Alfred Hugenberg. Due in part to Jung's influence, the idea was hatched to entrust Hitler with the chancellorship of the German Reich yet to "frame" the government with conservative ministers in such a way that Hitler and the National Socialist movement could be "tamed" and transformed into instruments of conservative politics.

After Hitler became Reich chancellor on January 30, 1933, Papen, who joined Hitler's cabinet as vice-chancellor, called on Jung, who gathered together a team of young conservatives in the vice-chancellery in order to implement the "taming plan": Fritz-Günther von Tschirschky and Count Kageneck worked as Papen's personal advisers; Friedrich Karl von Savigny was responsible for the Catholic Church; Herbert von Bose and Baron von Ketteler were in contact with the Reichswehr, the police, and the press; Jung functioned as the central intellectual figure, as Papen's political adviser, and as his speechwriter. Because the circle considered the maintenance of constitutionality to be an important task while the "taming plan" was being realized, the vice-chancellery quickly became the "Reich Office of Complaints," as it soon came to be called. In view of the activities of National Socialist organizations in all of Germany, however, the group around Jung recognized by the end of 1933 and beginning of 1934 at the latest that the "taming plan" had failed and had apparently been a chimera from the beginning.

This recognition initiated a change in political thinking that brought about a gradual warming to hitherto disdained western European and Anglo-Saxon political values. The circle around Jung began to discover the utility, indeed the indispensability, of the modern pluralistic constitutional state. The insight that Hitler's nationalistic, biologistic imperialism would inevitably end in a large European war even attenuated the nationalism of Jung and his friends.

Thoughts of a coup d'état arose in the vice-chancellery shortly after the end of 1933. A certain feeling of guilt within the circle also played a role. Jung said, "We bear part of the responsibility that this guy came to power; we have to get rid of him." The circle hoped to win over Reich President von Hindenburg, on whom Papen had great influence, and the Reichswehr, which felt increasingly threatened by the ambitions of the Storm Unit (SA), for a putsch under monarchist pretensions. The Jung Circle finally threw down the gauntlet publicly before Hitler when, on June 17, 1934, in Marburg, Papen gave a speech formulated by Jung that, proceeding from conservative premises, subjected the National Socialist system of rule to incisive and far-reaching criticism. Of course, this also sealed the fate of the circle.

Hitler, who wanted to act against the SA in an alliance with the professional military establishment, which was more important for his expansionist policy anyway, saw that it was now high time to make good on this alliance in order to concede to an oppositional tendency in the Reichswehr and thereby do away with conservative plotters in the Reich chancellery as well. With the help of the army, he attacked the SA in the so-called Röhm Putsch on June 30, 1934, and its most important leaders were murdered. Tolerated by the relieved Reichswehr, he was in fact able to extend the action to conservative opponents and especially to the circle around Jung. Edgar Jung himself was shot near Oranien-burg on June 30, 1934, and Herbert von Bose was also killed; Jung's remaining cohorts avoided this fate only by chance, yet Baron von Ket-teler, who had gone to Vienna together with Papen (now demoted as a special envoy), was killed there by a murder commando of the Security Service during the Anschluss of Austria in March or April 1938.

HERMANN GRAML

Bibliography

Graml, Hermann. "Vorhut konservativen Widerstands: Das Ende des Kreises um Edgar Jung." In *Widerstand im Dritten Reich. Probleme, Ereignisse, Gestalten,* edited by H. Graml, 172–83. Reprint. Frankfurt am Main, 1994.
Graß, Karl Martin. "Edgar Jung: Papenkreis und Röhmkrise 1933/34." Disser-tation, Heidelberg, 1966.

Éditions du Carrefours. *See* Exile and Resistance.

Elser's Assassination Attempt. *See* Bürgerbräu Assassination At-tempt.

Emergency League of Clergymen. *See* Opposition by Churches and Christians.

Erwin von Beckerath Task Force. *See* Freiburg Circles.

Essen Gallivanters. *See* Youth Opposition.

Everyday Acts of Dissent and Disobedience. Long overlooked by research on resistance, there was a wide spectrum of everyday acts of dissent and disobedience outside the circle of the political resistance by parties and groups. These acts mostly involved a large number of indi-vidual, clandestine patterns of behavior that could nevertheless assume a public as well as a collective character. Those who performed these acts came primarily from those milieus and political camps that had resisted National Socialism prior to 1933. The *Edelweiss Pirates and the Swing Youth notwithstanding, dissent and disobedience by youth remained limited.

Never before in a political system had the definition of loyalty to the system been so strict as in the Third Reich. The omnipresent legal mechanism for coercing that unreserved assent was the Law against Malicious Attacks on the Party and State and for the Protection of Party Uniformities (the so-called law against malicious gossip) of December 20, 1934, which, as the "muzzle of the small man," particularly made verbal statements of displeasure punishable. At the beginning of the war, it was complemented by the Special Wartime Penal Code, which introduced the crime of "military subversion," according to which even those statements could be punished that, in the view of the National Socialist wielders of power, had the potential to weaken or to subvert the "military might of the German people." Receiving information from any media except those controlled by the National Socialists was also forbidden. With the Decree concerning Extraordinary Radio Measures of September 1, 1939, listening to foreign radio broadcasts became punishable by death in extreme cases. In order to realize the National Socialist racial model, marriages and extramarital relations between Jews and "citizens of German or racially related blood" were made punishable by the Law for the Protection of German Blood and German Honor of September 15, 1935. Finally, it was forbidden to associate with POWs and allegedly racially inferior foreign workers.

Despite the tremendous threat of punishment, the ideal type of loyal and innerly convinced "fellow German" that these laws and decrees sought to realize remained propagandistic wishful thinking. Germans by the millions went against National Socialist maxims of belief and behavior without simultaneously being opponents of the National Socialist system. In hundreds of thousands of discussions involving malicious gossip in the form of jokes, satirical verses, and critical statements, people, in a sort of "bowel movement of the soul," spontaneously distanced themselves from individual aspects of National Socialism as the situation dictated, more often out of disappointment and discontentment than out of principled opposition and fundamental political criticism.

A particular variant of this minimalist form of social disobedience was the pastor's sermon, which generally attacked only specific items of the National Socialist overlords' church policy. The critical sermons by the bishop of Münster concerning euthanasia were an exception. Verbal expressions of displeasure and of doubts in the course of gossip were supplemented by a refusal to participate in National Socialist events; an attitude opposed to the National Socialist model of the "German people" and to the subsequently expected identity was supplemented by the maintenance of traditional forms of greeting and association as well as by the adherence to time-honored symbols and customs. The opposition to the removal of crucifixes from schools, which was especially intense in the Münsterland, Bavaria, and the Saarland and which escalated to school strikes and public demonstrations in 1936–37, was an expression of a collective, symbolic identity that stood juxtaposed to the National Socialists' claim to cultural and ideological hegemony. Especially within the Catholic milieu, an outright journalistic fight for the ecclesiastical rights and duties that had been proposed and secured by the concordat was ignited such that observers even spoke of a "new *Kulturkampf.*" People also attempted to preserve their identity and to evade the strong pressure to conform by maintaining associations outside of the coordinated National Socialist organizations in youth cliques, church associations, Social Democratic "tradition companies," and social events that did not fall within the National Socialist calendar of events.

Thus, away from coordinated public life, there immediately arose the rudiments of an informal counterpublic life that nourished itself by passing on flyers, with rumors and propaganda spread mouth to mouth, and, during the war, with Allied radio and flyer propaganda. Despite threats of the harshest of punishments, at least two million Germans sporadically or regularly listened to foreign radio broadcasts alone or together in groups and thereby showed their mistrust of the news supplied by National Socialist radio broadcasts.

In addition, many Germans also defied the racist principle of the "German people" by not participating in the exclusion and persecution of religious, ethnic, and social minorities and by showing their solidarity with them. In this manner, Jews who were endangered by police raids and deportations could be warned in time. Especially in large cities such as Berlin, Jews were hidden from the Gestapo and thereby saved from the machinery of annihilation (see *Assistance and Solidarity) in ways that were often daring and dangerous.

Escaped POWs were often helped by members of the "German *Volk.*" Associating with foreigners and POWs became a wide-scale offense beginning in 1940 and ranked significantly higher in the Gestapo's arrest statistics than arrests due to political opposition. The majority of the cases in which the police authorities determined "forbidden association" involved suspicion of sexual relations between foreigners and Germans. In these cases, sexual needs and humanitarian, charitable ideals were much stronger than the National Socialist ideal of the "German *Volk.*" In contrast to these seemingly nonpolitical acts, a "no" vote or the failure to participate in elections had a significant political character. Yet these remained isolated cases.

The nazification of factories also remained imperfect. Refusal to work and the failure to fulfill one's "duty of service" contradicted the ideal of the totalitarian productive community; labor disputes contradicted the image of the harmonious work community. Droves of workers maintained their own means of negotiating social conflicts and rejected the

National Socialist Councils of Confidence that had been newly introduced into factories as a result of the Council of Confidence elections of 1934–35. Particularly after full-employment was reached, collective strikes occurred again and again, especially in the construction industry, in agriculture, and in mining. In most cases, it was wage disputes and problems involving working hours and working conditions that motivated workers to social protest. Refusal by miners in the Ruhr and the Saar to work additional shifts in 1937 and 1938 caused a commotion. Workers drawn together from all areas of the Reich to work on the West Wall bulwark constituted an unruly crowd of a particular type, repeatedly calling attention to themselves by protests and strikes.

In order to avoid unnecessary risks, the most frequently practiced type of workers' opposition was not the outright strike but the work slowdown or, as it was then called, "passive resistance." Further, the working class's willingness to fight decreased markedly during the war. Intentional sabotage was not the concern of the German worker, but rather was reserved for groups of foreign workers. On the whole, work slowdowns and labor conflicts were more an expression of a lack of work morale, physical overwork, and unjust compensation than of political opposition. True, this also went against the propagated idea of the community, albeit without seriously endangering the planned goals of National Socialist economic policy or the armament program.

The desertion of hundreds of thousands of German soldiers and the defection to enemy armed forces and partisan groups (see *Military Subversion and Desertion) constituted a mass offense and disobedience of a particular sort. In 1944 alone, approximately two hundred thousand cases of desertion were counted. This does not necessarily indicate a rejection of the goals of National Socialist war policy, but it does indicate a lack of war euphoria and an increase in battle fatigue; in individual cases, it also shows a rethinking about the meaning of the war. Often spontaneous and dictated by the situation, these desertions and defections did not extend to collective mutiny. In contrast, the refusal primarily of young Bible students (see *Jehovah's Witnesses) to serve in the military and the refusal of soldiers and members of the SS to shoot civilians in occupied territories were conscious, religiously or humanitarianly motivated acts.

Forms of open and collective disobedience by German civilians did not appear until the final months of the war, when more and more Germans refused to serve in senseless battles, to dig trenches, and to follow evacuation measures; yet these actions were also not aimed offensively at the National Socialist overlords. In spite of all partial opposition and all disobedience, the basic political consensus between the German people and the National Socialist regime remained intact until the final days of the war.

National Socialist security authorities and postwar West German research placed a higher value on the forms of dissent and disobedience described as "popular opposition" and "resistance," which were thought to have hindered National Socialism, than on the political resistance of parties and groups, which were thought to have been unsuccessful in their opposition. This view assumed that society had been entirely coordinated and that the popular opposition indeed constituted conscious dissent or resistance against that system. The latter, however, was only very rarely the case. In fact, the society of the Third Reich, despite National Socialist attempts to gain a hegemony, was never fully coordinated: that is, the system provided loopholes, niches, and contradictions by means of which one could develop manners of behavior that ran against the system but that did not constitute full-blown dissent. In these noncoordinated areas, such behavior had little or nothing to do with intransigence or even with resistance. Strikes, desertion, and the reception of foreign radio broadcasts stood in the way of the National Socialist will to power only temporarily and in part at best.

The instances and variety of individual and civil courage were indeed often surprising, but they did not at all change the fact that, in key points of National Socialist rule, armament policy, and Jewish policy, the extent of dissent and disobedience was minimal and the manifestation of dissent and disobedience was primarily passive and verbal. The National Socialist overlords were altogether able to live on this consensual basis with malicious gossipers, critical pastors, striking workers, indeed even deserters. At the same time, political resistance groups did not succeed in politicizing the wide spectrum of dissent and disobedience and in organizing it with much consequence against the National Socialist regime.

GERHARD PAUL

Bibliography

Kershaw, Ian. " 'Widerstand ohne Volk?' Dissens und Widerstand im Dritten Reich." In *Der Widerstand gegen den Nationalsozialismus: Die deutsche Gesellschaft und der Widerstand gegen Hitler.* Edited by Jürgen Schmädeke and Peter Steinbach. Munich, 1986.

Mallmann, Klaus-Michael and Gerhard Paul. *Herrschaft und Alltag: Ein Industrierevier im Dritten Reich.* Bonn, 1991.

———. "Resistenz oder loyale Widerwilligkeit? Anmerkungen zu einem unstrittenen Begriff." *Zeitschrift für Geschichtswissenschaft* 41, no. 2 (1993): 99–116.

F Action. *See* Knöchel Organization.

Falkenhorst Group. *See* Youth Opposition.

***Fanal* (Beacon).** *See* Anarcho-Syndicalists.

The Fighter for Peace (*Der Friedenskämpfer*). *See* Communist Resistance; Knöchel Organization.

Foreign Contacts. Opponents of the National Socialist regime, whether individuals or groups, were able to maintain numerous contacts with friends, political allies, and potential cohorts abroad until the final phase of World War II. This shows that the totalitarian character of the regime — in contrast to contemporary and subsequent regimes in Communist countries — could be perfected neither in the years of peace nor in the years of war.

Social Democrats who had gone into exile built a network of confidence men and informants in Germany who supplied enough information that the party's executive committee in exile could publish *Deutschland-Berichte der Sozialdemokratischen Partei Deutschlands (Sopade)* (Reports on Germany by the Social Democratic Party of Germany [Sopade]) from April/May 1934 until April 1940, first in Prague and then in Paris. Communist resistance cells were also in contact — albeit irregularly — with the Comintern and the leadership of the Communist Party of the Soviet Union in Moscow. With the constant decimation of the socialist resistance by the Gestapo and with the increasingly tighter closing of the borders (particularly after the beginning of the war), foreign contacts by leftist groups gradually almost entirely ceased; however, individual cells continued to cooperate with places abroad in a political or — as in the case of the *Red Orchestra — news-related capacity into the war years via Sweden and Switzerland.

Bourgeois opponents had it easier, as they were almost without exception in important institutions of the state apparatus of power and of the economy or were able to have an effect through like-minded persons who were in those positions. Goerdeler disguised his trips abroad as being for the purpose of checking up on the interests of the industrialist Bosch, who, together with his general director, Walz, did indeed finance Goerdeler solely for purposes of resistance, and Hassell disguised his activities through his membership in the Central European Economic Conference, which was also sponsored by industry. Protestant resisters such as Dietrich Bonhoeffer and Hans Schönfeld were able to maintain ecclesiastical foreign contacts through Willem Visser't Hooft, the secretary general of the Ecumenical Council of the Church in Geneva, through Scandinavian representatives, and through Bishop Bell of Chichester; Catholic plotters used the international network of their church, including the Vatican. The group around Oster in the *Counterintelligence Office sent activists of the resistance, disguised as consulate workers, to Zürich (as in the case of Hans Bernd Gisevius) and Istanbul (as in the case of Dr. Paul Leverkuehn), where they were then able to make useful contacts with the Western allies through their colleagues in the British and American secret services. The circle within the Foreign Office had no trouble in placing its confidence men in important foreign missions, as in the case of Theodor Kordt, who was in London in 1938–39 and in Bern after the beginning of the war. Trott zu Solz, the "foreign minister" of the *Kreisau Circle, was himself a member of the Foreign Office, and other members of the circle, such as Count Moltke, managed again and again to find a justification for making foreign contacts in the service of the churches, the Counterintelligence Office, or the Foreign Office.

The purpose of the foreign contacts varied. Social Democrats and Communists sought primarily to uphold organizational integrity and to keep their groups alive as a political force until the end of National Socialist rule. Until the turn of the year in 1937–38, bourgeois opponents, on the one hand, pursued the simple goal of not allowing themselves to be entirely cut off from the outside world, as in the case of Hjalmar Schacht with his associations with Anthony Eden and various British and American statesmen and researchers. On the other hand, they tried to open the eyes of their foreign contacts to the true nature of the National Socialist regime, as in the case of Theodor Steltzer (who was later a member of the Kreisau Circle) and his connection with Austrian chancellor Kurt von Schuschnigg.

During the Sudeten crisis of 1938 — earlier manifestations of the crisis had led to the formation of resistance circles among bourgeois conservatives as early as 1934 — there arose the attempt, born of these groups' two goals of toppling Hitler and averting the threat of war, to make a sort of alliance with the Western powers and particularly with the British government. The Western powers were supposed to oppose Hitler's policy, which was directed toward the destruction of Czechoslovakia, with a decisiveness that even in the face of war would make it clear to the German people that Hitler intended to steer his nation toward a European war. If, as was expected, Hitler did not abandon his policy, then the group around Beck, Goerdeler, and Oster wanted to overthrow the government between the time that Hitler gave the order to attack and the actual beginning of hostilities; they also hoped that by maintaining the peace, they could win over the understanding of the German people for that overthrow. Goerdeler's very intensive contact with the London Foreign Office, conducted through the British industrialist A. P. Young and other middlemen, was directed toward those ends. The same was true of the trip to London (August 18–23, 1938), which had been promoted by Oster and approved by Beck, by the anti-Nazi estate holder Ewald von Kleist-Schmenzin, who was able to speak with Lord Lloyd, Sir Robert Vansittart, and Winston Churchill and, through them, to contact Foreign Minister Lord Halifax and Prime Minister Chamberlain. After the beginning of the war, contacts of this nature had two goals: an agreement by the Western allies not to take military advantage of a coup d'état in Germany and the negotiation of conditions for peace, primarily pertaining to territory, for a post-Nazi government. Examples of this are Hassell's meeting with an acquaintance of Halifax, James Lonsdale Bryans, in Arosa on February 22–23, 1940; Trott's visit to the United States from September to November 1939 and his subsequent frequent trips to Sweden and Switzerland; Bonhoeffer's and Schönfeld's meetings with Bishop Bell in Sigtuna on May 31, 1942, and in Stockholm on May 26, 1942; and the permanent contact that Hans Bernd Gisevius had with Allen W. Dulles, the head of the U.S. Office of Strategic Services in Switzerland, from 1941 to the summer of 1944 in Zurich.

The resistance groups' foreign contacts had no political effect, for three reasons. First, during the Sudeten crisis, the emissaries of the resistance not only made demands on their British contacts similar to those that Hitler had announced but also made demands that Hitler had not yet made at all (the latter included claiming the German borders of 1914), albeit with the acceptance that Germany would be a coguarantor of the peace in Europe after these demands were met. Second, the German envoys were not able to convince the Western powers of the strength of the resistance for overthrowing Hitler. Third, there was no coup d'état until the summer of 1944, when there was no longer any time for politics, which confirmed the skepticism of Western politicians. Between the campaigns in Poland and western Europe, the group around Oster and Beck, with the help of the Vatican contacts of the respected Munich attorney Dr. Josef Müller, was able through the mediation of Pope Pius XII to establish communication with the British Foreign Office. For the first and last time, that contact led to British willingness to discuss matters and thereby made possible an alliance between German resistance groups and the Western powers. At the end of 1940, however, Beck and Oster had to admit to the pope and British partners that they had not succeeded in winning over the leaders of the German army for a coup d'état and that this would also not be possible by the time of the German attack on western Europe, which was soon expected.

Three other contacts deserve mention. During the war, evangelical opponents of the regime and a certain Colonel Staehle, who was acting on Goerdeler's behalf, had contacts with the Résistance in the Netherlands through Visser't Hooft. Through the Dutch military attaché in Berlin, Colonel Sas, Colonel Oster informed the western and northern European countries of the date of the German attack on western Europe and on Denmark and Norway, thereby hoping to bring about a military setback that was supposed to mobilize the German general staff against Hitler; to convince the German people of the correctness of a coup d'état; and otherwise to avoid a long and bloody war. Finally, in December 1943, Count Moltke contacted representatives of the U.S. Office of Strategic Services in Istanbul and suggested a cooperative effort that involved accepting the defeat of Germany. But Oster's warnings fell on deaf ears, and Moltke's offer did not reach President Roosevelt.

HERMANN GRAML

Bibliography

Graml, Hermann. "Die außenpolitischen Vorstellungen des deutschen Widerstands." In *Widerstand im Dritten Reich: Probleme, Ereignisse, Gestalten.* Edited by Hermann Graml. Reprint. Frankfurt am Main, 1994.

Klemperer, Klemens von. *German Resistance against Hitler: The Search for Allies Abroad 1938–1945.* Oxford, 1992.

Young, A. P. *Die X-Dokumente: Die geheimen Kontakte Carl Goerdelers mit der britischen Regierung 1938/39.* Munich/Zurich, 1989.

Foreign Mission of German Trade Unions. *See* Socialist Resistance; Trade Union Resistance.

Foreign Office. On March 5, 1938, shortly after Joachim von Ribbentrop had become Reich foreign minister, he appointed the then-director of the Political Department of the Foreign Office, Baron Ernst von Weizsäcker, state secretary. As a conservative diplomat with patriotic values, Weizsäcker hoped to be able to uphold the traditions and political line of the Foreign Office vis-à-vis his superior, who was diplomatically inept but believed in National Socialism. Pursuant to this line, Weizsäcker was also for a revision of the Versailles Treaty (especially with respect to Germany's eastern borders); he approved of the annexation of Austria and the Sudeten regions and was thus for a "Greater Germany," but he was against a "large war" for the acquisition of Lebensraum, since this, in the opinion of diplomats of the Foreign Office, could not be won and would necessarily lead to the downfall of the Reich.

Weizsäcker had connections with opposition circles within the military; he initially hoped to be able to influence Ribbentrop and to have a moderating effect upon Hitler. As it became clear after the end of May 1938 that Hitler was steering toward a war with Czechoslovakia in which intervention by the Western powers was feared, Weizsäcker and a circle of young diplomats who were assembled closely around him and becoming quite conspiratorially active — especially Erich Kordt, his brother Theodor Kordt, and Albrecht von Kessel — sought to sabotage Hitler's policy of war. They tried primarily to move the British government to take a firm position against Hitler. With the help of the Italian ambassador in Berlin, Bernardo Attolico, they arrived at a suggestion for a compromise with Mussolini, which led to the Munich Pact of September 30, 1938. Weizsäcker praised this as a "great success," but he had lost credibility with Hitler and Ribbentrop because of his recommendation of a "nonmilitary acquisition of the Sudetenland," although he, too, sought a "chemical dissolution" of Czechoslovakia.

In view of Hitler's war plans and of the National Socialist regime's brutal persecution of the Jews, which was becoming manifest in November 1938, a circle of friends who wanted to work toward toppling the regime drew more closely together in the winter of 1938–39. Members of the Foreign Office in this circle were Albrecht von Kessel, Gottfried von Nostitz, and Adam von Trott zu Solz. They usually met in Count Peter Yorck von Wartenburg's house in Dahlem. A primary goal of the colleagues from the Foreign Office was to motivate the English to energetically oppose Hitler's further plans of annexation. After the forceful destruction of Czechoslovakia by Hitler in the middle of March 1939, the British government made a "guarantee" of Poland's "independence." In June and the middle of August 1939, the Kordt brothers tried in secret contacts to motivate the British government to warn Germany of a war in a public statement. They informed the English of Hitler's war intentions and pushed for a British-Soviet alliance. Ribbentrop foiled them with the German-Soviet Nonaggression Treaty of August 24, 1939, in which a large portion of eastern Europe was declared to be a Soviet area of interest.

Even if one can hardly describe Weizsäcker as a "man of the resistance," he nevertheless took steps through intermediaries (such as Carl Jacob Burckhardt) and through the approval of corresponding activities of his colleagues in the Foreign Office (such as those of the Kordt brothers, Kessel, and Nostitz) that bordered on treason in order to thwart Hitler's and Ribbentrop's war plans. In November 1939, Erich Kordt planned personally to assassinate Hitler, but the plan could not be carried out as a result of the *Bürgerbräu Assassination Attempt. With the beginning of the war, the Foreign Office lost much in the way of importance and influence. Opponents of the regime who were not in positions abroad attempted to become active in the resistance in other areas (as in the case of Adam von Trott zu Solz in the *Kreisau Circle).

HELLMUTH AUERBACH

Bibliography

Blasius, Rainer A. *Für Großdeutschland — gegen den großen Krieg: Staatssekretär Ernst Frhr. von Weizsäcker in den Krisen um die Tschechoslowakei und Polen 1938/39.* Cologne, 1981.

Thielenhaus, Marion. *Zwischen Anpassung und Widerstand: Deutsche Diplomaten 1938–1941. Die politischen Aktivitäten der Beamtengruppe um Ernst von Weizsäcker im Auswärtigen Amt.* Paderborn, 1985.

Fraternal Cooperation of Prisoners of War (BSV). The BSV was the most important resistance organization of foreigners in Germany. It was founded at the beginning of 1943 in the Schwanseestrasse camp for officer POWs in Munich-Giesing. The first plans were made by Roman Petruschel, a soldier, and Michael Kondenko, a major, who in March drew up a program for the prospective organization. Josef Feldmann, who had worked for the Russian secret service in Dnepropetrovsk until 1941 and was able to escape German captivity, joined this organizational core. Commissioned by the Communist Party to organize resistance among Soviet POWs, he enlisted as a "foreign worker" in Germany under the name Georg Fesenko and worked as an interpreter in the Schwanseestrasse camp. Together with Air Force Major Karl Osolin, he assumed leadership of the organization.

The BSV worked toward a comprehensive organization of all POWs, yet found interest only among Soviet POWs and "Eastern workers." Its espoused goals were acts of sabotage, resistance against enlistment in the collaborating Vlassov Army, preparations for an armed uprising in concert with opponents of Hitler, and the support of Soviet and Western troops after the expected invasion.

The BSV was able to take hold very quickly among Soviet POWs and workers from eastern Europe in the Munich area and then in Baden and Württemberg. Other contacts extended as far as Vienna, Hamburg, and Berlin. It cooperated especially closely with the *Anti-Nazi German People's Front (ADV) surrounding Karl Zimmet and Hans Hutzelmann, which was established in Munich in August 1943. The BSV was quite effective in its resistance against Vlassov recruits, in helping people to escape, and in putting pressure on authorities to improve the living conditions of prisoners and workers from the East.

The Gestapo succeeded in infiltrating the BSV's covert network with an informant at the end of 1943. In a wave of arrests lasting until the spring of 1944, a total of 383 persons was apprehended. The Gestapo employed brutal methods of torture during hearings. All ninety-two leading organizers and cell leaders were shot in Dachau on September 4, 1944; at least thirty-eight other BSV members were executed in Mauthausen at the beginning of October.

JÜRGEN ZARUSKY

Bibliography

Brodskij, Josif A. *Die Lebenden kämpfen: Die Organisation Brüderliche Zusammenarbeit der Kriegsgefangenen (BSW)*. Berlin, 1968.

Herbert, Ulrich. *Fremdarbeiter: Politik und Praxis des "Ausländer-Einsatzes" in der Kriegswirtschaft des Dritten Reiches*. Berlin/Bonn, 1985.

Streim, Alfred. *Sowjetische Gefangene in Hitlers Vernichtungskrieg*. Heidelberg, 1982.

Freedom (*Freiheit*). *See* Knöchel Organization.

Freedom Action of Bavaria (FAB). In Munich and its vicinity at the end of April 1945, various more or less closely associated individuals and groups of anti-Nazi persuasion attempted a putsch that was supposed to end National Socialist rule in Upper Bavaria and to end the war in that region. Under the command of the chief of the interpreters' company of the Seventh Army Corps Area, Captain Rupprecht Gerngross, segments of the Seventeenth Panzer Reserve Unit in Erding (ninety men with three tanks under the command of Major Alois Braun) and of the Nineteenth and Sixty-first Grenadier Reserve and Training Battalions, officers of Wehrmacht Headquarters in Munich and of the Seventh Air Regional Command, as well as members of the socialist underground organization "0 7" and of smaller resistance groups in Munich factories (Fa. Steinheil, BMW) took part in the so-called Freedom Action of Bavaria (FAB); it comprised approximately four hundred soldiers and civilians.

After the Americans had crossed the Danube on April 26 and 27, 1945, the FAB expected a quick advance on Munich and attacked. During the night of April 28, Major Braun and his soldiers succeeded in occupying the radio stations in Erding and Freimann. Other actions against Gauleiter Giesler's headquarters in the Ludwigstrasse in Munich, against the headquarters of Commander in the West Field Marshal Kesselring in Pullach near Munich, and against the headquarters of the Seventh Army Corps Area in Kempfenhausen near Starnberg failed, however. During that night, Gerngross himself drove to the quarters of Reich Governor General Franz Ritter von Epp in Starnberg in order to convince him, through the help of Major Günther Caracciola-Delbrück (Epp's contact officer with the Wehrmacht), to offer Bavaria's capitulation to the Americans. Epp hesitated, yet agreed to be taken by Gerngross and Caracciola to Major Braun in Freising.

During the early morning of April 28, the FAB began to broadcast calls to the people over the radio stations in Erding and Freimann. Gerngross very prematurely announced that the FAB had "taken over the government during the night," and he presented a generally reserved and conservatively tinged ten-point program: (1) the elimination of the bloody rule of National Socialism; (2) the elimination of militarism; (3) the restoration of peace; (4) a struggle against anarchy; (5) the guarantee of food; (6) the restoration of ordered economic conditions; (7) the reconstruction of the constitutional state; (8) the establishment of a social order; (9) the reintroduction of basic rights; and (10) the restoration of human dignity.

When Epp heard the second point of the program, he refused to take part in the action. Together with Caracciola, he went back to his quarters; they were arrested there and handed over to the Gauleiter. Caracciolo was shot, and Epp was taken into "honorary custody." The putschists had placed their bets on the wrong man insofar as Epp still enjoyed a certain popularity in Bavaria but had no command whatsoever over any troops — and was thus not in a position to speak with the Americans in the name of the Wehrmacht.

In the face of advancing SS troops, the rebels evacuated both radio stations that morning and fled to safety. At about ten in the morning, Munich mayor Fiehler and Gauleiter Giesler spoke to the people over the Freimann radio station. The putsch had thus collapsed after a few hours. Ignorant of the actual situation in Munich, however, courageous citizens in numerous areas surrounding Munich had followed the FAB's calls to a "pheasant hunt" of NSDAP functionaries and had arrested them and taken over the local government.

During the course of April 28, all these attempts to end the war and to shake off National Socialist rule were brutally put down by units of the SS and the Wehrmacht; the participants were arrested, and most of them were executed. The bloodiest acts of revenge by the National Socialist myrmidons were in the small mining town of Penzberg, where the uprising had been conducted by former SPD and KPD members (fourteen men and two women lost their lives), and in the Catholic pilgrimage site of Altötting, where seven people lost their lives. In all, forty-one persons who had taken part in the uprising or had followed its calls were victims of the National Socialist regime in these final days.

The FAB had entirely underestimated the situation of the war and the means of power still at the disposal of the National Socialist regime and had badly overestimated its own possibilities. The attempted uprising was insufficiently prepared and carried out in a very dilettantish manner. It accomplished nothing and produced only unnecessary victims. Claims that thousands of soldiers on the front north of Munich had laid down their weapons as a result of the proclamations broadcast over radio are greatly exaggerated. In view of the quick suppression of the putsch, the Americans believed that there were still powerful forces in the city and did not occupy Munich — and then rather hesitantly — until April 30, 1945.

HELLMUTH AUERBACH

Bibliography

Bretschneider, Heike. *Der Widerstand gegen den Nationalsozialismus in München 1933 bis 1945.* Munich, 1968.

Henke, Klaus-Dietmar. *Die amerikanische Besetzung Deutschlands,* Volume 2: *Ins Innere des Reiches.* Munich, 1994.

Troll, Hildebrand. "Aktionen zur Kriegsbeendigung im Frühjahr 1945." In *Bayern in der NS-Zeit*. Volume 4: *Herrschaft und Gesellschaft im Konflikt*, part C. Edited by Martin Broszat, Elke Fröhlich, and Anton Grossmann. Munich, 1981.

Free Germany (*Freies Deutschland*). *See* National Committee "Free Germany."

"Free Germany" Committee for the West. *See* Exile and Resistance.

Free Germany Movement (Freies Deutschland). *See* Exile and Resistance; National Committee "Free Germany."

The Free Word (*Das freie Wort*). *See* Hanno-Günther Group/Rütli Group; National Committee "Free Germany."

Free Workers' Union of Germany (FAUD). *See* Anarcho-Syndicalists.

Freiburg Circles. Three resistance groups that existed parallel to but independent of one another in Freiburg are referred to as the "Freiburg Circles": the Freiburg Council, the Bonhoeffer Circle, and the Erwin von Beckerath Task Force. They were personally connected by the economists Constantin von Dietze, Walter Eucken, and Adolf Lampe. Because the groups were connected in this way, the term "Freiburg Circles" (or "Freiburgers") is often used to refer to them collectively.

While the members of the Freiburg Circles were not immediate members of the circle of conspirators involved in the *July 20, 1944, assassination attempt on Hitler, they maintained contacts especially with Carl Goerdeler (see *Goerdeler Circle), Johannes Popitz, Count Peter Yorck von Wartenburg, General Thomas, and Jens Jessen. Since some of them (such as von Dietze, Eucken, Lampe, and Günter Schmölders) were consulted as experts in economic questions by the Kreisau Circle as well as by Goerdeler and Popitz, their basic ideas regarding a future economic order were accorded a place in the plans of the resistance groups involved in the July 20, 1944, assassination attempt against Hitler. Their neoliberal theory envisioned a state-"sponsored" competitive system as a middle path between laissez-faire liberalism and a centrally planned economy. By means of strict systemic policy, the state was supposed to bring about "real economic competition" by making it impossible for "particular interests" to govern the market.

The economists' cooperation in the Freiburg Circles was a result not only of their having done research and taught together at the university, but also of their membership in the *Confessing Church. On

Lampe's initiative, the Freiburg Council was formed at the end of 1938 for the purpose of discussing unresolved theological questions in a free exchange of ideas. The discussion group met regularly under the direction of the historian Gerhard Ritter until 1944. Members included von Dietze, Eucken, Lampe, Ritter, and their wives; pastors of the Confessing Church; and, later, Catholic theologians. In a memorandum, Ritter summarized the conclusion of the discussions concerning the question of how engaged Christians should behave vis-à-vis a government that openly disregarded God's commandments.

Von Dietze's connections with leading members of the Confessing Church in Berlin were partially responsible for the establishment of a smaller work group — the Freiburg Bonhoeffer Circle — from the ranks of the Freiburg Council at the end of 1942. On behalf of the Confessing Church's leadership, a closely knit circle was supposed to work out the principles for a new order in Germany (see *"Principles for the New Order") in a memorandum. The memorandum was supposed to serve as a topic for discussion at a world conference of churches planned for the period after the war. A core group consisting of Ritter, von Dietze, Eucken, and Lampe (all from Freiburg) wrote the main part of the pamphlet *Political System of the Community.* For the concluding discussion, Carl Goerdeler and others were brought in. After the July 20, 1944, assassination attempt against Hitler, parts of the pamphlet fell into the hands of the Gestapo, which led to the arrest of von Dietze, Lampe, and Ritter.

Their arrest ended the work of the last Freiburg circle, the Erwin von Beckerath Task Force, whose members included, in addition to von Dietze, Eucken, and Lampe, the economists Gerhard Albrecht, Erwin von Beckerath, Erich Preiser, Günter Schmölders, Heinrich von Stackelberg, and Theodor Wessels as well as Franz Böhm, Clemens Bauer, and Fritz Hauenstein. This circle had arisen in 1943 out of a committee of the Academy of German Law that had been officially suspended due to the war but that had continued its work privately. At issue in the numerous reports written by the task force was the question of how the economic problems of the transitional period could be solved. The political dimension was entirely excluded. In accordance with neoliberal theory, the reactivation of the market mechanism stood at the center of attention and accorded only secondary importance to social issues. The planned final report was not completed due to the arrest of the Freiburgers. As only a few members of the task force knew, the final report was meant for Goerdeler.

Otto Ohlendorf, an SS obergruppenführer and, since 1943, deputy state secretary in the Reich Ministry of Economics, was also interested in the activity of the Erwin von Beckerath Task Force; under his direction, similar plans for the postwar economy had been made in the Reich

Ministry of Economics. Yet he was not successful in closely integrating the Freiburgers into his ministry's work.

DANIELA RÜTHER-ZIMMERMANN

Bibliography

Blumenberg-Lampe, Christine. *Die wirtschaftlichen Programme der "Freiburger Kreise": Entwurf einer freiheitlich-sozialen Nachkriegswirtschaft.* Berlin, 1973.

———, ed. *Der Weg in die Soziale Marktwirtschaft: Referate, Protokolle, Gutachten der Arbeitsgemeinschaft Erwin von Beckerath 1943–1947.* Stuttgart, 1986.

Rübsam, Dagmar, and Hans Schadek, eds. *Der "Freiburger Kreis": Widerstand und Nachkriegsplanung 1933–1945: Katalog einer Ausstellung, mit einer Einführung von Ernst Schulin.* Freiburg im Breisgau, 1990.

Rüther-Zimmermann, Daniela. *Die wirtschaftspolitischen Vorstellungen des Widerstands im "Dritten Reich."* Scheduled for publication in 1996/97.

Freiburg Council. *See* Freiburg Circles.

Freies Deutschland (Free Germany). *See* National Committee "Free Germany."

Freiheit (Freedom). *See* Knöchel Organization.

Das freie Wort (The Free Word). *See* Hanno-Günther Group/Rütli Group; National Committee "Free Germany."

Der Friedenskämpfer (The Fighter for Peace). *See* Communist Resistance; Knöchel Organization.

Friends of Children (SPD). *See* Leipzig Hound Packs; Socialist Resistance; Youth Opposition.

Fritz List Sporting and Hiking Goods Store. *See* Youth Opposition.

Front National de le Libération (FNL). *See* Exile and Resistance.

Gegen den Strom (Against the Current). *See* German Communist Party/Opposition (KPDO or KPO).

gegner (opponent). *See* Red Orchestra.

Der Gerade Weg (The Straight Path). *See* Resistance against National Socialism before 1933.

German Boys' Club (d.j. 1.11). *See* Youth Opposition.

German Communist Party/Opposition (KPDO or KPO). Within the KPO, which was founded at the end of 1928 after the Sixth World Congress of the Comintern, there arose the so-called rightist opposition of the German Communist Party (KPD) surrounding Heinrich Brandler, August Thalheimer, and other (former) leading representatives, that is, particularly those KPD members who were not prepared to follow the ultraleftist course ordered by the Comintern leadership, for whom the "social-fascist" German Social Democratic Party (SPD) was the primary enemy. As one of the larger leftist splinter groups, the KPO initially had about thirty-five hundred members. Despite the KPO's harsh criticism of the KPD leadership and especially of the KPD leadership's stance on trade union solidarity and the SPD, the KPO's intended political goal was to take over the KPD, which placed strict limits on the KPO's organizational activities.

The KPO was subject to fierce internal, factional squabbles during the final years of the Weimar Republic. This led to its split at the end of 1931 over the question of its relationship to the *German Socialist Workers' Party (SAP): the majority, which saw itself as the cadre organization of a future reunited KPD, rejected cooperation with the SPD, while the minority considered itself to be the core of a new radical socialist party and pushed for the fusion of both organizations. After the split, the KPO minority for the most part went over to the SAP.

At the beginning of 1933, the KPO — which was the second largest of the leftist splinter groups after the SAP, albeit by a considerable margin — still had roughly three thousand members. In contrast to the other leftist splinter groups, it was hit relatively hard by the waves of arrests during the spring of 1933: it lost approximately one-fifth of its members. This occurred essentially because the KPO consisted primarily of dissident KPD cadres who had become politically prominent during the Weimar period and were thus known to the police and because the KPO continued its activist unity-front policy even during its initial underground phase, which to a certain degree went against desired covert security measures.

At the end of 1932, the KPO had decided to rearrange its organization in accordance with the circumstances of its being outlawed. The reformation of the top leadership was carried out the day after the Reichstag fire: the party's domestic leadership, the so-called Berlin Committee, was comprised of three leading party members, as was the party's leadership abroad, the Foreign Committee under Heinrich Brandler and August Thalheimer. The latter committee was formed at the beginning of March 1933 in Strasbourg, where the first exile issue of the KPO organ *Gegen den Strom* (Against the current) appeared in May 1933. The seat of the Foreign Committee was moved to Paris a little later; after the outbreak of the war in 1939, it was moved to Stockholm.

From 1933 to 1937, Hans Tittel, Erich Hausen, Karl Bräuning, Fritz Wiest, and finally Theo Gabbey functioned as the political leaders of the Berlin Committee. Following the model of the KPO's organizational hubs during the Weimar period, the outlawed KPO had its main bases in Berlin and in central Germany; in addition, there were significant groups in Hamburg, Frankfurt am Main, Stuttgart, and the Rhine-Ruhr region. Other groups with which the Berlin Committee was in contact existed in Thuringia, Saxony, East Prussia, Württemberg, Bavaria, and Bremen. Underground regional conferences within Germany are documented into 1935; the organization is said to have still had roughly twelve hundred members in 1936.

In February 1937, the Gestapo succeeded in arresting the central courier, Hans Löwendahl, and in coercing extensive statements from him. The result was the arrest of the domestic leadership and finally the destruction of the entire organization of the KPO. Local KPO groups in central Germany that escaped this wave of arrests continued to exist into wartime. After 1945, former KPO members formed the Workers' Policy Group in Berlin, which continued to exist as a small political organization for a long time.

HARTMUT MEHRINGER

Bibliography

Bergmann, Theodor. *"Gegen den Strom": Die Geschichte der kommunistischen Partei-Opposition.* Hamburg, 1987.

Foitzik, Jan. *Zwischen den Fronten: Zur Politik, Organisation und Funktion linker politischer Kleinorganisationen 1933 bis 1939/40.* Bonn, 1986.

Tjaden, K. H. *Struktur und Funktion der "KPD-Opposition" (KPO): Ein organisationssoziologische Untersuchung zur "Rechts" — Opposition im deutschen Kommunismus zur Zeit der Weimarer Republik.* Meisenheim am Glan, 1964.

German Communist Youth Organization (KJVD). *See* Youth Opposition.

German Freedom (*Deutsche Freiheit*). *See* Saar Battle (Status Quo Movement).

German Freedom Radio. *See* Committee for the Preparation of a German People's Front.

German Information (*Deutsche Informationen*). *See* Committee for the Preparation of a German People's Front.

German People's Front. In the Weimar Republic there had been repeated attempts to overcome the division within the German working class that had become manifest with the founding of the German Communist Party (KPD) on January 1, 1919. These attempts were based on the notion of creating a unity front made up of party leaders and then of the base. Particularly in the two central German states of Saxony and Thuringia, these attempts succeeded even to the point that members of the KPD worked together with state governments that were headed by the German Social Democratic Party (SPD) (Erich Zeigner in Dresden and Paul Frölich in Weimar). The Moscow Communist International's tactic of effecting a transition from the bourgeois-democratic form of a parliamentarily supported workers' government to a proletarian soviet republic — a tactic that was directed by Grigori Sinovyev and the Communist International's German protagonists (August Thalheimer, Ernst Thälmann, Walter Ulbricht) — failed in October 1923 due to social democracy's republican sense of responsibility and the Reichswehr's intervention.

The transfer of power to Hitler and the National Socialist German Workers' Party (NSDAP) on January 30, 1933, caused the KPD to revive the idea of a unity front of German workers' parties two years later. From exile in Moscow on February 11, 1935, it suggested a "unity-front pact" to the SPD's executive committee, which had emigrated to Prague. In August 1935, the Sixth Moscow Congress of the Communist International took up the suggestion again, and at its "Brussels Conference" three months later the KPD referred to "the active unity [of the KPD and SPD] as the surest way to bring about the political unity of the proletariat as well." With Otto Wels at its head, the exiled SPD rejected the offer, since it was still burdened with the memory of the "period of [the KPD's] unity-front maneuvers with all means of lying and deceit" in 1922–23.

In 1936, initiatives from abroad led former Social Democrats who had not emigrated from Germany after 1933 to make their own moves. Political events in France and Spain also gave the project the name "people's front." These events were: (1) the union of socialist groups that had taken place in France on November 3, 1935; this was initially a socialist-republican union that then joined with radical socialists and Communists in a people's front (June 5, 1936: the first people's front cabinet under Léon Blum); (2) the people's front government under Manuel Azaña that was founded by leftist parties (republicans, socialists, syndicalists, Communists) in Spain on February 16, 1936. Both events stood sponsor to the *Committee for the Preparation of a German People's Front, which, initiated by Willi Münzenberg and presided over by Heinrich Mann, was founded at Hotel Lutetia in Paris in February 1936; members included Rudolf Breitscheid, Walter Ulbricht, Paul Hertz, Arnold Zweig, and Lion Feuchtwanger.

In Berlin, these past and unfolding events led the Social Democrats Otto Brass, Hermann Brill, Oskar Debus, Franz Petrich (from the district of Gera), Johannes Kleinspehn (from Nordhausen), and Otto Jenssen (also from the district of Gera) to formulate a catalogue of ten points as the founding platform for a German People's Front on December 21, 1936. Communist sources maintain that Elli Schmidt (alias Irene Gärtner), the Berlin briefer of the Moscow Communist International and KPD member in Moscow, cooperated in this, but this cannot be indubitably demonstrated. Hermann Brill, who was born in Thuringia, was the theoretician.

Propagandistic wishful thinking introduced the platform with the claim that "the liberal, democratic, socialistic, and Communist groups of Germany" were joined together in the German People's Front. Its political content was moderate; it called for a "Reich of political, social, and economic democracy," a foreign policy of peace and reconciliation, and an economic policy "that serves solely the betterment of the German people" (the elimination of the law pertaining to entailed estates; the nationalization of heavy industry, the chemical industry, energy, and banks; and the breakup of large landed estates).

Brill provided considerable theoretical and programmatic grounding, and for this he wrote "German Ideology" (1937), "Establishment of a German People's Front Program" (1937), and "Freedom" (1938). They all rejected a deterministic Marxism and its one-sided theory of the socioeconomic contingency of new political orders and called for an intellectual, individual renaissance of the Germans: "A new man is coming into being, critical, active in thought and deed, creative and tragic in his experience of humanity."

Foreign contacts by the German People's Front with the exiled executive committee of the SPD in Prague in January 1937 and with the Brussels headquarters of the Socialist Workers' International in September 1937 had no effect; the necessary covert camouflage denied all activities a large-scale effect. The German People's Front remained limited to a narrow circle of theoretical disputants (there was loose contact with the group *New Beginning under Kurt Schmidt and Fritz Erler, but contact with the KPD in Moscow was intentionally avoided) who were successful only in maintaining their identity underground and not their actual capacity for resistance. The people's front was working toward a new Germany after the end of National Socialism; it did not have the power to topple the government.

In September 1938, the Gestapo broke up the group despite its camouflage. Brill was named the "head of this illegal circle." Its members were given long-term prison sentences in July 1939 "due to preparation

for high treason." Brill resumed his theoretical, covert work in Buchenwald and entered the public light after his liberation on April 13, 1945,
with his "Manifesto of Democratic Socialists of the Former Concentration Camp of Buchenwald." A new party, the League of Democratic
Socialists, was supposed to carry the political legacy of the German
People's Front into the future of Thuringia, the center of Germany. The
American occupation forces encouraged this path, yet the German Communists, with the assistance of the Red Army, put an end to it.

MANFRED OVERESCH

Bibliography

Overesch, Manfred. *Hermann Brill in Thüringen 1895–1946: Ein Kämpfer
gegen Hitler und Ulbricht.* Bonn, 1992.

German People's Front Group/Ten-Point Group. *See* German
People's Front; New Beginning; Socialist Resistance.

German Revolution (*Deutsche Revolution*). *See* Black Front.

German Socialist Workers' Party (SAPD or SAP). With respect to
its numerical strength and its programmatic role, the Socialist Workers' Party (SAP) was undoubtedly the most significant of leftist splinter
groups. It was founded in 1931 by left-wing SPD Reichstag representatives (including Kurt Rosenfeld and Max Seydewitz) who had left the
party after intense disputes arose within the organization following the
collapse of Hermann Müller's coalition government; it initially recruited
its members primarily from among left-wing members of the SPD surrounding the journal *Klassenkampf* (Class struggle). It saw itself as the
crystalized core of a renewed revolutionary workers' movement and, in
view of the growth of National Socialism, attempted primarily to form a
unity front of the workers' movement; it was also initially successful in
bringing in some of the leftist splinter groups such as the right wing
of the German Independent Social Democratic Party (USPD) around
Theodor Liebknecht. Nevertheless, it could not fulfill its goal of becoming a repository of all leftist splinter groups: despite the universally
recognized necessity for cooperation and unity, the personal and political differences among the many groups and factions that were involved
usually proved to be too strong.

Originally twenty-five thousand members strong, its membership
sank to roughly seventeen thousand by 1933 despite the numerically significant growth that it experienced at the beginning of 1932 due to the
division that had formed around Jacob Walcher and Paul Frölich within
the minority faction of the *German Communist Party/Opposition
(KPDO) at the end of 1931. Members of the KPDO faction had

switched to the SAP and had also quickly succeeded in gaining important positions in the SAP leadership. The SAP's stated policy of working toward a unity front — that is, of attempting to stir the workers' movement to form a common policy toward National Socialism through the propagation of a united front "from above" as well as "from below" — failed primarily due to the intransigent policy of the KPD, which denounced the SAP as the "most dangerous variety of social fascism."

Primarily due to obvious failures in the elections, violent disputes arose within the party during the course of 1932 that, after the Reichstag fire, led the Rosenfeld-Seydewitz wing to push through a resolution that would have dissolved the party, a resolution with which the overwhelming majority of the party did not comply. Even at the beginning of its time underground, the SAP, on the basis of its persistent and credible struggle for a unity front among the proletariat, enjoyed considerable confidence, which it then turned into one of the most important points of reference in the resistance of the workers' movement against National Socialism. (For more information on the SAP's resistance activity, see *Socialist Resistance.)

Hartmut Mehringer

Bibliography

Brandt, Willy. *Links und frei: Mein Weg 1930–1950.* Hamburg, 1982.

Bremer, Jörg. *Die Sozialistische Arbeiterpartei Deutschlands: Untergrund und Exile 1933–1945.* Frankfurt am Main and New York, 1978.

Drechsler, Hanno. *Die Sozialistische Arbeiterpartei Deutschlands (SAPD): Ein Beitrag zur Geschichte der deutschen Arbeiterbewegung am Ende der Weimarer Republik.* Meisenheim am Glan, 1965.

Foitzik, Jan. *Zwischen den Fronten: Zur Politik, Organisation und Funktion linker politischer Kleinorganisationen im Widerstand 1933 bis 1939/40.* Bonn, 1986.

German Youth Front. *See* Youth Opposition.

German Youth Strength. *See* Youth Opposition.

"The Goal" ("Das Ziel"). Next to the *"Principles for the New Order" by the *Kreisau Circle, the program "The Goal," which Carl Goerdeler wrote at the end of 1941 with help from Ludwig Beck, is the most important constitutional plan by the resistance. The period in which it was written explains the assumption that the German Reich would continue to exist within its territorial borders of 1938 (including Austria, Alsace, the Sudetenland, and the Polish Corridor). Although there are later versions by the *Goerdeler Circle, the program of 1941 best illustrates the program.

The program sought a reform of the German Reich in the spirit of the Prussian reform period of the nineteenth century; statements concerning election rights, the organization of the Reich from the bottom up, the strong emphasis on ideas of self-government, and the dominant position of the Reich chancellor are characteristic. Popular representation appears at the bottom among the constitutional institutions, virtually as an appendix of the Reich government. A nonelected Reich legislative house composed of representatives from the various classes of society was to stand on equal terms next to the Reichstag. Among key ministers, the minister of defense was most important; a ministry of labor was intentionally rejected. Goerdeler's and Beck's plan mixed patriarchal characteristics with moral postulates of the Enlightenment; a sense of responsibility and the "trust of decent men among one another" were more important values to the drafters of the program than formal democratic notions. "The dictatorial or tyrannical führer state" seemed to them "just as impossible as untethered, overly democratic parliamentism." For head of state, they considered possibilities such as a hereditary emperor, an elected emperor, or a "Reich leader" who was elected for a certain period of time, clearly preferring a hereditary monarchy.

WOLFGANG BENZ

Bibliography

Mommsen, Hans. *Gesellschaftsbild und Verfassungspläne des deutschen Widerstandes*. In *Widerstand im Dritten Reich*. Edited by Hermann Graml. Reprint. Frankfurt am Main, 1994.

Schramm, Wilhelm Ritter von, ed. *Beck und Goerdeler, Gemeinschaftsdokumente für den Frieden 1941–1944*. Munich, 1965.

Goerdeler Circle. Carl Goerdeler's resignation from his post as mayor of Leipzig — which occurred after the monument to Mendelssohn in front of the Gewandhaus was removed without his approval at the end of 1936 — was less the end of unconditional cooperation with the National Socialists than the beginning of an oppositional career that went from negative criticism to open opposition and conspiracy to do away with Hitler up to the preparation of and participation in a coup d'état and assassination attempt. The renowned national-conservative administrative lawyer and local politician, who was by no means unfavorably disposed toward empowerment laws and other dictatorial decrees in times of state emergency, had personally advised Hitler, who thought highly of Goerdeler as an administrative expert, on the new local level administrative system in 1935 and had already accepted the post of Reich price commissioner for the second time in November 1934.

Deeply convinced of the power of rational thought and economically an anti-Keynesian, he saw himself in this office as a counterweight to the unsound credit policy of Economics Minister Schacht. In two reports ordered by Hitler concerning the financial situation (October 1935 and September 1936), he criticized not only armament policy, which could hardly be financed, but also the devastating effect that the most recent laws concerning Jews were having abroad.

Goerdeler continued to criticize the economic course of the Reich government even when he no longer held public office. Now aware that he and Schacht agreed in their rejection of Hitler's course of armament after Schacht resigned in July 1937, Goerdeler repeatedly attempted to win over Schacht's successor, Funk, and Reich Finance Minister Schwerin von Krosigk for a change in financial policy. Supported by Robert Bosch and his oppositional Stuttgart Circle, but also with Göring's approval, he went on long trips abroad between 1938 and 1939 that served to establish contacts and to gather information. In detailed reports to Göring, he warned of underestimating England and France and pointed to the negative effects that National Socialist policy toward the church and Jews was having abroad.

After his resignation, Goerdeler renewed old relations with Ludwig Beck, the chief of the general staff, and General von Fritsch, commander of the army. He also extended his relations to other generals at the head of the Wehrmacht, such as Beck's successor, Franz Halder; the chief of Wehrmacht rearmament in the High Command of the Armed Forces, General Georg Thomas; and the commander of the Berlin military district, General Erwin von Witzleben. In the civilian sphere, he found critics of official German policy in the German ambassador in Rome, Ulrich von Hassell, in Prussian finance minister Johannes Popitz, and in the economist Jens Jessen, who was disappointed by the NSDAP; all were members of the learned Berlin Wednesday Society. Hans-Bernd Gisevius, who was then working in the Office of the Secret State Police (Gestapo), was an important informant and intermediary for contact with the group around Colonel Oster in Canaris's *Counterintelligence Office. These men, who were counted among the old national-conservative elite, were brought together by the realization that Hitler, going beyond the itemized revisions of the Versailles Treaty that they wholeheartedly endorsed, wanted quickly to set a coarse toward war, a war whose results for Germany at least Beck and Goerdeler were aware of at an early date.

At the beginning of the war, the two trade unionists Jakob Kaiser, a former representative of the Center Party, and Wilhelm Leuschner, the former Hessian minister of the interior who had already been held in Lichtenburg concentration camp in 1933–34, joined this group. Goerdeler's contact with the military resistance around Beck was Captain Hermann Kaiser, who worked for the commander of the Reserve Army and later had contact with Generals Olbricht, von Tresckow, and

Stauffenberg. The commanding officer of the Berlin-Frohnau veterans' hospital, Colonel Wilhelm Stähle, established contact with Dutch resistance circles; he was also in contact with the *Kreisau Circle through Adam von Trott zu Solz. Contacts to the circle around the industrialist Reusch developed through Carl Wenzel-Teutschenthal, the owner of an estate.

Goerdeler and Beck saw the first opportunity to stem the party's apparatus, specifically the Security Service (SD), during the crisis within the general staff and during the Sudeten crisis of 1938, a chance that was dashed by the Munich Pact. Next to Canaris's colleague Helmuth Groscurth, it was again Goerdeler who pressured the commanders of the three army groups in the west to carry out a coup d'état in order to hinder the further expansion of the war after the blitzkrieg against Poland. With the support of Generals Thomas and Oster, Goerdeler again attempted during the crucial year of 1942 to win over one of the highest army commanders for a coup d'état. After Field Marshal von Witzleben, one of the most resolute oppositionists within the military, was ousted by Hitler in February, Goerdeler's attempts concentrated on Field Marshal von Kluge. In the late autumn of 1942, Goerdeler convinced the commander of Army Group Middle on the eastern front to go along with the idea, having been helped by Tresckow, who was that commander's chief of staff. When Kluge decided against a coup d'état against Hitler after all, Goerdeler and his friends turned to military leaders in the Reserve Army, raising in the bargain a new legend of a stab in the back. General Friedrich Olbricht, the chief of the General Army Office who had been in the opposition since the spring of 1940, became the coordinator of military plans after Halder, too, was ousted by Hitler in September 1942.

Although the power within the resistance had shifted more toward younger officers since the worsening of the military situation in 1943 and although other groups were also active in the political sphere, the bourgeois camp had agreed relatively early (winter 1941–42) on a directorate with General Beck as head of state, Goerdeler as head of the government, and Field Marshal von Witzleben as commander in chief of the armed forces. The plotters' lists of ministers from 1943 and 1944 include other members of the Goerdeler group, such as Wilhelm Leuschner as vice-chancellor (and as Goerdeler's possible successor), von Hassell as foreign minister, as well as Hermann Kaiser and Fritz-Dietlof von der Schulenburg as state secretaries in the ministries of culture and of the interior. Johannes Popitz does not appear in later lists as minister of justice, as he had been rejected by the trade union wing as too reactionary. Eugen Bolz was to be the minister of culture.

Goerdeler and Popitz were monarchists and believed that Germany could become politically stable and a major European power again

only under authoritarian leadership. This explains the initial willingness of persons such as Beck to cooperate with Hitler. Jessen, whose
disciple Otto Ohlendorf became one of the key figures of the National
Socialist annihilation of the Jews, leaned toward state socialist ideas;
Hassell, though, returned to his *völkisch* element while the war was still
going on.

The Goerdeler group's ideas of a Germany and Europe after Hitler
can be discerned primarily in Goerdeler's numerous writings and proclamations (see *"The Goal" ["Das Ziel"]). On the one hand, Germany
was to have a strong central government with a parliament whose power
was limited to making the budget; on the other hand, Germany was to
have extensive self-government on the regional level. The introduction of
democratic institutions — with a monarchist head of state if possible —
was made conditional on the political maturity of the Germans after the
National Socialist criminals had been punished and after the rule of law
and individual freedoms had been restored in a Christian-oriented political system. With respect to foreign affairs, German-Polish reconciliation
stood in the foreground. For Alsace-Lothringen, Goerdeler foresaw a division according to language or the granting of autonomy. Germany was
to remain within its old borders, albeit with the inclusion of South Tyrol. In the next step, an alliance of European nations was to be created,
which meant, next to a European military, the creation of ministries
for foreign policy and economics and the inclusion of former German
colonies in a union of colonies of European states for the benefit of all of
Europe. Plans in the cultural sphere — conservative in their sociopolitical
orientation — existed only with respect to schools and institutions of
higher learning.

Since Goerdeler gave information about the plans of the people involved in the July 20, 1944, assassination attempt while he was in
custody, he was long spared execution. Himmler still planned to use
Goerdeler's contacts with Sweden to sound out Churchill. Yet Goerdeler
and Popitz were finally executed on February 2, 1945. Beck had taken
his own life on July 20, 1944. Of the members of the Goerdeler Circle
who were arrested, von Witzleben, von der Schulenburg, Leuschner, von
Hassell, Kaiser, Stähle, and Jessen were killed.

HERMANN WEISS

Bibliography

Müller, Klaus-Jürgen. "Struktur und Entwicklung der national-konservativen
    Opposition." In *Aufstand des Gewissens: Der militärische Widerstand
    gegen Hitler und das NS-Regime 1933*. Edited by the Research Office of
    Military History. Herford/Bonn, 1987.
Ritter, Gerhard. *Carl Goerdeler und die deutsche Widerstandsbewegung*. Stutt-
    gart, 1956.
Roon, Ger van. *Widerstand im Dritten Reich*. Munich, 1990.

Graphia Publishing House. *See* New Beginning; Socialist Resistance.

Green Reports (*Grüne Berichte*). *See* Exile and Resistance; Socialist Resistance.

Grüber Office. *See* Assistance and Solidarity.

Grüne Berichte (Green Reports). *See* Exile and Resistance; Socialist Resistance.

Gymnastics Youth. *See* Black Squad.

Hamburg Group of the White Rose. *See* White Rose.

Hanno Günther Group/Rütli Group. Hanno Günther, a baker's apprentice in Berlin, was a part of the proletarian resistance during the first two years of the war yet was not closely tied politically to the German Communist Party (KPD). His underground work was marked by extraordinarily independent and persistent efforts to adopt the principles of Marxism and to use them for the resistance struggle. His essential political achievement consisted in recognizing the National Socialist regime at the height of its power in the summer of 1941 as a "colossus on feet of clay" and in seeing the decisive power for toppling that regime in an armed struggle by the people.

Born in 1921 as the child of a grade school teacher and a bookstore owner, he went to a reform grade school (Rütli School) in the working-class district of Neukölln until 1933, became a member of the Communist Youth Pioneers after a short stint with the social democratic Red Falcons, and finished his schooling in 1936 in the ninth grade after being expelled from the Scharfenberg school manor, which had become a model National Socialist institution. Upon commencement of his baker's apprenticeship at Eastertime 1936, he left the Hitler Youth, which he had entered in 1933 due to his having been accepted at Scharfenberg. (He justified his withdrawal by citing professional obligations.)

During the first phase of his underground work (from the fall of 1939 until January 1941), Günther, together with Elisabeth Pungs, an early member of the Red Aid, and with Wolfgang Pander, a Youth Communist of Jewish descent, distributed hundreds of stickers with rhymed slogans against the blitzkriegs and six issues of the flyer series *Das freie Wort* (The free word). From the standpoint of the worker and the little person, these exposed the fascist propaganda of the "new order of Europe," the National Socialist regime's sociopolitical measures, which were very popular at the time, and the strategic inferiority of the Berlin air defense system. They also stressed the necessity of a workers' armed struggle to topple National Socialist rule. "We do not want to oppress any foreign peoples!" was a frequently recurring slogan against the blitzkriegs.

The second phase of Günther's underground work, which began after the work on flyers was stopped in January 1941, was marked by the intensive search for contact with the KPD and the simultaneous formation of a small group of like-minded classmates from the Rütli School, whom the Gestapo called the "Rütli Group." The youths listened to London radio broadcasts together, read Marxist texts, and discussed the current war situation. In this manner, a growing consciousness of resistance arose, even though it did not lead to the formation of a Marxist resistance group or to antifascist activities.

At the end of January 1941, Günther came into contact with Herbert Bochow, an experienced Communist functionary; he received critical advice from him on how to develop training in the Rütli Group and on how to conduct covert activities in the Wehrmacht, into which Günther had been drafted in April 1941, and was advised to stop the work on flyers, which was said to be too dangerous and ineffective.

On October 9, 1942, and in a second trial in 1943, the Second Panel of the People's Court sentenced Günther and his cohorts in the struggle against the National Socialist regime to death for treason and high treason. The first sentences were carried out on December 3, 1942, in Plötzensee, the last one on September 7, 1943. Only Günther's girlfriend, Dagmar Petersen, escaped this fate with seven years' imprisonment. Through skillful tactics by her lawyer and medical affidavits attesting to her being unfit to stand trial due to tuberculosis, Elisabeth Pungs avoided trial and a death sentence.

VOLKER HOFFMANN

Bibliography

Hoffmann, Volker. *Hanno Günther, ein Hitlergegner: Geschichte eines unvollendeten Kampfes.* Berlin, 1992.

Helmuth Hübener Group (Hamburg). *See* Juvenile "Gangs of Four."

The Herald (*Der Vorbote*). *See* Lechleiter Group.

Herbert Baum Group. The name "Herbert Baum Group" stands for several resistance circles that comprised a total of more than one hundred persons. Its specific character was determined by the young age of the majority of its members, most members' origin in the Jewish youth movement, the Communist orientation of the leading persons, and the relatively high proportion of female members. The makeup of the youth groups, which were led by the older members, changed over the course of years due to the emigration of the boys and girls.

The young Jews and Jewesses came from the German-Jewish Comrades' Hiking League, the leftist-Zionist Hashomer Hazair, the Black Gang, and the Habonim. Several youths, having a Zionist background, were oriented to socialism or communism; others had a leftist-Zionist orientation. Most of them were only between eleven and fourteen years old when the National Socialist period began. Only the four leading group members were already nineteen years old in 1933. Herbert Baum and Marianne Cohn, who later married each other, as well as Martin Kochmann and Sala Rosenbaum knew one another from their school days.

Their feeling of togetherness grew further due to their affinity to socialist and communist ideals as those ideals were understood at that time; after Germany's attack on the Soviet Union, this led to heightened engagement. There are reports that the group put up stickers, painted graffiti, and distributed illegal material as early as between 1933 and 1935, when the circle around Herbert Baum had widened. Cultural activities with Jewish youths played an important role in group life. At the beginning of 1941, the group widened even further when people were drawn into the oppositional circle. This occurred when approximately ten boys and girls who worked in a special section for male and female Jewish forced laborers in the Siemens-Schuckert Works' electric motor plant in Berlin-Siemensstadt, together with friends and acquaintances who worked in other factories, joined the group.

After many members of the enlarged group demanded clearly visible oppositional activities, a new phase began. This initially included ideological and political training and later the production and distribution of political literature and flyers, the painting of graffiti, acts of solidarity, attempts to evade the deportations and to make contact with other resistance groups, and the recruitment of foreign men and women forced laborers for the resistance.

After Jews were forced to wear the Star of David in September 1941, resistance activities, with the preparation for life underground and public actions, had two contrary goals. Carried out in concert with members of other resistance groups, the arson attack on the anti-Communist touring exhibition "The Soviet Paradise," which was opened on May 8, 1942, in the Berlin Lustgarten, should be seen as their most important act. After they decided that it would be too dangerous to lay out flyers due to the large number of visitors, they decided on arson. They wanted thereby to express their belief that the mistakes of a different society were being exploited for propagandistic purposes and that National Socialist crimes were being hushed up. The suggestion was accepted after a long discussion concerning the pros and cons of such an action. The majority of the group wanted to make a visible statement, even if doing so constituted putting their lives on the line.

The following secret report of May 19, 1942, to the Berlin security police concerning the attack has been preserved:

> Acts of sabotage against the anti-Bolshevist exhibition "The Soviet Paradise" in Berlin. At about 8 P.M. on May 18, 1942, as yet unidentified perpetrators attempted to set fire to the exhibition. A wad of cotton soaked in phosphorus and placed on a wooden post covered with cloth was set aflame at the site of the first fire. An incendiary device with two bottles of phosphorous carbon disulfide exploded in the farmhouse. Eleven people were injured. A sabotage committee of the State Police office in Berlin has begun necessary investigations without delay.

The minimal damages were repaired during the night; the overall impression of the exhibition was preserved; and the exhibit, almost unscathed, opened the following day.

Just four days later — perhaps due to betrayal — the participants in the attack were tracked down by a special Gestapo search commission and arrested. Several were directly hauled off from their workplaces at Siemens. After horrible tortures, group leader Herbert Baum died, probably from suicide. A series of trials that ended with death sentences in very many cases was opened. Only a few members of the Herbert Baum Group survived. Some dedicated themselves to commemorating the murdered men and women resistance fighters.

KURT SCHILDE

Bibliography

Kreutzer, Michael. "Die Suche nach einem Ausweg, der es ermöglicht, in Deutschland als Mensch zu leben." In *Juden im Widerstand: Drei Gruppen zwischen Überlebenskampf und politischer Aktion: Berlin 1939–1945.* Edited by Wilfried Löken and Werner Vathke. Berlin, 1993.

Brothers, Erich. "Wer war Herbert Baum? Eine Annäherung auf der Grundlage von 'oral histories' und schriftlichen Zeugnissen." In *Juden im Widerstand: Drei Gruppen zwischen Überlebenskampf und politischer Aktion: Berlin 1939–1945.* Edited by Wilfried Löken and Werner Vathke. Berlin, 1993.

Hofgeismar Circle. *See* Kreisau Circle.

Informationsdienst (Information Service). *See* Uhrig-Römer Group.

Information Service (*Informationsdienst*). *See* Uhrig-Römer Group.

International Antifascist Committee. *See* Schumann Group.

International Bible Students' Association (IBV). *See* Jehovah's Witnesses; Women between Dissent and Resistance.

International Socialist Combat League (ISK). With its specific ideology, the International Socialist Combat League (ISK) was one of the most peculiar leftist splinter groups. The history of its origin goes back to disputes within the German Youth Movement before World War I, disputes in which Leonard Nelson, the philosophical mentor and founder of the ISK and professor of philosophy at the University of Göttingen until his death in 1927, actively participated. Although the German workers' movement was politically committed and active within the German Social Democratic Party (SPD), and the SPD was intertwined with the ISK, the axioms of Nelson and his supporters were derived from German idealist philosophy, especially from Kantianism. They rejected Marxist historical determinism as well as the Enlightenment principle of democracy and proposed an ethical socialism that strove politically for a dictatorship of the ethical and intellectual elite in the state and in society. As a result of their criticism of Marxism, they particularly attacked the SPD's "superstition of necessity" (that is, the historically determined development of socialism) and propagated a "dictatorship of reason." The ISK was organized according to a principle of strictly hierarchical leadership and demanded of its members a vegetarian lifestyle, abstinence from alcohol and nicotine, as well as a break from the church.

The Nelsonians' youth-propelled activism — which still went by the name International Youth Alliance (IJB) during the first half of the 1920s — within the SPD and especially within the Young Socialists led to their being expelled from the SPD in 1925 and the founding of the ISK. In accordance with its elitist-voluntaristic ideology, the ISK had a strictly hierarchical, almost "Leninist" organizational structure and dedicated its primary attention to the training of its members for political leadership.

The ISK saw itself as an independent party; indeed, it consciously saw itself as a cadre party with high demands with respect to membership dues (which were prorated according to income) and the amount of time required of members for work in the party. It concentrated its political work on trade unions, free thinkers' organizations, the League of Abstinent Workers, and other cultural organizations within the workers' movement. The ISK's national headquarters continued to be in Göttingen, yet the organization had at its disposal branches and offshoots in many large and midsized cities in all of Germany. After Leonard Nelson's death, the uncontested leader of the ISK was Willi Eichler, who had been the ISK's secretary up to that point.

During the final phase of the Weimar Republic, the ISK had thirty-two regular local organizations and smaller groups of members directly under the national leadership and several hundred active members surrounded by sympathizers whose numbers varied according to locality and were sometimes much larger than the number of members in the actual organization. Significantly, the ISK's resistance activity in the Third Reich (see *Socialist Resistance) had many international contacts, especially to groups within the Labour Party.

HARMUT MEHRINGER

Bibliography

Foitzik, Jan. *Zwischen den Fronten: Zur Politik, Organisation und Funktion linker politischer Kleinorganisationen im Widerstand 1933 bis 1939/40.* Bonn, 1986.

Lemke-Müller, Sabine. *Ethischer Sozialismus und soziale Demokratie: Der politische Weg Willi Eichlers vom ISK zur SPD.* Bonn, 1988.

Link, Werner. *Die Geschichte des Internationalen Jugend-Bundes (IJB) und des Internationalen Sozialistischen Kampf-Bundes (IKB): Ein Beitrag zur Geschichte der Arbeiterbewegung in der Weimarer Republik und im Dritten Reich.* Meisenheim am Glan, 1964.

International Transport Workers' Federation (ITF). *See* Exile and Resistance.

Iron Front. *See* Resistance against National Socialism before 1933.

Jehovah's Witnesses. Although the Jehovah's Witnesses were outlawed just a few months after the National Socialist "seizure of power" and were persecuted with merciless severity in the Third Reich, their resistance and their persecution have remained largely unknown. The small Christian congregation had adopted its name in 1931; in Germany, though, it long remained common to use the older terms "Bible students" and "serious Bible students" when referring to them.

The origins of the religious community, which today numbers more than four and one-half million believers worldwide, go back to the 1870s. It was founded by Charles Taze Russell, an American. After Russell broke with the Adventists, he proclaimed that Christ, invisible, had returned for humanity, was gathering the faithful of the Lord around himself, and would establish his "Thousand-Year Kingdom" on earth with the promise of salvation after a forty-year "period of harvest." Russell's message was carried in the journal *Zion's Watch Tower,* which had been published in Pittsburgh since 1879. That message began to be heard on the European continent at the beginning of the 1890s.

The group's central organ, *The Watch Tower,* was published in a German-language edition beginning in 1897; the International Bible Students' Association (IBV) opened its first branch five years later in Elberfeld. At the end of World War I, when the IBV numbered 3,868 "messengers" in nearly one hundred congregations in the German Reich, church and state authorities began to become increasingly aware of the congregations' activities due to the growing number of Jehovah's Witnesses who refused military service.

The Jehovah's Witnesses, whose number grew greatly during the post-war years and increased sixfold to 22,535 believers by 1926, were afterward subject to the harshest attacks by church apologists who propagated a battle against "the confusion of sects" and especially by *völkisch* and, later, National Socialist adversaries. Their main points of criticism were: the new prophecies of salvation for the advent of the Christian kingdom of peace; changes in the credo under the IBV's second president, Joseph Franklin Rutherford, according to which Christians owed obedience to divine, not state, authority; the preaching of the final, decisive apocalyptic battle of Armageddon and of the impending destruction of the "old world" and the powers that ruled it, "politics, capital, and church"; the agitation against "Satan's worldly empire of false religions" and especially the demonization of the pope and Catholic spirituality; the doctrine of the equality of the races and the recognition of the Zionist movement as a clear sign of the Apocalypse; and the congregation's "foreign management" from the United States. The ecclesiastical "defense struggle" and continued *völkisch* and anti-Semitic provocations against the Jehovah's Witnesses as "forerunners of Jewish Bolshevism" finally led in 1931 to actions against the IBV in individual German states (Baden, Bavaria, and Württemberg) in the form of police ordinances and press bans.

Although the approximately twenty-five thousand Jehovah's Witnesses did not make up even five one-thousandths of the total population of Germany in 1933, they were seen by National Socialism as a serious threat to "people and state" and were the first religious group to be gradually banned in all German states (in Prussia on June 24, 1933) already beginning in April 1933. No other religious group fought National Socialist coercions with comparable determination and obstinacy. The resolute disobedience of numerous Jehovah's Witnesses vis-à-vis the regime's various demands — such as the obligations to give the Hitler salute, to take oaths, and to become members of National Socialist organizations — led to a clear escalation of the conflict.

A very large proportion of the Jehovah's Witnesses did not give in to the banning of their religious community. In spite of the high risk, far more than ten thousand Jehovah's Witnesses stubbornly continued their "missionary service" by using covert techniques. In doing so, they developed organizational structures that were suited to the conditions of life underground. With the help of couriers, they maintained foreign contacts and an extensive system for smuggling printed materials; in addition, they produced printed materials underground, which they used to supply IBV groups and cells throughout the Reich and to try to gain new believers. In addition, they even turned to the people in a flyer campaign in 1936–37 in order to protest against the restriction of their religious freedom and to inform the public about the criminal character of the National Socialist regime. With respect to their outer form, the activities of the Jehovah's Witnesses bore great similarities to the resistance struggle that was waged by political opponents of the regime.

The religious courage of the Jehovah's Witnesses, whose numbers were on the whole rather insignificant, engaged a surprisingly broad array of people; the highest offices of the justice system, police, and SS were at times occupied with the "Bible students question." Beginning especially in 1935, Jehovah's Witnesses were sent by the hundreds and the thousands to prisons and concentration camps. In the concentration camps, where the various groups of inmates were marked by the SS with chevrons of different colors, a violet chevron was used as a special category to mark "Bible students," while other colors designated "politicals," "criminals," "asocials," and "homosexuals." This exclusive marking indicated the position of the Jehovah's Witnesses within the concentration camp order, a position that was special in numerous respects.

In the camps, the Jehovah's Witnesses, who were subject to the particular whims of the SS (such as isolation, assignment to penal companies, and mistreatment, which were used to force them to break from the sect), displayed a strong will to assert themselves due to their feeling of solidarity and their religious faith. They developed a network of mutual help and strong organizational solidarity, as in the case of groups that were formed to collect money and food. They tried to practice their religion even in the concentration camps, holding services, converting fellow inmates, and so on. In the eyes of many fellow inmates, the Jehovah's Witnesses were "the most astonishing group that was in the concentration camps."

At the same time, the Jehovah's Witnesses in the Third Reich were the only group that, in its entirety, spoke out for a refusal of military service and, in great numbers, practiced this as well — despite the fact that the Wehrmacht justice system sentenced large numbers of the Jehovah's Witnesses to death for this reason after the beginning of the war (see *Military Subversion and Desertion). The religious community was also persecuted in occupied countries and in countries allied with the German Reich.

On the basis of recent research, the following figures can be given about the extent of the persecution of the Jehovah's Witnesses. Of the approximately 25,000 persons who claimed to be Jehovah's Witnesses at the beginning of the Third Reich, about 10,000 were imprisoned for varying periods of time, 2,000 of them in concentration camps. The number of dead among the German Jehovah's Witnesses is around 1,200, of whom 250 were executed, primarily as a result of Wehrmacht court convictions for refusal to serve in the military. Of groups that espoused a religion or worldview, the Jehovah's Witnesses — after members of the Jewish faith — were the group that was most harshly persecuted by the National Socialist regime.

The position of the Jehovah's Witnesses, which was nonconformist and radical yet not directed toward overthrowing the government, escapes categorization according to ruling paradigms in the study of the history of the resistance. Indeed, the faithful, who were eager in their mission and who, conscious of their own predestination, proclaimed the imminent victory of God over the forces of the devil in the apocalyptic battle of Armageddon, consciously made the decision to put their own lives on the line in the fight against the National Socialist regime but were certainly not "resistance fighters." Their activity was not directed toward changing the political order; rather, they were concerned in their religiously motivated opposition with the possibility of unrestricted religious freedom, with being faithful to the "Biblical commandment," and ultimately with the responsibility of the individual vis-à-vis God. For them, "resistance" was an act of faith, a requirement of religious self-assertion.

DETLEF GARBE

Bibliography

Garbe, Detlef. *Zwischen Widerstand und Martyrium: Die Zeugen Jehovas im "Dritten Reich."* Munich, 1993.

Graffard, Sylvie, and Léo Tristan. *Les Bibelforscher et le nazisme (1933–1945): Ces oubliés de l'Histoire.* Paris, 1990.

Imberger, Elke. *Widerstand "von unten": Widerstand und Dissens aus den Reihen der Arbeiterbewegung und der Zeugen Jehovas in Lübeck und Schleswig-Holstein.* Neumünster, 1991.

Jesuits. *See* Rösch Circle.

Jewish Resistance. Defamed, disenfranchised, and abandoned first to persecution and then to annihilation as a *minorité fatale,* Germany's Jews had only limited possibilities for resistance. Their strategies of defense and survival were expressed in various forms of self-assertion and opposition. When anti-Semitism was elevated to state doctrine in 1933 and the persecution of the approximately five hundred thousand assimilated German Jews began, Jewish representatives raised their voices against the injustice. Attempts were made to protect Jewish life in Germany — in a world in which the Jews felt at home. They continually defended themselves against hostile acts. And they did this not only in letters and petitions, speeches and writings, prayers and sermons, but also in public gestures of spontaneous anger and outrage. Nor was there any lack of defiance. Jews repeatedly defied National Socialist orders. Some refused to accept the names "Sarah" and "Israel" that had been forced upon them for purposes of identification. Others were not willing to be stigmatized by the palm-sized, yellow star.

Their protests were heard neither by the authorities nor by the public. After the November pogrom of 1938, they remained for the most part silent. The authorities took strict action against acts of defense, which they classified as "malicious baiting by Jews" or "behavior hostile to the state," as "treachery" or "high treason." Punishments were handed out accordingly. They ranged from a warning, to "protective custody," up to the death sentence. After Jews were forbidden to emigrate and were transported to the east, the remaining group of 164,000 decimated and elderly, isolated and impoverished Jews had two possible paths of escape from the persecutors' grasp after the end of 1941. One path led to suicide. When the expulsion and deportation orders went into effect, more than three thousand Jews decided to determine the end of their lives themselves. By suicide, an expression of utmost despair, they took leave of a vital German-Jewish community that had been destroyed forever. The other path led underground. Nearly ten thousand Jews decided to abandon their "legal" existence and to flee underground. In Berlin alone, five thousand looked for a hiding place: one-third of these persons survived.

From the beginning, Jews also participated in the general German resistance. Political and social positions and connections dictated that they ally themselves with politically organized antifascism. Members of leftist youth groups continued or began the struggle against National Socialism in 1933. More than two thousand party members or sympathizers joined the outlawed groups of the beaten and shattered workers' movement. Most felt bound to Communist antifascism. Several hundred German Jews of all stripes and colors hurried to Spain in 1936 to fight fascism. During World War II, refugees joined underground organizations or partisan groups in the occupied regions of Europe. In the concentration camps, too, there were sometimes opportunities to overcome demoralization and isolation and to make contact with resistance groups. German Jews in the safety of exile distinguished themselves by volunteering for military service. More than twenty thousand served in the armies of Great Britain, the United States, and other Allies. Youths in Germany mustered the strength to fight back even during the phase of the "Final Solution." A Zionist youth group that went by the name *Chug Chaluzi and went underground in 1942 had approximately forty members. A Communist-Jewish resistance organization that — isolated in the Berlin underground — became known in the history of antifascism as the *Herbert Baum Group recruited its members from among young forced laborers. Jews and non-Jews joined even in 1943 in the small *Community for Peace and Construction in order to assist refugees who had gone underground and to inform the populace through flyers.

Before and during World War II, there were many opportunities to save Jewish lives. Only a few were used. The Jews in Germany and in the occupied territories of Europe were not able alone to stop the destructive course of National Socialist policy toward the Jews. They would have needed help from non-Jews (see *Assistance and Solidarity). Persecution and expulsion occurred in front of everyone's eyes. Aside from the exceptions, they did not spark any opposition among the public. The Jewish resistance came up against barriers that had been set up by a barbaric regime and a hostile society. The limitations and failure of that resistance cannot — as has been done for years — be held against those people who defended themselves and resisted but rather must be held against those who ignored and squandered strategies for defense and survival.

Konrad Kwiet

Bibliography

Ainsztein, Ruben. *Jewish Resistance in Nazi-Occupied Europe.* London, 1974.
Kwiet, Konrad, and Helmut Eschwege. *Selbstbehauptung und Widerstand: Deutsche Juden im Kampf um Existenz und Menschenwürde.* Hamburg, 1986.
Paucker, Arnold. *Jüdischer Widerstand in Deutschland: Tatsachen und Problematik.* Berlin, 1989 (German Resistance Memorial).

July 20, 1944. When Colonel Count Claus Schenk von Stauffenberg assumed the post of chief of staff at the office of the chief of army armaments and commander of the army reserve, Brigadier General Fromm, he was given the chance to attend Hitler's military briefings in the "Führer Headquarters." This opportunity strengthened Stauffenberg's resolve to carry out the assassination of Hitler himself, although he was handicapped by the loss of an eye, his right hand, and two fingers of his left hand after having been badly wounded in North Africa. In view of the hopeless military situation in the summer of 1944 (that is, the Allied invasion in Normandy and the collapse of the central eastern front), some questioned whether an assassination of Hitler still made any sense, especially since no one had yet received any signals from the "enemy forces." Yet coconspirator Brigadier General von Tresckow expressly encouraged Stauffenberg: "The assassination must take place, *coute que coute* (whatever it might cost). After all, it no longer has to do with a practical purpose, but rather with German resistance making the decisive move before the world and before history."

Since not only Hitler but also Himmler and Göring were supposed to be killed in the planned attack, Stauffenberg passed up his first opportunities for an assassination when he briefed only Hitler at the Berghof near Berchtesgaden on July 6, 11, and 14. Although Göring and Himmler were not present on July 20, 1944, either, on that day Stauffenberg, together with his staff officer, First Lieutenant Werner von Haeften, set the timer of a bomb during a pause between several preliminary briefings in Hitler's "Wolf's Lair" headquarters near Rastenburg. Since they were disturbed while doing this, Stauffenberg was able to set only half of the explosives that he had brought with him to detonate. When he entered the conference barracks, he placed the explosive device, which was hidden in his briefcase, by the large map-table near Hitler, who had already begun the discussion of the military situation. Stauffenberg then left the room under the pretext that he had to make another telephone call. The bomb detonated at about 12:45 P.M., but the explosion was too weak to kill Hitler. The dictator was only slightly injured. Yet Stauffenberg assumed that Hitler as well as several other participants at the conference were dead.

In spite of the alarm that was sounded, Stauffenberg and Haeften succeeded in leaving Führer Headquarters and in flying back to Rangsdorf. They did not arrive in Berlin until nearly four hours later, however. The coconspirators around General Friedrich Olbricht and Colonel Mertz von Quirnheim had not yet sounded an alarm there. Not until Stauffenberg assured them that Hitler could not have survived the blast did they issue an alarm to military circles according to the "Walküre" plan and proclaim the death of Hitler. However, they could not move General Fromm, the commander of the army reserve, to cooperate with them. Instead, he had to be arrested by Stauffenberg, who arrived at the Army High Command (OKH) in the Bendlerstrasse at about 4:30 P.M. General Hoepner, who had been arbitrarily dismissed by Hitler in 1942 and was a coconspirator, took over Fromm's post. Although Stauffenberg repeatedly responded to the numerous questions from military circles, army staff headquarters, and front headquarters by stating that Hitler was dead and that General Beck and Field Marshal von Witzleben had assumed leadership, he could not silence doubts about his statement. As more and more commanders and officers — such as Major Remer, commander of the Berlin Guard Battalion — heard directly from Führer Headquarters that Hitler was alive and received their orders from there, the conspirators' plan started to go sour. It was lost when there was an official radio report that Hitler had survived the assassination attempt.

Orders from the Bendlerstrasse were not followed in most military circles; people preferred to wait things out. In Prague, Vienna, and Paris, however, there were arrests of local SS leaders. When the soldiers of the Berlin Guard Battalion switched over to the side of the dictator, a countermovement of officers loyal to Hitler formed from among Fromm's and Olbricht's staff on Bendler-Strasse. They succeeded in freeing Fromm. This resulted in a shooting spree in which Stauffenberg was hit. For his part, Fromm then arrested Retired General Beck, Retired General Hoepner, General Olbricht, Colonel von Stauffenberg, Colonel Mertz von Quirnheim, and First Lieutenant von Haeften shortly before midnight.

While Beck and Hoepner were given the opportunity to shoot themselves, an opportunity that Hoepner declined, Fromm had the remaining four arrested men summarily shot by a special commando in the yard of the OKH building after midnight. Hoepner and other coconspirators who were also being held in the building in the Bendlerstrasse were handed over to the SS commando that soon forced its way into the building. The attempted coup d'état led by von Stauffenberg was thus thwarted and failed.

GERD R. UEBERSCHÄR

Bibliography

Hoffmann, Peter. *Widerstand: Staatsstreich, Attentat: Der Kampf der Opposition gegen Hitler.* Munich, 1985.
Ueberschär, Gerd R., ed. *Der 20. Juli 1944: Bewertung und Rezeption des deutschen Widerstandes gegen das NS-Regime.* Cologne, 1994.

Jung Conservatives. *See* Edgar Jung Circle.

Juvenile "Gangs of Four." Independently and without knowledge of one another, small oppositional youth groups arose in Hamburg, Munich, and Vienna in 1941 and agitated in flyers and graffiti for toppling the National Socialist regime. Each of these groups was comprised of four male youths between the ages of sixteen and eighteen and had a clearly outstanding, active, and precocious leader: Helmuth Hübener in Hamburg, Walter Klingenbeck in Munich, and Josef Landgraf in Vienna. The members of all three groups came primarily from Christian-oriented families of the lower and lower-middle classes. Listening to so-called enemy broadcasters, especially programs of the BBC, played an important role for all of them. None of the three groups had a well-formulated political agenda, yet they all more or less fervently hoped for a victory by the Western opponents in the war.

Through contacts to youths from Communist families, the Hamburg administrative apprentice Helmuth Hübener had been motivated to listen to German-language broadcasts by the BBC and other broadcasters. He acquired his own receiving device at the end of April 1941. In the summer of 1941, Hübener invited his friends Karl-Heinz Schnibbe and Rudi Wobbe, individually and without their knowing of each other, to listen to foreign broadcasters. Schnibbe and Wobbe as well as Hübener were members of the Hamburg Mormon congregation.

In contrast to most other Christian denominations, the Mormons knew relatively well how to get along with the National Socialist regime. Hübener in fact secretly wrote his flyers on a typewriter from the Mormon congregation. He seems to have been motivated to begin preparing the flyers by a request from Schnibbe to transcribe news broadcasts for him that he had missed. At the beginning of August 1941, Hübener convinced Schnibbe and Wobbe to help in distributing the flyers in mailboxes, telephone booths, and building entrances in the Hamburg districts of Hammerbrook and Rothenburgsort. At the beginning of 1942, he also convinced his colleague Gerhard Düwer to help. The flyers produced by Hübener — between three to five copies of a total of approximately sixty — contrasted, among other things, official Wehrmacht reports with news reports from "enemy broadcasters," attacked antireligious National Socialist propaganda, criticized the "weekend detention" that had been introduced, or made fun of Joseph Goebbels in rhymes. In the flyer "Who Is Hounding Whom?" which was not completed because of his arrest, Hübener emphasized the defensive motives for America's entry into the war.

At the beginning of February 1942, Hübener was turned in by a supervisor who had seen Hübener unsuccessfully try to convince another apprentice to translate a flyer into French for distribution among foreign workers. On August 11, 1942, Hübener was sentenced to death by the People's Court in Berlin for preparations for high treason and other offenses. His three codefendants, Schnibbe, Wobbe, and Düwer, received prison sentences of between four to ten years. Hübener was decapitated in Berlin-Plötzensee on October 27, 1942.

Influenced by broadcasts from Vatican Radio, which he listened to with his father since the beginning of the war, and by the forced disbandment of his Catholic youth group, Walter Klingenbeck developed a critical stance toward the National Socialist regime quite early. Although listening to foreign broadcasters was outlawed in September 1939 and stood under the threat of draconian punishments, Klingenbeck continued to listen to Vatican Radio, the German-language service of the BBC, and other "enemy broadcasters." During the spring and summer of 1941, he told his friends Hans Haberl and Daniel von Recklinghausen about these broadcasts and invited them to listen to the broadcasts with him.

In the summer of 1941, Klingenbeck took up the BBC's appeal to spread the victory sign as a symbol of the Allies' victory and, assisted by Recklinghausen, painted this sign in large varnish letters on approximately forty buildings in Munich. He planned to distribute flyers with the motto "Hitler Can't Win the War, He Can Only Prolong It" and worked together with his friends, who not only had the same Catholic background as he but also shared his passion for building radios, in constructing their own radio for transmitting anti-Nazi propaganda.

After foolishly bragging about his having painted the victory signs, Klingenbeck was denounced and arrested on January 26, 1942; Haberl and von Recklinghausen were arrested shortly thereafter. On September 24, 1942, the People's Court sentenced the three to death and sentenced a fourth youth who was peripherally involved to eight years' imprisonment. Although Haberl's and von Recklinghausen's sentences were commuted to eight years' imprisonment on August 2, 1943, Klingenbeck was executed in Munich-Stadelheim on August 5, 1943.

Since the beginning of the war, the Viennese high school student Josef Landgraf listened to BBC broadcasts as well as to the broadcaster "European Revolution," which bore the stamp of socialist emigrés. At the beginning of September, he began to transcribe in flyers what he had heard. Although he was denounced and arrested after just three weeks, he produced on his father's typewriter no fewer than seventy flyers that were one-half to one page long and approximately the same number of leaflets and stickers.

Like Hübener, he contradicted German war propaganda with BBC reports on German losses and condemned the antireligious activities of the National Socialist German Workers' Party (NSDAP). Like Klingenbeck, Landgraf also started a V-campaign and proclaimed in one of his flyers, "The V-army's sole aim is the liberation from Hitler and his war." His schoolmates Ludwig Igalffy, Friedrich Fexer, and Anton Brunner helped him to a rather minimal extent in the production and distribution of the flyers.

Landgraf and Brunner were sentenced to death by the People's Court on August 23, 1942; the two other defendants were sentenced to eight and six years' imprisonment, respectively. One year later, Landgraf's sentence was commuted to seven years' imprisonment; after a retrial, Brunner was sentenced to five years' imprisonment.

JÜRGEN ZARUSKY

Bibliography

Schnibbe, Karl-Heinz. *Jugendliche gegen Hitler: Die Helmuth-Hübener-Gruppe in Hamburg 1941/42.* Berg am See, 1991.

Widerstand und Verfolgung in Wien. Volume 2. Vienna, 1975.
Zarusky, Jürgen. " '...nur eine Wachstumskrankheit?' Jugendwiderstand in Hamburg und München." *Dachauer Hefte 7* (1991).

Kameradschaft (Camaraderie). *See* Youth Opposition.

Kaufmann Group. Franz Kaufmann was a Jew who had been baptized as a Protestant and who was married to a non-Jew. Because of his Jewish origin, he lost his position as senior government counsel in Berlin in 1936. He was a member of the *Confessing Church and had contact through it with many other "half-breeds" and Jews living in "mixed marriages." When deportations began in October 1941, Kaufmann tried to stop or to delay the deportation of individual persons by creating jobs. When this became increasingly difficult, he began to supply some of his Jewish acquaintances with falsified identification cards in 1942. The circle of persons looking for help quickly grew larger.

With help from Ernst Hallermann and Edith Wolff, both "half-breeds," and several other contact persons, some of whom were from the *Chug Chaluzi group, Kaufmann then began to purchase postal identification cards, factory identification cards, driver's licenses, identity cards, and food ration stamps and to sell them to Jews who were living underground. The cost of the falsified documents exactly covered the costs of purchase and of the graphic artists who altered the documents.

In addition, Kaufmann gave shelter to fleeing Jews and provided them with money and food. He cooperated in this with several members of the Confessing Church who had also established contact with the graphic artists. In addition to many individual persons, members of the Chug Chaluzi group also obtained falsified documents from Kaufmann via contact person Edith Wolff.

Kaufmann was able to supply a large circle of Jews who were living underground with personal documents for approximately one year until the denunciation by a Jewish woman who was living underground and who possessed falsified documents from Kaufmann led to the arrest of Kaufmann, Hallermann, and Edith Wolff in August 1943. During the course of investigations, approximately fifty other people, assistants and Jews living underground, were arrested.

The Jews were deported to concentration camps; the non-Jews and "half-breeds" were taken into custody for questioning. In November 1943, eleven prisoners were charged with breaking the War Economy Decree and falsifying documents. In January 1944, seven of those charged were sentenced — they included Ernst Hallermann, who was sentenced to eight years' imprisonment, and Edith Wolff, who was sentenced to two years' imprisonment. Kaufmann himself was not charged because punishable acts committed by Jews were no longer handled by the justice system at this point but by the police. He was held in custody until the verdict was announced against the seven persons who had been charged. He was sent to Sachsenhausen concentration camp in February 1944 and was immediately shot there.

MARION NEISS

Bibliography

Kroh, Ferdinand. *David kämpft: Vom jüdischen Widerstand gegen Hitler.* Reinbek bei Hamburg, 1988.

Kittelbach Pirates. *See* Edelweiss Pirates.

***Klassenkampf* (Class Struggle).** *See* German Socialist Workers' Party (SAPD or SAP).

Klingenbeck Group. *See* Juvenile "Gangs of Four."

Knöchel Organization. In January 1942, central committee member Wilhelm Knöchel was the only leading KPD cadre to succeed in illegally returning to the German Reich from emigration. He followed the instructions of the party leadership in exile in Moscow to revive domestic German resistance after the outbreak of war and especially after the attack on the Soviet Union. Three other leaders who were supposed to work in the central domestic leadership that had ceased to exist in 1935 but that was now to be established anew had already been arrested; among them was Herbert Wehner, with whom Knöchel, in the Netherlands, had sought to discuss how to proceed in Germany. Knöchel, who was supported by a Dutch news group of the Comintern in making his thorough preparations, concentrated on activity in western Germany, as had been discussed. Three instructors who had succeeded in entering the Rhine-Ruhr area in 1941 were supposed to provide lodging and contacts with former comrades in mines and armament factories. Knöchel himself found lodging in Berlin, which had been provided by his colleague Alfred Kowalke.

By February 1942, the first issue of the monthly underground newspaper *Der Friedenskämpfer* (The fighter for peace) was ready for distribution; Knöchel described the newspaper as politically neutral, as beholden to "no particular political, economic, or any other interest group," as written "by German working people for the productive people of Germany," and as serving "only Germany and its people." The title was a platform: the expressed goal was the quick ending of the war with an honorable peace. A type of underground referendum for peace, the "F-Action," was suggested. The letter *F*, the sign for peace, freedom, and progress (*Friede, Freiheit, Fortschritt*), was supposed to inundate the entire country. Parallel to this, *Der Friedenskämpfer* called for the disruption of armament production (using the watchword "work slowdown"), for the sabotage of machines and materials, for the disruption of the transportation system, and for the disregard of appeals to save and to give to winter assistance collections. Like leitmotivs, these calls course through further issues as well as through the newspapers *Freiheit* (Freedom) and *Ruhr-Echo,* which Willi Seng in Wuppertal and Alfons Kaps in Düsseldorf published in 1942.

In addition, the organization, which had taken on two more briefers who had come afterward from the Netherlands, made small posters, flyers, and stickers that were distributed in factories and residential areas by the growing network of contacts. Via various routes, Knöchel distributed information about armament production, the effects of air raids, the mood of the public, and so on. Knöchel also sent copies of his writings to Amsterdam, from where they made their way to Moscow. Party chairman Wilhelm Pieck noted at the time, "We have a man in Germany again." Since Knöchel was the only central committee member on the domestic German front, he was named domestic director by the distant exile leadership in the summer of 1942 — an action without practical consequence, as he continued to concentrate his group's work on western Germany. There is no evidence of any contacts with the Communist organizations that had begun to form in Berlin, Hamburg, Saxony, and Thuringia in 1940–41.

Knöchel's wife, Cilly Hansmann, who, working in Amsterdam, had maintained contacts and provided the group with all of the additional people and material necessary for the group's survival, had just crossed the Dutch border in January 1943 when the organization fell victim to the Gestapo. She was able to return without being noticed and to warn those people in Amsterdam who were endangered: German emigrés and Dutch contacts. Knöchel, who was already ill with tuberculosis before his arrest, made a *va banque* bet against the Gestapo that finally failed due to suspicion on the part of the Gestapo. In the summer of 1944, he was sentenced to death and executed as a terminally ill man in Brandenburg prison. The same sentence was given to twenty-two group members, contacts, and providers of lodging from the circle of more than two hundred persons who were arrested.

BEATRIX HERLEMANN

Bibliography

Herlemann, Beatrix. *Auf verlorenem Posten: Kommunistischer Widerstand im Zweiten Weltkrieg: Die Knöchel-Organisation.* Bonn, 1986.

Kreisau Circle. The term "Kreisau Circle" was first used in the "Kaltenbrunner Reports" of the Reich Security Main Office. These documents, written for Martin Bormann, concerned the July assassination attempt against Hitler. The circle got its name from the Moltke family estate of Kreisau in the Lower Silesian county of Schweidnitz.

About twenty active members of the circle and almost as many sympathizers had connections with the youth movement, especially in Silesia (Silesian Young Men's Club, Boberhaus Circle); with socially active circles such as the Löwenberg Task Force surrounding the "father of the Kreisau Circle," Professor Rosenstock-Huessy (Peter Yorck von Wartenburg, Heinrich von Einsiedel, Helmuth James von Moltke, Carl Dietrich von Trotha, Adolf Reichwein, and Hans Peters); with the Hofgeismar Circle of the Young Socialists (Carlo Mierendorff, Theo Haubach, and Gustav Dahrendort); and with the Jesuit-initiated Catholic Youth Movement New Germany (Father Alfred Delp and Father Lothar König). This is evidence of a young elite that was aware of its intellectual, social, and Christian responsibility in the years of political and economic crisis after World War I.

This elite found its teachers and role models not only in Rosenstock-Huessy but also in the Protestant theologian Paul Tillich, the Social Democratic lawyer Gustav Radbruch, the Christian socialist professor Adolf Löwe, the Jesuit priest Gundelach, and others. After the National Socialist assumption of power, some of these teachers had no other alternative than emigration. Their socialist protégés Reichwein, Mierendorff, and Haubach were sent to concentration camps; bourgeois members such as Hans Lukaschek, the president of the province of Upper Silesia, were removed from office or withdrew to their circles of friends.

A remarkably large number of the members of the Kreisau Circle could look back on rich experiences abroad. Of the inner circle, von Moltke, Adam von Trott zu Solz (a Rhodes scholar), von Einsiedel, von Trotha, Hans-Bernd von Haeften, Eugen Gerstenmaier, Paul van Husen, and the Jesuits Alfred Delp, Lothar König, and Augustin Rösch had studied abroad; others such as Reichwein or the later prison pastor Harald Poelchau had become acquainted with life outside of Germany while on trips abroad.

Independently of each other, Moltke and Yorck had gathered around themselves oppositionally minded friends several years before the war; Yorck had done so in the so-called Counts' Circle. The first meeting between the two groups took place in 1940; beginning in August, Kreisau became the preferred location for the meetings.

The Kreisau Circle was systematically expanded to include coconspirators who had an area of expertise. Einsiedel brought in the agricultural scientist Fritz Christiansen-Weniger; von der Gablentz, an old acquaintance of Einsiedel, brought in the former Rendsburg district magistrate

Theodor Steltzer. In the spring of 1941, Hans-Bernd von Haeften and Adam von Trott zu Solz, who worked in the Foreign Office, joined the circle; a few months before the outbreak of war, Trott had had discussions with British prime minister Neville Chamberlain, foreign minister Lord Halifax, and others about the plans of oppositional circles in Germany. Van Husen, a lawyer in the High Command of the Armed Forces, also began to participate in the meetings in 1941.

The Jesuit provincial of Upper Germany, Father Augustin Rösch (see *Rösch Circle), and his fellow Jesuits Delp and König were won over through Baron Karl-Ludwig von und zu Guttenberg. Also in 1941, Moltke renewed old contacts with the constitutional lawyer Hans Peters, and he formed new contacts with Otto John, who was working in the Counterintelligence Office at the time, and with Pastor Poelchau, who, along with Peters, quickly became a member of the inner circle. In the following year, Moltke made a greater effort to win over the churches. Of his contacts with high Catholic officials (such as those with Faulhaber in Munich, Bertram in Breslau, Gröber in Freiburg, and Dietz in Fulda), that with Berlin bishop Count Preysing turned out to be the most valuable, as can be seen in van Husen's remarks concerning oaths and resistance law at the third Kreisau meeting.

Eugen Gerstenmaier — who worked in the service of the Foreign Office but had been a member of the Ecclesiastical Foreign Office of the evangelical church — made contact with State Bishop Wurm, one of the exponents of church resistance among Protestants. Discussions with the bishops made it clear, however, that the churches were not prepared to resist the National Socialist state openly.

The stated goal of the Kreisau Circle was to supersede National Socialism with an ethically founded concept of the state and government based on human rights; further, it intended, on this basis, to train a capable elite that was aware of its responsibility. In order to do this, it was necessary to mobilize all segments of society, including the working class. Moltke was able to convince the reform pedagogue Reichwein, whom he knew from the days of the Silesian labor camp movement, to help, as well as the former SPD Reichstag representative Carlo Mierendorff and Theo Haubach, Carl Severing's former press agent. Because of the controversy among the members of the circle surrounding central trade unions, there never was any close cooperation with the respected former Hessian minister of the interior Wilhelm Leuschner, who sent Hermann Maass to the circle as a representative. Leuschner also backed Carl Goerdeler, who, after a personal exchange of views in January 1943, was rejected as too reactionary by the other Social Democrats but also by Delp and finally by Moltke and Yorck.

Of the contacts to other resistance circles and figures — such as the Freiburg circle of professors around Walter Eucken (see *Freiburg Circles), the Speer Circle in Bavaria, former Merseburg president Ernst von Harnack, Albrecht Haushofer, and others — the contact with Fritz-Dietlof von der Schulenburg remained especially important after his participation in the discussions of Yorck's Counts' Circle. Through von der Schulenburg, contacts were made with the national-conservative camp around Goerdeler and Beck; despite doubts, Beck and the others agreed on Goerdeler as the future Reich chancellor.

The Kreisau Circle's activities were not confined solely to working out theoretical concepts. Von Moltke, in particular, had called for Hitler's overthrow; he did this quite early on through Beck, through Halder in the winter of 1941–42, and, one year later, through Field Marshal von Kluge. The generals' uncertainty about the behavior of the younger officers and the troops, as well as the rejection of assassination as a means of getting rid of Hitler, proved to be substantial impediments to the realization of this idea.

Nor was there any support from abroad. All of von Moltke's and von Trott's attempts to find paths of cooperation with the Allies through contacts in England (Lionel Curtis, Lord Lothian, and Michael Balfour) and Sweden failed due to the governments' mistrust even after the beginning of the war. The same is true of von Trott's efforts to make contact with government circles in Turkey through old acquaintances (Ambassador Kirk and Dorothy Thompson). Contacts with resistance organizations in the occupied countries of Norway, the Netherlands, and Denmark were more positive.

At the meetings in Kreisau, at Yorck's estates in Klein-Öls and Kauern, and at Ernst von Borsig's estate in Gross-Behnitz in the vicinity of Berlin, the participants frequently came together, for security reasons, in small workgroups that had been set up to discuss problems such as the structure of the state, foreign policy, economics, agriculture, social policy, and culture. The first large meeting of the members was on Whitsunday 1942 and was dedicated to the relation between church and state, specifically to the concordat and the reform of the educational and university system; the second meeting in October 1942 addressed the future structure of the state and of the economy. Next to questions of economic regulation (self-government, factory trade unions), the primary topic of discussion at the third meeting in June 1943 concerned the punishment of the National Socialist war criminals by special courts.

The conclusions of the Kreisau meetings were summarized in the summer of 1943 in the *"Principles for the New Order" and in a new version of "Punishment of Violators of Justice." The "First Instruction for Governors," which was drawn up at the same time, addressed a circle of persons (including Lukaschek for Silesia) who were supposed to take over civil administration in the states, in the Prussian provinces, and in Austria when the National Socialist regime was toppled.

In the foreground of the plans stood the renewal of the state and its relation to the individual, the economy, labor, and the churches. The concept of the proposed state was basically the exact opposite of the National Socialist criminal state, although it did emphasize that humankind's depersonalization in modern liberal mass society had to be overcome by integration with the historically mature *Volk*. In view of the experiences of the Weimar Republic, the executive branch was granted no legislative powers; the Reich chancellor with his cabinet consisting strictly of specialized ministers was supposed to be capable of being toppled only by a constructive vote of no confidence. With the dissolution of Prussia and Bavaria, the states were to correspond to the old German tribes and regions, and Germany was to be integrated into a European federal state. A condition for this European state — which was also to exclude Russia — was the rapprochement with France and Poland. There was no consensus on the question of the possible secession of regions of Germany (such as Silesia).

The economy, like the state, was supposed to be organized from the bottom up and run by organs of self-government. There was to be state control to protect against unhealthy social developments as well as to determine salaries and prices. Central trade unions remained a point of contention. As a precondition for the people's participation in political life, there were to be appropriate training and education, and these were to be realized by, among other methods, the restraint of the influence of the state and the strengthening of parents' rights and of the churches' role in education. Christianity was to be the formative basis of all aspects of culture.

In the course of the Gestapo's investigations of the *Counterintelligence Office (Abwehr), von Moltke was arrested in January 1944 and sent to Ravensbrück concentration camp. After Leber and Reichwein were turned in by an informant for having contacts with a Communist group, von Yorck and Haubach pushed the military to carry out the assassination of Hitler quickly. Von Yorck, von Trott zu Solz, and von Haeften offered their assistance to the assassins on July 20, 1944. They were executed in August 1944. Reichwein and Leber also lost their lives. The Gestapo did not recognize Moltke's role in the Kreisau Circle until late; he was executed in January 1945 with Haubach and Sperr. In February 1945, Father Delp was the last person of the Kreisau Circle to be executed. Steltzer survived his death sentence due to the intervention of Swedish friends. Most of the others were liberated from prisons by Allied troops; some remained unfound by the authorities until the end of the war.

HERMANN WEISS

Bibliography

Graml, Hermann. "Die außenpolitischen Vorstellungen des deutschen Widerstandes." In *Der deutsche Widerstand gegen Hitler.* Edited by W. Schmitthenner and H. Buchheim. Cologne, 1966.

Moltke, Albrecht von. "Die wirtschafts-und gesellschaftspolitischen Vorstellungen des Kreisauer Kreises innerhalb der deutschen Widerstandsbewegung." Ph.D. diss., Cologne, 1989.

Roon, Ger van. *Neuordnung im Widerstand: Der Kreisauer Kreis innerhalb der deutschen Widerstandsbewegung.* Munich, 1967.

Landgraf Group. *See* Juvenile "Gangs of Four."

League of German Bible Study Groups. *See* Youth Opposition.

Lechleiter Group. From 1940 to 1942, this Communist underground network functioned in the Rhine-Neckar region. It was named after its leader, Georg Lechleiter. Lechleiter, a trained typesetter, was a cofounder of the German Communist Party (KPD) in Mannheim in 1919 and afterward was a full-time party functionary; he was secretary of the KPD's regional directorate in Baden from 1920 to 1922 and a member of the Baden state parliament from 1925 to 1933. He was arrested in March 1933 and spent two years in the concentration camps of Ankenbukhoff and Kislau. After his release, he worked as a digger and again as a typesetter beginning in 1937.

The loose personal contacts that he made with former KPD members and fellow political prisoners after his release from prison solidified in 1940 to form a stable network (a network of "Red Aid") for helping the families of political prisoners. After the German attack on the Soviet Union in 1941, the network was developed into a KPD underground organization on the basis of factory groups consisting of three persons. From September to December 1941 in Mannheim and Heidelberg, the group leadership, together with Jakob Faulhaber, produced between fifty and two hundred copies of four issues of the underground platform *The Herald: Informational and Militant Organ Against Hitler's Fascism; Publisher: Communist Party.* It was distributed to reliable people in large Mannheim factories and especially to former Communists, but also to Social Democrats and persons without political affiliation.

In February and March of 1942, fifty to sixty group members were arrested, and thirty-two of them were put on trial. Nineteen members were sentenced to death and executed; three others died while in custody for questioning.

JAN FOITZIK

Bibliography
Matthias, Erich, and Hermann Weber, eds. *Widerstand gegen den National-sozialismus in Mannheim.* Mannheim, 1984.

Leftist Splinter Groups. *See* Anarcho-Syndicalists; German Communist Party/Opposition (KPDO or KPO); German Socialist Workers' Party (SAPD); International Socialist Combat League (ISK); New Beginning; Red Militants; Socialist Resistance; Trotskyites.

Left Opposition of the KPD (Bolsheviks-Leninists). *See* Trotskyites.

Leipzig Hound Packs. Oppositional groups operated in Leipzig from 1937 to 1939 and were called "hound packs" by the police. Their members were usually youth workers, some of whom had belonged to the Hitler Youth for years. They rejected National Socialism and demonstrated this — with variations from "hound" to "hound" — by their behavior and their clothing (youth movement shoes, white knee-high stockings, short leather or ski pants, checkered shirts or blouses, and so on), which had their origins in the youth movement. Some of the approximately five hundred boys and girls who comprised the hound packs came from the outlawed or disbanded children's and youth groups of the workers' movement, such as the Red Young Pioneers (KPD), Red Falcons, and Friends of Children (SPD), or had contact with the Communist resistance movement.

The three largest groups had formed independently of one another in the working-class districts of Leipzig in 1936–37. The hound packs that have so far become known took their various names from the places where they met, such as "Hundestart" (from a dog-walking area in an old cemetery in the district of Kleinzschocher), "Lille" (based on the name Lilienplatz in Reudnitz), and "Reeperbahn" (from an area in Lindenau that had many cinemas and pubs). Some hound pack members put up political resistance, such as those who were arrested by the Gestapo in June 1939. The youth of the "Reeperbahn" pack were accused of distributing leaflets saying "Down with Hitler," and they were also accused of tearing down swastika banners and of damaging showcase windows with a glass-cutter (the display had been specially decorated for the führer's birthday). Of the thirty-three identified members of this pack, three were twenty years old, two were nineteen, seven were eighteen, nine were seventeen, eight were sixteen, and four were only fifteen years old.

In Leipzig and Dresden between 1938 and 1940, there were several trials against the criminalized and targeted core groups of the hound packs. Most of the trials ended with long-term prison and penitentiary sentences or with commitment to the Mittweida youth correctional camp.

KURT SCHILDE

Bibliography

Gruchmann, Lothar. "Jugendopposition und Justiz im Dritten Reich: Die Probleme bei der Verfolgung der 'Leipziger Meuten' durch die Gerichte." In *Miscellanea: Festschrift für Helmut Krausnick zum 75. Geburtstag.* Edited by Wolfgang Benz. Stuttgart, 1980.
Kircheisen, Sabine. "Jugendliche Opposition gegen den Hitlerfaschismus: Die Leipziger Meuten 1937–1939." *Jugendgeschichte* (University of Rostock) 12 (1990).

Leninist Organization (LO). *See* New Beginning; Socialist Resistance.

Lenin League. *See* Socialist Resistance; Trotskyites.

Liberal Resistance. *See* Strassmann Group.

Löwenberg Task Force. *See* Kreisau Circle.

Lutetia Circle. *See* Committee for the Preparation of a German People's Front; Exile and Resistance.

Malik Publishing House. *See* Resistance against National Socialism before 1933.

Michael. See Youth Opposition.

Military Subversion and Desertion. During World War II, the attempt by draftees and soldiers to evade military service, to desert, or to oppose the conduct of the war in another way was usually prosecuted by courts-martial of the Wehrmacht justice system as military subversion or desertion.

After the attack on Poland, individual German and Austrian Catholics and Protestants refused military service for religious reasons — without the support of their churches. Most conscientious objectors were *Jehovah's Witnesses, who, already before the war, had opposed the National Socialist state's claim to omnipotence by steadfastly refusing all military or coerced service. Between 1939 and 1945, the Reich Court-Martial sentenced more than 250 religiously motivated conscientious objectors. Some conscientious objectors were handed over to a penal battalion of the *parole units for particularly severe service.

The basis for prosecution was the Special Wartime Penal Code of August 26, 1939. It was seen as a penal "mobilization measure" and was made increasingly severe during the course of the war. The code sought to nip in the bud any "agitation hostile to the military" or other "manifestations of subversion" (that is, any resistance whatsoever) in order to "achieve final victory." The infamous paragraph 5 of the code included an entire batch of activities under the rubric "subversion of military potential." This included "defeatist" statements, public doubt or criticism of the leadership, self-mutilation, fakery or other forms of evading military service, as well as incitement to desertion or "subversion." There were nearly thirty thousand court-martial convictions, including approximately five thousand death sentences, for military subversion. The People's Court and the Special Courts ma ie use of this provision especially during the second half of the war ь. order to suppress growing discontent within the population.

Paragraph 70 of the Military Penal Code provided for the death sentence or severe prison sentences in case of desertion during wartime. Hitler's guidelines of April 14, 1940, called for the death sentence if the deserter had acted out of fear for his personal safety or if the "maintenance of military discipline" required it. During the course of the war, decrees by the Wehrmacht leadership required increasingly severe action in the case of desertion. Since it constituted a violation of the unilateral obligation of the soldier's Wehrmacht oath of "unconditional obedience" and categorical loyalty to the person of Adolf Hitler, desertion was considered to be "disloyalty," a crime against the "military and *Volk* community." Eminent military lawyers branded deserters as "social parasites," "psychopaths," and "subversives" and called them "inferior." The Wehrmacht justice system pronounced approximately thirty-five thousand sentences for desertion, including twenty-two thousand death sentences, of which roughly fifteen thousand were carried out.

The motives and reasons for avoiding military action were manifold and many-layered. Next to conscious political opposition, there were the personal desire to be free and the rejection of the hard military discipline in the Wehrmacht. Especially after the attack on the Soviet Union in June 1941, men were incited to desert because of the circumstances that accompanied the war, the witnessing of war crimes, years of absence from their homeland due to deployments in faraway theaters of war, love for a woman, or familial problems that arose as a result of the bombing war. The frequently inhuman treatment in parole units, special units, and penal battalions was also a motivation for attempts to evade a threatening persecution by fleeing. Many Luxembourgers or Alsatians and Poles who were considered to be "ethnic Germans" refused to be forcefully recruited into the German Wehrmacht. Deserters usually went underground in their homeland or in occupied territories, often in large cities, but also in inaccessible areas within the German Reich. Often supported by women, they had to try to survive underground.

In this manner, many made contact with other groups of persecuted persons and with the resistance. In areas occupied by the Germans, primarily in France and in the Balkans and especially in Greece, deserters joined national resistance groups. Some joined the *National Committee "Free Germany" in the Soviet Union or the Free Germany Movement in western Europe. In addition, the Allies gained in strength by the individual as well as collective desertion of German soldiers to the military foe, after which they were put in POW camps. In the case of the *Parole Units, there were organized desertions of entire companies.

Comparatively few soldiers succeeded in fleeing to neutral foreign countries due to strict border security. Not seldom for political reasons, hundreds sought haven in Switzerland, Sweden, or even in the Vatican. During the final phase of the war, deserters included younger and younger soldiers who had originally been influenced by the National Socialist regime's propaganda about being tough and resolute. Confronted with the reality of collapsing fronts, fear and desperation arose within them, as well as the recognition of the senselessness of the war. Their desertion was usually an expression of their concern for family members, a rejection of the destruction of their homeland, and a statement against a prolongation of the war at any price. By the end of the war, well over one hundred thousand soldiers had deserted the Wehrmacht.

NORBERT HAASE

Bibliography

Haase, Norbert. *Das Reichskriegsgericht und der Widerstand gegen die nationalsozialistische Herrschaft.* Berlin, 1993 (German Resistance Memorial).

Monarchist Resistance in Bavaria. Supported by wide segments of the Bavarian People's Party, an attempt at the end of February 1933 to restore the monarchy under Crown Prince Rupprecht in order to fend off a National Socialist takeover of power in Bavaria failed. The leader of the Bavarian monarchists, Baron Erwein von Aretin, paid for this action by spending many years in "protective custody."

From the circle around the Bavarian Federation for Fatherland and King, there arose under Baron Karl-Ludwig von und zu Guttenberg the journal *Weiße Blätter* (White pages), which, from 1934 until 1942, offered authors such as Reinhold Schneider, Ulrich von Hassell, and Oswald Spengler space for articles stealthily critical of National Socialism. After the federation's self-dissolution in July 1938, a resistance group that drew attention to itself through its oral propaganda primarily in Upper Bavaria formed under the attorney Baron Adolf von Harnier. Josef Zott, a gardener and member of the group, developed the idea of a social monarchy supported primarily by the working class. Crown

Prince Rupprecht, who was for many people a hub of oppositional groups, rejected any association with this group.

Already by 1936, the Gestapo succeeded in planting an informant in this group, which was financed by Prince Erich Waldburg-Zeil. The Gestapo, which, as is shown by surviving documents, was specifically informed of all meetings, bided its time until the group made contact with Communist groups through Alfred Loritz in Switzerland. Between August 3 and 5, 1939, 125 persons were arrested in Munich and Upper Bavaria. The trial was delayed until 1944. Zott was sentenced to death on October 26 and executed on January 16, 1945; many other members of the group were given sentences ranging from three to five years' imprisonment.

There was a special rubric, "actions of Bavarian monarchists," in reports by the Bavarian president until 1945. This led Heydrich to push for the revocation of Crown Prince Rupprecht's citizenship with the argument that Rupprecht was a hub of all oppositional groups in Bavaria. This idea was dropped due to the intervention of Reich Governor von Epp, although the crown prince was refused reentry into Germany after he visited the Italian king in 1940. His family and the family of his son were arrested in 1944 and sent to various concentration camps.

Even though the Harnier/Zott resistance group never had any close contact with the crown prince, there was another monarchically oriented resistance group around Franz Sperr, the former Bavarian envoy in Berlin. Belonging to this group were former Reich defense minister Gessler and Prince Joseph Ernst Fugger-Glött, who made contact with the *Kreisau Circle. This group, which expressed considerable doubts about the plans worked out by Count Helmuth James von Moltke for a new federalistic organization of Germany, was in constant contact with Crown Prince Rupprecht, who was living in Florence.

KARL OTMAR VON ARETIN

Bibliography

Aretin, Karl Otmar von. "Der bayerische Adel von der Monarchie zum Dritten Reich." In *Bayern in der NS-Zeit*. Volume 3: *Herrschaft und Gesellschaft im Konflikt,* edited by Martin Broszat, Elke Fröhlich, and Anton Grossman, 513—64. Munich, 1981.
Bretschneider, Heike. *Der Widerstand gegen den Nationalsozialismus in München 1933–1945*. Munich, 1968.

Mormons. *See* Juvenile "Gangs of Four."

National Committee "Free Germany." Created by the Soviet Union and existing from the summer of 1943 until the autumn of 1945, the National Committee "Free Germany" (NKFD) was an umbrella movement of Communist German emigrés and German officer POWs whose value as a resistance organization against Hitler and the National Socialist regime is debated in historical research and in public opinion.

Accorded great value in the German Democratic Republic (GDR) on the basis of the German Socialist Unity Party's pretenses of having been the "political and organizational center of the German antifascist resistance struggle" and consequently celebrated in journalism and history books as the progressive "militant alliance" of Communists with representatives of the bourgeoisie and nobility, the NKFD and its military members were, in contrast, widely accused in the FRG of high treason and treason. Since resistance was, as a rule, identified with the *July 20, 1944, assassination attempt on Hitler and with the people on the periphery of that assassination attempt — a periphery with which the NKFD had no contact — the "Free Germany" movement was thus, in Scheurig's words, "outcast from the beginning."

This does not change the fact that many military members of the NKFD thought of themselves as opponents of Hitler and his Third Reich. The example of the survivors of the Battle of Stalingrad, who saw their soldierly merits shamefully abused by Hitler, was decisive for this attitude. The horrible experiences and images of the defeat of an entire army still before their eyes, plagued, furthermore, by self-doubts, yet as prisoners of war well-treated psychologically by the Soviet safekeepers in the camps, not a few officers were ready to do something in order to save their comrades and, not last, the German people from a fate similar to that of the Sixth Army. In demonstrative opposition to the National Socialist regime, they wanted to do their part to save large parts of Germany and the German people even by the limited means of "resistance behind barbed wire." All this justified expanding the spectrum of the military segment of the German resistance against National Socialism to include those officers and soldiers who did not want to look on in the Soviet POW camps while Hitler drove the Third Reich into the abyss.

The "Free Germany" movement did not form spontaneously in the summer of 1943 in the Soviet Union. The Soviets had made attempts to motivate German soldiers to resistance against Hitler and his Third Reich at the beginning of the Russian campaign. In doing this, people in Moscow initially counted largely on the supposed strength of the usual "antifascist" slogans to incite disruption and rebellion; these slogans, though, quickly proved to be without success. Not until the conclusion of an arduous process did those persons in the Head Political Administration of the Red Army who were responsible for working with German POWs push for the formation of an umbrella movement consisting of members of the German Wehrmacht who had been taken as POWS and of Communist German emigrés. That arduous process depended on the successful state of military operations on the German-Soviet front (including the Sixth Army's capitulation in the pocket of Stalingrad at the beginning of February 1943), on the negative result of German-Soviet overtures for peace in 1942–43, and on Stalin's disappointment with his Anglo-American allies' failure to open a "second front." Based on the unity and popular front policy that had been agreed upon at the Seventh World Congress of the Communist International and stressing watchwords pertaining to nation rather than to class struggle, a campaign for winning over German POWs began in the early summer of 1943. Stalin's wish to join "all antifascist Germans" in a national committee — a wish that was communicated to the German Communists in Moscow at the beginning of July 1943 by Dmitri Manuilski, the representative of the Central Committee of the Communist Party of the Soviet Union at the Head Political Administration of the Red Army — hastened the development. After Soviet intervention ironed out disagreements between the Communist emigrés and the POWs concerning the phrasing of the founding platform (which was largely in accord with the generally nationally oriented POWs), the National Committee "Free Germany" was established on July 12–13, 1943, in the assembly room of the local council of Krasnogorsk near Moscow.

Approximately three hundred persons took part in the meeting, which was held under the black, white, and red colors of the German Imperial Reich and was, in J. von Puttkamer's words, a "hybrid of a patriotic citizens' meeting and a Marxist party debate." Laying out basic principles in his speech, the writer Erich Weinert (a KPD member) recalled the historic traditions of German-Russian alliance in the Wars of Liberation. At the same time, he called for saving the German fatherland, for toppling Hitler, and for forming "a truly German government" and spoke up for a "strong democratic state power that has nothing in common with the impotence of the Weimar regime." The ratified founding platform ended in the call to German soldiers and officers on the eastern front to remain under arms and, "under conscientious leaders who are at one with you in the struggle against Hitler," to press forward "on the path toward the homeland, toward peace."

Initially belonging to the NKFD were thirteen Communist emigrés (W. Ulbricht, W. Pieck, A. Ackermann, W. Florin, H. Mahle, E. Hoernle, M. Arendsee, G. Sobottka, E. Weinert, F. Wolf, J. R. Becher, W. Bredel, and Baron G. von Wangenheim), twelve officers (including Majors K. Hetz, H. Homann, and H. Stösslein, Captain Dr. E. Hadermann, First Lieutenants E. Charisius, F. Reyher, and F. Rücker, as well as Lieutenants Count H. von Einsiedel, E. Kehler, and B. von Kügelgen), and thirteen junior officers and rank-and-file soldiers (including Corporal M. Klein, Private First Class F. Luddeneit, Privates J. Eschborn, L. Helmschrott, and H. Zippel, and the soldiers O. Sinz, R. Fleschhut, H. Kessler, and E. Kühn). The Communist writer E. Weinert was elected president of the NKFD; Major K. Hetz and Lieutenant Count H. von Einsiedel functioned as vice presidents.

Several high-ranking German officers who had been taken as prisoners of war were also present as guests, yet they refused to become members because of the preponderance of Communist emigrés and other members who had come from the antifascist movement, which was generally controlled by Communists. For that reason, an attempt was made, allegedly by Soviet functionaries, to establish an alliance comprised only of officers and tailored to "the heads of the Wehrmacht." With the Soviets' verbal promise that the Soviet government would back a German Reich "within the borders of 1937" if this officers' alliance succeeded in instigating a coup d'état against Hitler, prominent generals were convinced to cooperate. The path to the establishment of the Alliance of German Officers (BDO) was thus open, and the BDO was created on September 11–12, 1943, in Lunyovo, near Moscow, in the presence of approximately one hundred participants. General W. von Seydlitz-Kurzbach was elected president; Major General A. Edler von Daniels and Colonels Hans-Günther van Hooven and L. Steidle functioned as vice presidents. Members of the executive committee also included Brigadier Generals Dr. O. Korfes and M. Lattmann.

Plans for making the officers' alliance into a POW interest group for purposes such as fulfilling demands, registering prisoners, preparing lists of the dead, and protecting the rights of POWs in accordance with the Geneva and Hague Conventions quickly proved to be illusory. Already apparent at the BDO's founding meeting, efforts to merge the BDO into the NKFD were quickly realized on September 14, 1943. In so doing, the NKFD had to bow to the BDO's demand that it restrict its activities to the Wehrmacht leadership and avoid any acts of sabotage. This expanded the National Committee to include eleven members from the BDO (von Seydlitz, Lattmann, Korfes, Edler von Daniels, Steidle, van Hooven, Major E. von Frankenberg und Proschlitz, the Wehrmacht pastors J. Kayser and J. Schröder, court-martial adviser I. von Knobelsdorff-Brenkenhoff, and First Lieutenant H. Gerlach), three emigrés (R. Herrnstadt, H. Matern, and T. Plivier), and three members of the antifascist movement (junior officers G. Klement and T. Grandy and Private H. Gossens); the NKFD's presidium was expanded to include Generals von Seydlitz and Edler von Daniels as well as M. Emendörfer, a soldier.

The merger of the NKFD and BDO to form the "Free Germany" Movement had no effect on the generally "left-wing" position of the committee's members and on the generally "right-wing" stance of the representatives from the officers' alliance. Their differing importance was also manifest in their separate accommodations: while the members of the military were housed in their POW camplike area in Lunyovo

(Camp Number 20), the Communist emigrés resided in a building in Moscow (Institute Number 99), which housed the office of the committee's president, Weinert, the editorial offices of the newspaper and radio stations, and the office of the Soviet liaison. The political emigrés no doubt had a greater influence on the city committee, the NKFD's actual nerve center; toward the end of the war, this "left-wing" of the "Free Germany" Movement clearly determined its political direction.

The great publicity in the radio and in the press that the Soviets made of the founding of the NKFD and the BDO gave rise to the impression that the movement was a means by which Moscow wished to pressure its Western allies finally to open the "second front." Even though the establishment of the NKFD was seen this way in London and Washington, there is much to be said for the idea that the "Free Germany" Movement was primarily intended in the summer of 1943 to incite the German Wehrmacht leadership or the domestic German opposition to topple Hitler and to bring about a cessation of hostilities. These steps were to be made easier by the surprising establishment of the NKFD; directed toward the demand of unconditional capitulation, the establishment of the NKFD ran counter to the "anti–Hitler coalition's" policy principle toward Germany, was supposed to make these steps easier, and was to give the German people a signal of Moscow's general willingness to work together with a Germany without Hitler. Most of all, a sign was to be given to the Wehrmacht or to a domestic German front in order to provide the conditions for an immediate cessation of hostilities on the German-Soviet front by toppling the dictator. If Hitler were eliminated, then it was primarily the officers' alliance that could make it easier for Moscow to establish contact with a new Reich government; on the other hand, the "Free Germany" Movement was to be assigned the task of training cadres for a new Germany.

In accordance with its original goal, the NKFD's first main tactical slogan, which was aimed at the elites in the Wehrmacht and in Germany and remained in force until the end of 1943, called for the "pushing back of the army to the borders of the Reich against Hitler's orders and under conscientious leadership" (the NKFD's call of September 24, 1943). After it became clear from the Tehran conference near the end of 1943 that there was general agreement concerning the "anti-Hitler coalition's" war aims, the NKFD leadership saw itself forced at the beginning of January 1944 to change its existing "plan for subversion" (in Scheurig's words), which had hitherto been seen as being valid until the end of the war; this plan included the cessation of hostilities and a desertion to and alliance with the NKFD. Both propaganda plans were expressed in the NKFD's founding proclamation (its manifesto) of July 1943 and in the "Twenty-five Articles for Ending of War" of March 1944.

According to its statutes, the NKFD was composed of a plenary and a Management Committee. The plenary was supposed to meet whenever there were important events and at least once each month. It came together a total of seventeen times, issued statements about current tasks, and agreed on necessary measures. The Management Committee was the executive body of the NKFD and answered to the plenary; it was composed of a president and a vice president from the NKFD, additional elected members, the leading editors of the newspaper, and the radio broadcaster. The Management Committee's tasks included the implementation of the resolutions of the NKFD's plenary; the preparation of the agenda for full meetings of the NKFD; the formulation of immediate responses in the event of new political problems; the issuing of instructions and guidelines for the work of the operational division, editorial offices, and specialist groups; correspondence with agents on the front and in camps; and the care and control of all NKFD publications. The president of the NKFD was simultaneously the chairman of the Management Committee and, as such, maintained contacts with the Soviet authorities.

The Management Committee had the power to entrust appropriate members of the movement with the training and management of specialist groups. Such groups existed for economics (directed by Captain C. Fleischer), social policy (directed by Vice President M. Emendörfer), culture (directed by Brigadier General Dr. O. Korfes), law, ideology, and history. They were initially supposed to compile propaganda and training material for these areas; later, they were to work out instructions for activity in the new Germany. A special task group for ecclesiastical issues, comprised of three Protestant and three Catholic Wehrmacht clerics, was formed in June 1944.

After the NKFD was founded, the POW newspaper *Das freie Wort* (The free word) was replaced by the newspaper *Freies Deutschland* (Free Germany). Beginning on July 19, 1943, it was published weekly and had four pages and a circulation of fifty thousand. Its management answered to an editorial staff that was named by the plenary of the NKFD and that was comprised of free and POW members of the NKFD who had their accommodations in Moscow (L. Bolz, K. Maron, E. Held, and A. Kurella) and Lunyovo (K. Hetz, Lance Corporal Dr. G. Kertzscher, H. Gerlach, and I. von Knobelsdorff-Brenkenhoff). The first editor in chief was R. Herrnstadt, who was replaced by A. Kurella in May 1945; Comintern functionary E. Gerö worked as censor. The Soviet authorities provided the wherewithal for the newspaper's production, especially printing presses and paper.

Capable of being heard in all of Germany, the radio station that was set up specially for the NKFD, "Free Germany," which was located on the outskirts of Moscow and had to answer to the Soviet censor, began broadcasting on July 20, 1943. Most broadcasts were twenty minutes long; there were initially four broadcasts daily on seven shortwave bands and one middlewave band. Beginning in January 1944, there were six broadcasts daily on ten shortwave bands and two middlewave bands. Beginning in May 1945, there were again four broadcasts daily. The theme tune was Ernst Moritz Arndt's "Der Gott, der Eisen wachsen ließ..." (The God who let iron grow...). The station was managed by an editorial staff that was appointed by the NKFD, and its members worked in a Moscow "city editorial office" (K. Fischer, F. Erpenbeck, M. Keilson, and Baron G. von Wangenheim) and in Lunyovo (E. Hadermann and L. Achilles); the editor in chief was A. Ackermann. The broadcasting equipment, recording devices, and power were provided by the Soviets.

The NKFD concentrated its energy on activities of organization on the front and on operations in the POW camps; organization on the front played a special role in its goals. In September 1943, it numbered 350 to 400 people; at the end of 1944, it numbered approximately 1,500 people and, at the end of the war, roughly 1,800 to 2,000 people. Dependent on extensive help from the Red Army, whose own flyer activities competed with the activities of the NKFD, and supported by staffs comprised of dependable "antifascist" POWs, agents of the NKFD were charged with organizing propaganda activities at specific segments of the front. Some were responsible for an entire segment of the Soviet front; some were responsible for a segment of an army; there were also division assistants, who were responsible for a segment of a division; in addition, there were graduates of antifascist schools, agents for POW camps near the front, and technical assistants such as typesetters, printers, electricians, and radio engineers.

Next to flyers, megaphones, and NKFD newspapers, persons working at the front also had at their disposal printing presses, loudspeaker vehicles ("for broadcasting addresses and record albums to the forward positions of the enemy in a dynamic manner"), radio sets, and the Red Army's reconnaissance ("for the dispatching of propaganda material and letters to commanders and family members of POWs in the homeland"). The NKFD's agents at the front were also authorized to return newly captured POWs to German positions ("where, as living witnesses, they could defuse the lie about bad treatment by the Red Army"), to send POWs as envoys when Wehrmacht units were "in particularly hopeless situations," such as encirclements, or "to send through the front line reliable antifascist POWs who carried detailed instructions so that they could work on behalf of the NKFD in the enemy's hinterland." In isolated cases, there is evidence that units of the NKFD, misusing the name "Free Germany," participated in combat against German troops, such as in the battles for Königsberg, Graudenz, Thorn, Danzig, and Breslau.

Because, in Bodo Scheurig's words, Lunyovo and the German army in the east were separated by "unbridgeable gaps," the NKFD's numerous attempts to contribute to a hastening of the defeat of the National Socialist regime by means of propaganda, subversion, or combat were ultimately unsuccessful. Even the entry of Field Marshal F. Paulus, the highest German officer in Soviet captivity, into the BDO after long hesitation did nothing to change this. A typical failure of the BDO's work at the front was the attempt—supported by the personal engagement of President von Seydlitz—to win over the two German corps that were encircled near Tscherkassy in February 1944; the corps preferred to try to break out rather than go over to the side of the NKFD.

The modest successes of the propaganda activity in the camps provided no compensation for the failure of work at the front. Recruitment activities sought to win over new members for the NKFD and the BDO. The BDO's recruitment efforts were carried out by camp agents who concentrated on the four officer camps (Yelabuga, Oranki, Susdal, and Camp 150) and at first met up against a nearly total boycott. In the camps, the NKFD agents who were selected by President Weinert and presidium member Ulbricht showed absolutely no ability to empathize with the situation of the camp inmates, which was characterized by hunger, corruption, exploitation, extortion, and informant activities; in addition, they avoided frank, leavening discussion and counted unquestioningly on the supposed strength of their Marxist-Leninist agitation in lectures, meetings, and group work. They considered it a success if an apathetic crowd of participants at the meetings unanimously approved prepared "resolutions." The crimes committed by the Red Army as it pushed forward into the eastern German territories crippled the NKFD's work and ultimately rendered it untrustworthy.

After the end of the war, there were no longer any reasons for the NKFD's existence, and its dissolution became inevitable. The return of political emigrés and "reliable antifascist" officers and soldiers to Germany left the NKFD and the BDO with a skeleton staff. Weinert's summary report at the last full meeting on November 2, 1945, contained the admission that the goal that had been set — "the overthrow of Hitler by forces from the German people" — had not been reached. In extravagant exaggeration of the work in the camps, though, he stated that the NKFD had become "the political master teacher for millions of POWs in the Soviet Union" and called the cooperation of the NKFD and BDO a model for the new Germany. In addition, Weinert stated that it was not a coincidence that men who had come from the NKFD were now "in leading positions in Germany." Yet he considered the continued existence of the NKFD to be "superfluous" and thus proposed its self-dissolution. The president of the BDO, General von Seydlitz, made statements to the same effect. It was subsequently decided to dissolve the

NKFD and the BDO and to cease publication of the newspaper *Freies Deutschland.*

Whereas Communist emigrés without exception went on under Soviet occupation rule to have careers in the German Communist Party (KPD) and German Socialist Unity Party (SED) and in the state, economy, and society of the Soviet Occupation Zone and the German Democratic Republic (GDR), members of the military establishment who had been in the NKFD and BDO took various paths: graduates of the antifascist schools and other officers and soldiers who were reliable in an "antifascist" sense eventually returned to the Soviet Occupation Zone in order to assume particular functions there (such as the formation of the armed forces in the zone beginning in 1948); the others were sent off to various prisoner camps. Many of them who had made no secret of their anti-Communist views, including many members of the BDO, were accused of war crimes on trumped-up charges and were confronted with long-term prison sentences, as in the case of General von Seydlitz, who, as vice president of the NKFD and president of the BDO until the end, was at first sentenced to death but then had the sentence reduced to twenty-five years' imprisonment.

ALEXANDER FISCHER

Bibliography

Frieser, Karl-Heinz. *Krieg hinter Stacheldraht.* Mainz, 1981.
Scheurig, Bodo. *Freies Deutschland: Das Nationalkomitee und der Bund Deutscher Offiziere in der Sowjetunion 1943–1945.* Revised edition. Berlin, 1993.
———, ed. *Verrat hinter Stacheldraht? Das Nationalkomitee "Freies Deutschland" und der Bund Deutscher Offiziere in der Sowjetunion 1943–1945.* Munich, 1965.
Weinert, Erich. *Das Nationalkomitee "Freies Deutschland."* East Berlin, 1957.

Navajos. *See* Youth Opposition.

Neroth Hikers. *See* Youth Opposition.

Neubauer Group (Neubauer-Poser Group). Communist underground circles around Theodor Neubauer and Magnus Poser were active in Thuringia between 1940 and 1944 under this umbrella term. Theodor Neubauer was a high school teacher and a volunteer in World War I from 1914 to 1917. Having come to the German Independent Social Democratic Party (USPD) via the German Democratic Party and to the German Communist Party (KPD) via the USPD in 1920, he became a member of the Thuringian state parliament in 1921 and was a member of the Reichstag from 1924 to 1933. Active underground after Hitler's assumption of power, he was arrested in August 1933 and imprisoned until April 1939. As an employee in an auto repair shop in Tabarz in Thuringia, he drew together a network of Communist underground circles and resistance groups in Thuringia (including in Gotha, Eisenach, Erfurt, Langensalza, Mühlhausen, and Ruhla), until the end of 1941.

From January 1942, Neubauer worked with Magnus Poser, who had built up Communist underground organizations in Jena, Bad Salzungen, Zella-Mehlis, Suhl, Erfurt, and Weimar. There were ultimately connections in almost fifty locations in Thuringia in the fall of 1943, from which between 560 and 1,500 copies of illegal flyers in German and Russian were distributed.

As of the fall of 1942, Neubauer was also in contact with Franz Jacob and Anton Saefkow in Berlin (*see Saefkow-Jacob Group), Georg Schumann in Leipzig (*see Schumann Group), and Martin Schwantes in Magdeburg (see *Danz-Schwantes Group). At the end of 1943, Neubauer authored the programmatic platform "Situation Report," which constituted the basis of the manifesto "We Communists and the National Committee 'Free Germany,'" which Neubauer worked out together with Jacob, Saefkow, and Schumann between the end of 1943 and the beginning of 1944. Independently of the Moscow KPD leadership's line, the manifesto set down the KPD's old goal of a "dictatorship of the proletariat" in Germany.

Magnus Poser and Theodor Neubauer were arrested on July 14, 1944, in the course of investigations that, in September 1943 and June 1944, led to arrests prior to the assassination attempt on Hitler.

JAN FOITZIK

Bibliography
Glondajewski, Gertrud, and Heinz Schumann. *Die Neubauer-Poser-Gruppe.* East Berlin, 1957.

Neue Politische Briefe **(New Political Letters).** *See* International Socialist Combat League (ISK); Socialist Resistance.

Die Neue Rundschau **(The New Review).** *See* Resistance against National Socialism before 1933.

Neuer Vorwärts **(New Forward).** *See* Exile and Resistance; Socialist Resistance.

New Beginning. With some justification, the Leninist Organization (referred to as the LO and also as the ORG), has a special place of importance among leftist splinter groups. The group, whose history went back to the late 1920s, believed that it could heal the division within the working class in a new, revolutionary unity party. It became known in 1933 as "New Beginning," a name derived from the title of its manifesto. This manifesto was published by Graphia Publishing House — the publisher of the exiled German Social Democratic Party's executive committee — in Czechoslovakia in October 1933. It bore the subtitle "Fascism or Socialism: A Basis for Discussion among Germany's Socialists." It caused an enormous stir in the socialist public abroad and — having been smuggled into Germany in large numbers — among the socialist underground in the Reich because it seemed to offer a theoretical response to the novel practical necessities of underground activity and, most of all, corresponded exactly to the mood and plans of socialists who were underground in the Reich.

Behind the pseudonym "Miles" hid the Berlin left-wing socialist Walter Loewenheim. The child of a Jewish merchant family, Loewenheim had originally been a member of the German Communist Youth Organization (KJVD) and the German Communist Party (KPD), had broken with the KPD in 1927, and had joined the German Social Democratic Party (SPD) in 1929 — certainly not due to social democratic convictions, but rather because he saw in the SPD a corresponding field for political action. His theoretical ideas stood diametrically opposed to the common convictions of the workers' movement that historical development as a whole was moving by natural necessity in the direction of socialism and proletarian revolution and, what was much more, that a chain of fascist dictatorships and new European wars were to be expected, especially as a result of the worldwide economic crisis. Loewenheim believed this could be avoided only if people succeeded in progressively overcoming the historical division in the workers' movement; this, he held, was possible only on the basis of a self-liberation of scientific consciousness and of planned political action derived from it, action by members of the elite who would have to create a new proletarian-revolutionary unity party that would have not only to overcome the division within the working class but also to represent the indispensable subjective factor in the historical process. Only in this manner could the development of society be propelled in the direction of the revolution that was the only guarantee for the continued existence of human culture. And the fight against fascism — according to the analysis after the National Socialist takeover of power — was not a matter of short duration and of foolhardy mass agitation that assumed a rapid collapse of the new system, but rather was a matter that demanded long-term perspectives, careful organizational work, training, and, most of all, a comprehensive system for reporting information.

On the basis of these ideas, which, in view of the historical defeat of the workers' movement at the hands of National Socialism, were comprehensively formulated and explained in the manifesto "New Beginning," Loewenheim began building up the LO in about 1929 by engaging in the most confidential plots and by strictly orienting himself toward the LO's principles. The organization had its hub in Berlin but was soon domiciled in the students' and intellectuals' milieu of Frankfurt and other large German cities through supporters and sympathizers. There is documented evidence that the organization had contact networks in Mannheim, Düsseldorf, and Breslau as well as connections with Thuringia and possibly with Munich.

Prior to 1933, recruits came primarily from activists and participants in the political training programs of the two large workers' parties, but also from disappointed KPD and especially German Communist Party/Opposition (KPO) members (see *German Communist Party/Opposition [KPDO or KPO]); in 1931, the LO was also successful in co-opting a series of leading functionaries from the Berlin Socialist Workers' Youth. The organization's goal was to infiltrate and, in the long term, to take control of the management of the workers' organizations in a covert fashion in order thereby to create the conditions for a revolutionary unity party led by LO/New Beginning cadres.

Of course, these connections cannot be viewed in the sense of normal memberships that existed, for example, in the SPD and KPD. The core of the LO/New Beginning was a highly developed and covertly operating organization of probably no more than 150 cadres, frequently — quite in harmony with the infiltration strategy pursued by New Beginning — functionaries of other workers' organizations or informants who were not members of any organizations and were from the political and economic elites active in sensitive areas. A central committee called the "Circle" was at the top; its members were the brothers Walter and Ernst Loewenheim, Eberhard and Wolfgang Wiskow (the latter had been a former Reichswehr officer and member of the KPD's military or counterintelligence apparatus), as well as Walter Dupré and Franz Schleiter. In 1933, Richard Löwenthal, a former key functionary in the German Communist Youth Organization, and Karl Frank, a former KPD functionary, joined; Frank built up and directed New Beginning's foreign office in Prague. One must also mention Edith Schumann and Vera Franke, who assumed key functions within the organization.

Around this relatively small organization there formed a so-called periphery of sympathizers and co-workers of the most diverse origins and orientations, from the political trade union area to the ecclesiastical area. Until their emigration, Hans Gottfurcht, a member of the Berlin central directorate of the underground employees' trade unions, as well as Hans Jahn from the leadership of the underground Railroad Workers' Trade Union, were in close, if not always unacrimonious, contact with the LO/New Beginning in the years after 1933. Further, in Berlin already by 1933, there were good contacts with the approximately one-hundred-member group called the Religious Socialists, whose leading representative, Erich Kürschner, an evangelical prison-pastor in Berlin-Tegel, was admitted into the cadre organization. The former KPD functionary Werner Peuke, who had built up underground factory groups in Berlin independent of the KPD apparatus after the National Socialist takeover of power, joined New Beginning in the spring of 1934 at the latest and immediately began to play a central role.

The originally sharp separation between the core and the periphery of the organization paled markedly after 1933; the strength of the LO/New Beginning during its initial months underground is estimated at approximately five hundred activists. From underground, the group had already announced its claim to leadership of the workers' movement in the so-called Whitsunday Theses of 1933 and even more clearly in Loewenheim's manifesto "New Beginning." In exile, New Beginning entered into an organizational struggle with the SPD's exiled executive committee, a struggle in which the latter was indeed able to prevail in the long run even though three of its border secretaries, Waldemar von Knoeringen, Erwin Schoettle, and Franz Bögler, secretly belonged to New Beginning (see *Socialist Resistance). Knoeringen even became responsible for the group's entire domestic operation and recruited a network of roughly one dozen underground groups in southern Bavaria for New Beginning's organization.

These tensions in exile were not the least reason why a sharp conflict arose within New Beginning in 1934–35, a conflict in which primarily the old "Circle" around Walter Loewenheim and the foreign office around Karl Frank as well as elements of the domestic cadre organization were at loggerheads. In essence, the issue probably concerned a difference in the estimation of and perspectives for underground work, toward which the Loewenheim group took a generally defensive and defeatist position and the group around Karl Frank assumed a more offensive position.

During the summer of 1935, there was a sort of inner-organizational putsch and a formal deposition of the leadership around Loewenheim; Karl Frank, Richard Löwenthal, and Werner Peuke afterward constituted the new Reich leadership of New Beginning.

HARTMUT MEHRINGER

Bibliography

Joitzik, Jan. *Zwischen den Fronten: Zur Politik, Organisation und Funktion linker politischer Kleinorganisationen im Widerstand 1933 bis 1939/40.* Bonn, 1986.

Kliem, Kurt. *Der sozialistische Widerstand gegen das Dritte Reich, dargestellt an der Gruppe "Neu Beginnen."* Marburg, 1957.

Mehringer, Hartmut. *Waldemar von Knoeringen: Eine politische Biographie.* Munich, 1989.

"New Beginning" ("Aufbruch"). *See* Uhrig-Römer Group.

New Forward (*Neuer Vorwärts*). *See* Exile and Resistance; Socialist Resistance.

New Germany. *See* Kreisau Circle; Rösch Circle.

New Political Letters (*Neue Politische Briefe*). *See* International Socialist Combat League (ISK); Socialist Resistance.

The New Review (*Die Neue Rundschau*). *See* Resistance against National Socialism before 1933.

October 3rd Club. *See* Resistance against National Socialism before 1933; Strassmann Group.

Office of Counterespionage. *See* Counterintelligence Office (Abwehr).

Operation Walküre. *See* July 20, 1944.

opponent (*gegner*). *See* Red Orchestra.

ORG (Leninist Organization). *See* New Beginning.

The Other Germany (*Das andere Deutschland*). *See* Resistance against National Socialism before 1933.

The Other Germany (group). *See* Exile and Resistance.

Paris Daily News (*Pariser Tageblatt*). *See* Exile and Resistance.

***Pariser Tageblatt* (Paris Daily News).** *See* Exile and Resistance.

Parole Units. The history of the parole units is part of the history of the resistance because they included thousands of opponents of the regime who were forced into military service by the National Socialist regime and because numerous resistance activities began in them. On the basis of a Führer Decree issued on December 21, 1940, soldiers who had been convicted by court-martial were deployed for the "maintenance of the front" in temporary suspension of their punishment.

Parole Unit 500 was set up exclusively for soldiers from all three branches of military service who were punished by court-martial and

who, not infrequently, had come into conflict with the military justice system due to insubordination and resistance. The total strength
of Parole Unit 500, which was established in April 1941, was approximately forty thousand to fifty thousand men, including five thousand
Wehrmacht prisoners from the Emsland camps who were sent to "500"
after having completed an aptitude test in the Wehrmacht prison at
Torgau/Fort Zinna. Especially risky deployments of Special Infantry Battalions 500, 540, 550, 560, and 561 on the eastern front were made
at "critical points" and places of "partisan action." Real possibilities
for "parole" hardly existed. Desertions and attempts to defect were
punished with death sentences as a "deterrent." Some members of Parole Unit 500 joined the *National Committee "Free Germany" or the
antifascist committees in Soviet POW camps.

By a decree of the High Command of the Armed Forces of October 2,
1942, offshoots of Parole Unit 999 were established at the military training grounds in Heuberg/Schwäbisch Alb in the middle of October 1942
and in Baumholder in the Palatinate at the end of 1943. They consisted
mostly of persons who had been sentenced by civil courts and persons
who had been excluded from military service as "not fit for duty." Persons who had been sentenced to prison for political reasons or criminal
offenses were deprived of their civil rights and were proclaimed to lack
"worthiness for military service." Of the approximately twenty-eight
thousand "soldiers unfit for military service" in Parole Unit 999, one-
third were victims of political persecution in a strict sense. They included
the entire spectrum of resistance, especially from the workers' movement. Many of them knew one another from the underground and from
the time when they had been persecuted and cooperatively sought contact with the civilian populations and resistance movement in occupied
territories.

Riflery Regiments 961 and 962 were combined into Africa Division
999; via Belgium, France, and Italy, they were then transported to North
Africa to take part in combat there. In addition, there were twelve fortress infantry battalions that were entrusted primarily with garrison and
coast guard duties in Greece as well as several building pioneer battalions that were primarily deployed on German territory until the end of
the war.

Due to the political undependability of the members of Africa Division 999, their combat value was seen as minimal, and the idea of their
being used in the Soviet Union was quickly dismissed. After being stationed in the Aegean Sea and on the Greek mainland and during the
course of retreats in the Balkans, many soldiers in parole units defected
to partisans despite reprisals. Beginning in August 1944, Wehrmacht and
SS prisoners were drafted into "parole"; in November 1944, approximately eight hundred concentration camp prisoners were again placed

in the infamous SS special unit "Dirlewanger." Many of these soldiers defected to the Red Army in December 1944.

The term "parole" conceals the actual character of the parole units as penal units. Being in such units affected soldiers especially with respect to visitation and furlough limitations, and they were subject to spiteful and ruthless treatment, up to the point of severe punishments and death sentences. The parole units were a part of a totalitarian system that placed punishment in the service of the conduct of the war.

NORBERT HAASE

Bibliography

Klausch, Hans-Peter. *Die Geschichte der Bewährungsbataillone 999 unter besonderer Berücksichtigung des antifaschistischen Widerstandes.* 2 Volumes. Cologne, 1987.

People's Front Strategy. *See* Committee for the Preparation of a German People's Front; Communist Resistance; Resistance against National Socialism before 1933.

Popular Opposition. *See* Everyday Acts of Dissent and Disobedience.

"The Prague Manifesto." As the result of long debates, Sopade (the executive committee of the German Social Democratic Party [SPD] in exile) published a programmatic statement in Prague on January 28, 1934, as a document of resistance against the National Socialist dictatorship and as a call to a revolutionary orientation of socialism. A first draft, written by Friedrich Stampfer, Curt Geyer, and Erich Rinner, went through numerous revisions beginning in November 1933. Rudolf Hilferding played a crucial part in the final version, which was approved on January 20, 1934.

Emphasizing Marxist theoretical positions, the "Prague Manifesto of Sopade" of 1934 saw Hitler's dictatorship as a victory of the counterrevolution that had to be overcome by a new revolutionary struggle in order to restore a semblance of the initial situation of 1918. According to the manifesto, the reinstatement of democratic rights had become "a necessity in order to make the workers' movement again viable as a mass movement and to conduct the socialist struggle for liberation again as a conscious movement of the masses themselves." The "struggle for democracy" had thus grown to be a "a struggle for the complete overthrow of the National Socialist state power."

The SPD leaders in exile envisioned a renewed democratic state and a socialist society after the immediate measures that would be taken after the elimination of National Socialism. To this end, the old political apparatus was supposed to be destroyed, and the elites in the bureau-cracy, the justice system, the police, and the military were to be replaced. There was to be a separation of church and state. The immediate con-fiscation of large estates and of heavy industry without compensation as well as the socialization of the large banks seemed to be indispensable as conditions of the revolutionary change. "The despotic system of cen-tralized state power will be broken by the institution of a genuine, free self-government within the unified branched state." The intended social-ization of the entire economy would then be the "means to the final goal of realizing true freedom and equality, human dignity, and the complete development of the individual."

Overcoming the opposition between state and society was propa-gated as an ideal: "Instead of the power state, which rules its subjects by the military, bureaucracy, and the justice system, there will be the self-government of society in which everyone is called upon to work on common tasks." In contrast to the *Goerdeler Circle, which understood the concept of "self-government" primarily to refer to the jurisdictions of the Prussian state parliament, the Social Democrats associated the concept with elements of direct democracy. "The Prague Manifesto" concluded with the impassioned appeal to the German working class to shake off the chains of bondage.

WOLFGANG BENZ

Bibliography

Mit dem Gesicht nach Deutschland: Eine Dokumentation über die Sozial-demokratische Emigration. From the previously unpublished works of Friedrich Stampfer. Edited by Erich Matthias and revised by Werner Link. Düsseldorf, 1968.

"Principles for the New Order." The most important document of the *Kreisau Circle is dated August 9, 1943. Its authors were Count Hel-muth James von Moltke and Count Peter Yorck von Wartenburg. The "Principles for the New Order" summarizes the conclusions of the three large Kreisau meetings and presents a program for Germany's rebuilding in the spirit of Christianity. The working class and the church stand at the center of this program. The document's guiding principles were the restoration of the constitutional state, the guaranty of human rights, and the abandonment of the National Socialist principle of sovereignty in fa-vor of an international order. Self-government with a federal structure from the local level up to the Reich and individual joint responsibility were to constitute the formative elements of the new state. The docu-ment offered an interesting variant on the right of suffrage: the head of every family was supposed to have an additional vote for every child who was not eligible to vote. Political civil servants and men in uniform were to be ineligible for election to the Reichstag, whose members were to be elected indirectly by the state parliaments. The economic program was determined by the principles of state economic control, free competition under state supervision, and the socialization of key industries and by the idea of workers' participation in factory management in factory associations, chambers, and a "German trade union."

WOLFGANG BENZ

Bibliography

Mommsen, Hans. "Gesellschaftsbild und Verfassungspläne des deutschen Widerstandes." In *Widerstand im Dritten Reich: Probleme, Ereignisse, Gestalten.* Edited by Hermann Graml. Reprint. Frankfurt am Main, 1994.
Roon, Ger van. *Neuordnung im Widerstand: Der Kreisauer Kreis innerhalb der deutschen Widerstandsbewegung.* Munich, 1967.

Quakers. *See* Assistance and Solidarity.

Rechberg Group. This underground organization named after the pseudonym of the Heidelberg writer and journalist Emil Henk, who founded the organization, comprised numerous local resistance circles of leftist oppositional Social Democrats in 1933–34. Henk had first studied economics and then the history of literature and was a member of the circle of friends around Carl Zuckmayer, Carlo Mierendorff, and Theodor Haubach. In these surroundings, he drew near to socialist ideas without becoming a party member. Additionally motivated by the arrest of some of his friends, Henk, together with the trained economist Otto Calvi, gathered around themselves in the Heidelberg/Mannheim area a circle of sympathizers after the National Socialist takeover of power. Disappointed by the policy of the leadership of the German Social Democratic Party (SPD), this group worked toward a new socialist beginning underground and wanted to contribute to a quick overthrow of the National Socialist regime.

The Rechberg Group recruited mostly younger activists from the Socialist Workers' Youth and from the Reichsbanner Black Red Gold. According to Henk's plan, the socialist underground apparatus was to consist of a comprehensive system of "elite," strictly covertly operating "nests of resistance" that could be mobilized at a moment's notice for particular actions, such as the liberation of concentration camp inmates. Through couriers, such as future Frankfurt mayor Willi Brundert, who established and maintained contact with groups in Hesse, the ringleaders, based in northern Baden, succeeded in forming a network of resistance circles. Although political training and instruction in covert techniques were initially in the foreground of its work, the Rechberg Group heightened its public propaganda in the spring of 1934 and increasingly cooperated with Sopade (the executive committee of the SPD in exile) resistance in Mannheim and in the Palatinate. The group cooperated with Sopade in order to gain access to its resources (such as underground writings and financial assets). This connection became the group's downfall.

After the Gestapo uncovered the Social Democrats' underground organization in the Palatinate at the end of September 1934, it arrested the leading functionaries of the Rechberg Group shortly afterward. Henk and Calvi were sentenced to twenty months' imprisonment on March 29, 1935. By the end of the 1930s, Emil Henk was in close contact with Mierendorff and Haubach and was a member of the *Kreisau Circle.

GÜNTER BRAUN

Bibliography

Braun, Günter. "Die Sozialdemokraten." In *Widerstand gegen den Nationalsozialismus in Mannheim*. Edited by Erich Matthias and Hermann Weber, with the assistance of Günter Braun and Manfred Koch. Mannheim, 1984.

Red Aid. *See* Hanno-Günther Group/Rütli Group; Lechleiter Group.

Red Banner (Die Rote Fahne). *See* Communist Resistance; Red Orchestra.

Red Falcons. *See* Hanno-Günther Group/Rütli Group; Leipzig Hound Packs.

Red Militants. Even though one must clearly assign the Red Militants to the socialist spectrum among leftist splinter groups, their origins and their self-image go back to radical leftist and soviet traditions within the workers' movement at the end of World War I. They recruited their members primarily from those circles of radical leftist socialists who had returned to the German Social Democratic Party (SPD) via the Spartacus League, the German Communist Party (KPD), and the German Communist Workers' Party (KAPD) during the 1920s and initially assembled primarily around Paul Levi, the former cochairman of the KPD who died in 1930, and around the journal that he published, *Socialist Policy and Economy*. From this circle, which was especially active in training (young) socialists, the Social Scientific Union formed at the end of the 1920s with its seat in Berlin; at that time it had more than eight hundred members who were recruited from all socialist parties and groups. The criteria for acceptance were an interest and cooperation in theoretical questions concerning the workers' movement and sponsorship by an active member.

Like other left-wing socialist groups that saw the danger of National Socialism more realistically than the KPD, this circle, which strove to build itself up as a cadre organization beginning in about 1930 and which, based in Berlin, spread out over the entire area of the Reich, gained ground in all organizations of the workers' movement, sometimes in a covert manner. The name "Red Militants" was derived from a left-wing social democratic journal of the same name in western Germany that came under the group's influence in 1931.

In 1933, the Red Militants, who had begun preparing in the middle of 1932 to go underground, comprised a series of groups in Berlin, Saxony, and the Rhine-Ruhr area and numbered roughly four hundred members, primarily young workers, under the Reich leadership in Berlin, of which Arthur Goldstein, Karl Schröder, Alexander Schwab, and Kurt Stechert were members; Bernhard Reichenbach was another influential personality. The goal of their program was to build up a movement on sound, soviet bases. For information about resistance by the Red Militants under National Socialism, see *Socialist Resistance.

HARTMUT MEHRINGER

Bibliography

Foitzik, Jan. *Zwischen den Fronten: Zur Politik, Organisation und Funktion linker politischer Kleinorganisationen im Widerstand 1933 bis 1939/40.* Bonn, 1986.

Ihlau, Olaf. *Die Roten Kämpfer: Ein Beitrag zur Geschichte der Arbeiterbewegung in der Weimarer Republik und im Dritten Reich.* Meisenheim am Glan, 1969.

Red Orchestra. "Red Orchestra" is a general term that was used by German military counterintelligence for various groups in France, Belgium, Holland, and Switzerland that worked for the Soviet military information service during the initial years of World War II. Information pertinent to the war was passed on to Moscow on a large scale.

One must distinguish the Red Orchestra in Germany from these groups. In August 1942, the decoding department at Army High Command (OKH) deciphered a radio address that had been broadcast from Moscow in October 1941. In the address, the Moscow Head Office had called on its resident in Brussels, "Kent," to go to Berlin. Subsequently, follow-up investigations of Adam Kuckhoff and Harro Schulze-Boysen, who were named in the address, began. The department of the Reich Security Main Office that was conducting the investigation (which was looking into "acts of sabotage, parachute and radio agents, and counterfeiting") classified the largest proportion of the women and men of Berlin resistance circles who had been arrested at the end of 1942 and beginning of 1943 as belonging to the western European network of the "Red Orchestra." After 1945, this view of an espionage organization working in the service of an enemy power largely determined disputes over the historical position of the group around Arvid Harnack and Harro Schulze-Boysen in the German resistance against National Socialism.

New studies of groups and individuals in the resistance make it clear that stylized Western interpretations of espionage and treason, which were closely tied in to the political development of postwar history, and eastern European interpretations of a resistance group that was oriented toward the decisions of the KPD leadership in Moscow and served as a spy group for the Soviet Union were erroneous. The German groups had roots that belie these erroneous assumptions. Indeed, the first contacts of individual women and men from the older resistance groups already existed during the final period of the Weimar Republic. In school reform projects, in groups of the youth movement, in the Communist Youth League, in the editorial offices of *Die Rote Fahne* (The red banner), and in the artists' milieu, the first friendships and discussion contacts formed in circles outside of traditional political institutions, such as around the journal *gegner* (opponent), which was published by Harro Schulze-Boysen, and the Arplan Society, which was founded by Arvid Harnack and was devoted to the study of the Soviet planned economy.

As early as 1933, a circle met in the home of Arvid and Mildred Harnack and included academics, artists, and students, particularly from the Berlin night school. The training and education work practiced by Harnack was supposed to enable the participants to understand economic and political realities and to prepare them for the period after National Socialist rule. The Religious Socialist and former Prussian minister of culture Adolf Grimme sometimes took part in the discussions. Arvid Harnack, who began working in the Reich Ministry of Economics in 1935, had confidential exchanges of opinion with representatives of the American and Soviet embassies.

After his entry into the Reich Aviation Ministry in April 1934, Harro Schulze-Boysen surrounded himself with a large circle of friends. In the middle of the 1930s, a smaller discussion group formed. Its members were Harro and Libertas Schulze-Boysen; Walter Küchenmeister, who was a communist but not a member of the party; the physician Elfriede Paul; Gisela von Pöllnitz, who worked for United Press; the sculptor Kurt Schumacher and his wife, Elisabeth; the Communist Walter Husemann, who was released from Buchenwald in the fall of 1938, and his wife, Marta; the writer Günther Weisenborn; and the dancer Oda Schottmüller. Evening social gatherings and group excursions, a regular exchange of opinions concerning artistic, political, and philosophical questions, help for Republican Spain and the families of persecuted persons, and the production of flyers strengthened the group's solidarity and were the manifestation of its initial organized oppositional activities.

A particular intellectual and artistic milieu set the tenor for loose forms of meeting and communication that got along largely without rigid organization or covert rules. The internal differentiation was heightened by the exchange of opinions that began between Schulze-Boysen and Harnack in 1940, by the joining of the groups surrounding the two men, and by the expansion of the group to include the circle of Youth Communists around the worker Hans Coppi, the group around the psychoanalyst John Rittmeister, and the discussion group around the actor Wilhelm Schürmann-Horster. Young people such as Cato Bontjes van Beek, Horst Heilmann, Liane Berkowitz, Eva-Maria Buch, Heinz Strelow, Fritz Thiel, and others joined; the decisive phase of their socialization lay in the period of National Socialism. Some of them participated in activities such as the drafting and distribution of the flyer "Concern about Germany's Future Pervades the People" and the pasting up of stickers against the anti-Soviet propaganda exhibition "The Soviet Paradise." After 1939, contacts were strengthened though Wilhelm Guddorf and John Sieg, former editors of *Die Rote Fahne,* with cells of the Communist resistance in Berlin and Hamburg that were operating independently of the party leadership in Moscow.

At the beginning of the 1940s, the various resistance circles, which partially overlapped and also influenced one another, came together on the basis of personal contacts to form an umbrella movement that can be called an organization. Its members gave information to one another, analyzed the reality of the National Socialist state, documented crimes against humanity as evidence material, and described crimes in flyers, thereby addressing a small public and attempting to win new recruits for their struggle. Meetings and social gatherings were often the pretense for coming together discreetly with other opponents of the National Socialist regime. New contacts were opened to a group in Heidelberg, to the group around Robert Uhrig (see *Uhrig-Römer Group), and to French forced laborers in Berlin. There were discussions with Albrecht Haushofer, with men of the *Kreisau Circle such as Horst von Einsiedel, Hans Peters, Carl Dietrich von Trotha, Adam von Trott zu Solz, and Count Fritz-Dietlof von der Schulenburg, as well as with Curt Bley, Hans Zehrer, and others.

In the autumn of 1940, Alexander Korotkow, who was employed in the Soviet embassy in Berlin and worked for the Soviet news service, established contact with Arvid Harnack. At the end of March 1941, Harro Schulze-Boysen joined the discussions and reported what he knew of military plans and preparations for the attack on the Soviet Union. Harnack and Schulze-Boysen worked out policy options for eastern Europe that would secure Germany's national sovereignty and a German role as mediator between eastern and western Europe. They wanted to use these ideas as a basis of confidence for negotiations that would end the war and restore a consensus with Stalin regarding foreign policy. In May and June 1941, Schulze-Boysen pushed for the procurement of radios for communication in wartime. Radio contact with Moscow did not get passed the trial stage. From his discussion with Harro Schulze-Boysen during his onetime visit in Berlin, "Kent" brought information that he then gave to Moscow via eight radio transmissions from Brussels in November 1941. Other information from Berlin apparently did not reach Moscow.

Parachutists coming from Moscow during the summer of 1942 were again supposed to establish an information connection. They mostly encountered people who had no contact with resistance groups but who, for the most part, had already been engaged for many years in gathering news for the Soviet Union.

Far more than 150 women and men of various generations and different occupations, embodying numerous traditions and origins and having quite specific motivations and differing philosophical and political positions, can be counted as part of the "Red Orchestra" resistance network in Germany. Between August 31, 1942, and March 1943, 126 of them were arrested. Five men opted for suicide. Five of those arrested were killed without having had a trial. Ninety-one were brought before the Reich Court-Martial and the People's Court. Forty-eight of them were murdered in Plötzensee, Tegel, Halle, and Brandenburg at the end of 1942 and in 1943.

HANS COPPI

Bibliography

Coppi, Hans. *Harro Schulze-Boysen: Wege in den Widerstand: Eine biographische Studie.* Koblenz, 1993.

Sahm, Ulrich. *Rudolf von Scheliha 1897–1942: Ein deutscher Diplomat gegen Hitler.* Munich, 1990.

Scheel, Heinrich. *Vor den Schranken des Reichskriegsgerichtes: Mein Weg in den Widerstand.* Berlin, 1993.

Schilde, Kurt, ed. *Eva Maria Buch und die "Rote Kapelle."* Berlin, 1992.

Red Shock Troop. *See* Socialist Front; Socialist Resistance; Youth Opposition.

Red Youth Pioneers (KPD). *See* Black Squad; Leipzig Hound Packs.

Reichsbanner Black Red Gold. *See* Rechberg Group; Socialist Resistance; Resistance against National Socialism before 1933.

"Reinhart Letters." *See* Socialist Resistance.

Religious Socialists. *See* New Beginning.

Reports on Germany (*Deutschland-Berichte*). *See* Exile and Resistance; Foreign Contacts; Socialist Resistance.

Resistance: Notes for National-Revolutionary Politics (*Widerstand: Blätter für nationalrevolutionäre Politik*). *See* Resistance against National Socialism before 1933.

Reusch Circle. *See* Goerdeler Circle.

Revolutionary Socialists. *See* Exile and Resistance.

Robinsohn-Strassmann Group. *See* Strassmann Group.

Rösch Circle. Father Augustin Rösch, S.J., became the provincial of the southern German province of the Jesuits and thus was from the beginning confronted with National Socialism, for which "Jews, Jesuits, and Freemasons" were enemies of the state. Already by 1935, special instructions were issued by the Political Police in Munich to observe the activities of Jesuits in particular. Rösch soon had to endure the ordeal surrounding Father Rupert Mayer, S.J., in Munich. Mayer was sentenced to six months' imprisonment by the Munich Special Court on July 23, 1937, for violating the pulpit paragraph and the law against malicious gossip. Rösch had to accept the disbandment of several Jesuit facilities in his province.

This "cloister storm," which Martin Bormann had hatched, led in 1941 to Rösch's first activity, which was played out primarily within the penumbra of the church but had import for ecclesiastical policy. Rösch assembled a group of engaged members of orders (Laurentius Siemer, O.P., Odilo Braun, O.P., and Lothar König, S.J.) and a layperson (Dr. Angermaier). This group, the Committee for the Affairs of Religious Orders of the Bishops' Conference, has not yet been much noted in historical research.

On Rösch's initiative, a base for collecting information about National Socialist activity against the church and cloisters was first set up. Due to the disquieting state of affairs, the committee had two goals: (1) to steer the Catholic bishops onto a collision course with the National Socialist regime and thereby to stop the course of church policy set by the chairman of the bishops' conference, Cardinal Adolf von Betram; and (2) to commit the superiors of orders themselves to common action in the "cloister storm."

Three texts resulted from these efforts. In the fall of 1941, the committee worked out the "Human Rights Pastoral Letter," which clearly emphasized the violation of human rights by the Third Reich and which was ultimately approved by twenty diocese bishops. It was not read from pulpits due to the veto of the chairman of the bishops' conference. Nevertheless, a statement was sent to the Reich chancellery in which the group strongly protested on December 10, 1941, against the violation of human rights, and that statement was strengthened when the Protestant church sent a note of protest at the same time. In the summer of 1942, the Catholic group issued a pastoral letter that aimed to strengthen members of orders in their calling despite oppression and persecution. In 1943, they participated in drawing up the "Decalogue Pastoral Letter," which is the German bishops' harshest statement concerning injustice in the Third Reich and which was read from pulpits on September 12, 1943. Father Rösch was the hub of these activities and had the brave help of Father König as a messenger and aid.

Rösch's second activity, in the *Kreisau Circle, assumed a decisively political direction beginning in the winter of 1941. Rösch became acquainted with the founder of the Kreisau Circle, Helmuth James von Moltke, in October 1941. Von Moltke requested his help. Rösch agreed and participated in the first meeting in Kreisau in Lower Silesia during the spring of 1942. He then brought in two of his fellow priests: Father Lothar König, S.J., and Father Alfred Delp, S.J. König again assumed the role of messenger. Delp concerned himself primarily with the social order after the demise of the Third Reich and acquainted the members of the Kreisau Circle with the demands of papal encyclicals concerning social issues. Between 1942 and 1944, the Jesuit provincial's office in Munich developed into a covert meeting point, especially for the discussions in August 1942 in which expectations were explained to churches during this time of injustice.

Rösch was in the background of other activities as well: in contacts with the Vatican, with Pope Pius XII; in contacts with the Sperr Circle, a rather conservatively oriented covert group in Munich that had gathered around Franz Sperr, the former Bavarian envoy in Berlin; in contacts with the Catholic Workers' Movement in Cologne (which involved Bernhard Letterhaus, Nikolaus Gross and Otto Müller); in connections with Austria, Salzburg, and Vienna; and in discussions with German bishops (Cardinal Faulhaber of Munich, Bishop von Preysing of Berlin, Archbishop Gröber of Freiburg, and Bishop Dietz of Fulda). There were also contacts with members of the military, such as General Halder. Cooperation ceased when connections between Munich and Berlin were broken after the arrest of von Moltke on January 19, 1944. Father Lothar König seems to have been the only person who was informed of the exact planning of the *July 20, 1944, assassination attempt on Hitler. After

July 20, 1944, interrogations by the Gestapo revealed that the Kreisau Circle had a "Bavarian group" in Munich, as is documented by the "Kaltenbrunner Reports."

After Father Delp was arrested by the Gestapo on July 28, 1944, Rösch and König went underground. A warrant was issued for their arrest on September 30, 1944. Father König was not found for the entire duration of the Third Reich. Father Rösch was found and arrested in his hiding place in Hofgiebing east of Munich on January 11, 1945, the day on which Father Delp was sentenced to death by the People's Court in Berlin for high treason. Rösch was sent to Berlin via Dachau and was interrogated in the Reich Security Main Office. A trial was apparently planned against the churches, whose complicity in the resistance had become known to the Gestapo through the interrogations. But this trial did not take place: Father Delp was executed in Berlin-Plötzensee on February 2, 1945. Rösch was liberated from the Lehrter Strasse prison in Berlin on April 25, 1945, and, after a four-week march by foot, returned to Munich on June 8, 1945.

Father Rösch saw to it that the drafts of writings in the Kreisau Circle were collected. After König's death on May 5, 1946, this "File: Kreisau Circle" was kept in a safe at Berchman Collegium in Pullach near Munich. After Rösch's death on November 7, 1961, it was forgotten for a decade; it was rediscovered in 1971 and was edited in 1986. It is documentation of the Rösch Circle's activity in the Kreisau Circle. The activities of the committee that was composed of members of orders are currently being assessed by historians.

ROMAN BLEISTEIN

Bibliography

Bleistein, Roman. *Alfred Delp: Geschichte eines Zeugen.* Frankfurt, 1989.

————, ed. *Dossier: Kreisauer Kreis: Dokumente aus dem Widerstand gegen den Nationalsozialismus.* Frankfurt, 1987.

Leugers, Antonia J. "*...entsetzlich geschwiegen zu so Vielem und Furchtbarem": Der Ausschuß für Ordensangelegenheiten und seine kirchenpolitische Konzeption (1941–1944).* Münster, 1986.

Rösch, Augustin. *Kampf gegen den Nationalsozialismus.* Edited by Roman Bleistein. Frankfurt, 1985.

"Spiegelbild einer Verschwörung": Geheime Dokumente aus dem ehemaligen Reichssicherheitshauptamt. Volumes 1 and 2. Stuttgart, 1984.

Die Rote Fahne **(The Red Banner).** *See* Communist Resistance; Red Orchestra.

Ruhr-Echo. *See* Knöchel Organization.

Rütli Group. *See* Hanno-Günther Group/Rütli Group.

Saar Battle (Status Quo Movement). After the Council of the League of Nations, on June 4, 1934, had set January 13, 1935, as the day on which a vote would be taken on the future of the Saar region, which had been separated from the German Reich in 1920 and was administered by an international governing commission, the Social Democratic Party (SPD) and the Communist Party in the Saar region joined together on July 2, 1934, after long labor pains to form an alliance against the threatened reincorporation of the Saar region into Hitler's Germany. Under the motto "We'll Beat Hitler on the Saar — Status Quo!" this first German unity front called for interim maintenance by the disliked League of Nations administration — the status quo — as the lesser political evil. The Saar region was never to be given up to Hitler and his course toward war. A programmatic demand was made to fight for securing the freedoms of assembly, demonstration, press, and coalition and against the process by which the administration, justice system, and executive would be made fascist. The "status quo motto" was accompanied with the hope of putting a brake on Hitler's expansionist plans and of supporting the domestic German resistance by achieving victory in the vote on January 13.

The anti-Hitler coalition was represented by Max Braun, the chairman of the Saar SPD, which had broken with the SPD's executive committee in exile and had formed a revolutionary organization for agitation, and by Fritz Pfordt, the leader of the Saar Communists, who, only after long hesitation, had broken away from their motto of a "Red Saar in a red soviet Germany." The alliance was supported by the numerous leading politicians of both parties who had emigrated to the Saar region and by renowned leftist writers, journalists, and artists.

Despite intense efforts, the unity front did not grow into a popular front. Rejecting the Saar Center Party's course toward reincorporation and coming together in November 1934 to form a people's alliance for a Christian-social community, a small group of oppositional Catholics around the Center Party politician and future prime minister of the Saarland, Johannes Hoffmann, spoke up for the status quo solution but kept away from the alliance between Social Democrats and Communists.

In form and content, the Status Quo Alliance as a popular movement opposed National Socialism and the Third Reich. It was supported primarily by the ranks of independent and red trade union organizations. With a plethora of publications, demonstrations, and mass rallies in which tens of thousands of people took part — such as the one on August 26, 1934, in Sulzbach and the one at Kieselhumes Stadium in Saarbrücken on January 6, 1935 — both leftist parties pushed for the idea of a German Saar region without Hitler. A press that, in contrast with the rest of Germany, was still free reported clearly what the Saarlanders could expect if the Saar region were reincorporated. Along with the Communists' Red Militant Front League, the Social Democrats' Socialist Defense League, which had been patterned on the Republican Defense League in Austria, fought against the daily terror unleashed by supporters of reincorporation. Melees in halls and streets were an everyday affair. Especially among younger Social Democrats and Communists, the battle of the Saar gave reason for radicalization and militancy, which were later continued through the participation of a high proportion of Saarlanders in the ranks of the International Brigades in the Spanish Civil War and within the Résistance.

Since the Saar region was supposed to become, in Max Braun's words, a "final refuge of German freedom against Hitler's despotism," the Saar region, along with Prague, developed into the most important center of exile resistance against the Third Reich. Published here for a long time were the central organ of the German Communist Party (KPD), which was forbidden in the Reich, and *Deutsche Freiheit* (German freedom), the journalistic mouthpiece of the Saar SPD, a party that viewed itself as revolutionary and distanced itself from German social democracy's path of accommodation. From the Saar region a great number of other writings were smuggled into Germany by the KPD and SPD through border offices. Numerous pockets of resistance in the Reich were also supported logistically from the region.

The Status Quo Movement agitated people's political reasoning and their desire for freedom, but that desire was only weakly developed, even in the Saar region. Intimidated by the threats and terror of supporters of reincorporation or beholden to their own nationalistic needs, thousands of Social Democrats and Communists drifted over into the camp of those who favored reincorporation, especially during the final weeks of the battle for the Saar. In contrast to the emotional and easily remembered slogans used by supporters of reincorporation, the formula of the Status Quo Movement proved to be too abstract and hardly conveyable. Finally, the movement was largely isolated with respect to foreign policy and remained without support.

The results of the vote of January 13, 1935, were thus not surprising. Only 46,613 eligible voters (or 8.8 percent) voted for the status quo solution, that is, against a reincorporation of the Saar region. Two-thirds of former KPD and SPD members had thus turned their backs on their parties. In the view of Sopade (the SPD's exile executive committee in Prague), the battle for the Saar had shown "that the present apathy of the wide mass of people toward the loss of freedom cannot be overcome by short-term propagandistic means" and that the battle for the Saar had not provoked "an explosion of the will to freedom" even within the working class of the Saar region. Sopade saw this as a warning against all "revolutionary hopes for a miracle."

In view of threats previously made to settle accounts, roughly six thousand Saarlanders emigrated after January 13, 1935, mostly to neighboring France; among them was almost the entire body of functionaries of both status quo parties. In the following years, hundreds of status quo supporters continued their resistance against National Socialism and the Third Reich in the KPD's and SPD's border operations, which were organized in Forbach in Lorraine; in various unity front organizations such as the Saar People's Front, which was formed in Metz in 1937; in the Spanish Civil War; and within the Résistance.

GERHARD PAUL

Bibliography

Mühlen, Patrik von zur. *"Schlagt Hitler an der Saar!" Abstimmungskampf, Emigration und Widerstand im Saargebiet 1933–1935.* Bonn, 1979.
Paul, Gerhard. *"Deutsche Mutter — heim zu Dir!" Warum es mißlang, Hitler an der Saar zu schlagen: Der Saarkampf 1933–1935.* Cologne, 1984.
Schock, Ralph, ed. *Haltet die Saar, Genossen! Antifaschistische Schriftsteller im Abstimmungskampf 1935.* Berlin and Bonn, 1984.

Saar People's Front. *See* Committee for the Preparation of a German People's Front.

Saefkow-Jacob Group. This group, led by the trained machine builder Anton Saefkow, was one of the large Communist resistance organizations in wartime Germany. It was not until shortly before the beginning of the war in 1939 that Saefkow, who had been a functionary of the German Communist Party (KPD) during the Weimar Republic, was released from incarceration; he had been in prison and a concentration camp since 1933. It is said that after he again began to gather a circle of sympathizers around him, he began cooperating with the Communist Uhrig resistance group around 1941. The Gestapo broke up the *Uhrig-Römer Group in Berlin and Munich in February 1942, however. When the Communist resistance group around Bernhard Bästlein (*see Bästlein Group) and Franz Jacob in Hamburg also fell victim to the Gestapo in October 1942, Jacob, a former representative in the Hamburg city government, escaped to Berlin and made contact there with Saefkow.

Beginning in 1943, Saefkow and Jacob then attempted to gather together the remaining members of the Berlin organization who had not been found. They set up a new network of underground cells by the dozens in large Berlin factories, especially in the armaments sector. In these factories, the group pushed primarily for passive work attitudes and sabotage in armament production. For their underground activity, the Saefkow-Jacob Group established an infrastructure in which there was a division of labor, such as for making copies of flyers, for securing underground accommodations and false documents, and for making sure that activities and meetings were safe. Communists, trade unionists, members of workers' athletic clubs, and Social Democrats were in the Saefkow-Jacob Group.

The Saefkow-Jacob Group intensively sought out contacts with other Communist resistance groups in Thuringia, Saxony, and Anhalt, such as the *Schumann Group and the *Neubauer Group. A new KPD domestic leadership arose in the autumn of 1943 out of the coordination of this common resistance. The Communists' stance toward the *National Committee "Free Germany" (NKFD), which had been formed in July 1943, was frequently debated by the leaders of the three groups. In accordance with the NKFD's goals, all antifascists were now supposed to be mobilized for a broad resistance movement. The Saefkow-Jacob Group often signed its flyers, in which the group called for an end of the war, the toppling of the National Socialist dictatorship, and a democratic Germany, with "NKFD — Berlin Committee."

Members made numerous contacts and connections with other groups — including groups of the Social Democratic and bourgeois resistance — within and outside of Berlin, with prisoners of war and foreign forced laborers, and with sympathizers. Bästlein began working in the direction of the Saefkow-Jacob Group in May 1944. He had been hidden by the Saefkow-Jacob Group after he had taken advantage of an Allied bombing raid to escape from Berlin-Plötzensee prison in January 1944. During this phase, the group, which up to this point had depended on manual methods for making copies of flyers, increased the distribution of its propaganda for ending the war with the help of a press that it had acquired in the meantime. The "Soldier Letters" were directed specifically to members of the Wehrmacht. In addition, the group assisted in the formation of small NKFD groups in Wehrmacht support organizations in Berlin, such as in the Office of Army Clothing and Accessories.

The discussions that had been initiated between the Saefkow-Jacob Group and the Social Democrats Julius Leber and Adolf Reichwein, who were members of the *Kreisau Circle, could no longer be intensified. The discussion about the conditions for a coordinated resistance against the National Socialist regime and the perspectives after its elimination was broken off by the Gestapo's wave of arrests that began against both groups at the beginning of July 1944.

The People's Court sentenced Saefkow, Jacob, and Bästlein to death on September 5, 1944. The sentence was carried out on September 18, 1944, in Brandenburg-Görden prison. More than sixty members of the group, which had been active between 1942 and 1944, were murdered before the end of the war.

WOLF GRUNER

Bibliography

Nitzsche, Gerhard. *Die Saefkow-Jacob-Bästlein-Gruppe: Dokumente und Materialien des illegalen antifaschistischen Kampfes (1942–1945)*. Edited by the Institut für Marxismus-Leninismus beim ZK der SED. Berlin, 1957.

***Schriften der jungen Nation* (Writings of the Young Nation).** *See* Youth Opposition.

Schumann Group. This large Leipzig resistance group, which was active between 1939 and 1944, was led by rather unorthodox Communists. Georg Schumann, a trained toolmaker, longtime functionary of the German Communist Party (KPD), and Reichstag representative, rebelled against the dogmatic policy of the KPD leadership at the end of the 1920s. Otto Engert, a trained carpenter and representative in the Thuringian state parliament, had been expelled from the KPD as a nonconformist during the same phase.

After Schumann was released from Sachsenhausen concentration camp during the summer of 1939 after having been imprisoned for several years, he, Engert, and Kurt Kresse, who knew one another from their editorial work at the *Sächsiche Arbeiter-Zeitung* (Saxon workers' news), which was published in Leipzig prior to the National Socialist period, began in 1939–40 to gather together underground groups in Leipzig that existed mostly without having contact with one another. In Leipzig and its vicinity, the Schumann Group was active in dozens of armament factories that were important for the war, including at the I. G. Farben Leuna Synthetic Rubber Works. In Leipzig, the group cooperated with more than 120 former members of Communist and Social Democratic youth organizations, which disguised their meetings as those of "Strength through Joy" groups. The group had contacts with antifascists in Dresden, Halle, Magdeburg, Breslau, and even in concentration camps.

Flyers distributed in factories demanded the end of the war and of National Socialist rule, called for passive behavior by workers in factories, and appealed for solidarity with prisoners of war and foreign forced laborers. Later, sabotage of armament production was especially supported. Group members who were employed in a disinfection company, for example, gained access to armament factories that were off limits, to POW barracks, and to foreign forced laborers. In this manner, the resistance group also established connections in the General Government (German-dominated Poland) and in Austrian factories of the Hugo Schneider Company of Leipzig.

The Schumann Group's stated goals were a socialist republic, the control of factories by elected workers' commissions, cooperative unity among workers' parties, and free and independent trade unions. During this phase, the leadership cooperated more intensively with the *Saefkow-Jacob Group in Berlin and the *Neubauer Group in Thuringia. Several meetings took place in 1943–44; discussions focused on the Schumann and Saefkow-Jacob Groups' theoretical "platforms" concerning the Communists' position toward the *National Committee "Free Germany" (NKFD), on perspectives for ending National Socialist rule, on postwar politics, and on the expansion of connections with one another and the centralization of the Communist resistance.

In the meantime, there had been contacts and cooperation with resistance organizations comprised of foreign forced laborers and POWs in Leipzig, such as the International Antifascist Committee, as well as with members of the intelligentsia. In 1943–44, the Schumann Group produced flyers concerning various topics, such as passive behavior after bombing raids on factories and opposition to the introduction of a seventy-two-hour work week. Beginning in March 1944, three issues of the flyer "Resistance against War and Nazi Rule" appeared; the flyer not only was supposed to mobilize all opponents of Hitler for a broad resistance movement but also concretely called for the installment of a people's government after the overthrow of National Socialist rule and for the reintroduction of basic democratic rights.

The group operated for nearly five years without being uncovered. It was not until the middle of July 1944 that the Gestapo arrested the leadership and more than one hundred members of the Schumann Group. A number of resistance fighters, including Schumann, Engert, and Kresse, were executed in Dresden on January 11 and 12, 1945, after receiving death sentences. Those resistance fighters who escaped the wave of arrests and continued to operate as the Leipzig NKFD are said to have played a part in the Allies' bloodless occupation of Leipzig by directly appealing to the mayor and the police in April 1945.

WOLF GRUNER

Bibliography

Krause, Ilse. *Die Schumann-Engert-Kresse-Gruppe: Dokumente und Materialien des illegalen antifaschistischen Kampfes (Leipzig 1943 bis 1945)*. Edited by the Institut für Marxismus-Leninismus beim ZK der SED. Berlin, 1960.

Serious Bible Students. *See* Jehovah's Witnesses.

Silesian Young Men's Club. *See* Kreisau Circle.

Socialist Action (*Sozialistische Aktion*). *See* Socialist Front.

Socialist Front. In the records of Sopade (the executive committee of the German Social Democratic Party [SPD] in exile), the Socialist Front (SF) is often mentioned in one breath with other oppositional Social Democratic resistance groups in the Reich, with the group *New Beginning, the Red Shock Troop, and the *Rechberg Group in Mannheim. In fact, the founder of the SF, Werner Blumenberg, had caused the so-called Western Front Conference — a meeting in Mannheim of representatives from Social Democratic resistance organizations from western Germany — to fail not only by refusing to allow his organization to distribute the *Sozialistische Aktion,* the underground periodical of Sopade, but also by refusing to let the SF be incorporated into the organization of Sopade. Instead, he demanded the creation of an independent underground Reich executive body that he, as representative of the largest organization, also bluntly laid claim to head.

The SF was at the highpoint of its development at this time. It had formed through a rather long process involving the dispute of a group of activists, mostly younger Social Democrats from Hannover, with the legalistic local party executive committee. The actual force behind its development was Blumenberg, who, born in 1900, was both the son of a pastor in Hannover and the editor of the Social Democratic *Volkswillen* (People's will). His legitimacy was derived from his having been named the director of the Hannoverian organization of the so-called pioneer system at a conference of SPD department chiefs in the summer of 1932. The pioneer system, which had also been recommended by the SPD executive committee in the spring of 1932, was intended to mobilize young active party members primarily for propaganda activities. There is no longer any specific evidence of the extent to which this organization had already made plans in 1932 for its possible underground existence. Yet it is certain that this task assigned to Blumenberg by the party gave him the opportunity to establish contacts with especially active party members. Among them was, in particular, the worker Franz Nause, who, three years younger than Blumenberg, was a former regional party treasurer and member of the Defensive Formations (Schufo). Nause became Blumenberg's closest associate. By means of copied circulars and their first flyers during the months of the party's semilegality beginning in the spring of 1933, both tried — in vain — to convince the Hannover party leadership to take the party underground.

In spite of these preparations, the formation of the SF's underground organization after the party was outlawed at the end of June 1933 apparently turned out to be largely a reconstruction from scratch. In addition to Blumenberg and Nause, Willy Wendt, who, like Nause, was a worker and former regional party treasurer, played a leading role. In contrast to Blumenberg's later idealized portrayal, the SF's decisive organizational unit was not, as was the case among other underground groups, the usual covert five-man group, but rather, as was the case in local SPD organizations prior to 1933, the department. There apparently were plans to divide Hannover into twelve departments, which would have resulted in considerably fewer than the forty departments within the local organization. Yet only eleven departments were formed, some of which were quite different from one another with respect to size, internal structure and jurisdiction.

On the whole, the SF was far from being a thoroughgoing covert organization constructed on the basis of a unitary system. That it nevertheless succeeded in operating without great losses until the middle of 1936 is probably due not least to the fact that it worked almost exclusively within the Social Democratic–oriented workers' milieu of Hannover. Indeed, the SF recruited its members without exception from organizations of this milieu: the political (SPD, Socialist Workers' Youth [SAJ], and Reichsbanner with the Schufo and Young Banner), trade union, and cultural periphery organizations. In spite of Blumenberg's pretension of seeing the SF itself as the realization of the unity front, this exclusively Social Democratic tendency actually grew during the course of the SF's development. At the time of its greatest strength in roughly the middle of 1935, more than seven hundred members were firmly attached to the organization. This was only approximately 4 percent of the members of the SPD's local organization in Hannover, yet, in terms of membership numbers, the SF was thus probably the largest resistance organization in the Reich.

In accord with the dominant concept of the Social Democratic resistance, the SF also entirely desisted from spectacular public activities. This large organization was essentially nothing but a distribution organization and a reader's association for the flyers that were published more or less regularly every four to six weeks from April 1934 to August 1936 and that, by August 1936 at the latest, bore the standardized title *Sozialistische Blätter* (Socialist notes). This publication originally had a circulation of about 200 copies; an exception was in 1935, when circulation was at nearly 1,000 copies. With the assistance of several other people, Nause and Wendt took care of production and distribution. The largest proportion of copies was circulated in Hannover and its vicinity, but approximately 100 to 150 copies were always sent outside of the city to Göttingen, Münster, Hamburg, Magdeburg, Berlin, Leipzig, and other cities as well as to Amsterdam and London. One of the duties of the journalist Walter Spengemann consisted in sending out the publication. He also felt that the *Sozialistische Blätter* should be distributed only within the organization or within its milieu at most.

The *Sozialistische Blätter* was consequently not directed toward a wide public. For Blumenberg, who wrote nearly all the articles himself, the publication was rather a means of communication for the mobilization, solidification, and organization of those segments of the working class that were prepared to work against the fascists. As he wrote in a memorandum to Sopade in 1936, he saw the purpose of his underground work as consisting in "gathering together only those forces that can come into question as the leadership of an antifascist front, namely, socialist workers." For him, the SF was the beginning of a new German workers' movement that was supposed to replace the old parties whose time, in his opinion, had come to an end, since their leaderships had failed in the task of the antifascist struggle. This new movement was supposed to gather the best forces of the socialist working class and to assume the leadership of the working class. After the overthrow of Hitler, its task was to consist in bringing about the realization of socialism with the assistance of a "socialist dictatorship." In Blumenberg's view, only this goal justified the sacrifices that underground work necessarily entailed. He also stuck to this idea, which was essentially Leninist, when Sopade again backed down from altogether similar positions in * "The Prague Manifesto" of 1934. Indeed, despite the emphasis on the SF's autonomy and independence, Blumenberg was in constant loose contact with the party executive committee in Prague after he had participated in Sopade's "Antwerp Conference" at the beginning of December 1934.

By simple means of camouflage (the *Sozialistische Blätter* contained no news from Hannover and pretended to be published at constantly changing places, for example) and by the general limiting of its activities to members and personally known individuals (an attempt made in the summer of 1934 to expand the SF systematically throughout Hannover had little success and was not tried again), the SF leadership succeeded for a long time in leaving the Gestapo in the dark as to the SF's actual organization. Isolated penetrations into the organization, of which Willy Wendt became a victim in February 1935, were initially without much consequence. The end of the SF did not come until a wide-scale wave of arrests in Hildesheim in the summer of 1936 succeeded in tracking down Franz Nause and until a Gestapo agent, planted from without, simultaneously penetrated the leadership circle. While Blumenberg and several other members succeeded in fleeing abroad, this was not a realistic possibility for most. Thus, more than three hundred persons were arrested in the weeks following the end of August 1936; more than two hundred were finally brought to court in several trials.

The trial against the primary defendants, who included Nause, Spengemann, Auguste Breitzke, and Brunhilde Schmedes, took place before the People's Court in September 1937; the mass trial against the more than two hundred other defendants took place between October and December of the same year in four court divisions before the Higher

Regional Court of Hamm, which convened in Hannover. Blumenberg's attempts to reorganize the SF from Amsterdam failed.

HANS-DIETER SCHMID

Bibliography

Rabe, Bernd. *Die "Sozialistische Front": Sozialdemokraten gegen Faschismus 1933–1936*. Hannover, 1984.

Schmid, Hans-Dieter. "Sozialdemokratischer Widerstand." In *Widerstand im Abseits: Hannover 1933–1945*. Edited by Herbert Obenaus et al. Hannover, 1992.

Socialist Notes (*Sozialistische Blätter*). *See* Socialist Front; Socialist Resistance.

Socialist Workers' Youth (SAJ). *See* Rechberg Group; Socialist Resistance.

Social Scientific Union. *See* Red Militants.

"Soldier Letters." *See* Saefkow-Jacob Group.

Solf Circle. During World War II, critics and opponents of the National Socialist system of rule met at the home of Hanna Solf, the widow of Dr. Wilhelm Solf, who had been the German ambassador in Tokyo and had died in 1936. Given the hostess, it is no surprise that former and active diplomats dominated in this circle, which was held together by common views and met of its own accord. One must particularly mention Reichstag Legation Councilor Dr. Richard Kuenzer; Reichstag Embassy Councilor Count Albrecht von Bernstorff; Reichstag Legation Secretary Herbert Mumm von Schwarzenstein; Ambassador Dr. Otto Kiep; Legation Councilor Dr. Hilger van Scherpenberg, the son-in-law of former Reichsbank President and Minister of Economics Hjalmar Schacht; Elisabeth von Thadden, the daughter of Countess Hanna Solf von Ballestrem; Irmgard Zarden; the industrialist Nikolaus von Halem; and Baron Karl-Ludwig von Guttenberg, who was the publisher of the *Weisse Blätter* (White notes), a Catholic journal that held oppositional views insofar as this was publicly possible up to the beginning of the war.

The circle itself by no means made plans and preparations for assassination and an overthrow of the government. Its members met in order to create from time to time an island of humanity in discussions and an exchange of opinion, an island on which the intellectual, cultural, and political principles and standards of a Germany free of National Socialist perversion could be kept alive and thereby weather the storm.

Yet the circle also served some of its members as a source of strength for individual acts of resistance or opposition. Thus, Count Bernstorff tirelessly and bravely attempted to help politically and racially persecuted non-Jews and Jews to leave the Reich and to save their possessions; for this purpose, he joined the A. E. Wasserman firm, a bank that had previously been directed by Germans of Jewish origin. The spirit of the circle and the personalities of some of its members also had a constant and profound influence on other oppositional groups; Kiep, for example, had an influence on young diplomats around State Secretary von Weizsäcker who sought to counteract Hitler's policies in the *Foreign Office or in the foreign legations, as well as on the *Kreisau Circle around Count von Moltke.

Through Fabian von Schlabrendorff, Nikolaus von Halem had contacts with anti-Nazi forces within the army, including with the group around Tresckow in the staff of Army Group Middle. It became his downfall that he encouraged and supported the retired captain and former leader of the Freikorps "Oberland," Dr. Joseph ("Beppo") Römer (see *Uhrig-Römer Group), who, having become a Communist and being the leader of a group of Communists, doggedly planned *assassination attempts against Hitler. Römer was arrested at the beginning of February 1942; Halem was arrested on February 25, 1942, together with Herbert Mumm von Schwarzenstein, who was involved in this matter. After spending more than two years in prison, Halem and Mumm were sentenced to death on June 16, 1944, and executed four months later.

Most of the other members of the Solf Circle also fell victim to the regime. On September 10, 1943, the circle had a "tea party" — in fact, a birthday party — at the home of Elisabeth von Thadden at which the usual discussions hostile to the regime came up. One of the participants, the Berlin physician Dr. Paul Reckzeh, turned out to be an informant for the Gestapo who made reports about the group. When Count von Moltke warned the circle in September 1943 that Dr. Reckzeh was a Gestapo agent, it was already too late.

During the course of 1944, the Gestapo arrested nearly all members of the group. Because of repeated postponements of their trials, Mrs. Solf, her daughter Countess Ballestrem, Hilger van Scherpenberg, and Irmgard Zarden were able to survive the final phase of the war; Elisabeth von Thadden, Otto Kiep, Kuenzer, Bernstorff, Guttenberg, and others were executed or simply murdered. It is characteristic of the spirit of the circle that Nikolaus von Halem shouted, "A ship can go down, but it doesn't have to haul down its flag," at the president of the People's Court, Roland Freisler, who, with derisive comments, had just sentenced him to death.

Hermann Graml

Bibliography

Hoffmann, Peter. *Widerstand, Staatsstreich, Attentat: Der Kampf der Opposition gegen Hitler.* Munich, 1985.
Zeller, Eberhard. *Geist der Freiheit: Der 20. Juli.* Munich, 1963.

Solidarity. *See* Assistance and Solidarity.

Die Sonntags-Zeitung **(The Sunday Times).** *See* Resistance against National Socialism before 1933.

Sopade. *See* Exile and Resistance; Foreign Contacts; Socialist Resistance.

Sozialistische Aktion **(Socialist Action).** *See* Socialist Front.

Sozialistische Blätter **(Socialist Notes).** *See* Socialist Front; Socialist Resistance.

"Spark" Group. *See* Trotskyites.

Sperr Circle. *See* July 20, 1944; Kreisau Circle; Monarchist Resistance in Bavaria; Rösch Circle.

Status Quo Movement. *See* Saar Battle (Status Quo Movement).

Stäuber Gangs. *See* Edelweiss Pirates.

Storm Troops. *See* Youth Opposition.

The Straight Path (*Der Gerade Weg***).** *See* Resistance against National Socialism before 1933.

Strassmann Group. The Strassmann Group, which was called the Robinsohn-Strassmann Group until the end of 1938, was the only Reich-wide liberal democratic resistance group that lasted for any considerable length of time. It was formed on Whitsunday 1934, was rigidly organized, operated covertly, and ceased to exist in 1942 with Strassmann's arrest. Its founders, Berlin judge Ernst Strassmann, Hamburg businessman Dr. Hans Robinsohn, and Berlin journalist Dr. Oskar Stark, came from the German Democratic Party (DDP) and the German Democratic Youth (DDJ). The group recruited from the field of leading persons of outlawed democratic leftist organizations: the DDP/DDJ, the German Social Democratic Party (SPD), the German Peace Society, humanitarian and reformed Freemasons, and the October 3rd Club. Robinsohn and Strassmann had fought together with younger Social Democrats (Theodor Haubach and Gustav Dahrendorf) for a strong republican-democratic and social-political course from 1924 to 1933 (see *Resistance against National Socialism before 1933). The underground network of connections covered large areas of Germany until the end of 1937. Strongly consolidated groups quickly formed in Berlin and Hamburg; there were additional centers in Lachmund in Mecklenburg, in Hoernigk in central Germany, and in Dehler in northern Bavaria. Not only the group's leadership but also a large proportion of the group's members came from the DDP/DDJ. The first contacts were made with the Social Democratic resistance in Hamburg, Mecklenburg, Wilhelmshaven, and Kiel in 1934 and, in 1937, with the Social Democratic resistance in Berlin as well. Social Democratic allies in northern Germany were later joined by conservatives in other regions, those in central Germany by members of the German National People's Party/Steel Helmet, and those in southern Germany by members of political Catholicism. Former members of the national-liberal German People's Party were represented in very small numbers.

During its period of consolidation, the group worked out a liberal democratic program for after the overthrow of the government, a program that was expressly conceived as a counterprogram to Hitler's reckless policy of risk. Dependability and predictability were to be the hallmarks of German policy, which was to include the return to a constitutional state of law, equal rights for Jews, a putting in order of state finances, the encouragement of international trade (instead of the policy of autarky), and disarmament beginning unilaterally with Germany. Economic reform was to be directed toward the traditional subsidizing of heavy industry and large farms. A strong social component was to raise the broad masses' standard of living. With respect to defense policy, the group sought the formation of a small, defensive militia instead of a "standing army."

The group's activity consisted in gathering information in order to break the government's monopoly on information, in fostering the group's own organizational growth, in helping persecuted persons, and in establishing and maintaining contacts with other resistance groups and persons in the government apparatus and with emigrés and government circles abroad. Through the establishment of contact with, on the one hand, representatives of the Social Democratic resistance (Haubach, Leber, and Leuschner) and with, on the other hand, the conservative Goerdeler already at the beginning of 1938 and the military opposition (Beck and Oster), the group assumed a key position within the resistance movement roughly between 1938 and 1940.

After 1938, the group worked toward participation in the first transition government after the overthrow of the National Socialist system. The group's first foreign policy activity was during the Austrian crisis of 1938, when it sought to cooperate with opponents of National Socialism within the government as well as within the outlawed Austrian Social Democratic Party. Robinsohn's emigration to Denmark as a Jew at the end of 1938 made it possible for him to establish the first contacts with the British government, and he pushed for an end to the policy of appeasement. In May and June of 1939, this led to a visit of a small delegation of the Strassmann Group in London at which the delegation had a conference with the head diplomatic adviser of the foreign minister, Robert Vansittart, and others; Vansittart, for his part, was close to Churchill and the British secret service. This contact remained intact until Strassmann's arrest. The group was drawn into plans for an overthrow of the government during the winter of 1939–1940; parallel to Josef Müller's establishment of contact with British officials via the Vatican, a messenger of the Strassmann Group traveled to Stockholm in order to win British support for a post-Hitler government to be established by the resistance.

The group's centrally organized work ended with Strassmann's arrest in 1942. He remained imprisoned until 1945. In contrast to other resistance groups, Strassmann's arrest did not lead to any mass arrests in the group; this was because of the protection offered by people in the Counterintelligence Office of the High Command of the Armed Forces. Individuals and associated local groups continued to operate until 1945; individual leading members were privy to the plans for an overthrow of the government by the conspirators who were involved in the *July 20, 1944, assassination attempt against Hitler, and Strassmann's mediator to Goerdeler, Dr. Fritz Elsas, paid for this with his life. After 1945, members in some regions showed preferences for the Free German Youth, primarily in Hamburg; Strassmann joined the SPD, and Robinsohn remained politically unaffiliated.

HORST R. SASSIN

Bibliography

Sassin, Horst R. *Liberale im Widerstand.* Hamburg, 1993.

Stuttgart Circle. *See* Goerdeler Circle.

The Sunday Times (*Die Sonntags-Zeitung*). *See* Resistance against National Socialism before 1933.

Swing Youth. *See* Youth Opposition.

Das Tage-Buch (The Diary). *See* Resistance to National Socialism before 1933.

Tea Party. *See* Solf Circle.

Ten-Point Group. *See* German People's Front; New Beginning; Socialist Resistance.

Trade Union Resistance. In view of the National Socialists' breakup of the trade union organizations, the term "trade union resistance" cannot be applied to the continuation of traditional trade union work. Under the conditions of terror and persecution, surveillance and spying, there were indeed nevertheless attempts to develop trade union activities — up to the point of strikes — in individual areas. Yet every attempt to establish an underground organization was bound to fail. This is shown by the initial attempts of the German Communist Party (KPD) to maintain the idea of the "formation of cells," which led to mass arrests in 1933–34. And the initial attempts to establish covert trade union work, which were undertaken within the German Workers' Front (DAF) according to "Trojan horse" tactics, remained without success; in addition, these attempts, with the — alleged — cooperation of Communists in the DAF, contributed to an unsettling of the working class.

Trade union resistance was thus the attempt of individual trade unionists to engage in political work directed against the National Socialist regime as such. The first precondition for this was to stay in contact in order thereby to strengthen political conviction against the growing pressure of National Socialist propaganda and to exchange information. Due to clever camouflage, well-known trade union leaders (including Alwin Brandes, Fritz Husemann and Jakob Kaiser) were able to accomplish this. They built up a network in which numerous groups comprised mostly of former trade union functionaries were in contact with one another and exchanged information. Members transported camouflaged written materials and news, and they printed and distributed flyers in order to penetrate the National Socialist monopoly on information. For this, relatively good conditions presented themselves to workers in the transportation sector, who were actively supported in part by the International Transport Workers' Federation (ITF) under Edo Fimmen.

Neither the covert meetings in which communication was solely by word of mouth nor the groups that became active were safe from attack by the Gestapo. The networks of the trade union resistance groups were almost entirely broken up by 1937. In the Underground Reich Leadership of German Trade Unions (that is, in circles of former top-level functionaries), the trade union resistance subsequently restricted itself basically to discussing plans for "afterward." The trade union leaders certainly did not have extensive contacts, but they did indeed have a covert information network, which made the leaders important partners especially for trade unionists who had fled abroad.

Bases in neighboring countries were set up early and served as the initial reception points for trade unionists who had been driven out of Germany. Their primary task consisted in coordinating work there. The Saar region served as a refuge for exiled trade unionists until it was annexed to the German Reich in 1935; this function was then assumed by Czechoslovakia until 1938 and by the border regions of the Netherlands, Belgium, France, and Denmark.

In Sweden and England, which, together with Switzerland, were the most important countries that took in trade unionists, national groups of German trade unionists were formed that assisted refugees in securing the most basic necessities; they supported the resistance in Germany, gathered and distributed information, and attempted to influence the Allies' policy toward Germany, especially by working with the trade unions of the respective host country, by publicizing their own work, and by working with the Allies' information services. The latter were often of the opinion that the National Socialist dictatorship could be beaten only from without. Finally, national representatives worked out plans and programs for the rebuilding of the trade unions as well as for the organization of the labor market and the "post-Hitler period" political order as a whole.

These groups could not directly aid in ending the war or in toppling the dictatorship. But this was exactly the goal of individual trade unionists who had contact with resistance groups in Germany itself that were involved in the *July 20, 1944, assassination attempt on Hitler. In particular one must mention Wilhelm Leuschner of the Free Trade Unions and Jakob Kaiser of the Christian Trade Unions. The July 20, 1944, assassination attempt on Hitler failed, and the people who had planned it had to count on the severest punishment: Jakob Kaiser was able to go underground in time and to remain hidden until the end of the war, yet Wilhelm Leuschner was arrested, sentenced to death, and executed. His oft-quoted last word was "Unite!"

MICHAEL SCHNEIDER

Bibliography

Beier, Gerhard. *Die illegale Reichsleitung der Gewerkschaften 1933–1945.* Cologne, 1981.

Peukert, Detlev J. K. "Die Lage der Arbeiter und der gewerkschaftliche Widerstand im Deutschen Reich." In *Geschichte der deutschen Gewerkschaften: Von den Anfängen bis 1945.* Edited by Ulrich Borsdorf. Cologne, 1987.

Travail Anti-Allemand. *See* Exile and Resistance.

Trotskyites. The history of the organized Communist leftist opposition goes back to 1925 and the Comintern's famous "Open Letter," which started the purge of the Sino- and Trotskyite opposition within the German Communist Party (KPD). This purge was essentially complete by 1927 and led to the formation of a huge number of leftist oppositional organizations, groups, and small coteries, the most important of which was the Lenin League under Ruth Fischer and Hugo Urbahns, which was formed in 1928 and had five to six thousand members. Yet the Lenin League fell apart during the early 1930s and no longer played a role in the resistance against National Socialism after 1933. The Trotskyite minority was expelled from the Lenin League in 1930 and formed the United Opposition of the KPD (Bolshevists-Leninists), the first Trotskyite organization in Germany; its leading representative was Anton Grylewicz. In 1931, a minority group around Kurt Landau, Alexander Müller, and Hans Schwalbach broke off and formed its own organization. Both groups, which were recognized by Trotsky himself as Trotskyite organizations of equal standing, called themselves the Left Opposition of the KPD (Bolshevists-Leninists) and could be distinguished only by their respective central organs, *Die Permanente Revolution* and *Der Kommunist*. The first group had about six hundred members, the second approximately one hundred; both had their organizational basis primarily in Berlin.

While underground, the first and larger Trotskyite group concentrated itself primarily on work in factories, by no means limiting itself to Berlin. Its leading representative was Erwin Ackerknecht, who emigrated to Paris in the early summer of 1933 to form a foreign committee. Primarily due to its acquisition of dissatisfied KPD members, the group grew during these months to roughly one thousand sympathizers, a number that again quickly declined, however. Leading representatives of the group's Reich leadership, which divided into two factions while the group was underground, included Joachim Unger and Walter Nettelbeck. In addition to Berlin, the organization had groups in Hamburg, Saxony (Magdeburg, Halberstadt, Leipzig, and Dresden), western Germany (Gelsenkirchen, Neuss, Solingen, Essen, and Cologne), Mainz, Frankfurt am Main, and Munich as well as in the Free City of Danzig, which was administered by the League of Nations. All these groups, which totaled a good two hundred cadres, were broken up by the Gestapo between 1934 and 1936.

The second Trotskyite group also sought its success in work in factories, yet remained largely limited to Berlin. Its leading representative was the Austrian Kurt Landau until he emigrated to Paris in March 1933, where he formed a foreign central office; he was succeeded by

Hans Schwalbach, Erich Rätzke, and Reinhold Schedlich. Called the Spark Group after its underground publication, the group, which was approximately forty members strong and had originally formed from the ultraleftist so-called Wedding Opposition, was mopped up by the Gestapo in March 1934; approximately 170 members and sympathizers were arrested, including Henry Jacoby, who had played a key role in the group's underground work. The particular tragedy of the Trotskyite groups was that, due to their positions at the front of the workers' movement, they had already been observed and attacked by the KPD's intelligence apparatus prior to 1933. The KPD's intelligence archives fell into the hands of the Gestapo in December 1933 and offered the Gestapo the basis for long-term surveillance, which in some cases was carried out over the course of months and years, and ultimately for the complete elimination of Trotskyite groups and organizational footholds. The number of persons from this spectrum who were arrested totaled several hundred.

Hartmut Mehringer

Bibliography

Foitzik, Jan. *Zwischen den Fronten: Zur Politik, Organisation und Funktion linker politischer Kleinorganisationen im Widerstand 1933 bis 1939/40.* Bonn, 1986.

Schafranek, Hans. *Das kurze Leben des Kurt Landau: Ein österreichischer Kommunist als Opfer der stalinistischen Geheimpolizei.* Vienna, 1988.

Zimmermann, Rüdiger. *Der Leninbund: Linke Kommunisten in der Weimarer Republik.* Düsseldorf, 1978.

Uhrig-Römer Group. In Berlin, the toolmaker Robert Uhrig began in 1940 to lead one of the largest Communist resistance groups. Released from Luckau prison in 1936 after having been convicted of illegal activity, he at first continued his personal resistance in a circle of Communists he had befriended in Berlin. In subsequent years, Uhrig established contacts among underground groups that were eventually supposed to constitute the core of a widespread antifascist organization.

The Communist-led Uhrig Group, which was one of the few groups that continued to receive sporadic courier news from the leadership of the German Communist Party (KPD) abroad, embraced a wide political spectrum of members. Next to its own network of groups in factories and residential areas, it had contacts with other resistance groups not only within Berlin but also elsewhere, including in Hamburg, Mannheim, Leipzig, Essen, Munich, Vienna, and the Tyrol. More than eighty illegals are said to have belonged to the Uhrig Group's underground factory organization in the German Weapons and Armaments Works AG of Borsigwalde alone.

In 1940–41, Uhrig developed especially close contacts with Josef ("Beppo") Römer's resistance group. A retired captain, former leader of the Freikorps "Oberland," and onetime member of the National Socialist German Workers' Party, Römer had moved in the direction of the KPD toward the end of the 1920s via national-Bolshevist views. Leftist intellectuals came together in "Aufbruch" ("New Beginning") work groups, which were named after the journal that Römer began heading in 1932. After two arrests in 1933 and 1934, Römer was not released from Dachau until 1939. He again immediately formed a resistance group in Munich whose members came from the Oberland organization and the working class. In 1940, Römer also assembled a resistance group in Berlin that was comprised of friends from the "Aufbruch" work groups and thereby used his expanded contacts to the military and industry.

In September 1941, after Germany's attack on the Soviet Union, Uhrig's and Römer's loosely cooperating groups were united to form a single organization under a single leadership. In several meetings, Uhrig and Römer coordinated political principles for common activities. While Uhrig favored the gathering of information about the mood of the people and armament production, the publication of flyers against the war, and intensive contacts with other Communist organizations, Römer pushed for a common political "general position" with the goal of taking over power after the overthrow of the National Socialist dictatorship and for sabotage in armament factories and the training of "battle and action groups."

Uhrig and Römer now published together the monthly bulletin *Informationsdienst* (Information service), which had been written by the Römer Group since 1940 and which was directed particularly to organized resistance fighters. As of the summer of 1941, the bulletin was published twice monthly. The bulletin formulated the group's general goals (a people's revolution and socialism), analyzed the economic and military situation, and gave concrete directions for acts of sabotage. The primary elements of illegal activity by hundreds of antifascists of both groups were the distribution of flyers, assistance for forced laborers, sabotage in armament factories, and antiwar propaganda in the Wehrmacht.

Beginning in February 1942, the Gestapo succeeded in systematically uncovering the organization despite extensive security measures. In Berlin and Munich alone, more than two hundred members of the Uhrig-Römer Group were arrested and sent to concentration camps. Sixteen of them were murdered before court proceedings. Between November 1942 and October 1944, more than twenty trials were held against at least 105 resistance fighters — including fifteen women — of the Uhrig-Römer Group. Uhrig was executed in Brandenburg-Görden on August 21, 1944, Römer on September 25, 1944. Despite massive repressions, many of the undiscovered members continued to be active, such as in the newly formed *Saefkow-Jacob Group in Berlin.

WOLF GRUNER

Bibliography

Bindrich, Oswald, and Susanne Römer. *Beppo Römer: Ein Leben zwischen Revolution und Nation.* Berlin, 1991.

Kraushaar, Luise. *Berliner Kommunisten im Kampf gegen den Faschismus 1936–1942: Robert Uhrig und Genossen.* Berlin (GDR), 1981.

Underground Reich Leadership of German Trade Unions. *See* Trade Union Resistance.

United Opposition of the KPD (Bolshevists-Leninists). *See* Trotskyites.

Viennese Shufflers. *See* Edelweiss Pirates; Youth Opposition.

Vitus-Heller Movement. *See* Youth Opposition.

***Der Vorbote* (The Herald).** *See* Lechleiter Group.

Wedding Opposition. *See* Trotskyites.

Wednesday Society. *See* Goerdeler Circle.

***Weisse Blätter* (White Notes).** *See* Monarchist Resistance in Bavaria.

***Welt am Montag* (World on Monday).** *See* Resistance against National Socialism before 1933.

White Notes (*Weisse Blätter*). *See* Monarchist Resistance in Bavaria.

White Rose. Going by the name "White Rose," a small group of students in Munich distributed flyers against Hitler and National Socialism during the summer of 1942. The name very quickly became associated with the entire resistance circle. Medical students Alexander Schmorell and Hans Scholl were the core of this group; Christoph Probst, Sophie Scholl, Willi Graf, and Professor Kurt Huber gradually became actively involved in various ways in the activities that were critical of the regime. Other members from the circle of friends, such as the students Traute Lafrenz, Gisela Schertling, Katharina Schüddekopf, Hubert

Furtwängler, the architect Manfred Eickemeyer, and the painter Wilhelm Gayer, were not active but participated insofar as they knew of the group's activities.

Between June 27 and July 12, 1942, the group's first four flyers appeared in Munich in the mailboxes of a select intellectual elite; the flyers, entitled "Flyers of the White Rose," called for passive resistance against the regime. The authors were Hans Scholl and Alexander Schmorell. The texts were written at a high level and appealed to Christian values. Apocalyptic passages from the Bible coursed through the flyers in an almost overpowering manner. This striking and unusual style of the first four flyers reflects the interests that bound and characterized the circle of friends surrounding the group.

All the students came from rather conservative-bourgeois, Christian-oriented families. A great deal of all the participants' leisure time was devoted to literature, philosophy, religion, music, and art. Willi Graf and Hans Scholl were members of various youth groups that had been associated with the Youth Movement, which Hitler had outlawed. The two Catholic journalists Professor Carl Muth and Theodor Hacker had a strong influence on the students during the period of the group's activity between the early summer of 1942 and February 1943; Muth and Hacker devoted much time to discussing philosophical and political questions with the students and provided them with stimulation that influenced the content of the first four flyers.

The induction of the Student Company into service on the eastern front, on July 23, 1942, which directly affected Willi Graf (who, along with Sophie Scholl, had in the meantime become a participant in the group's activities), Alexander Schmorell, and Hans Scholl, brought about an interruption of the group's underground work. Inspired by their impressions in Russia — impressions of the Russian people, their culture, and their literature — and horrified by the senseless atrocities of the war at the same time, they intensified their resistance activities after their return in November 1942.

The formation of a network of resistance circles in several university cities was planned and put into action. Through Falk Harnack, the students tried to make contact with central resistance circles in Berlin, including the *Red Orchestra and the Bonhoeffer brothers. They were able to win over their university professor Kurt Huber for assistance in writing the flyers (numbers five and six) that now followed, the first of which was circulated in several cities; the students had become aware of Huber's critical stance toward the regime through his lectures and his participation in evening discussion groups.

The fifth and sixth flyers were no longer crowned with the romantic symbol of the White Rose and were clearly different from the initial flyers in terms of style and content. The title of the fifth flyer, "Fly-

ers of the Resistance Movement in Germany: A Call to All Germans,"
signaled the change. The flyers are decidedly more political; their language is clearer; they address all social strata and students of all types.
Concrete plans for postwar Germany are presented. The defeat at Stalingrad, which shook the population, or a notable speech by Gauleiter
Giesler before the student body of Munich were effectively employed in
gripping headlines. In contrast to the previous flyers, the final flyer addressed to students was by Professor Huber. Huber rejected the version
that was printed, however, since the students had deleted the passage
that he had deemed central: "Place yourselves tirelessly in the service of
our glorious Wehrmacht."

When the Sixth Army's defeat at Stalingrad became known after February 3, 1943, Willi Graf, Alexander Schmorell, and Hans Scholl on
several occasions used tar to paint slogans for peace on university buildings and the fronts of houses in the university quarter under cover of
darkness — an extremely risky action.

The final flyer was placed in a stairway and in empty hallways of
the University of Munich on February 18, 1943. The Scholls were observed in the act by the university janitor and arrested. The Munich
Gestapo, which had already formed a special committee to investigate
the events at the university and had gathered evidence, interrogated the
two students and searched their apartment. Christoph Probst, who, as
a married father, had had no part in the actual activities, was dismissed
from his company in Innsbruck after a flyer that he had drafted was
discovered; he was also arrested. After long interrogations and initial
denials, the three gave confessions. The trial quickly began on February 22 before the People's Court. Chairman Roland Freisler, who had
come from Berlin specially, presided over the trial. The verdict was
announced after three and one-half hours: the death sentence for all
three defendants. The sentence was carried out by guillotine three hours
later.

The second trial against the White Rose took place on April 19,
1943. Having fourteen defendants and lasting fourteen hours, it was
on a considerably larger scale, since, in contrast to the first trial, the
defendants insisted on their right to a defense. One should mention Professor Kurt Huber's defense speech, which, preserved in a manuscript,
accurately characterizes his beliefs and emphasizes his exceptional position within the circle of the resistance group as well as his resolution in
deed. Of the fourteen defendants, Willi Graf, Kurt Huber, and Alexander Schmorell received the death sentence; the other defendants from the
circle of friends came away with comparatively minor prison sentences
of between six months and ten years. This was surprising insofar as the
defendants from the Scholls' circle of friends in Ulm — Heinrich Guter,
the siblings Hans and Susanne Hirzel, and Franz Joseph Müller — had

actively copied and distributed flyers, as had Willi Bollinger, whom Willi Graf had been able to recruit for an expansion of flyer-related activities in his hometown of Saarbrücken. Eugen Grimminger, a friend of the Scholl family who lived in Stuttgart and had financially supported the White Rose, came away with a ten-year prison sentence. Falk Harnack was the only person who was acquitted, probably due to tactical reasons. Alexander Schmorell and Kurt Huber were executed on July 13, 1943; Willi Graf had to wait for his death until October 12, since the Gestapo hoped to receive more information from him.

A third trial in conjunction with the White Rose took place against Harald Dohrn, Manfred Eickemeyer, Wilhelm Geyer, and Joseph Söhngen before the First State Court of Munich on July 13, 1943. Only Söhngen was convicted, and he was given a six-month prison sentence; the others were acquitted despite the serious charges against them.

Although the core of the student resistance group was silenced by police persecution, the students' activity was continued to a certain extent in an institute at the University of Munich and especially in Hamburg. In the Institute of Chemistry at the University of Munich, Jewish and "half-Jewish" students were able to study despite existing regulations; a model director of the institute, Nobel Prize winner Heinrich Wieland, had made this possible. With other oppositional students there, Hans Leipelt, a student from Hamburg, continued to distribute the final flyer with an appendix, "Their Spirit Lives On," and started a collection to benefit Kurt Huber's widow. These activities were reported and became the subject of a trial before the People's Court that took place in Donauwörth on October 13, 1944. Hans Leipelt was sentenced to death and guillotined on January 29, 1945.

Resistance activities in Hamburg were of a different nature. The circle, which is referred to as the Hamburg branch of the White Rose, was comprised of rather small, individual groups, all of whose members did not know one another and some of which had already been working underground against the National Socialist state longer than the Munich students. Traute Lafrenz, a woman from Hamburg, established contact with the Munich group and brought flyers by the White Rose from Munich to Hamburg at the end of 1942; in Hamburg, her school friend Heinz Kucharski distributed the flyers among circles of friends. After the White Rose in Munich had been smashed, the Hamburg group expanded flyer activities. As a result of Leipelt's arrest, the oppositional students in Hamburg became known to the Gestapo and were brought before the People's Court in Hamburg on April 17, 1945. Kucharski was sentenced to death but was able to flee while en route to his execution and to save his life. Of the other members of the Hamburg White Rose who received prison sentences, Gretha Rothe, Reinhold

Meyer, and Friedrich Geussenhainer died while in custody in the Nazis' prisons and concentration camps.

The courageous deeds of the White Rose became known beyond the borders of Germany even during the war. Thomas Mann, among others, honored them over the BBC in June 1943. In a flyer by the *National Committee "Free Germany" that was distributed at the front, the names Scholl and Schmorell appear as a "wake-up call by the heroes of freedom from faraway Munich," and the English dropped several thousand of the flyers over Germany. The call of the fifth flyer, "Support the Resistance Movement, Distribute These Flyers," thus did not go unheard.

MONIKA MAYR

Bibliography

Graf, Willi. *Briefe und Aufzeichnungen.* Edited by Anneliese Knoop-Graf and Inge Jens. Reprint. Frankfurt, 1994.

Petry, Christian. *Studenten aufs Schafott: Die Weiße Rose und ihr Scheitern.* Munich, 1968.

Schneider, Michael, and Winfried Süß. *Keine Volksgenossen.* Munich, 1993.

Scholl, Hans, and Sophie Scholl. *Briefe und Aufzeichnungen.* Edited by Inge Jens. Frankfurt, 1994.

Scholl, Inge. *Die Weiße Rose.* Expanded edition. Frankfurt, 1982.

White Rose Foundation, comp. *Die Weiße Rose: Der Widerstand von Studenten gegen Hitler: München 1942/43.* Munich (private printing), 1991.

Widerstand: Blätter für nationalrevolutionäre Politik (Resistance: Notes for National-Revolutionary Politics). *See* Resistance against National Socialism before 1933.

Wild Cliques. *See* Youth Opposition.

Winzen Group. *See* Socialist Resistance.

Workers' Illustrated News (Arbeiter-Illustrierte-Zeitung). *See* Resistance against National Socialism before 1933.

World on Monday (Welt am Montag). *See* Resistance against National Socialism before 1933.

Writings of the Young Nation (Schriften der jungen Nation). *See* Youth Opposition.

X Report. *See* Black Chapel.

Young Church. *See* Youth Opposition.

Young Fighters. *See* Youth Opposition.

Young Front. *See* Youth Opposition.

Young Guard. *See* Youth Opposition.

Zazous. *See* Youth Opposition.

"Das Ziel." *See* "The Goal" ("Das Ziel").

Zossen File Discovery. *See* Counterintelligence Office (Abwehr).

Part III

Biographical Sketches

Compiled by Marion Neiss
with the cooperation of
Maren Krüger and
Martina Voigt

Page numbers at the end of the following entries refer to discussions in parts 1 and 2 above.

Abshagen, Robert (1911–44) Insurance salesman; became member of KPD in 1931; did propaganda work at regional head office of KPD in Wasserkante; imprisoned in 1933–34; arrested again in fall of 1934; sentenced to two and one-half years' imprisonment; imprisoned in Sachsenhausen concentration camp from 1937 to 1939; arrested for third time in October 1942; sentenced to death by People's Court in May 1944; executed in July 1944. *22, 125, 126.*

Achilles, Leo (Leopold) Teacher; participated in Russian campaign as lance corporal; returned to Germany (West) in 1945. *210.*

Ackerknecht, Erwin (born 1906) Physician, journalist; member of KPD until 1932; became leader of the Left Opposition of KPD in 1932; editor of *Permanente Revolution;* went into exile in Republic of Czechoslovakia, Turkey, and France in 1933; director of Foreign Committee of the International Communists of Germany until 1934; member of SAPD from 1935 to 1937; internment in France in 1940; professor in Madison, Wisconsin, from 1947 to 1957. *246.*

Ackermann, Anton (1905–73) Politician; became member of KPD in 1926; attended Lenin School in Moscow from 1928 to 1932; became member of central committee and politburo of KPD in 1935; became member of the foreign administration of KPD in Paris in 1938; became editor in chief of newspaper *Das freie Wort* (The free word) in Moscow in 1941; became member of central committee of SED in 1946; became state secretary of Ministry of Foreign Affairs of GDR in 1949; dismissed in 1953; rehabilitated in 1956. *206, 210.*

Albrecht, Gerhard (1889–1971) Economist; became professor in Erlangen and Jena in 1927; transferred to Marburg in 1935; became director of Department for Social Issues in government of North Rhine-Westphalia in 1945; rector of University of Marburg from 1948 to 1950. *165.*

Angermaier, Georg (1913–45) Lawyer, ecclesiastical judge of diocese of Würzburg and diocese of Bamberg; legal adviser of Order of Bavaria; soldier 1939–40 and 1942. *227.*

Arendsee, Martha (1885–53) Politician; became member of SPD in 1906, member of USPD in 1917, member of KPD in 1920; member of Prussian state parliament from 1921 to 1924; member of Reichstag from 1924 to 1930; spent six months under arrest in 1933; in Moscow in 1934 (at Radio Moscow/German People's Broadcasting); became director of Department of Social Policy of the German Free Trade Union

Alliance (GDR) in 1945; chairwoman of Welfare Insurance Institute of East Berlin 1949–50. *206.*

Aretin, Baron Erwein von (1887–1952) Journalist, chairman of Bavarian Federation for Fatherland and King from 1924 to 1929; imprisoned in 1933–34 and in 1938 (including in Dachau); banished from Munich and forbidden to practice his profession from 1934 to 1945; became member of constitutional committee in Bavaria in 1946. *203.*

Ballestrem, Countess Lagi von (1909–55) Daughter of Hanna Solf; arrested in 1944; survived until end of war due to repeated postponement of court appearance date. *239.*

Barth, Karl (1886–1968) Protestant theologian, clergyman; founder of dialectical theology; became professor of systematic theology in Göttingen in 1921; transferred to Münster in 1925 and to Bonn in 1930–35; became member of SPD in 1931; dismissed as university professor in 1935; transferred to Faculty of Theology in Basel. *47, 50.*

Bästlein, Bernhard (1894–1944) Precision toolmaker, editor, and politician; became member of SPD in 1912, of USPD in 1918, and of KPD in 1920; in Soviet Union from 1921 to 1923; became member of Prussian state parliament in 1932; elected to Reichstag in March 1933; arrested in May 1933; imprisoned in penitentiary and concentration camp from 1933 to 1940; arrested again in 1942; escaped in January 1944; arrested in May 1944 and sentenced to death by People's Court; executed in September 1944. *22, 125, 126, 232, 233.*

Bauer, Clemens (1899–1984) Historian; university lecturer in Munich from 1932 to 1933; professor in Riga from 1933 to 1935 and in East Prussia and Braunschweig from 1936 to 1937; became professor at University of Freiburg in 1938 and rector in 1962. *165.*

Baum, Herbert (1912–42) Electrician; became member of KJVD in 1931; director of Ring Alliance of German-Jewish Youth in 1932; barred from further education due to his Jewish origin in 1935; forced labor in Berlin in 1941; arrested in May 1942; allegedly committed suicide in June 1942 while in detention for questioning in Berlin-Moabit. *23, 70, 179, 180.*

Baum, Marianne (née Cohn) (1912–42) Wife of Herbert Baum, member of the German-Jewish Youth Community and of KJVD; began forced labor in Berlin in 1941; arrested in May 1942; sentenced to death by Special Court of the Provincial Court of Berlin in July 1942; executed in Berlin-Plötzensee in August 1942. *179.*

Bavaud, Maurice (1916–41) Swiss citizen, technical drafter; attended missionary school in France; went to Germany in 1938; imprisoned in 1938–39 due to ticket counterfeiting; arrested again in 1939; sentenced to death by People's Court in December 1939; executed in Berlin-Plötzensee in May 1941. *121.*

Becher, Johannes R. (1891–1958) Writer; became member of USPD in 1917 and of KPD and Spartacus League in 1918–19; fled to Republic of Czechoslovakia in 1933, then to Soviet Union in 1935, where he was in the central committee of KPD; returned to Germany (East) in 1945; Minister for Culture of GDR from 1954 to 1958. *206.*

Becher, Walter (born 1912) Political scientist, journalist; active in the youth movement of the Sudeten German Party; spent six months imprisoned in concentration camp; became soldier in 1940; after 1945, became active in movement of Germans who had been expelled from former eastern territories of Germany (Sudeten German Countrymen's Organization) and in extreme right-wing German Community; member of CSU from 1965 to 1980. *135.*

Beck, Ludwig (1880–1944) Career officer; became member of General Staff in 1911, promoted to major general in 1932, then to general; chief of Troop Office in Ministry of Reichswehr from 1933 to 1935; chief of General Staff of Army from 1935 to 1938; resigned in August 1938; shot on July 20, 1944. *36–38, 60–64, 67, 121, 127–28, 157–58, 172–76, 188–89, 197, 242.*

Beckerath, Erwin von (1889–1964) Economist; professor in Rostock and Kiel from 1920 and in Bonn from 1939 to 1957; director of Research Group for Economics of the Academy of German Law; became chairman of academic advisory committee in Federal Ministry of Economics in 1949. *164, 165.*

Beimler, Hans (1895–1936) Politician; became member of KPD in 1918; city councilman in Augsburg from 1929 to 1931; member of Bavarian state parliament from 1930 to 1932; became member of Reichstag in 1932; arrested in 1933; escaped from Dachau and fled to Paris; director of "Red Aid for Underground Germany" in Zurich from 1935 to 1936; political commissioner of all German battalions of International Brigades in Madrid in 1936; died in Spanish Civil War. *16.*

Berkowitz, Liane (1923–43) Student in Berlin; arrested in Berlin in September 1942; sentenced to death by Reich Court-Martial in January 1943; appeal for clemency rejected in July 1943; executed in Berlin-Plötzensee in August 1943. *225.*

Bernhard, Georg (1875–1944) Journalist, politician, member of SPD; expelled from SPD in 1906; became editor in chief of *Vossische Zeitung* in 1914; city councilman in Charlottenburg district of Berlin from 1915 to 1918; became member of DDP in 1924 and member of that party's executive committee in 1927; member of Reichstag from 1928 to 1930; fled to Paris in 1933; emigrated to the United States in 1941. *8.*

Bernstorff, Count Albrecht von (1890–1945) Diplomatic adviser; became co-owner of banking house A. E. Wassermann in 1933; arrested in conjunction with July 20, 1944, assassination attempt on Hitler; sentenced to death by People's Court; executed in Lehrter Strasse prison in Berlin in April 1945. *239, 240.*

Bertram, Adolf (1859–1945) Catholic cleric; ordained as priest in 1881; became bishop of Hildesheim in 1906; appointed cardinal in 1916; became chairman of the Fulda Bishops' Conference in 1919; became prince-bishop of Breslau in 1930; metropolitan of diocese. *51, 52, 54, 196.*

Blaskowitz, Johannes (1883–1948) Career officer; became commander in chief of Army Group East in December 1939, commander in chief of Army Group West in May 1944, and finally commander in chief of occupied Netherlands; indicted by American court-martial in 1948; committed suicide. *63, 64.*

Bley, Curt (1910–61) Lawyer, journalist; while studying law, he was chairman of Socialist Students' Organization and German Republican Students' League; member of SPD from 1929 to 1933; cofounded Red Shock Troops in 1933–34; transferred in 1940 to diplomatic service, where he worked as an academic adviser in Foreign Office in Berlin, Rome, and Copenhagen; arrested in April 1943 and dismissed from Foreign Office; soldier until end of war; became deputy editor in chief of *Die Welt* (The world) in 1946 and an attorney in Bonn in 1945. *225.*

Bloch, Ernst (1885–1977) Philosopher and writer; in 1933, fled to Vienna, Paris, and Prague; emigrated to the United States in 1938; became professor of philosophy in Leipzig in 1949; moved to FRG in 1961; professor at University of Tübingen. *138.*

Blumenberg, Werner (1900–1965) Journalist; became member of SPD in 1920; founded Socialist Front in Hannover in 1933; publisher of *Sozialistische Blätter* (Socialist notes) from 1934 to 1936; fled to the Netherlands in 1936; worked on *Deutschland Berichte* (Reports on Germany); in underground in Amsterdam from 1940 to 1945; after 1945, worked in German Department of International Institute for Social History in Amsterdam. *30, 236–39.*

Bochow, Herbert (1906–42) Studied philosophy in Leipzig; became member of KPD in 1929; worked as white-collar employee and writer; arrested in March 1933; imprisoned in concentration camp; arrested again in November 1934; sentenced to eighteen months' imprisonment; arrested for third time in June 1941; sentenced to death by People's Court in March 1942; executed in Berlin-Plötzensee in June 1942. *178.*

Bodelschwingh, Friedrich von (1877–1946) Protestant clergyman; in 1910, became director of Bodelschwingh Institutes in Bethel, which his father had founded; elected as Reich bishop of German Evangelical Church in May 1933; resigned in June 1933; member of central committee for the Home Mission and of German Evangelical Missionary Council. *48.*

Bögler, Franz (1895–1976) Politician; became member of SPD in 1921 and member of Bavarian state parliament in 1933; member of Reichsbanner Black Red Gold; fled to Saarbrücken in 1933 and to France in 1938; arrested and incarcerated in 1939; fled to Switzerland in 1942; became SPD politician in Rhineland-Palatinate after war and member of that party's executive committee in 1962. *216.*

Böhm, Franz (1895–1977) Lawyer, politician; university lecturer in Freiburg from 1933 to 1935 and in Jena from 1936 to 1938; barred from teaching in 1940 and suspended; Hessian minister of culture in 1945–46; professor in Frankfurt am Main from 1946 to 1962; head of reparations negotiations with Israel and world Jewish organizations in 1952; member of CDU in Bundestag from 1953 to 1965. *165.*

Bohm-Schuch, Clara (1879–1936) Clerk in Berlin; active in socialist women's movement; member of SPD; member of National Assembly in 1919; member of Reichstag from 1920 to 1933; spent fifteen days under arrest in August 1933 and was subsequently under police surveillance. *111.*

Bollinger, Heinrich (Heinz) (1916–90) Assistant at University of Freiburg and product of Catholic youth organization "The New Germany"; arrested in March 1943; indicted in April 1943 and sentenced by People's Court to seven years' imprisonment; incarcerated in penitentiary at Ludwigsburg until April 1945; held several professorships at teachers' colleges in Germany (West) after 1945. *252.*

Bollinger, Willi (1919–73) Chemist; medical orderly during war; counterfeited and obtained furlough certificates and military driver's licenses; arrested in March 1943 and sentenced by State Court of Saarbrücken to three months' imprisonment; after end of war, worked as chemist in German industrial concerns. *252.*

Bolz, Eugen (1881–1945) Lawyer, politician, member of Center Party; from 1912 to 1933, member of Württemberg state parliament and Reichstag; minister of justice from 1919 to 1924; minister of interior in 1923; state president of Württemberg from 1928 to 1933, resigned in 1933; imprisoned in concentration camp for several weeks; arrested after July 20, 1944, assassination attempt on Hitler; executed in Berlin-Plötzensee in January 1945. *175.*

Bolz, Lothar (1903–86) Politician, lawyer, member of KPD; alleged to have worked in Soviet secret service; barred from practicing law in 1933; fled to Soviet Union; returned to Germany (East) in 1948; cofounder of NDPD, of which he was chairman until 1972; became member of Volkskammer in 1950; deputy prime minister of GDR from 1950 to 1967; minister for foreign affairs of GDR from 1953 to 1965. *209.*

Bonhoeffer, Dietrich (1906–45) Protestant theologian, students' minister in Berlin; permission to teach was revoked in 1936; drafted into Counterintelligence Office of High Command of the Armed Forces in 1940; arrested in 1943; imprisoned for two years at Berlin-Tegel; murdered in Flossenbürg concentration camp in April 1945 after SS summary court proceeding. *47, 50, 55–56, 143–45, 156, 158, 164–65.*

Bontjes van Beek, Cato (1920–43) Moved to Amsterdam in 1927, returned to Germany in 1933; studied business in 1937–38; office worker in Bremen; moved to Berlin in fall of 1939; labor service in 1940; arrested in September 1942; sentenced to death by Reich Court-Martial in January 1943; executed in Berlin-Plötzensee in August 1943. *225.*

Borsig, Ernst von (1906–45) Grandchild of August Borsig (the founder of the locomotive and machine factory in Berlin); cofounder of central task force group composed of top employers' and workers' unions. *197.*

Börth, Friedrich (born 1914) Member of SPD and SAJ; director of SAJ in Hamburg-Eimsbüttel; arrested in January 1935; sentenced to three years' imprisonment by Hamburg Court of Appeals in November 1935; imprisoned in Sachsenhausen concentration camp from 1938 to 1945. *70.*

Bosch, Robert (1861–1942) Industrialist; founded Precision Tools and Electronics Works in Stuttgart in 1886 (renamed Robert Bosch GmbH in 1937); achieved social-political and philanthropic aims in his company; rejected honors offered by National Socialist regime. *156, 174.*

Bose, Herbert von (1893–1934) High-level government adviser; became von Papen's press agent in 1934; shot in his office on June 30, 1934, in conjunction with Röhm Putsch. *150, 151.*

Brand, Walter (born 1908) Politician, leading functionary of Sudeten German Party, Konrad Henlein's foreign policy adviser; arrested in

December 1933 and imprisoned for several months; later directed press office of Sudeten leadership in London. *135.*

Brandes, Alwin (1866–1949) Locksmith; became chairman of executive board of German Metal Workers' Union in 1919; member of Reichstag (SPD) from 1912 to 1924 and 1928 to 1933; arrested in 1934; held in Oranienburg concentration camp; arrested again in 1936 and acquitted by People's Court; held in Sachsenhausen concentration camp until October 1937; participated in formation of trade unions in Germany (East) after end of war. *244.*

Brandler, Heinrich (1881–1967) Politician; member of SPD from 1901 to 1915 and of KPD from 1918 to 1928; sentenced to five years' confinement in a fortress in 1921; fled to Soviet Union; returned to Germany in 1922; member of KPDO; fled to France in 1933; confined in 1939; fled to Mexico and Cuba in 1941; settled in London in 1947 and in Hamburg in 1949. *167.*

Brandt, Willy (1913–92) Journalist, politician; member of SAJ from 1927 to 1931; became member of SPD in 1930 and member of SAPD in 1931; fled to Norway in 1933 and to Sweden in 1940; switched party allegiance in 1944 from SAPD to SPD; returned to Germany in 1947; member of House of Representatives in West Berlin from 1950 to 1966; mayor of Berlin from 1957 to 1966; state chairman of Berlin from 1958 to 1962 and chairman of SPD from 1964 to 1987; German foreign minister from 1966 to 1969; German chancellor from 1969 to 1974. *96, 138.*

Brass, Otto (1875–1950) File cutter; became member of SPD in 1895; founding member of USPD; member of National Assembly in 1919–20; became member of KPD in 1920 and member of SPD in 1922; director of publishing company in Berlin from 1920 to 1933; arrested in September 1938; sentenced to twelve years' imprisonment by People's Court in 1939; became member of SPD in 1945 and of SED in 1946. *33, 170.*

Braun, Alois (born 1892) Career officer, commanding officer of the Seventeenth Panzer Reserve Unit in Erding; held rank of major; after 1945, senior government adviser in Bavarian State Ministry for Education and Culture. *162.*

Braun, Leo (Father Odilo) (1899–1981) Catholic clergyman, Dominican; ordained in 1933; clergyman in Worms in 1934 and in Cologne from 1938 to 1940; became general secretary of Superiors' Union of Berlin in 1940; sought by Gestapo after July 20, 1944, assassination attempt on Hitler; arrested in Berlin in October 1944 and released in February 1945 after having been held for questioning. *227.*

Braun, Max (1892–1945) Journalist, politician; became member of SPD in 1919, secondary chairman of Saarbrücken branch of SPD from 1925 to 1928, and primary chairman from 1928 to 1935; escaped assassination attempt by National Socialists in 1933; fled to France in 1935; worked at *Pariser Tageblatt* (Paris daily news); later emigrated to England and interned there. *138, 230, 231.*

Bräuning, Karl (1886–1962) Politician; became member of SPD in 1906, of USPD in 1917, and of KPD from 1920 to 1929; imprisoned from 1923 to 1925; became member of KPDO in 1929; fled to the Saar in 1933; began working for exile KPDO in Republic of Czechoslovakia in 1934; fought in Spanish Civil War in 1936; emigrated to the United States in 1941; returned to Germany in 1955; member of SPD. *168.*

Bredel, Willi (1901–64) Writer; became member of KPD in 1919; imprisoned in a fortress from 1930 to 1932 for "literary high treason"; imprisoned in Fuhlsbüttel concentration camp in 1933–34; fled to the Soviet Union via Prague in 1934; fought in Spanish Civil War in 1937; emigrated to the Soviet Union in 1939; returned to Germany (East) in 1945; became president of the German Academy of Arts in Berlin in 1962. *206.*

Breitenbuch, Eberhard von (born 1910) Professional soldier, cavalry captain, staff officer attached to Field Marshals Kluge and Busch. *122.*

Breitscheid, Rudolf (1874–1944) Economist, politician; became member of SPD in 1912, of USPD from 1917 to 1922, and of SPD in 1922; city councilman from Wilmersdorf district in Berlin from 1914 to 1920; member of Reichstag from 1920 to 1933 (first in USPD, then in SPD); member of executive committee of SPD from 1931 to 1933; fled to Switzerland and France in 1933; deported in 1941; imprisoned in a concentration camp; allegedly was killed during a bombing raid in Buchenwald. *92, 137, 138, 170.*

Breitzke, Auguste (1908–82) Worker in Hannover; became member of SPD in 1926; became leading figure in Socialist Front in 1933; arrested in 1936; sentenced by People's Court in September 1937 to two years' imprisonment, which was spent in women's prison at Lübeck-Lauerhof. *238.*

Bretschneider, Hein (1904–44) Carpenter in Hamburg; became member of KPD in 1930; sentenced in 1931 to one and one-half years' confinement in a fortress; sentenced in 1933 to twenty-one months' imprisonment, then to four years' imprisonment in concentration camp; arrested in October 1942; failed to return from prison furlough; arrested again in March 1944; sentenced to death by People's Court in May 1944 and executed in June 1944 in Hamburg prison. *125.*

Brill, Hermann (1895–1959) Lawyer; became member of SPD in 1922; member of Thüringen state parliament from 1920 to 1932 and in 1933; dismissed from state service in 1933; arrested in September 1938; sentenced by People's Court to twelve years' imprisonment in July 1939; confined in Brandenburg prison and Buchenwald; became member of regional executive board of Thüringen branch of SPD in 1945; state secretary and director of the Hessian Chancery from 1946 to 1949; member of Bundestag from 1949 to 1953. *33, 170, 171.*

Brockdorff-Ahlefeldt, Count Walter von (1887–1943) Professional soldier, infantry general, commanding officer of Potsdam garrison in 1938–39, commanding officer of the Twenty-third Infantry Division from September 1939 until June 1940. *61.*

Brundert, Willi (1912–70) Lawyer and politician; member of SPD; head of Ministry of Economics of Saxony-Anhalt from 1946 to 1950; sentenced to 15 years' imprisonment in Dresden in April 1950; early release from prison in 1957; settled in FRG; chief of the Hessian Chancery in 1963–64; member of SPD; mayor of Frankfurt am Main from 1964 to 1970. *221.*

Brüning, Heinrich (1885–1970) Politician, member of Center Party; executive director of Alliance of Christian Trade Unions from 1920 to 1930; entered Reichstag in 1924; Reich chancellor from 1930 to 1932; fled to Netherlands in 1934, settled in the United States in 1935; became professor at Harvard University in 1939; appointment at University of Cologne in 1951; returned to the United States in 1955. *3.*

Brunner, Anton (born 1923 or 1924) High school student, school friend of Josef Landgraf; arrested in January in 1942; sentenced to death by People's Court in August 1942; sentence commuted to five years' imprisonment after retrial. *191.*

Buch, Eva-Maria (1921–43) Bookseller; became student at German Institute of Foreign Studies in Berlin in 1940; arrested in October 1942; sentenced to death by Reich Court-Martial in February 1943; executed in Berlin-Plötzensee in August 1943. *225.*

Bussche-Streithorst, Baron Axel von dem (1919–93) Career officer; held rank of major; witnessed a mass shooting of Jews in Dubno in 1942; escaped arrest in July 1944; began study of law after 1945; adviser in German embassy in Washington from 1954 to 1958. *122.*

Calvi, Otto (born 1902) Economist; became member of SPD in 1926; teacher at Labor School in Leipzig from 1931–1933; taken into "protective custody" during March/April 1933; temporary work in Heilbronn from July 1933 to 1934; arrested in October 1934; sentenced to twenty months' imprisonment in 1935; later emigrated to South America. *221, 222.*

Canaris, Wilhelm (1887–1945) Career officer; organizer of citizens' militia during 1919–20; commander of naval base at Swinemünde; director of Counterintelligence Office from 1935 to 1944; promoted to admiral; dismissed in 1944; arrested in July 1944; held in Flossenbürg concentration camp; murdered in Flossenbürg in April 1945 after SS summary court trial. *60, 62, 127, 128–29, 143, 144, 145, 174, 175.*

Caracciola-Delbrück, Günther (1898–1945) Career officer; General von Epp's contact to Wehrmacht; arrested and shot during attempted putsch by "Bavarian Freedom Action" in April 1945. *162–63.*

Charisius, Eberhard (born 1916) Career officer; entered Hitler Youth at end of 1931; later entered SS; in Soviet POW camp as first lieutenant; accompanied Red Army during its advance into Germany; went to the GDR as commander of the National People's Army after 1945; became professor of military science at Dresden Military Academy. *206.*

Christoffers, Hans (1905–42) Ship's carpenter in Hamburg; became member of KPD in 1930; arrested in 1933 and sentenced to three years' imprisonment; confined in Sachsenhausen concentration camp from 1936 to 1939; became soldier in 1941; died of typhus as watch guard in POW camp at Wietzendorf. *125.*

Coppi, Hans (1916–42) Lathe operator; member of KJVD; sentenced in 1934 to one year's imprisonment in juvenile penitentiary; arrested in September 1942 with his wife, Hilde; sentenced to death by Reich Court-Martial in December 1942 and executed in Berlin-Plötzensee. *225.*

Dahlem, Franz (1892–1981) Journalist, politician; became member of trade union in 1911, of SPD in 1913, of USPD in 1917; became member of KPD's central committee and politburo in 1920; member of Prussian state parliament from 1921 to 1924; entered Reichstag in 1928; moved to Paris in 1933; director of political commission of International Brigades in Madrid from 1937 to 1939; internment in France from 1939 to 1942; extradited to Germany in 1942 and held in Mauthausen concentration camp until 1945; after 1945 in central committee of KPD; after 1946 in executive committee of SED; after 1950 in central committee and politburo of SED; removed from all offices in 1953; rehabilitated in 1956. *16.*

Dahrendorf, Gustav (1901–54) Politician, editor; became member of SPD in 1918; member of Hamburg city council from 1928 to 1933;

member of Reichstag in 1932–33; confined in Fuhlsbüttel concentration camp in 1933; became salesman in Berlin in 1934; arrested after July 20, 1944, assassination attempt on Hitler; sentenced by People's Court to seven years' imprisonment in October 1944; liberated from Brandenburg prison in April 1945. *9, 242.*

Daniels, Lord Alexander von (1891–1960) Career soldier; held rank of major general; participated in Russian campaign. *207.*

Danz, Hermann (1906–45) Locksmith; became member of KPD in 1923; entered Lenin School in Moscow in 1928; returned to Germany in 1931; became head of regional administration of KPD in Magdeburg-Anhalt in 1933; arrested twice in 1933; sentenced to three years' imprisonment in 1934; arrested again in July 1944; sentenced to death by People's Court in November 1944 and executed in Brandenburg prison in February 1945. *23, 145–46.*

Debus, Oskar (1896–1942) Social Democrat, functionary of cooperative society; arrested in 1939 and sentenced to five years' imprisonment; died in Brandenburg prison in December 1942. *170.*

Dehler, Thomas (1897–1967) Lawyer, politician; cofounded Reichsbanner Black Red Gold in 1924; member of executive committee of DDP/DSP; in forced labor camp in 1944; member of Bundestag from 1949 to 1967 (FDP); federal minister of justice from 1949 to 1953; chairman of the FDP in Bundestag from 1953 to 1956; national chairman of FDP from 1954 to 1957; vice president of German Bundestag from 1960 to 1967. *242.*

Delp, Alfred (1907–45) Jesuit priest; ordained in 1937; began editing Catholic journal *Stimmen der Zeit* (Voices of the time) in 1939; pastoral work in Munich from 1941 to 1944; arrested in July 1944; sentenced to death by People's Court in January 1945 and executed in Berlin-Plötzensee in February 1945. *42, 43, 55, 195, 196, 198, 228, 229.*

Dietz, Johannes B. (1879–1959) Catholic clergyman; ordained in 1905; became assistant priest in Bayreuth in 1907; became suffragan bishop of Fulda in 1936; became bishop of Fulda in 1939; became papal inspector of diocesan and order seminaries in Germany in 1940. *196, 228.*

Dietze, Constantin von (1891–1973) Economist; taught in Göttingen and Rostock; professor in Jena from 1927 to 1933, then in Berlin from 1933 to 1937; forbidden to teach in 1937; arrested and charged; became professor in Freiburg im Breisgau; suspended in 1944–45; held in detention from September 1944 until April 1945 in concentration camps (including in Ravensbrück); rector of University of Freiburg im Breisgau from 1946 to 1949. *55, 164, 165.*

Dirks, Walter (1901–91) Catholic journalist; editor of features section of *Rhein-Mainische Volkszeitung* (Rhine-Main people's news) from 1924 to 1934; worked for features section of *Frankfurter Zeitung* (Frankfurt times) from 1935 to 1943; became cofounder of CDU in Frankfurt am Main after end of war; coeditor of *Frankfurter Hefte* (Frankfurt journal); director of Main Cultural Division at West German Radio in Cologne from 1956 to 1967. *47.*

Dohnanyi, Hans von (1902–45) Lawyer; became personal press agent of Reich minister of justice in 1929; dismissed in 1938 and transferred to Leipzig as a justice of the Reich; became special director in Counterintelligence Office at High Command of Armed Forces in 1939; arrested in 1943 due to alleged foreign currency improprieties; murdered in Sachsenhausen concentration camp after a SS summary court proceeding in April 1945. *128, 144, 145.*

Dohrn, Harald (1895–1945) Father-in-law of Christoph Probst; tried before Special Court in State Court in Munich in July 1943 and acquitted; murdered in Perlach Forest on April 29, 1945. *252.*

Dupré, Walter (born circa 1904) Member of KPD in 1920s, afterward member of KPDO and SPD; before 1933, member of Leninist Organization; fled to France after Leninist Organization split; returned to Germany (West) in 1945; member of SPD. *215.*

Düwer, Gerhard (born 1924) Administrative apprentice, member of Hitler Youth; arrested in 1942; sentenced by People's Court to four years' imprisonment in August 1942; imprisoned at Hamburg-Glasmorr and in prison camp at Graudenz; forced labor in underground airplane factories; imprisoned in Hannover youth penitentiary; drafted into Wehrmacht in 1945; taken as POW by British. *190.*

Ebeling, Hans (1897–1968) Writer; founding member of Young National League in 1921; fled to the Netherlands in 1934; moved to Brussels in 1936; editor of *Kameradschaft: Schriften junger Deutscher* (Camaraderie: The writings of young Germans) until 1940; established ties to British military authorities in 1939; worked with exile government of Republic of Czechoslovakia; returned to Germany (West) in 1950. *75–76.*

Eichler, Willi (1896–1971) Journalist, politician, member of SPD; expelled from party in 1925; fled to France in 1933 and to England in 1939; worked at BBC; returned to Germany (West) in 1945; editor in chief of *Rheinische Zeitung* (Rhine news); member of executive board of

SPD from 1946 to 1968; member of North Rhine-Westphalian state parliament from 1947 to 1948; member of Bundestag from 1949 to 1953. *32, 181.*

Eickemeyer, Manfred (1903–78) Painter and architect in Munich; became soldier in General Government in 1940; made his gallery available to the White Rose; arrested in April 1943; acquitted before a Special Court of the Munich State Court in July 1943. *250, 252.*

Einsiedel, Count Heinrich von (born 1921) Journalist, career soldier, lieutenant; as a fighter pilot, taken as POW by Soviets on eastern front in August 1942; returned from the Soviet Union in July 1947; journalist in East Berlin; moved to West Germany in 1948; works as journalist and translator. *195, 206, 207.*

Einsiedel, Horst von (1905–47 or 1948) Studied law; became member of SPD in 1930; began working at Reich Office of Statistics in 1934, dismissed, then worked at the Reich Office of Chemistry until 1945; entered economic administration of Berlin magistrate in 1945; arrested by Soviet secret police in October 1945; presumably died in Soviet internment camp at Sachsenhausen in 1948. *225.*

Elsas, Fritz (1890–1945) Lawyer, local politician (DDP); vice president of German Towns' Conference in 1926; mayor of Berlin from 1931 to 1933; relieved of office in 1933; arrested in 1937; arrested again in 1944; murdered in Sachsenhausen concentration camp in January 1945. *243.*

Elser, Johann Georg (1903–45) Furniture maker; unemployed from 1930 to 1933, then worked as cabinetmaker and at odd jobs; arrested in Constance in 1939; imprisoned in Sachsenhausen and Dachau; murdered in Dachau in April 1945. *x, 132–34.*

Emendörfer, Max (1911–74) Shoemaker, member of KPD; arrested several times after 1933; imprisoned in Esterwegen concentration camp from 1935 to 1937; began serving on eastern front in December 1941; deserted to Red Army in 1942; in Siberian prison camp after 1945; returned to GDR in 1956; editor of the SED's newspaper *Freiheit* (Freedom). *207, 209.*

Engert, Otto (1895–1945) Carpenter; became member of SPD in 1912 and member of KPD in 1919; member of Thüringian state parliament from 1924 to 1928; expelled from KPD in 1928; imprisoned in Coldnitz and Sachsenhausen concentration camps in 1933–34; arrested again in July 1944; sentenced to death by People's Court in November 1944; executed in Berlin-Plötzensee in January 1945. *234, 235.*

Erler, Fritz (1913–67) Politician; member of SPD and SAJ; became city inspector in Berlin in 1935; dismissed in 1937; imprisoned from 1938 to 1945; member of Bundestag from 1949 to 1966; became member of executive board of SPD in 1956; SPD chairman in German Bundestag in 1964. *33, 170.*

Erpenbeck, Fritz (1897–1975) Writer, actor at the Piscator-Bühne in Berlin; editor of the socialist journal *Roter Pfeffer* (Red pepper) from 1930 to 1933; fled to Prague in 1933 and to Moscow in 1935; returned to Germany (East) in 1945; began working as theater critic in 1946; head dramatic producer of Volksbühne of East Berlin from 1959 to 1962. *210.*

Eschborn, Jacob Student of Catholic theology; member of the Order of the Heart of Jesus; volunteer in Russian campaign; taken by Soviets as POW. *206.*

Eschen, Heinz (1909–38) Medical student; member of KJVD and KPD; imprisoned in Dachau in 1933; block elder in Dachau from February 1937 until his death. *83.*

Eucken, Walter (1891–1950) Political economist; professor in Tübingen from 1925 to 1927 and in Freiburg im Breisgau from 1927 to 1950; became member of Academic Advisory Council within Bizone and at Federal Ministry of Economics in 1948. *164, 165, 196.*

Fabian, Walter (1902–92) Journalist; member of SPD from 1924 to 1931; worked at social democratic newspapers; cofounded SAPD in 1931 and became member of party's executive board in 1932; fled to France via Switzerland in 1933 and worked in exile administration of SAPD in Paris; expelled from party in 1937; became SDS member in Switzerland in 1945; returned to West Germany in 1957 and became an honorary professor at the University of Frankfurt. *31.*

Faulhaber, Jacob (1900–1942) Locksmith, gardener in Mannheim; became member of SPD in 1922 and of KPD in 1930; in "protective custody" from March 1933 until 1935; later opened a nursery in Mannheim; arrested in February 1942; sentenced to death by People's Court in May 1942; executed in Stuttgart in September 1942. *196, 199.*

Faulhaber, Michael von (1869–1952) Catholic clergyman; ordained in 1892; professor in Strasbourg from 1903 to 1910; became bishop of Speyer in 1910 and archbishop of Munich-Freising in 1917; named cardinal in 1921. *228.*

Feuchtwanger, Lion (1884–1958) Writer; citizenship revoked while on a visit to the United States in 1933; in southern France until 1940; visited Soviet Union in 1936–37; interned in France in 1940; fled to

New York via Spain and Portugal; settled in California in 1943. *5, 92, 138, 170.*

Feurstein, Heinrich (1877–1942) Catholic clergyman; ordained in 1899; pastoral work in Donaueschingen in 1906; taken into "protective custody" in January 1942; forbidden to teach; imprisoned in Dachau in June 1942, where he was presumably murdered in August 1942. *54.*

Fexer, Friedrich (born 1924) High school student in Vienna; school friend of Josef Landgraf; arrested in January 1942; sentenced to imprisonment by People's Court in August 1942. *191.*

Fischer, Kurt (1900–1950) Politician; became member of KPD in 1919; emigrated to the Soviet Union in 1920; after return to Germany, became KPD secretary in Mecklenburg; fled to the Soviet Union in 1933, where he entered Red Army; worked for secret service; returned to Dresden in 1945, where he became mayor; became member of Saxony state parliament in 1946; deputy prime minister and minister of the interior of Saxony from 1946 to 1948. *210.*

Fischer, Ruth (1895–1961) Politician, journalist; cofounded Austrian Communist Party in 1918; chairperson of KPD in Berlin in 1921; member of Reichstag from 1924 to 1928; expelled from KPD in 1926; member of Reich administration of Left Opposition of KPD; cofounded Lenin League in 1928; fled to Paris in 1933 and to the United States in 1940; returned to Europe and taught in Paris after 1945. *246.*

Fleischer, Carl Economist; member of Steel Helmet; participated as captain in Russian campaign; taken as POW by Soviets. *209.*

Fleschhut, Reinhold (born 1908) Salesman; participated as soldier in Russian campaign; deserted to Red Army; returned to Germany (East) in 1945; mayor of Leipzig from 1955 to 1957; director of German Tobacco Goods Export/Import in Leipzig. *206.*

Florin, Wilhelm (1894–1944) Politician; became member of USPD in 1917 and of KPD in 1920; member of Reichstag from 1924 to 1933; became member of central committee of KPD in 1925 and member of that party's politburo in 1929; city councilman in Essen from 1928 to 1932; fled to France in 1933; participated in forming of exile administration of KPD in Paris; settled in the Soviet Union in 1935; secretary of executive committee of Communist International from 1935 to 1943; became chairman of International Control Commission in 1937. *16, 206.*

Frank, Karl Borromäus (1893–1969) Psychologist, journalist; became member of Austrian Communist Party in 1919; settled in Berlin in 1920; member of KPD; held leading functions in KPD and Austrian Communist Party from 1920 to 1928; switched to KPDO in 1929;

became member of SAPD in 1932 and later of SPD; emigrated to Republic of Czechoslovakia via Austria in 1933, to France in 1938, and to the United States via England in 1939; worked as psychoanalyst in New York. *215, 216.*

Franke, Vera Member of Leninist Organization and secretary in its head office; began working in its provincial department in 1935; fled to Prague in fall of 1935, to Paris at beginning of 1936, and to Spain probably in 1940; later settled in New York, where she worked as an editor. *215.*

Frankenberg und Proschlitz, Egbert von (born 1909) Career soldier; became member of NSDAP in 1931 and of SS in 1932; member of Legion Condor in 1938–39; became major in 1942; taken as POW by Soviets in May 1943; returned to Germany (East) in 1947; NDPD functionary; representative in GDR's Volkskammer from 1951 to 1954. *207.*

Frei, Bruno (1897–1988) Austrian writer; became member of Social Democratic Workers' Party in 1918; began working at *Weltbühne* (The world stage) in 1929; editor in chief of *Berlin am Morgen* (Berlin in the morning) from 1929 to 1933; fled to Prague in 1933; became member of KPD in 1934; fled to Paris in 1936; interned from 1939 to 1941; emigrated to Mexico via the United States in 1941; returned to Austria in 1946. *138.*

Fricke, Bruno (born 1900) Banker, member of NSDAP, SA leader; in Paraguay in 1931–32; returned to Germany in 1932; follower of Otto Strasser; fled to Paraguay before Hitler's assumption of power; settled in Argentina in 1935, where he was editor of journal *Die Schwarze Front* (The black front); became vice president of Free Germany Movement in 1941; imprisoned in 1943; fled to Paraguay in 1945; later returned to Hannover. *130.*

Frieb, Hermann (1909–43) Economist; head of socialist students' group at the University of Munich until 1933; after 1933, established contacts with Sopade and New Beginning leadership in Prague; drafted into military service in 1941; arrested on front in March 1942; sentenced to death by People's Court in May 1943 and executed in Munich-Stadelheim in August 1943. *33.*

Frölich, Paul (1884–1953) Journalist, politician; became member of SPD in 1902, of KPD in 1919, and of Spartacus League; in central committee of KPD from 1919 to 1924; member of Reichstag from 1921 to 1924 and from 1928 to 1930; expelled from KPD in 1928; cofounder of KPDO; expelled from party in 1932 and entered SAPD; arrested in

1933 and imprisoned in concentration camp; fled to Republic of Czechoslovakia 1934 and to France, where he was interned; fled to the United States in 1941; returned to FRG in 1950 and entered SPD. *31, 169, 171.*

Fuchs, Emil (1874–1971) Protestant theologian, pastor; member of executive committee of League of Religious Socialists; professor at Pedagogic Academy of Kiel from 1931 to 1933; dismissed in 1933; sentenced to one month in prison; professor and director of Religious Sociological Institute of University of Leipzig from 1949 to 1958. *47.*

Fugger von Glött, Prince Joseph Ernst (1895–1981) Agricultural scientist; arrested in 1944; sentenced by People's Court to three years' imprisonment in January 1945; imprisoned in Berlin-Tegel and Bayreuth; cofounder of CSU in 1945; party chairman of CSU; member of Bundestag from 1949 to 1953; member of Bavarian state parliament from 1954 to 1962. *204.*

Furtwängler, Hubert (born 1918) Student in Munich, confidant of the White Rose; interrogated several times by Gestapo in February and April 1943; became pediatrician in Munich after 1945. *249–50.*

Gabbey, Theo (1891–1938) Typesetter; became member of SPD in 1911, of USPD in 1919, of KPD in 1920, and of KPDO in 1929; arrested in February 1937; sentenced by People's Court to eight years' imprisonment in November 1937; confined in Brandenburg prison; early release in 1938; died as result of imprisonment. *168.*

Gablentz, Otto Heinrich von der (1898–1972) Political scientist; sympathizer of Religious Socialists; became press agent in Reich Office of Statistics in Berlin in 1925; dismissed in 1934; worked at Economic Group of Chemical Industry from 1934 to 1945; escaped arrest after July 20, 1944, assassination attempt on Hitler; became director of Department of Political Theory in 1948 and director of German College of Politics in West Berlin in 1955. *195.*

Galen, Count Clemens August von (1878–1946) Catholic clergyman; ordained in Münster in 1904; served in Berlin from 1919 to 1929; president of Association of Fellows in Berlin; became bishop of Münster in 1933; named cardinal in 1946. *52.*

Gehre, Ludwig (1895–1945) Career soldier, held rank of captain; associate of Hans Oster; able to flee after July 20, 1944, assassination attempt on Hitler; confined in Buchenwald from February to April 1945; murdered in Flossenbürg concentration camp after SS summary court proceeding in April 1945. *145.*

Gerlach, Heinrich (born 1908) Educator and writer; entered Wehrmacht in 1939; taken prisoner as first lieutenant by Soviets in 1943;

returned to FRG in 1950; teacher in North Rhine-Westphalia from 1951 to 1973. *6, 207, 209.*

Gerlach, Hellmut von (1866–1935) Lawyer, journalist; member of DDP from 1918 to 1922; editor in chief of *Welt am Montag* (World on Monday) until 1931; leading member of Reichsbanner Black Red Gold; as member of executive committee of *Weltbühne* (The world stage), defended Carl von Ossietzky; fled to Paris in 1933; worked at *Pariser Tageblatt* (Paris daily) and *Neue Weltbühne* (New world stage). *8.*

Gerlich, Fritz Michael (1883–1934) Journalist, cofounder of journal *Die Wirklichkeit* (Reality); editor in chief of *Münchner Neueste Nachrichten* (Latest Munich news) from 1920 to 1928; publisher of Catholic *Illustrierter Sonntag* (Sunday illustrated); taken into "protective custody" in 1933; confined in Dachau in 1934, where he was murdered as part of Röhm Putsch. *8–9.*

Gerngross, Rupprecht (born 1905) Studied law in Munich and London, lawyer; held rank of captain; wounded in Russia in 1941; became head of Interpreter Company of Army Corps Area VII at beginning of 1942. *162.*

Gersdorff, Baron Rudolf-Christoph von (1905–80) Career officer; successful completion of course of study at Academy of War in Berlin in 1938–1939; counterintelligence officer in Army Group Middle from 1941 to 1943; chief of staff of Seventh Army in 1944–45; evaded Gestapo; in American POW camp from 1945 to 1947. *66, 121–22.*

Gerstenmaier, Eugen (1906–86) Protestant clergyman, politician; began working in ecclesiastical Foreign Office of Protestant Church in Berlin in 1936; called to serve in cultural-political department of Foreign Office in 1940; arrested on July 20, 1944; sentenced by People's Court to seven years' imprisonment in January 1945; became member of synod of German Evangelical Church in 1948; became member of Bundestag (CDU) in 1949; president of Bundestag from 1954 to 1965; became deputy chairman of CDU in 1956. *195, 196.*

Gessler, Otto (1875–1955) Politician; cofounder of DDP in 1918; Reich minister for reconstruction in 1919; Reich defense minister from 1920 to 1928; left DDP in 1927; retreat into private life in 1933; arrested after July 20, 1944, assassination attempt on Hitler; spent seven months imprisoned in Ravensbrück concentration camp; became president of German Red Cross in 1950. *204.*

Geussenhainer, Frederik (1912–45) Medical student in Hamburg; arrested in July 1943; held in police prison at Fuhlsbüttel and in

Neuengamme concentration camp; sentenced by People's Court to imprisonment in April 1945; died in Mauthausen concentration camp in 1945. *253.*

Geyer, Curt (1891–1967) Politician; became member of USPD in 1917 and of KPD in 1920; member of Reichstag from 1920 to 1924; expelled from KPD in 1921; became member of SPD in 1922; editor of SPD newspaper *Vorwärts* (Forward); fled to Prague in 1933; member of exile executive committee of SPD from 1938 to 1942; moved to England in 1939; correspondent of *Süddeutsche Zeitung* (South German news) in London from 1947 to 1963. *219.*

Geyer, Wilhelm (1900–1968) Painter in Munich; tried before a Special Court of State Court of Munich in July 1943; acquitted. *250, 252.*

Gisevius, Hans Bernd (1904–74) Adviser in Reich Ministry of Interior; became counterintelligence officer under Canaris in 1939; worked at German Consulate General in Zürich from 1940 to 1944; traveled to Berlin shortly before July 20, 1944, assassination attempt on Hitler and fled to Switzerland after that attempt. *144, 156, 158, 174.*

Goerdeler, Carl Friedrich (1884–1945) Lawyer, politician; mayor of Leipzig from 1930 to 1936; Reich commissioner for price control in 1931 and 1934/35; adviser to Bosch Company; went underground before July 20, 1944, assassination attempt on Hitler; arrested in August 1944; sentenced to death by People's Court in September 1944 and executed in Berlin-Plötzensee in February 1945. *37, 38, 40, 42, 43, 61, 63, 121, 156, 157, 164, 165, 172, 173–76, 196, 197, 242, 243.*

Goldstein, Arthur Journalist; became member of SPD in 1914, of USPD in 1917, and of KPD in 1919; cofounded KAPD in 1920 and served as its representative in executive committee of Communist International in Moscow; became member of SPD in 1922; fled to Paris in 1933, where probably was murdered by SS during the war. *32, 223.*

Gossens, Hans (1921–72) Student; served as volunteer in Russian campaign; taken prisoner by Soviets in July 1941; returned to Germany (East) after end of war; functionary of Free German Youth; became major in border police in 1957; held ranks of lieutenant colonel and colonel in National People's Army. *207.*

Gottfurcht, Hans (1896–1982) Trade unionist; became member of SPD in 1913 and trade union employee in 1919; established connection with Sopade in Prague after 1933; imprisoned in 1937; fled to London via Holland in 1938; became member of Labour Party; became member of KPD in 1941; general secretary of International Association of Free

Trade Unions in Brussels from 1952 to 1963; moved to Switzerland in 1961. *33, 215.*

Götze, Ferdinand (born 1907) Became member of Reich executive committee of outlawed FAUD after Hitler's assumption of power; fled to Republic of Czechoslovakia in 1934, to Spain in 1935, to Norway via France in 1939, and to Sweden in 1940, where he was interned; remained in Sweden after the war. *118.*

Graf, Willi (1918–43) Member of Catholic youth league New Germany and of boy's group Grey Order; began studying medicine in Bonn in 1937; became medical orderly in Wehrmacht in 1940; soldier in Russia in 1942; arrested in 1943; sentenced to death by People's Court in April 1943 and executed in October 1943. *249–52.*

Grandy, Theo Electrician; participated in Russian campaign as noncommissioned officer; returned to Germany (East) after 1945. *207.*

Grimme, Adolf (1889–1963) Cultural politician, Religious Socialist; became member of SPD in 1922; senior civil servant in Prussian Ministry of Culture in 1928–29; vice president of Provincial School Collegium of Berlin and Brandenburg in 1929–30; dismissed from his offices in 1932; arrested in 1942; imprisoned; minister of culture in Lower Saxony from 1946 to 1948. *224.*

Grimminger, Eugen (1892–1986) Accountant; dismissed in 1935; helped friends flee with falsified passports; arrested in March 1943; sentenced by People's Court to ten years' imprisonment in April 1943; held in Ludwigsburg prison; president of Württemberg Raiffeisen Cooperatives from 1946 to 1958. *252.*

Groscurth, Helmuth (1898–1943) Career officer, held rank of lieutenant colonel; began working for Counterintelligence Office in 1935; became head of Department for Special Assignments in High Command of Armed Forces in 1939; became head of Department of Troop Affairs in High Command of Armed Forces in 1940; became head of General Staff of army corps outside of Stalingrad in 1942; died of typhus in Soviet POW camp in 1943. *63–64, 144, 175.*

Gross, Nikolaus (1898–1945) Miner, cofounder of Christian Miners' Movement, trade union secretary, editor of *Westdeutsche Arbeiterzeitung* (Western German workers' news); began social work in 1941; imprisoned in August 1944 and held in Ravensbrück concentration camp and in Berlin-Tegel; sentenced to death by People's Court in January 1945 and executed. *55, 228.*

Grosz, George (1893–1959) Painter and graphic artist; member of KPD from 1918 to 1923; fled to the United States in January 1933; his works were exhibited as "degenerate art" in Munich in 1937; German citizenship revoked in 1938; returned to West Berlin in 1959. *4, 5.*

Grüber, Heinrich (1891–1975) Protestant clergyman; became pastor in Berlin in 1934; arrested in 1940 and imprisoned in Sachsenhausen and Dachau concentration camps until 1943; became provost in Soviet sector of Berlin after end of war; German Evangelical Church's authorized agent in GDR government from 1949 to 1958. *51, 124.*

Grün, Fancia (1904–45) Secretary of Jewish Congregation of Berlin; went underground in 1943; arrested in 1943 and deported to Theresienstadt, from where she escaped; arrested again in 1944; murdered in Theresienstadt in 1945. *140.*

Grylewicz, Anton (1885–1971) Politician; became member of SPD in 1912 and of USPD in 1917; chairman of USPD in Berlin in 1920; member of KPD from 1920 to 1927; member of Prussian state parliament and of Reichstag in 1924; in central committee of KPD in 1924–25; in Left Opposition of KPD in 1926; Reich director of organization of Lenin League in 1928; fled to Prague in 1933, to Paris in 1937, and to Cuba in 1941; returned to FRG in 1955; member of SPD. *246.*

Guddorf, Wilhelm (1902–43) Journalist, member of KPD, editor in chief of *Die Rote Fahne* (The red banner); arrested in 1934; held in prisons and concentration camps until 1939; afterward employed in a bookstore in Berlin; taken into police custody for one month in 1939; arrested again in October 1942; sentenced to death by Reich Court-Martial in February 1943 and executed in May 1943. *126, 225.*

Gumbel, Emil Julius (1891–1966) Mathematician, pacifist; joined New Germany League (later the German League for Human Rights) in 1915; taught at University of Heidelberg from 1923 to 1932; dismissed from university post and emigrated to Paris in 1932; moved to the United States in 1940. *5, 6.*

Gundelach, Gustav (1888–1962) Politician; became member of SPD in 1909, of USPD in 1919, and of KPD in 1920; Hamburg city council from 1924 to 1933; fled to Copenhagen in 1934; arrested in Switzerland and extradited in 1936; fought in Spanish Civil War in 1937–38; lived in Denmark in 1938–39; settled in the Soviet Union in 1940; returned to Germany in April 1945; left Soviet Occupation Zone for Hamburg in 1946; member of executive committee of KPD and of Bundestag from 1949 to 1953. *195.*

Günther, Hanno (1921–42) Baker; became member of Young Pioneers in 1930; became member of Young Folk in 1933 and of Hitler Youth in 1935; left Hitler Youth in 1936; drafted into Wehrmacht in 1941;

arrested in July 1941; sentenced to death by People's Court in October 1942 and executed in December 1942. *69, 177–78.*

Guter, Heinrich (born 1925)   Student; architect in Munich after 1945. *251.*

Guttenberg, Baron Karl-Ludwig von und zu (1902–45)   Land owner, monarchist, publisher of *Weisse Blätter* (White notes), mouthpiece of monarchist-conservative opposition in Bavaria; worked in Counterintelligence Office in High Command of Armed Forces; murdered in Berlin on April 23, 1945. *35, 196, 203, 239, 240.*

Haas, Johann Otto (1906–44)   Intermediate school teacher in Vienna; worked for Revolutionary Socialists and New Beginning from 1936 to 1942; arrested in July 1942; sentenced to death by People's Court in December 1943 and executed in August 1944. *33.*

Haberl, Hans (born 1924)   High-frequency engineer, member of Catholic Fellows' Association; arrested in January 1942; sentenced to death by People's Court in September 1942; death sentence commuted to eight years' imprisonment in summer of 1943. *190, 191.*

Hadermann, Ernst (1896–1968)   Teacher; forbidden to teach history in 1933; became member of NSDAP in 1937; volunteered for Wehrmacht in 1939; attained rank of captain; taken as POW by Soviets in 1941; became professor in Potsdam in 1948; professor in Halle-Wittenberg from 1955 to 1962. *206, 210.*

Haecker, Theodor (1879–1945)   Journalist, translator, philosopher; converted to Catholicism in 1921; forbidden to speak publicly in 1935; forbidden to publish in 1938. *250.*

Haeften, Hans-Bernd von (1905–44)   Lawyer; became member of Confessing Church in 1933; worked in German diplomatic service in Copenhagen, Vienna, and Budapest; became deputy director of cultural-political department in Foreign Office in Berlin in 1940; arrested in July 1944; sentenced to death by People's Court and executed in August 1944. *195, 196, 198.*

Haeften, Werner von (1908–44)   Brother of Hans-Bernd von Haeften; corporate lawyer at a bank in Hamburg; first lieutenant in reserves; participated in Russian campaign; became adjunct of von Staffenberg in November 1943; summarily executed in Berlin during night of July 20–21, 1944. *188, 189.*

Halder, Franz (1884–1972)   Career officer; became major in 1924, colonel in 1931, brigadier general in 1934, and major general in 1936; Chief of General Staff of the Army from 1938 to 1942, then dismissed;

arrested in 1944; imprisoned in concentration camp during 1944–45; director of martial law research staff of U.S. Army from 1946 to 1961. *37, 61, 63, 64, 121, 128, 144, 174, 175, 197, 228.*

Halem, Nikolaus Christoph von (1905–44) Lawyer; left civil service in 1933, then worked in industry; arrested in 1942; imprisoned in penal camp at Wuhlheide, in Sachsenhausen concentration camp and in Brandenburg-Görden; sentenced to death by People's Court in 1944 and executed in October 1944. *121, 239, 240.*

Hallermann, Ernst (born 1911) Clerk; expelled from Wehrmacht in 1940 as so-called mongrel; arrested in Berlin in 1943; sentenced to eight years' imprisonment in January 1944 due to violations of war economic code; held in Brandenburg prison until end of war; has been living in Cologne since 1945. *192.*

Hallgarten, Constanze (1881–1969) Politician; director of Munich regional group of International Women's League for Peace and Freedom from 1919 to 1933; member of German Society for Peace and German League for League of Nations; fled to the United States via Austria, Switzerland, and France in 1933; returned to Germany in 1945. *6.*

Hansmann, Cilly (1908–64) Bookkeeper, wife of Wilhelm Knöchel; lived in Cologne until 1935; in face of threat of arrest, fled to Amsterdam in September 1935, where she worked as secretary of miners' union; repeatedly returned to the Ruhr after 1939; chairwoman of KPD in Cologne after 1945. *194.*

Harnack, Arvid (1901–42) Lawyer; director of task force for study of Soviet planned economy; task force dissolved in 1933; began working in Reich Ministry of Economics in 1935; became senior government adviser in 1942; pro forma entry into NSDAP in 1937; arrested in September 1942; sentenced to death by Reich Court-Martial and executed in December 1942. *22, 23, 126, 224–26.*

Harnack, Ernst von (1888–1945) Administrative lawyer; became member of SPD in 1919; became president of Merseburg in 1929; placed on temporary leave in 1932 and on permanent leave in 1933; under police surveillance in Berlin after two weeks in "protective custody"; began working as, among other things, commercial representative in 1937; arrested in September 1944; sentenced to death by People's Court in February 1945 and executed in March 1945. *197.*

Harnack, Falk (1913–91) Theater director, actor, dramatic producer; conscripted into military service in 1941; tried before People's Court in April 1943 and acquitted; became soldier in partisan movement E.L.A.S.

in Greece; returned to Germany (West); worked as theater and film director in East Berlin from 1949 to 1952; moved to West Berlin in 1952. *250, 251.*

Harnack, Mildred (1902–43) Lived in the United States as U.S. citizen until 1929 and subsequently moved to Germany with husband, Arvid; began teaching at University of Berlin in 1941; arrested in September 1942; sentenced by Reich Court-Martial in December 1942 to six years' imprisonment, which was changed to death sentence in January 1943; executed in Berlin-Plötzensee in February 1943. *224.*

Harnier, Baron Adolf von (1903–45) Lawyer; represented mostly emigrants in Munich; monarchist; arrested in October 1939; sentenced to ten years' imprisonment in June 1944 after five years in custody for investigation; died in Straubing prison in May 1945. *203, 204.*

Hassell, Ulrich von (1881–1944) Lawyer, diplomat; became vice-consul in Genoa in 1911; general consul in Barcelona from 1921 to 1926; ambassador in Copenhagen from 1926 to 1930, in Belgrade from 1930 to 1932, and in Rome in 1932; recalled in 1937 and began working in private sector; arrested after July 20, 1944, assassination attempt on Hitler; sentenced to death by People's Court and executed in September 1944. *37, 38, 39, 61, 156, 158, 174, 175, 176, 203.*

Haubach, Theodor (1896–1945) Journalist, member of SPD; in executive committee of Reichsbanner Black Red Gold in Hamburg; editor of *Frankfurter Echo* from 1924 to 1929; became press agent in Reich Ministry of Interior in 1929; dismissed from civil service in 1933; repeatedly arrested; imprisoned in Esterwegen concentration camp from 1934 to 1936; arrested again in August 1944; sentenced to death by People's Court and executed in January 1945. *9, 12, 34, 42, 195, 198, 221, 222, 242.*

Hauch, Fritz *130.*

Hauenstein, Fritz (1896–1979) Economist, journalist; began working at *Schwäbischer Merkur* (Swabian mercury) in 1926; editor of *Kölnische Zeitung* (Cologne news) from 1933 to 1945; conscripted into Wehrmacht in 1939; copublisher of journal *Die Gegenwart* (The present) from 1946 to 1958; editor of *Börsen- und Wirtschaftshandbuch* (Guide to stocks and economics) from 1950 to 1967; worked at *Frankfurter Allgemeine* (Frankfurt general) from 1959 to 1971. *165.*

Hausen, Erich (1900–1973) Politician; became member of trade union and USPD in 1919; member of KPD from 1920 to 1928; became member of KPDO in 1929; worked with Swiss Communist Party/Opposition in 1929–30; fled to Rastatt in 1933, but returned illegally that same year; taken into custody in 1934 due to infractions involving foreign currency, but not recognized by authorities; fled to France after 1934; interned in 1939; emigrated to the United States in 1941. *168.*

Haushofer, Albrecht (1903–45) Geographer, politician, writer; professor in Berlin from 1933 to 1940; honorary associate of Foreign Office; foreign policy adviser to Rudolf Hess until 1941; went underground after July 20, 1944, assassination attempt on Hitler; arrested at end of 1944; murdered by SS commando in Berlin prison in Lehrter Strasse in April 1945. *197, 225.*

Heartfield, John (1891–1968) Graphic artist, member of Dadaist movement; worked at Malik Publishing House and other places; became member of KPD in 1919; fled to England via Prague in 1933; settled in GDR in 1950. *4, 5.*

Heber, Karolus (born 1883) Leather tailor; became member of Reich executive committee of outlawed FAUD in Erfurt in May 1933; arrested in March 1937 and sentenced to three years' imprisonment. *118.*

Heckert, Fritz (1884–1936) Politician; became member of SPD in 1902; cofounder of Spartacus Group in Chemnitz in 1916; became member of USPD in 1917; cofounder of KPD; member of Reichstag from 1924 to 1933; became member of central committee of KPD in 1920 and member of that party's politburo in 1927; representative of KPD in Comintern in Moscow from 1932 to 1934; fled to the Soviet Union in 1933; became member of executive committee of Communist International in 1935. *15.*

Heiden, Konrad (1901–66) Writer, journalist, member of SPD; fled to Switzerland in 1933 and to Paris in 1934; contributor to *Pariser Tageblatt* (Paris daily); interned in 1939–40; fled to the United States via Lisbon in 1940; worked for Süddeutschen Rundfunk (South German Radio) from 1953 to 1962. *7.*

Heilmann, Horst (1923–42) Became member of Hitler Youth in 1937; began studying at University of Berlin in 1940; volunteered for army in 1941; studied at School of Counterintelligence and Translation in Meissen in 1941–42; worked in decoding department of Army High Command in 1942; arrested in September 1942; sentenced to death by Reich Court-Martial in December 1942 and executed in Berlin-Plötzensee. *225.*

Heinrich, Walter (1902–84) Political scientist, economist; member of Sudeten German Youth Movement; founder of Fellowship League for Folk and Sociopolitical Education in 1925; assistant of Othmar Spann; became general secretary of national board of directors of Home Guards in 1930; became professor in Vienna in 1933; dismissed in 1938; imprisoned for eighteen months in Dachau; professor at College of World Trade in Vienna from 1949 to 1972. *134, 135.*

Heinz, Friedrich Wilhelm (1899–1968) Career officer; member of "Ehrhardt Brigade"; SA leader until end of 1923; member of national executive board of Steel Helmet from 1925 to 1928; expelled from NSDAP; lieutenant colonel in Counterintelligence Office of High Command of Armed Forces; became commanding officer of Fourth Regiment of Brandenburg Division in 1941. *61, 121.*

Held, Ernst Stage producer; participated in Russian campaign; editor of *Freies Deutschland* (Free Germany), newspaper of National Committee "Free Germany." *209.*

Held, Heinrich (1897–1957) Protestant clergyman; pastor in Essen-Rüttenscheid from 1930 to 1946; repeatedly arrested, first time at beginning of July 1933; taken into custody for questioning in 1937; became member of council of German Evangelical Church in 1945; became superintendent and senior church adviser in 1946; president of Evangelical Church in Rhineland from 1948 to 1957. *108.*

Helmschrott, Leonhard Farmer; participated as volunteer in Russian campaign; returned to Germany (East) in 1945. *206.*

Henk, Emil (1883–1969) Writer and journalist; studied economics in Munich and Heidelberg; worked at *Frankfurter Zeitung* (Frankfurt times) and elsewhere; not a member of a political party, although sympathized with SPD; sentenced to twenty months' imprisonment in March 1935; released from prison in 1936, then established a pharmaceutical company. *221, 222.*

Herman-Friede, Eugen (born 1926) Schoolboy; went underground in 1943; arrested in 1944; after end of war, worked as journalist at *Märkische Volksstimme* (Brandenburg people's voice) in Potsdam; imprisoned in Soviet Occupation Zone during 1948–49; emigrated to Canada in 1950; returned to FRG in mid-1950s. *140.*

Hermann, Liselotte (Lilo) (1910–38) Studied biology and chemistry in Stuttgart and Berlin; member of KJVD; expelled from university in 1933; arrested in December 1935; sentenced to death by People's Court in June 1937 and executed in June 1938. *103.*

Herrnstadt, Rudolf (1903–66) Journalist, politician; member of KPD; editor and correspondent of *Berliner Tageblatt* (Berlin daily news) in Prague, Warsaw, and Moscow from 1928 to 1936; began working for Soviet news service in 1933; returned to Germany (East) in 1945; editor in chief of *Neues Deutschland* (New Germany) from 1949 to 1953; in central committee of SED from 1950 to 1953; in GDR's Volkskammer until 1954; expelled from party in 1954; academic assistant in central archives in Merseburg until 1966. *207, 209.*

Hertz, Paul (1888–1961) Politician; became member of SPD in 1905; of USPD in 1917; and again of SPD in 1922; editor of USPD newspaper *Die Freiheit* (Freedom) from 1918 to 1922; member of Reichstag from 1920 to 1933; became member of executive committee of SPD in 1933; fled to Prague, to Paris in 1938, and to the United States in 1939; returned to West Berlin in 1949; senator for Marshall Plan and credit system from 1951 to 1953; senator for economics and credit from 1955 to 1961. *170.*

Herzfelde, Wieland (1896–1988) Writer, publisher; grew up in Switzerland; moved to Berlin in 1914; worked as director of Malik Publishing House and elsewhere; became member of KPD in 1918; fled to Prague in 1933 and to New York via London in 1939; returned to Germany (East) in 1949; professor in Leipzig. *5.*

Hespers, Theodor (1903–43) Politician; became member of Christian Social Reich Party in 1925; joined International Workers' Relief in 1927 and Revolutionary Trade Union Opposition in 1932; fled to Netherlands in 1933; in underground until 1942; arrested in February 1942; sentenced to death by People's Court in July 1943 and executed in Berlin-Plötzensee in September 1943. *75, 76.*

Hesse, Helmut (1916–43) Began study of theology at Ecclesiastical College of Berlin (which had been founded by Confessing Church) in 1936; imprisoned with his father Hermann A. Hesse in Dachau at end of 1943, where he died in November 1943. *54.*

Hesse, Hermann Albert (1877–1957) Protestant clergyman; became pastor in Wuppertal-Elberfeld in 1916; became moderator of Reformed Federation for Germany in 1934; headmaster of Theological College of Confessing Church in Wuppertal-Elberfeld; arrested in June 1943; imprisoned in Dachau from November 1943 until April 1944. *54.*

Hetz, Karl (born 1906) Engineer; became member of NSDAP in 1937; participated in Russian campaign as major; taken as POW by Soviets; returned to Germany (East) after 1945; president of executive board of Reichsbahn (East German railways) in Halle. *206, 207, 209.*

Heuss, Theodor (1884–1963) Journalist, politician; lecturer at German College of Politics in Berlin from 1920 to 1933; member of Reichstag from 1924 to 1928 (DDP) and from 1930 to 1932 and 1933 (German State Party); minister of culture in Württemberg-Baden in

1945–46; chairman of FDP in 1948; first president of FRG from 1949 to 1959. *6, 7.*

Hilferding, Rudolf (1877–1941) Physician, politician, journalist; became member of USPD in 1917; member of executive committee of SPD from 1922 to 1933; member of Reichstag from 1924 to 1933; Reich minister of finance in 1923 and 1928–29; fled to Switzerland via Denmark in 1933; worked in Sopade (helping write "The Prague Manifesto"); settled in Paris in 1938; turned over to Gestapo in 1941; died in Gestapo custody. *219.*

Hiller, Kurt (1885–1972) Writer, member of Expressionist movement; founder and president of Revolutionary Pacifists in 1926; imprisoned in Sachsenhausen concentration camp in 1933; released in 1934 and fled to Prague; citizenship revoked in 1935; settled in London in 1938 and in Hamburg in 1955; became chairman of New Socialist Federation in 1956. *6.*

Hirsch, Helmut (1916–37) Student; as a Jew, went to study architecture in 1935 in Prague, where he had contact with the Black Front; planned a bomb attack on the Reich Party Day grounds in Nuremberg; due to betrayal, immediately arrested after entering Germany on December 21, 1936; sentenced to death by the People's Court in March 1937 and, despite U.S. intervention (Hirsch had American citizenship), executed on June 4, 1937. *75, 120–21, 130.*

Hirschfeldt, Edith (born 1903) Secretary; emigrated to the United States in 1948; returned to West Berlin in 1973. *140–41.*

Hirzel, Hans (born 1924) Student; sentenced by People's Court to five years' imprisonment in April 1943; after 1945, editor at *Frankfurter Hefte* (Frankfurt journal); secretary of journalist Walter Dirks; academic assistant to Theodor H. Adorno; member of CDU until 1993; became member of "Republikaner" in 1993. *251.*

Hirzel, Susanne (born 1921) Student at Stuttgart College of Music; sentenced by People's Court to six months' imprisonment in April 1943; living in Stuttgart since 1945. *251.*

Hoepner, Erich (1886–1944) Career officer; officer of General Staff from 1928 to 1930; became general and commander in chief of Fourth Panzer Army in 1938; expelled from Wehrmacht in January 1942 due to insubordination; arrested and executed in Berlin-Plötzensee in 1944. *188, 189.*

Hoernigk, Frank (born 1908) Lawyer; member of DVP prior to 1933; lawyer at State Court in Naumburg; conscripted into Wehrmacht in 1939; in American POW camp until 1946; member of FDP in FRG from

1946 to 1975; became adviser in Hessian Ministry of Justice in 1946; later became district magistrate in Bad Hersfeld. 242.

Hoernigk, Rudolf (1905–78) Economist; member of DDP from 1928 to 1930; in German State Party from 1930 to 1933; assistant at University of Halle from 1934 to 1937; expelled in June 1937 for political reasons; conscripted into Wehrmacht in September 1940; member of German Liberal Democratic Party from 1945 to 1948; became director of state insurance agency of Saxony-Anhalt in 1945; moved to Frankfurt am Main in 1948 and became member of FDP; became adviser in Federal Ministry of Labor in 1949 and director of state insurance agency in Hesse in 1953. 242.

Hoernle, Edwin (1883–1952) Politician; became member of SPD in 1910; became editor in chief of *Die Rote Fahne* (The red banner) in 1918 and cofounded KPD in Stuttgart; member of Reichstag from 1924 to 1933; fled to Moscow via Switzerland in 1933; agrarian policy maker; returned to Germany (East) in 1945. 206.

Hoffmann, Johannes (1890–1967) Politician; became editor in chief of *Saarbrücker Landeszeitung* (Saarbrücken state news), the organ of Center Party, in 1929; dismissed in 1933; became founder and director of *Neue Saarpost* (New Saar post) in 1934; fled to Luxembourg in 1935 and to Brazil in 1941; returned to Germany (West) in 1945; chairman of Christian People's Party from 1945 to 1956; prime minister of Saarland from 1947 to 1955. 230.

Höltermann, Karl (1894–1955) Journalist; cofounded Reichsbanner Black Red Gold in 1924 and served as its national director beginning in 1932; initiated "Protective Formation" in 1930; member of Iron Front; began working in Armed Services Commission of SPD in 1928; member of Reichstag in 1932–33; fled to Amsterdam in 1933 and to England in 1935; withdrew from exile politics in 1942. 12.

Homann, Heinrich (born 1911) Career officer, held rank of major; became member of NSDAP in 1933; taken as POW by Soviets in 1943; cofounder of NDPD in Soviet Occupation Zone in 1948; began serving in GDR's Volkskammer in 1950; vice president of Volkskammer from 1952 to 1954; became a deputy chairman of GDR's State Council in 1960. 206.

Honecker, Erich (1912–94) Politician; became member of KJVD in 1926 and of KPD in 1929; attended Lenin School in Moscow in 1930–31; arrested in December 1935; sentenced to ten years' imprisonment in June 1937; confined in Brandenburg-Görden prison until 1945; cofounded FDJ in 1946 and served as its chairman until 1955; became member of politburo of SED in 1950; became first secretary of central committee of SED in 1971; became chairman of GDR's state council in 1976; resigned from all offices in 1989; emigrated to Chile in 1992 and died there. *69.*

Hooven, Hans-Günther van (1896–1964) Travel agent; participated in Russian campaign as colonel; last head of communications of Sixth Army at Stalingrad. *207.*

Horion, Emma (1889–1982) Chairwoman of Catholic German Women's Organization in Düsseldorf from 1923 to 1942; active in helping women and girls; subjected to several Gestapo hearings after Hitler's assumption of power; given a "state warning" in 1943; cofounder of Mother's Convalescence Center after 1945. *108.*

Hörsing, Friedrich Otto (1874–1937) Member of SPD; regional secretary of SPD in Oppeln/Opole from 1908 to 1914; member of Workers' and Soldier's Council in Upper Silesia; president of Prussian province of Saxony from 1920 to 1927; federal chairman of Reichsbanner Black Red Gold in 1924; expelled from SPD and Reichsbanner in 1932. *12.*

Hübener, Helmuth (1925–42) Administrative apprentice in Hamburg; member of Mormon Church; entered Young Folk in 1938 and later Hitler Youth; arrested in February 1942; sentenced to death by People's Court in August 1942 and executed in Berlin-Plötzensee in October 1942. *78, 189, 190, 191.*

Huber, Kurt (1893–1943) Musicologist; became professor in Munich in 1926; named to post at Archives of German Music Research in Berlin in 1937; had conflicts with leadership of student groups and Hitler Youth; returned to Munich in 1938; arrested in February 1943; sentenced to death by People's Court in April 1943 and executed in Munich-Stadelheim in July 1943. *249–52.*

Huber, Rupert (1896–1945) Printer; member of Christian Socialist Reich Party; arrested in June 1944; sentenced to death by People's Court in December 1944; executed in Brandenburg-Görden prison in January 1945. *119, 120.*

Husemann, Friedrich (1873–1935) Trade unionist; member of SPD; became secretary of Miners' Union in 1902 and its chairman in 1919; became member of Prussian state assembly in 1920; member of Prussian state parliament from 1919 to 1924; became member of Reichstag in 1924; arrested several times in 1933; arrested again in 1935; shot in Papenburg-Esterwegen concentration camp in April 1935. *244.*

Husemann, Marta (1913–60) Tailor, actress; became member of KJVD in 1928 and of KPD in 1931; first interrogated by Gestapo in

1935; arrested in November 1936; imprisoned in Moringen concentration camp from March to June 1937; arrested again in September 1942; sentenced by Reich Court-Martial to four years' imprisonment in January 1943; worked in regional administration of KPD in Berlin after 1945. *224.*

Husemann, Walter (1909–43) Toolmaker; became member of KPD in 1928; editor in Essen and Mannheim; went underground in 1933; arrested in November 1936; imprisoned in Sachsenhausen and Buchenwald concentration camps; released in 1938; arrested again in September 1942; sentenced to death by Reich Court-Martial in January 1943 and executed in Berlin-Plötzensee in May 1943. *224.*

Husen, Paulus van (1891–1971) Lawyer; became deputy district magistrate in Silesia in 1920; member of Center Party; worked as lawyer in High Command of the Armed Forces in 1941; arrested in August 1944; sentenced by People's Court to three years' imprisonment in April 1945; judge in Germany (West) after 1945. *195, 196.*

Hutzelmann, Emma (1900–1944) Bookkeeper; became member of German Christian Social Reich Party in 1928; arrested in 1944; escaped from prison in summer of 1944; died in a hiding place during an air attack in 1944. *119, 120.*

Hutzelmann, Hans (1906–45) Mechanic; with his wife, became member of German Christian Social Reich Party in 1928; visited the Soviet Union in 1929 and 1931; arrested in June 1944; sentenced to death by People's Court in December 1944 and executed in Brandenburg prison in January 1945. *119, 120, 161.*

Igalffy, Ludwig (born 1924) High school student in Vienna, school friend of Josef Landgraf; arrested in January 1942; sentenced to prison by People's Court in August 1942. *191.*

Jacob, Berthold (1898–1944) Journalist, worked for *Weltbühne* (World stage); became member of SPD in 1928 and of USPD in 1931; emigrated to Strasbourg in 1932; kidnapped by Gestapo in 1935 and brought from Basel to Germany; settled in Paris in 1935; interned in 1939; fled to Lisbon via Spain in 1941; again kidnapped by Gestapo in Lisbon; died while Gestapo prisoner in Jewish Hospital in Berlin. *6.*

Jacob, Franz (1906–44) Mechanical engineer; became member of SPD in 1920 and of KPD in 1925; began serving in Hamburg city council in 1932; confined in prison and concentration camp from 1933 to 1940; fled from Hamburg to Berlin in 1942; arrested in July 1944; sentenced to death by People's Court and executed in September 1944. *x, 22, 23, 24, 125, 126, 145, 213, 232–33, 235.*

Jacoby, Henry (Heinz) (born 1905) Writer, member of Free Youth; became member of KPD in 1930; joined illegal KPD Opposition Group in 1933; arrested in 1934 and sentenced to two and one-half years' imprisonment; fled to France via Prague in 1936; interned in 1939; emigrated to the United States in 1941; worked with UN Food and Agriculture Organization after 1945. *247.*

Jahn, Hans (1885–1960) Politician, trade unionist (German Rail Workers' Union); dismissed in 1933; in Task Force Committee for Provisionary Reich Administration for Rebuilding of Trade Unions; arrested in 1935; fled to London in 1940 via Prague, Austria, Switzerland, Holland, and Belgium; returned to Germany (West) in 1945; chairman of Rail Workers' Trade Union from 1949 to 1959. *215.*

Jahres, Georg (1903–44) Locksmith; member of KPD; arrested at end of 1943; died during interrogation in January 1944. *119, 120.*

Jenssen, Otto (born 1885) History teacher at Workers' Educational Institute in Leipzig; Social Democrat; known as SPD ideologue due to his book *Friedrich Engels und die Naturwissenschaft* (Friedrich Engels and natural science); history teacher in Tinz from 1922 to 1933; began living in Gera after 1945; member of SED. *170.*

Jessen, Jens Peter (1895–1944) Political scientist; held professorships in Göttingen, Kiel, and Marburg beginning in 1932 and in Berlin beginning in 1935; captain in reserves under general quartermaster of army; arrested in August 1944; sentenced to death by People's Court and executed in Berlin-Plötzensee in November 1944. *37, 164, 174, 176.*

John, Otto (born 1909) Lawyer; fled to England via Madrid and Portugal after July 20, 1944, assassination attempt on Hitler; interned; began working at Calais Soldiers' Radio in 1944; worked at Foreign Office (UK) after 1945; became provisional director of Federal Office for Protection of the Constitution in 1950 and its president in 1952; in GDR for unknown reasons in 1955; sentenced to four years' imprisonment in FRG in 1956. *196.*

Joseph, Fred (1911–43) Arrested in 1934 for being youth leader of Würzburg Catholic Boy Scouts of St. George; arrested again in 1941; sentenced to one year's imprisonment; murdered in Auschwitz in 1943 after having been arrested again. *72.*

Jovy, Ernst Michael (1920–84) Student; member of outlawed Bündische Jugend (the reconstituted German Youth Movement); arrested in 1939; sentenced by People's Court to six years' imprisonment in September 1941; assigned to "Parole Unit 999" in November 1944; fled to

American army; earned doctorate with dissertation on Youth Movement in 1952 and later worked in diplomatic service of FRG. 76.

Jung, Edgar J. (1894–1934) Journalist, lawyer; fought in Freikorps Epp against soviet republic in Bavaria in 1919; attorney in Zweibrücken; extradited from the Palatinate in 1923; private adviser to Franz von Papen in 1933–34; shot near Oranienburg on June 30, 1934. *x, 149–51.*

Kaas, Ludwig (1881–1952) Catholic clergyman, politician; ordained in 1906; represented Center Party in Constitutional Committee of National Assembly in 1919; as chairman of Center Party, advocated cooperation with NSDAP in 1931; participated in Reich concordat negotiations in Rome in 1933. *128.*

Kageneck, Count Heinrich von (1886–1957) Conservative; personal adviser to von Papen when von Papen was vice president; fortuitously escaped being murdered in 1934. *150.*

Kaiser, Hermann (1885–1945) Teacher; early member of NSDAP; reserve officer; transferred to High Command of Armed Forces in 1940; kept war diaries at headquarters of commanding officer of Home Army; arrested after July 20, 1944, assassination attempt on Hitler; sentenced to death by People's Court and executed in Berlin-Plötzensee in January 1945. *174, 175, 176.*

Kaiser, Jakob (1888–1961) Trade unionist, politician; member of executive board of German Christian Trade Unions from 1924 to 1933; member of Reichstag in 1933 (Center Party); went underground in 1944–45; cofounded CDU in Soviet Occupation Zone and Berlin in 1945; federal minister for pan-German affairs from 1949 to 1957; deputy federal chairman of CDU until 1958. *37, 47, 55, 174, 244, 245.*

Kampffmeyer, Paul (1864–1945) Journalist, historian, member of SPD; began working at *Sozialistische Hefte* (Socialist notebooks) in 1885; became archive director and literary consultant of Dietz Publishing House in Berlin in 1921. *5.*

Kapelle, Heinz (1913–41) Printer; became member of KJVD in 1931; arrested and sentenced to two years' imprisonment in 1934; arrested again in October 1939 and sentenced to death by People's Court; executed in Berlin-Plötzensee in July 1941. *69.*

Kaps, Alfons (1901–43) Waiter, politician; fled to the Netherlands in 1934; instructor at KPD Western Divisional Administration in Amsterdam from 1937 to 1939; went to Ruhr area to reorganize KPD in 1941; worked for underground journals *Der Friedenskämpfer* (The fighter for peace) and *Freiheit* (Freedom); arrested in January 1943 and committed suicide while in detention. *194.*

Kaufmann, Franz (1886–1944) Senior government adviser; participated in Epp's attempt to overthrow government in 1918; worked in Prussian Ministry of Interior in 1922; dismissed after eight months due to political differences with Severing and subsequently worked in Reich Ministry of Finance; in Reich Park Commission from 1928 to 1936; dismissed; arrested in August 1943; murdered in Sachsenhausen concentration camp in 1944. *123, 192–93.*

Kautsky, Benedikt (1894–1960) Economist, writer, Austrian social democratic journalist; imprisoned in Buchenwald from 1938 to 1942, Auschwitz from 1942 to 1944, and again in Buchenwald in 1945; became secretary of Vienna Workers' Chamber after end of war. *84.*

Kay, Ella (1895–1988) Municipal politician; became member of SPD in 1919; worked as social worker until 1933 and was then forbidden to do so; placed under police surveillance; imprisoned in Ravensbrück concentration camp; city councilwoman from Prenzlauer Berg district of East Berlin from 1946 to 1950; senator for youth and sport in West Berlin from 1955 to 1962; member of Berlin House of Representatives from 1958 to 1967. *111.*

Kayser, Josef (1895–1993) Textile industry engineer, mining engineer, Catholic clergyman; ordained in 1931; chaplain in Dortmund; participated in Russian campaign as Wehrmacht minister; taken by Soviets as POW on January 15, 1943; curate in Dortmund after end of war; minister in Bosseborn from 1949 to 1954; later worked as hospital minister in Eickelborn in diocese of Paderborn. *207.*

Kehler, Ernst (born 1913) Postal inspector; participated in Russian campaign as lieutenant; taken as POW by Soviets in 1941; deputy ward mayor of Center City district of Berlin and director of Department of Post and Telecommunications at municipal council of Berlin after 1945. *206.*

Keilson, Max (1900–1953 or 1955) Graphic artist, journalist, politician; cofounded German Association of Revolutionary Visual Artists in 1928; went to the Soviet Union via Republic of Czechoslovakia and France in 1933; editor at German People's Radio of Moscow; returned to Berlin (East) in 1945; journalist; director of the USSR Department in GDR's Ministry of Foreign Affairs; arrested in 1953; said to have died in 1953 or 1955. *210.*

Kertzscher, Günther (born 1913) Assistant teacher, journalist; became member of NSDAP in 1937; taken as POW by Soviets in 1941; sentenced to death in absentia by German court-martial in 1944; returned to Germany (East) in 1945; member of KPD/SED; editor in chief of *Berliner Zeitung* (Berlin news) from 1949 to 1955; sat in Volkskammer from 1954 to 1958; deputy editor in chief of *Neues Deutschland* (New Germany) from 1955 to 1983. *209.*

Kessel, Albrecht Theobald von (1902–76) Diplomat; director of Office of State Secretary in Foreign Office from 1937 to 1941; became legation councilor in 1939; at German consulate general in Geneva from 1941 to 1943; at embassy in Vatican from 1943 to 1945 and in Paris and Washington from 1950 to 1958. *159, 160.*

Kessler, Heinz (born 1920) Machine fitter; became member of Young Pioneers in 1926; soldier in Russia; joined Red Army in 1941; attended Antifascist Central School in Moscow; returned to Germany (East) in 1945; became member of party committee and central committee of SED in 1946; sat in GDR's Volkskammer from 1950 to 1989; became brigadier general in National People's Army in 1956; minister of defense of GDR from 1985 to 1989; resigned from all offices in 1989; expelled from party. *206.*

Ketteler, Baron Wilhelm Emanuel von (1906–38) Diplomat; became attaché at German embassy in Vienna in 1934; murdered on Heydrich's orders in March 1938. *150, 151.*

Kiep, Otto Carl (1886–1944) Lawyer, diplomat; at consulate general in New York from 1930 to 1933; German representative in London Nonintervention Committee for Spain from 1937 to 1939; became officer in Counterintelligence Office at High Command of Armed Forces in 1939; arrested in January 1944; sentenced to death by People's Court in July 1944 and executed in Berlin-Plötzensee in August 1944. *239, 240.*

Klein, Matthäus (born 1911) Protestant clergyman, curate in Haag/Baden, pastor; participated in Russian campaign as noncommissioned officer; taken as POW by Soviets in July 1941; returned to Germany (East) in April 1945; became director of Department of History of Philosophy at the Institute of Philosophy in the German Academy of Sciences in East Berlin in 1964. *206.*

Kleinspehn, Johannes (1880–1945) Metal worker; became member of SPD in 1903; editor of *Nordhäuser Volkszeitung* (Nordhäuser people's news) from 1910 to 1933; represented USPD in constitutional committee of Prussian state assembly in 1919; became member of SPD in 1920; became member of Prussian state legislature in 1921; arrested in 1939; sentenced to three years' imprisonment; died in Sachsenhausen concentration camp. *170.*

Kleist-Schmenzin, Ewald von (1890–1945) Holder of estate, lawyer, conservative; chairman of Farmers' Union Employers' Group in district of Belgard (Pomerania); arrested several times between 1933 and 1944;

sentenced to death by People's Court in March 1945 and executed in Berlin-Plötzensee in April 1945. *35, 122, 157–58.*

Klement, Gerhard Noncommissioned officer; participated in Russian campaign; returned to Germany (East) after 1945. *207.*

Klingenbeck, Walter (1924–43) Mechanic in Munich, member of Catholic Youth Flock; arrested in January 1942; sentenced to death by People's Court in September 1942 and executed in August 1943. *78, 189, 190–91.*

Klinkhammer, Karl (born 1903) Catholic clergyman; ordained in 1929; known as the "Red Ruhr Chaplain"; worked in Essen and Cologne-Ehrenfeld; prohibited to stay in Essen at end of 1933; arrested six times and spent two years in prison after April 1933; began working in diocese of Speyer in 1936, then in Düsseldorf-Heerdt in 1941. *47.*

Kloppe, Fritz (born 1891) Teacher; member of Freikorps of Central Germany and in outlawed National Union of German Officers; chairman of Werwolf Youth Club, which was founded in 1923; editor in chief of journal *Werwolf* from 1922 to 1933; later imprisoned in concentration camp. *129.*

Kluge, Hans Günther von (1882–1944) Career officer; became major general in 1934 and field marshal in 1940; commander in chief of Army Group Middle from December 1941 to October 1943; became commander in chief of western front in France in July 1944; committed suicide in France in August 1944. *66, 175, 197.*

Knobelsdorff-Brenkenhoff, Isenhardus von (1902–55) Lawyer, court-martial adviser; participated in Russian campaign. *207, 209.*

Knöchel, Wilhelm (1899–1944) Politician; became member of SPD in 1919 and of KPD in 1923; expert on German issues for Red Trade Union International in 1934–35; member of central committee of KPD in 1935; fled to Prague and Amsterdam in 1935; in Berlin in 1942–43; arrested in January 1943; sentenced to death by People's Court in June 1944 and executed in Brandenburg prison in July 1944. *22–23, 193–94.*

Knoeringen, Baron Waldemar von (1906–71) Politician; became member of SPD in 1926 and of Reichsbanner Black Red Gold; fled to Austria in 1933; director of Southern Bavarian Border Secretariat of Sopade in Czechoslovakia in 1934; fled to France in 1938; emigrated to London in 1939; worked at European Revolution Radio from 1940 to 1942; returned to Germany (West) in 1946; became member of SPD and member of Bavarian state parliament; member of Bundestag from 1949 to 1951. *33, 216.*

Kochmann, Martin (1912–43) Studied business in Berlin; white-collar worker until 1935, then manual laborer; became member of KJVD in 1933; indicted and acquitted in August 1934; went underground in February 1942; arrested in October 1942; sentenced to death by People's Court in June 1943 and executed in Berlin-Plötzensee in September 1943. *179.*

Kochmann, Sala (née Rosenbaum) (1912–42) Kindergarten teacher; worked in Jewish youth movement; became member of KJVD in 1932 and later worked in Ring Alliance of German-Jewish Youth; arrested in May 1942; sentenced to death by Special Court of Berlin County Court in July 1942 and executed in August 1942. *179.*

Koebel, Eberhard (1907–55) Journalist, politician; founded German Boys' Club of November 1 in 1929; joined KJVD and KPD in 1932; arrested at beginning of 1934; fled to England via Sweden; returned to Germany (East) in 1948; worked in FDJ and Free Germany Movement; member of SED from 1948 to 1951. *74, 75.*

Koestler, Arthur (1905–83) Writer, journalist, Near East correspondent of Ullstein Publishing House; became member of KPD in 1931; became foreign correspondent in Moscow, Paris, and Zurich in 1932; journalist in Spanish Civil War; taken prisoner in 1937 and freed due to British intervention; left KPD in 1937; fled to England in 1940; served in British army in 1941–42. *96.*

Kogon, Eugen (1903–87) Political scientist, journalist; worked for Catholic journal *Schönere Zukunft* (A better future) in Vienna; imprisoned from 1938 to 1945 (in Buchenwald as of 1939); coeditor of *Frankfurter Hefte* (Frankfurt notebooks) after 1945; professor in Darmstadt from 1951 to 1968. *84, 87.*

König, Lothar (1906–46) Jesuit priest; ordained in 1936; became professor of cosmology in 1938; member of Committee for Clerical Affairs of the Bishops' Conference from 1941 to 1944; went underground after July 20, 1944, assassination attempt on Hitler. *55, 195, 196, 227–29.*

Kordt, Erich (1903–69) Diplomat, administrative lawyer; brother of Theodor Kordt; diplomatic adviser second-class in German embassy in London from 1936 to 1938; director of ministerial office of Reich minister of interior from 1938 to 1941; ambassador in Tokyo and Nanking from 1941 to 1945; became lecturer at University of Cologne in 1951 and later ministerial adviser of state government in North Rhine-Westphalia. *121, 159, 160.*

Kordt, Theodor (1893–1962) Administrative lawyer; entered diplomatic service in 1923; councilor at German embassy in London in

1938–39; became adviser at German embassy in Bern in 1939; director of Regional Department in Foreign Office from 1950 to 1953; FRG's ambassador in Athens from 1953 to 1958. *157, 159, 160.*

Korfes, Otto (1889–1964) Political scientist, archivist; began working at Research Institute of Military History of Army in 1935; taken as POW by Soviets; returned to Germany (East) in 1948; member of founding committee of NDPD; worked in establishment of central state archives of GDR until 1952; brigadier general with Barracks People's Police from 1952 to 1956. *207, 209.*

Kowalke, Alfred (1907–44) Carpenter, politician; became member of KJVD in 1921 and of KPD in 1925; in Moscow during 1932–33; fled to Prague in 1933; instructor of Czechoslovakian Communist Party in Sudetenland from 1934 to 1937; middleman to Communist Party in Danzig; in Amsterdam during 1937 under auspices of central committee of KPD; arrested in February 1943; sentenced to death by People's Court in November 1943 and executed in Brandenburg prison in March 1944. *193.*

Kresse, Kurt (1904–45) Book printer; became member of KPD in 1924; served in West Saxon regional administration of KPD; chairman of Fichte Workers' Sport Club in Leipzig; editor of *Sächsische Arbeiter Zeitung* (Saxon workers' news); imprisoned for several months in 1933 and 1935; arrested in July 1944; sentenced to death by People's Court in November 1944 and executed in Dresden in January 1945. *234, 235.*

Kucharski, Heinz (born 1919) Student of philosophy, ethnology, and Oriental studies in Hamburg and, during 1939–40, in Berlin; arrested in November 1943; sentenced to death by People's Court in April 1945; succeeded in fleeing to Soviet army while being transported to execution site. *252.*

Küchenmeister, Walter (1897–1943) Trained lathe worker; became member of SPD in 1918 and member of KPD from 1920 to 1926; freelance writer and journalist; settled in Berlin in 1929–30; arrested twice in 1933–34 and held, among other places, in Sonnenburg concentration camp; arrested in September 1939; sentenced to death by Reich Court-Martial in February 1943; executed in Berlin-Plötzensee in May 1943. *224.*

Kuckhoff, Adam (1887–1943) Journalist, writer; worked at *Kölnische Zeitung* (Cologne news) and *Frankfurter Zeitung* (Frankfurt times) from 1913 to 1917; director and dramatic producer at various theaters in Frankfurt am Main and Berlin editor of newspaper *Die Tat* (The deed); arrested in September 1942; sentenced to death by Reich Court-Martial in February 1943; executed in Berlin-Plötzensee in August 1943. *223.*

Kuenzer, Richard (1875–1945) Legation adviser; in Peace Alliance of German Catholics; expelled from diplomatic service in 1923; directed Center Party's newspaper *Germania* for several years and later worked in public sector; murdered by Gestapo on April 24, 1945. *239, 240.*

Kügelgen, Bernt von (born 1914) Publisher, journalist; became lieutenant in Wehrmacht in 1939; held by Soviets as POW from 1942 to 1945; went to Soviet Occupation Zone of Germany in 1945; member of KPD/SED; editor in chief at *Berliner Zeitung* (Berlin news) from 1945 to 1948; editor in chief of *Sonntag* (Sunday) from 1957 to 1977. *206.*

Kühn, Erich (died 1944) Cashier in Berlin; drafted into Wehrmacht; became soldier on eastern front in summer of 1941; taken as POW by Soviets in October 1941. *206.*

Kurella, Alfred (1895–1975) Writer, politician; became member of executive committee of KJVD and of Free Socialist Youth in 1918; founding member of KPD; secretary of Communist Youth International from 1919 to 1924; director of party school of central committee of French Communist Party from 1924 to 1926; became editor in chief of *Monde* (World) in 1932; in Moscow from 1935 to 1951; became member of politburo of central committee of KPD in 1944; returned to Germany (East) in 1954; member of central committee of SED from 1958 to 1975. *209.*

Kürschner, Erich (1889–1966) Protestant minister; SPD's 1924 Reichstag candidate from East Prussia; prison clergyman in Berlin-Tegel from 1928 to 1933; became member of Leninist Organization in 1933; arrested in November 1938; sentenced to seven years' imprisonment; lived in East Berlin after end of war; member of SED. *216.*

Küster, Fritz (Friedrich) (1889–1966) Publisher, politician; founded first regional group of German Peace Society in Hagen in 1919; member of DDP in 1920 and of SPD from 1921 to 1931; founded monthly *Der Pazifist* in 1921; founded western German regional organization of German Peace Society in 1924 and served on its executive committee until 1929; became member of SAPD in 1931; arrested in 1933 and held in Buchenwald until 1938; executive chairman of German Peace Society in 1945–46; member of SPD; expelled from SPD in 1951. *8.*

Lachmund, Hans (1892–1972) Judge; became senior legal adviser in Mecklenburg Ministry of Justice in 1929; became member of DDP in 1919, of German State Party in 1930, and of SPD in 1931; repeated disciplinary transfer during time of Nazi rule due to his affiliation with Freemasons; arrested by People's Commissariat of Internal Affairs (the secret police of the Soviet Union as of 1941) in May 1945 and sentenced to twenty-five years' imprisonment; pardoned in 1954; became judge in West Berlin. *242.*

Lafrenz, Traute (born 1919) Medical student in Hamburg, Berlin, and Munich; first arrested in March 1943; sentenced to one year's imprisonment by People's Court in April 1943; released from Rothenfels juvenile prison in March 1944 and then arrested for second time; held for questioning in Cottbus, Leipzig, and Meusdorf prisons; emigrated to the United States after 1945. *249, 252.*

Lampe, Adolf (1897–1948) Economist; became economic adviser of Chamber of Industry and Commerce in 1923; assistant professor in Freiburg im Breisgau from 1926 to 1944 and from 1945 to 1948; entered Workers' Association for Economics in Academy for German Law in 1943; arrested in September 1944 and incarcerated until 1945. *55, 164, 165.*

Landau, Kurt (born 1903, missing since 1937) Politician; member of Austrian Communist Party from 1921 to 1926; in Austrian Communist Party-Opposition in 1927–28; cofounded Communist Opposition/Marxist-Leninist Left in 1928; settled in France in 1934 and in Barcelona in 1936; arrested after Partido Obrero de Unificación Marxista (Workers' Party of Marxist Unification) was broken up; afterward missing. *246.*

Landgraf, Josef (born 1924) High school student in Vienna; arrested in September 1941; sentenced to death by People's Court in August 1942; death sentence commuted to seven years' imprisonment in September 1943. *78–79, 189, 191.*

Langbehn, Carl Julius (1901–44) Attorney; arranged meetings between Popitz and Himmler in 1943; sentenced to death by People's Court and executed in October 1944. *37.*

Langbein, Hermann (born 1912) Journalist, politician; became member of Austrian Communist Party in 1933; arrested in 1935 and 1936; escaped to Spain via France in 1938; fought in Spanish Civil War; emigrated to France in 1939; interned; imprisoned in Dachau in 1941, in Auschwitz from 1941 to 1944, and in Neuengamme in 1944; fled in 1945; first secretary of International Auschwitz Committee from 1954 to 1962. *80.*

Lattmann, Martin (born 1896) Career officer; actively supported National Socialism; brigadier general in Russian campaign; taken as POW by Soviets in 1943; brigadier general of Barracks People's Police in Soviet Occupation Zone after 1945; had leading functions in various economic commissions of GDR; became deputy chairman of Workers' Association of Former Officers in 1958. *207.*

Leber, Julius (1891–1945) Journalist, politician; became member of SPD in 1912; became editor in chief of SPD's *Lübecker Volksboten* (Lübeck people's courier) in 1921; member of Reichstag from 1924 to 1933; prison and concentration camp incarceration from 1933 to 1937; arrested in July 1944; sentenced to death by People's Court in October 1944 and executed in Berlin-Plötzensee in January 1945. *24, 34, 38, 40, 198, 233, 242.*

Lechleiter, Georg (1885–1942) Typesetter; cofounder of KPD in Mannheim; editor of *Die Rote Fahne* (The red banner); secretary of Baden region of KPD from 1920 to 1922; member of Baden state parliament until 1933; arrested in 1933; concentration camp incarceration until April 1935; arrested again in February 1942; sentenced to death by People's Court in May 1942 and executed in Stuttgart in September 1942. *199.*

Leiber, Robert (1887–1967) Jesuit priest, church historian; personal secretary to Eugenio Pacelli from 1924 to 1958; followed Pacelli, the Berlin papal nuncio, to Rome in 1930; professor of church history at Gregoriana in Rome; one of closest assistants of Pope Pius XII. *127–28.*

Leipelt, Hans (1921–45) Student; volunteered for military service in 1939; expelled from Wehrmacht in August 1940 as so-called mongrel; studied chemistry in Hamburg and, as of 1941–42, in Munich; arrested in autumn of 1943; sentenced to death by People's Court in October 1944 and executed in January 1945. *252.*

Lessing, Theodor (1872–1933) Philosopher, writer; became member of SPD in 1904; became assistant professor in Hannover in 1908; suspended in 1926; fled to Republic of Czechoslovakia at beginning of 1933; reward of eighty thousand Reichmarks offered for his capture; shot by National Socialists in Marienbad in August 1933. *6.*

Letterhaus, Bernhard (1894–1944) Politician, secretary of Western German Catholic Workers' Movement; became member of Central Union of Christian Textile Workers in 1921; became member of Prussian state parliament (Center Party) in 1928; arrested numerous times after National Socialist assumption of power; became captain in Counterintelligence Office at High Command of Armed Forces in 1939; arrested after July 20, 1944, assassination attempt on Hitler; sentenced to death by People's Court in November 1944 and executed. *55, 228.*

Leuschner, Wilhelm (1890–1944) Politician, Social Democrat; became member of Hessian state parliament in 1924; served in Hessian

Ministry of Interior from 1928 to 1933; became deputy chairman of General German Federation of Labor in 1932; held in Lichtenburg concentration camp in 1933–34; small manufacturer in Berlin from 1934 to 1944; surrendered to Gestapo in August 1944 after arrest of his wife; sentenced to death by People's Court in September 1944 and executed. *33, 34, 37, 40, 55, 174, 175, 176, 196, 242, 245.*

Leverkuehn, Paul (1893–1960) Lawyer, diplomat; served as Reich commissioner for release of German assets in German embassy in Washington from 1928 to 1930; German consul in Persia in 1940; served in Foreign Office in Paris in 1941, then in German embassy in Ankara until 1944; became attorney in Hamburg after 1945. *157.*

Levi, Paul (1883–1930) Attorney, politician; became member of SPD in 1909; became one of leaders of Spartacus League in 1918; cofounder and cochairman of KPD; member of Reichstag from 1920 to 1930; expelled from KPD and again became member of SPD in 1922; leader of left wing of SPD. *222.*

Lichtenberg, Bernhard (1875–1943) Catholic clergyman; ordained in 1899; became cathedral pastor in 1932 and provost of St. Hedwig's Cathedral in Berlin in 1938; arrested in October 1941; sentenced to two years' imprisonment by Special Court in 1942; died in November 1943 while being transferred to Dachau. *51, 54.*

Liebknecht, Theodor (1870–1948) Politician; member of USPD; became member of Prussian state parliament in 1921; member of party executive committee of right wing of USPD until 1931; fled to the Netherlands in 1936 and worked from 1936 to 1939 in the founding of the International Institute for Social History in Amsterdam. *171.*

Lilje, Hanns (1899–1977) Protestant clergyman, pastor in Berlin; general secretary of the German Christian Student Organization from 1927 to 1936 and of the Lutheran World Council from 1935 to 1945; became member of council of Evangelical Lutheran Church of Germany in 1937; became member of council of German Lutheran Church in 1945; president of Lutheran World Federation from 1952 to 1957; bishop of Evangelical State Church in Hannover from 1947 to 1971. *73.*

Litten, Hans Achim (1903–38) Lawyer, attorney in Berlin; politically unaffiliated; defended socialists and communists; arrested on February 28, 1933; spent five years imprisoned in the concentration camps at Esterwegen, Lichtenburg, Buchenwald, and Dachau, where he died, presumably by suicide. *11.*

Loeper, Friedrich-Wilhelm von (1888–1983) Career soldier; commandant of army training ground at Senne from 1933 to 1935; with rank of brigadier general, became commanding officer of the Light Division in Wuppertal in 1938; became major general in 1940; commanding officer of Tenth Infantry Division from 1940 to 1942. *66.*

Loewenheim, Ernst (1898–1984) Businessman, member of German Youth Movement, Free Socialist Youth, Spartacus League; member of KPD from 1919 to 1927; expelled from and readmitted to KPD several times after 1921; later became member of Leninist Organization; resided in Soviet Union in 1927 and 1929; left KPD for good in 1929; member of outlawed Reich directorate of New Beginning; fled to Republic of Czechoslovakia in 1935 and to England in 1936; interned in 1940–41; director of engineering office in Great Britain after 1945. *215, 216.*

Loewenheim, Walter (1896–1977) Politician; member of Spartacus League in 1918; became member of KJVD and KPD in 1919; broke with KPD in 1927; became member of SPD in 1929; leader of Leninist Organization until 1934; fled to Republic of Czechoslovakia in 1935 and to England in 1936; interned in 1940–41; after 1945, retreated from political life, became active in publishing and worked with brother Ernst in managing engineering office in England. *32, 214–15.*

Loritz, Alfred (1902–79) Attorney, politician; in Reich Party of German Middle Class from 1928 to 1932; expelled from bar in 1939 and fled to Switzerland; returned to Munich in 1945; member of Bavarian state parliament from 1946 to 1950 (Economic Reconstruction Association); Bavarian state minister for special tasks (Denazification) in 1946–47; imprisoned in 1947 for inducement to perjury and black-market activities; member of Bundestag from 1949 to 1953. *204.*

Löwe, Adolph (Lowe) (born 1893) Economist, Religious Socialist; in Reich Office of Statistics from 1924 to 1926; at Institute for World Economy in Kiel from 1925 to 1931; professor in Frankfurt am Main from 1931 to 1933; dismissed in 1933; fled to England; lecturer in Manchester and London from 1933 to 1940; moved to the United States in 1940. *195.*

Löwendahl, Hans (born 1905, died before 1945) Lawyer; KPDO functionary; worked for KPDO in Algeria and Tunisia prior to 1933 and served as its foreign courier after 1933; sentenced by People's Court to ten years' imprisonment in 1937; eventually imprisoned in Auschwitz, where he was murdered. *168.*

Löwenthal, Richard (1908–91) Economist, journalist; member of KPD until 1929 and of KPDO from 1929 to 1931; became member of Leninist Organization in 1932; fled to Prague in 1935; in London during 1936–37; in Paris in 1938; in London in 1939; worked for Radio of the European Revolution from 1940 to 1942; began working for Reuters news agency in 1942; became member of SPD in 1945; professor at Free University of Berlin and at Harvard University from 1961 to 1974. *107, 215, 216.*

Luckner, Gertrud (born 1900) Studied philosophy and economics; pacifist; member of Peace Alliance of German Catholics; began working in German Caritas Union in Freiburg im Breisgau in 1938, where she was active for many years as adviser for assistance of persecuted persons; arrested in November 1943 and held at Ravensbrück concentration camp until end of war. *51.*

Luddeneit, Fritz Itinerant worker in East Prussia; participated as corporal in Russian campaign. *206.*

Lukaschek, Hans (1885–1960) Lawyer; member of Center Party; became president of Upper Silesia and Oppeln in 1929; expelled from office in 1933; subsequently became attorney in Breslau; arrested after July 20, 1944, assassination attempt on Hitler and imprisoned in Ravensbrück concentration camp; acquitted by People's Court in April 1945; founding member of CDU; first federal minister for German refugees from 1949 to 1953. *195, 197.*

Lutter, Kurt Ship carpenter, Communist; planned a bomb attack on Hitler in March 1933 while Hitler was in Königsberg, but arrested while conducting preliminary discussions with cohorts; released at end of 1933 due to lack of evidence. *120.*

Maass, Hermann (1897–1944) Social Democrat, trade unionist; director of Reich Committee on German Youth Organizations from 1924 to 1933; began working in Wilhelm Leuschner's armature company in 1934; arrested in August 1944; sentenced to death by People's Court in October 1944 and executed in Berlin-Plötzensee. *196.*

Mahle, Hans (born 1911) Politician; member of KJVD and KPD; became member of central committee of KJVD and resided in Moscow in 1932; returned to Germany in 1933; fled to Moscow via Republic of Czechoslovakian in 1935; began working for Radio Moscow in 1939; returned to Berlin (East) in 1945; general director of radio broadcasters of Soviet Occupation Zone/GDR from 1947 to 1951; became SED functionary in Berlin (West). *206.*

Maier, Reinhold (1889–1971) Attorney, politician; became member of DVP in 1912; became chairman of DDP in Stuttgart in 1924; became minister of economics in Württemberg in 1930; became member of Württemberg state parliament and Reichstag in 1932; in executive committee of State Party in 1932–33; barred from practicing law in 1938;

forced labor; became prime minister of Württemberg-Baden in 1946; member of Bundestag (FDP) from 1953 to 1959. *6.*

Maltzan, Countess Maria von (born 1909) Studied natural sciences; received doctorate in Munich in 1933; worked as journalist; moved to Berlin in 1938; began studying veterinary medicine in 1940; not prosecuted despite numerous denunciations and hearings; now a veterinarian in West Berlin. *123–24.*

Mann, Heinrich (1871–1950) Writer; became president of Literature Division of Prussian Academy of Sciences in 1931; expelled from academy in 1933; fled to France; fled to the United States via Spain and Portugal in 1940. *20, 95, 137, 169.*

Mann, Klaus (1906–49) Writer and journalist; fled to Paris in 1933; moved to the United States in 1936; worked as journalist in Spanish Civil War in 1938; became soldier in the United States Army in 1942; participated as soldier in the United States Army in Allied campaign in Italy in 1944–45; committed suicide in France. *92, 99, 138.*

Mann, Thomas (1875–1955) Writer; received Nobel Prize for Literature in 1929; began living in exile in southern France and Switzerland in 1933; moved to California in 1938; German citizenship revoked in 1936; returned to Switzerland in 1952. *8, 92, 253.*

Maron, Karl (1903–75) Politician; became member of KPD in 1926; fled to Copenhagen in 1934; worked as editor in press department of the executive committee of the Communist International in Moscow from 1936 to 1943; returned to Germany (East) in 1945; deputy mayor of Berlin (East) from 1945 to 1961; in central committee of SED from 1954 to 1975. *209.*

Materlink, Hubert (1895–1944) Worker; became member of USPD in 1918 and of KPD in 1920; worked as driver and installer of electrical machines; KPD functionary in Magdeburg-Anhalt; arrested in March 1939; sentenced to fifteen months' imprisonment by Supreme Court in Berlin in March 1941; early release from prison in Magdeburg in November 1941; arrested again in July 1944; died while trial proceedings were underway. *146.*

Matern, Hermann (1893–1971) Politician; member of SPD from 1911 to 1914; became KPD functionary in 1919; member of Prussian state parliament in 1932–33; arrested in 1934; escaped from protective custody and fled to Republic of Czechoslovakia; leading functionary of Red Aid; fled to the Soviet Union via France, Holland, Norway, and Sweden in 1941; returned to Dresden in 1945; SED functionary; entered National Defense Council of GDR in 1960. *207.*

Mayer, Rupert (1876–1945) Jesuit priest in Munich; ordained in 1899; warned in 1936; forbidden to speak publicly in 1937, which he contested; imprisoned for five months in Landsberg; released in 1938; arrested again in 1939; interned in Sachsenhausen concentration camp; under house arrest in Benedictine cloister at Ettal in 1940. *227.*

Metzger, Max Josef (1887–1944) Catholic clergyman; ordained in 1911; cofounded Peace Alliance of German Catholics in 1919 and served as its general director until 1944; cofounded fraternity Una Sancta in 1938; repeatedly arrested; last arrest in June 1943; sentenced to death by People's Court in October 1943 and executed in April 1944. *55.*

Meyer, Reinhold (1920–44) Arrested in December 1943 and held in police prison at Fuhlsbüttel; interned in Neuengamme concentration camp at beginning of June 1944 and held for several months; died as inmate in Fuhlsbüttel. *252, 253.*

Mierendorff, Carlo (1897–1943) Politician, journalist; became member of SPD in 1920; became press chief and assistant of Hessian minister of the interior Leuschner in 1929; became member of Reichstag in 1930; in concentration camp from 1933 until 1938; subsequently worked in personnel department of Brown Coal and Gasoline Company in Berlin; died in December 1943 during a bombing raid on Leipzig. *12, 34, 195, 196, 221, 222.*

Moltke, Count Helmuth James von (1907–45) Lawyer, owner of estate; became attorney in Berlin in 1934; worked in Counterintelligence Office at High Command of Armed Forces from 1939 to 1944; expert on questions of international law and on association between Wehrmacht and Counterintelligence Office; acquired possession of estate in Kreisau in 1939; arrested in January 1944; sentenced to death by People's Court and executed in January 1945. *35, 37, 38, 39, 42, 44, 55, 67, 144, 157, 159, 195–98, 204, 220, 228, 240.*

Muckermann, Friedrich (1883–1946) Jesuit priest; ordained in 1914; forbidden to speak or write publicly in 1933; fled to the Netherlands in 1934, where he was publisher of journal *Der deutsche Weg* (The German way); emigrated to Italy in 1936 and, in 1937, to Paris via Vienna; began residing in Switzerland in 1943. *94.*

Mühsam, Erich (1878–1934) Writer, journalist; leading participant in Munich soviet republic in 1919; confined to fortress from 1920 to 1924 and afterward active in Berlin as journalist and writer; publisher of anarchistic journal *Fanal* (Beacon); arrested on February 28, 1933; murdered in Oranienburg concentration camp after being tortured. *10.*

Mulert, Christian Herrmann (1879–1950) Protestant theologian; member of so-called Liberal Protestants; became professor in Kiel in 1920; publisher of *Christliche Welt* (Christian world); early retirement in 1935; professor in Freiberg (Saxony) after 1945. *47.*

Müller, Alexander Member of Reich leadership of Left Opposition of KPD; became copublisher of *Der Kommunist* in 1931; arrested in January 1934; further whereabouts unknown. *246.*

Müller, Franz-Joseph (born 1924) Sentenced to five years' imprisonment by People's Court in April 1943; member of research group of Persecuted Social Democrats and chairman of White Rose Foundation after 1945. *251.*

Müller, Hermann (1876–1931) Politician; became member of SPD in 1893; editor of *Volkszeitung* (People's news) from 1899 to 1906; city councilman in Görlitz from 1903 to 1906; became member of executive committee of SPD in 1906; became member of Reichstag in 1916; became member of executive council of Workers' and Soldiers' Councils in Berlin in 1918; member of National Assembly; Reich foreign minister in 1919–20; in executive committee of SPD in 1919 and 1928; Reich chancellor in 1920 and from 1928 to 1930. *171.*

Müller, Josef (1898–1979) Politician; began working as attorney in Munich in 1927; member of Bavarian People's Party; became counterintelligence officer in 1939; arrested in 1943; interned in Gestapo prison in Berlin and in Buchenwald, Flossenbürg, and Dachau; cofounder of CSU in 1945 and one of its state chairmen in 1946; deputy prime minister from 1947 to 1950 and minister of justice in Bavaria from 1947 to 1952. *64, 127–28, 144, 158, 243.*

Müller, Otto (1870–1944) Catholic clergyman, priest; cofounder of *Westdeutsche Arbeiterzeitung* (West German workers' news) in 1897; became president of West German Workers' Associations in 1917; founded Ketteler House in Cologne; arrested in September 1944; died in prison in Berlin-Tegel in October 1944. *47, 55, 228.*

Mumm von Schwarzenstein, Herbert (1898–1945) Lawyer, retired legation adviser; arrested together with Nikolaus von Halem in 1942; sentenced to death by People's Court in February 1944 and executed in 1945. *239, 240.*

Münzenberg, Willi (1889–1940) Journalist, politician; became member of Spartacus League and of KPD in 1919; owner and director of Neuer Deutscher Verlag (New German Press, also known as Münzenberg-Konzern or Münzenberg Group) in Berlin; member of Reichstag from 1924 to 1933; became member of central committee of

KPD in 1927; fled to Paris in 1933, where he was in central committee of KPD; expelled from KPD in 1937; interned in May 1940; his death in summer of 1940 remains unexplained. *20, 92, 96, 138, 169.*

Muth, Carl (1867–1944) Journalist; editor of newspaper *Elsässer* (The Alsatian) in Strasbourg from 1893 to 1895, afterward publisher of *Die Alte und Neue Welt* (The old and new world); founded Catholic periodical *Hochland* (Highland) in Munich in 1903; newspaper outlawed in 1941; died in Bad Reichenhall in November 1944. *250.*

Nause, Franz (1903–43) Worker; became member of SAJ in 1919 and of SPD in 1921; cofounder and leader of Socialist Front in Hannover; arrested in June 1936; sentenced to ten years' imprisonment by People's Court in September 1937; died in Brandenburg-Görden prison. *236, 237, 238.*

Nettelbeck, Walter (1901–75) Politician, journalist, photographer; became member of KJVD in 1922 and member of KPD from 1924 to 1933; worked in Moscow for *Arbeiter-Illustrierte-Zeitung* (Workers' illustrated news) in 1930–31; joined Leninist Organization; fled to Paris in 1935; interned in September 1940; in detention in Berlin in 1941; sentenced to six years' imprisonment by People's Court in 1942; held in Sachsenhausen concentration camp until end of war; director of Krefeld Department of Social Welfare from 1946 to 1966. *246.*

Neubauer, Theodor (1890–1945) Teacher, politician, member of KPD; member of Thuringian state parliament from 1921 to 1924; member of Reichstag from 1924 to 1933; concentration camp imprisonment from 1933 to 1939; arrested again in July 1944; sentenced to death by People's Court in January 1945 and executed in February 1945. *23, 145, 212–13, 235.*

Niekisch, Ernst (1889–1967) Politician, journalist; became member of SPD in 1917 and member of USPD from 1919 to 1922; opposition leader and deputy chairman of opposition in Bavarian state parliament in 1921–22; publisher of periodical *Widerstand — Blätter für national-revolutionäre Politik* (Resistance — journal for national-revolutionary politics), which was outlawed in 1934; arrested in 1937; sentenced to life imprisonment by People's Court in January 1939; became member of KPD in 1945; entered People's Congress as member of SED in 1947; entered GDR's Volkskammer in 1949; moved to Berlin (West) in 1953. *7.*

Niemöller, Martin (1892–1984) Protestant clergyman; director of Inner Mission in Münster from 1924 to 1931; pastoral work in Berlin-Dahlem in 1931; arrested in 1937; after eight months in detention, spent rest of time until end of war in Sachsenhausen and Dachau; president of

Ecclesiastical Foreign Office of German Evangelical Church from 1945 to 1956; church president of Evangelical Church in Hesse and Nassau from 1947 to 1965; became one of presidents of Ecumenical Council of Churches in 1961. *49, 54, 142.*

Nolden, Julius (1895–1973) Locksmith; became member of FAUD in 1923; unemployed from 1931 to 1936; entered FAUD Provincial Labor Exchange in Rhineland in 1932; arrested in 1937; sentenced to ten years' imprisonment by People's Court in November 1937. *118.*

Nostiz-Drzewiecki, Gottfried von (1902–76) Diplomat; legation secretary in Vienna from 1934 to 1938; became consul in Geneva in 1941; began doing charitable work for German Evangelical Church in 1946; entered foreign service in 1950; became embassy counselor in The Hague in 1953; became consul general in São Paulo in 1957 and afterward ambassador to Chile. *160.*

Olbricht, Friedrich (1888–1944) Career officer; became chief of staff of Dresden Division in 1933; became chief of General Staff in 1935; commander in chief of Twenty-fourth Infantry Division from 1938 to 1940; head of General Army Office of the Army High Command from 1940 to 1944; shot during the night of July 20–21, 1944. *38, 65, 174, 175, 188, 189.*

Ossietzky, Carl von (1889–1938) Journalist; secretary of German Peace Society in 1919–20; became editor of *Weltbühne* (World stage) in 1926 and its director in 1927; sentenced to eighteen months' imprisonment in 1931; arrested in 1933; interned in Sonnenburg concentration camp and, in 1934, in Papenburg-Esterwegen concentration camp; awarded Nobel Peace Prize in absentia in 1936; under Gestapo supervision in hospital from 1936 to 1938. *4, 8.*

Oster, Hans (1888–1945) Career officer; began working in counterintelligence division of Ministry of Reichswehr in October 1933; became chief of Central Division of Counterintelligence Office in High Command of Armed Forces in 1938; suspended from service in 1943; court-martial proceedings initiated; arrested on July 21, 1944; murdered in Flossenbürg concentration camp in April 1945 after SS summary court trial. *59–64, 121, 127, 128, 144, 145, 156–59, 174, 175, 242.*

Oster, Joachim (1914–83) Career officer; son of Hans Oster; held rank of major; in commanding unit of Fourteenth Panzer Corps in Italy in 1944; brigadier general in Bundeswehr after 1945. *44.*

Ottwalt, Ernst (1901–43) Writer, journalist; worked for *Deutsche Allgemeine Zeitung* (German general news) and Berliner Volkszeitung

(Berlin people's news); fled to Prague in 1933; cosigned Saar Proclamation in 1934; fled to the Soviet Union in 1934; worked for various exile newspapers; arrested in Moscow in 1936 and deported to Siberia. *5.*

Paetel, Karl Otto (1906–75) Journalist, member of Youth League; detained numerous times after 1933; forbidden to publish; fled to Prague in 1935; worked at *Neue Weltbühne* (New world stage); fled to Paris via Stockholm in 1938; interned in 1939; fled to southern France; went to New York via Spain and Lisbon in 1941; worked in publishing in New York. *75, 76.*

Pander, Wolfgang (1917–42) Became worker after being forced to quit school; became member of KJVD in 1930; arrested in 1937 for illegal border crossing; sentenced to two years' imprisonment; confined in Sonnenburg concentration camp from 1939 to 1940; arrested again in August 1941; sentenced to death by People's Court in October 1942 and executed in Berlin-Plötzensee in December 1942. *177.*

Paul, Elfriede (1900–1981) Physician; became member of youth movement in 1917 and of KPD in 1921; later with International Workers' Assistance; school service in Hamburg from 1921 to 1923; physician in Berlin after 1934; arrested in September 1942; sentenced to six years' imprisonment by Reich Court-Martial in February 1943; country physician in Hannover after 1945; began helping rebuild GDR's health care system in Berlin (East) in 1947. *224.*

Paulus, Friedrich von (1890–1957) Career officer; held rank of field marshal; became commander in chief of Sixth Army outside of Stalingrad in January 1942; taken as POW by Soviets in January 1943; held in the Soviet Union until 1953, after which he returned to Germany (East). *211.*

Perels, Friedrich-Justus (1910–45) Lawyer; member of Christian Student Association; became ecclesiastical judge of Emergency League of Clergymen and of Confessing Church in 1936; arrested in October 1944; sentenced to death by People's Court in February 1945; dragged from his cell and shot on street in April 1945. *143.*

Peters, Hans (1896–1966) Political scientist; became professor in Berlin in 1928; member of Center Party in Prussian state parliament in 1932–33; became member of executive committee of Catholic Görres Society in 1933; in Luftwaffe planning staff in Berlin from 1940 to 1942; member of CDU in All-Berlin City Representatives Assembly from 1946 to 1948; in Cologne city council from 1952 to 1961; rector of University of Cologne in 1964–65. *195, 196, 225.*

Petersen, Dagmar (born 1920) Stenographer; friend of Hanno Günther; arrested in August 1941; sentenced to seven years' imprisonment by People's Court in October 1942. *178.*

Petrich, Franz (1889–1945) Editor; member of SPD; member of Reichstag from 1932 to 1933; first arrested in 1933; arrested again in September 1939; sentenced to eight years' imprisonment in 1940; held in Sonnenburg prison; shot in April 1945. *170.*

Peuke, Werner (1905–49) Technician; became member of KPD in 1921; became party secretary in 1927; became part of inner-party opposition in 1930; went underground in 1933; fled to Prague in 1935; arrested while returning to Berlin in 1936; held in Sachsenhausen concentration camp from 1936 to 1939; became engineer in Berlin (East) in 1945; moved to West Berlin in 1948. *216.*

Pfempfert, Franz (1879–1954) Journalist; founded political-literary journal *Die Aktion* in 1911 (journal was published until 1932); cofounded Antinational Socialist Party in 1915; participated in founding congress of KPD in 1918–19; cofounded KAPD in 1920; expelled in 1921; fled to the United States via Republic of Czechoslovakia and Paris in 1933; began residing in Mexico City in 1941. *8.*

Pfordt, Fritz (1900–1957) Politician; chairman of KPD in the Saar region from 1933 to 1935; publisher of *Arbeiterzeitung* (Workers' news); spent short time in the Soviet Union; broke with KPD in 1939; interned in Sweden; in executive committee of Mouvement pour le Rattachement de la Sarra à la France from 1946 to 1949; cofounded Saarland-French Economic Union of Free Saar in 1952. *230.*

Pfülf, Antonie (1877–1933) Teacher, politician; became member of SPD in 1902; sat for SPD in National Assembly and Constitutional Committee in 1919; member of Reichstag from 1920 to 1933; active in school and women's politics; held under arrest for short time in 1933; committed suicide after being released in June 1933. *110, 111.*

Philippson, Julius (1894–1943) Teacher; member of SPD from 1921 to 1925; entered ISK in 1926; relieved of school teaching duties in 1934; arrested in August 1937; sentenced to life imprisonment in December 1938; deported to Auschwitz in May 1943 and murdered there. *32.*

Pieck, Wilhelm (1876–1960) Politician, cofounder of KPD; member of central committee of KPD; member of Reichstag from 1928 to 1933; fled to Paris in 1933; became chairman of KPD in exile in 1935; moved to Moscow; returned to Berlin (East) in 1945; became chairman of SED in 1946; first president of GDR from 1949 to 1960. *16, 138, 194, 206.*

Plivier, Theodor (1892–1955) Writer; published anarchistic flyers at beginning of Weimar Republic; supporter of KPD; fled to France via Republic of Czechoslovakia in 1933; went to Sweden and the Soviet Union in 1934 and to Tashkent in 1941; went to Soviet Occupation Zone in 1945, to Munich in 1947, and to Switzerland in 1953. *207.*

Poelchau, Harald (1903–72) Protestant clergyman; became prison chaplain in Berlin-Tegel in May 1933, and later in prisons in Plötzensee and Brandenburg; worked in formation of Evangelical Relief Organization after 1945; served in administration of prison system in Berlin (East); became prison clergyman in Tegel (West Berlin) in 1949; assumed post of social welfare incumbency; active in formation of factory workers' congregations. *195, 196.*

Poller, Walter (1900–1975) Journalist, publisher; member of SPD; arrested in 1933; sentenced to four years' imprisonment in 1935; from 1938 to 1940 in Buchenwald, where he was medical clerk in inmates' infirmary; journalist and editor in Germany (West) after 1945. *84.*

Pöllnitz, Gisela von (1911–39) Member of KJVD prior to 1933; began working as editorial assistant at United Press in Berlin in 1936; arrested at beginning of 1938; released from Gestapo custody during course of 1938; died of tuberculosis in 1939. *224.*

Popitz, Johannes (1884–1945) Lawyer; began working in Reich Ministry of Finance in 1919, where he was state secretary from 1925 to 1929; Reich minister without portfolio in 1932–33; Prussian minister of finance from April 1933 to July 1944; arrested after July 20, 1944, assassination attempt on Hitler; sentenced to death in October 1944 and executed in Berlin-Plötzensee in February 1945. *37, 38, 39, 164, 174, 175, 176.*

Poser, Magnus (1907–44) Cabinetmaker; became member of KJVD in 1919 and of KPD in 1928; arrested in 1933; sentenced to two years and three months' imprisonment in April 1934; held in Ichtershausen prison until July 1936; arrested again in July 1944; detained by Gestapo in Weimar; injured after attempted escape; died in Buchenwald in July 1944. *212, 213.*

Preiser, Erich (1900–1967) Economist; became professor in Rostock in 1937, in Jena in 1940, in Heidelberg in 1947, and in Munich in 1956; member of academic advisory committee in Federal Ministry of Economics. *165.*

Preysing, Count Konrad von (1880–1950) Catholic clergyman; studied law in 1898; legation councilor of Bavarian delegation in Rome; afterward studied theology; ordained in Munich in 1912; became bishop of Eichstätt in 1932 and of Berlin in 1935; named cardinal in 1946. *51, 196, 228.*

Probst, Christoph (1919–43) Began studying medicine in Munich in 1939; drafted into a student company in 1939 (finally in Innsbruck); arrested in Munich in February 1943; sentenced to death by People's Court and executed. *249, 251.*

Pungs, Elisabeth (1896–1945) Housewife; became member of Red Aid in 1931; interrogated several times after 1933 and under police surveillance; arrested in August 1941; inmate in sanitarium from 1942 to 1945; died in August 1945. *177, 178.*

Quirnheim, Albrecht Ritter Mertz von (1905–44) Career officer, held rank of colonel; Stauffenberg's successor as chief of staff in Army High Command; shot during night of July 20–21, 1944, after summary court proceeding. *67, 188, 189.*

Radbruch, Gustav (1878–1949) Philosopher of law, politician; became member of SPD in 1918; became professor in Kiel in 1919; member of Reichstag from 1920 to 1924; Reich minister of justice in 1921–22 and 1923; became professor in Heidelberg in 1926; dismissed in 1933; guest professor at Oxford in 1935–36; participated in rebuilding of Faculty of Law at University of Heidelberg after 1945. *195.*

Rade, Martin (1857–1940) Protestant theologian; became professor in Heidelberg in 1900; cofounded liberal journal *Christliche Welt* (Christian world) in 1886 and served as its editor until 1931; member of Reichstag from 1919 until 1921 and deputy chairman of DDP; became member of German State Party in 1930; dismissed from university in November 1933. *47.*

Rätzke, Erich (born 1910) Bookbinder; charged in February 1934 and sentenced to two years' imprisonment by Supreme Court of Berlin; assigned to "Parole Unit 999"; has been living in western Germany since 1945. *247.*

Recklinghausen, Daniel von (born 1925) High school student in Munich; in Catholic Young Men's Association; inducted into Hitler Youth in 1936; after completing school, began apprenticeship to become high-frequency engineer; arrested in 1942; sentenced to death by People's Court in September 1942; sentence commuted to eight years' imprisonment in summer of 1943; emigrated to the United States after 1945. *190, 191.*

Regler, Gustav (1898–1963) Writer; member of KPD from 1928 to 1939; fled to France in 1933; worked on *Braunbuch über Reich-*

stagsbrand und Hitlerterror (Brown book about the Reichstag fire and Hitler's terror); fought in Spanish Civil War in 1937; returned to France in 1937, where he was interned; emigrated to Mexico via the United States in 1940. *96.*

Reichenbach, Bernhard (1888–1975) Politician, journalist; became member of USPD in 1917; represented KAPD at executive committee of Communist International in Moscow in 1921; expelled from KAPD in 1922; became member of SPD in 1925 and of SAPD in 1931–32; forbidden to practice profession as journalist in 1934; fled to England in 1935; entered Labour Party; interned in 1940–41; London correspondent for German media after 1945. *223.*

Reichwein, Adolf (1898–1944) Educator; became professor of history and civics in Halle in 1930; dismissed in April 1933; afterward worked as country school teacher and museum guide; arrested in July 1944; sentenced to death by People's Court in October 1944 and executed in Berlin-Plötzensee. *24, 195, 196, 198, 233.*

Reincke, Oskar (1907–44) Quartermaster; became member of KJVD in 1924 and of KPD in 1929; became director of KPD subdistrict Flensburg in 1932; in detention from 1933 to 1935; in "protective custody" in 1937; arrested in October 1942; sentenced to death by People's Court in July 1944 and executed in Berlin-Plötzensee. *125.*

Rembte, Adolf (1902–37) Baker, editor; became member of SAJ in 1919 and of KPD in 1922; attended Lenin School in Moscow in 1927; returned to Germany in 1930; arrested in 1931 and sentenced to two years' confinement in a fortress; granted amnesty in 1932; KPD district leader in Halle-Merseburg until 1933; began working at head regional administration of KPD in Düsseldorf in May 1934; member of state-level administration of KPD in Berlin until March 1935; arrested in March 1935; sentenced to death by People's Court in June 1937 and executed in Berlin-Plötzensee in November 1937. *18.*

Reyer, Friedrich Career officer; participated in Russian campaign as first lieutenant; became mayor of Pirna (Saxony) in November 1945. *206.*

Riesterer, Albert (born 1898) Catholic clergyman; pastoral work in Mühlhausen; watched by local NSDAP members; interrogated by Gestapo for statements made in sermons; held for several months in "protective custody" in 1941; banished from September-October 1941; held in Dachau from November 1941 until April 1945. *54.*

Rinner, Erich (1902–82) Politician, SPD secretary in Reichstag; became member of party's executive committee in 1933; fled to Republic of Czechoslovakia in 1933 and to Paris in 1938, then to New York via Lisbon; worked at Office of War Information; worked for a private New York bank after 1945. *219.*

Ritter, Gerhard (1888–1967) Historian; professor in Freiburg from 1925 to 1956; began working in Research Group for Economics of the Academy of German Law in 1943; arrested in November 1944; held for questioning in Berlin and imprisoned in Ravensbrück concentration camp; delegate at First World Conference of Churches in Amsterdam in 1948. *42, 55, 165.*

Rittmeister, John (1898–1943) Psychoanalyst, physician in Zurich and Bern; expelled from Switzerland in 1938; became chief physician at Waldhaus Clinic in Berlin in 1938; became director of outpatients' clinic of German Institute of Psychotherapy in Berlin in 1939; arrested in September 1942; sentenced to death by Reich Court-Martial in February 1943 and executed in Berlin-Plötzensee in May 1943. *225.*

Robinsohn, Hans (1897–1981) Businessman in Hamburg; member of DDP from 1918 to 1930; fled to Denmark in 1938 and to Sweden in 1943; returned to Hamburg in 1958; director of Research Institute for the History of National Socialism in Hamburg from 1960 to 1963; member of executive committee of Humanistic Union from 1967 to 1975 and its chairman from 1973 to 1975. *9, 10, 241–43.*

Rödel, Fritz (1888–1945) Metal worker; became member of KPD in 1920; began working in KPD's regional administration in Magdeburg-Anhalt in 1924; editor of KPD's regional organ *Tribüne* until 1933; arrested in June 1933; sentenced to two and one-half years' imprisonment in 1934; sentenced to death by People's Court in November 1944 and executed in Brandenburg prison in February 1945. *146.*

Römer, Josef (Beppo) (1892–1944) Lawyer, career soldier; leader of Freikorps "Oberland" in 1919–20; became member of KPD and publisher of Communist Party periodical *Aufbruch* (Awakening) in 1932; in "protective custody" (including in Dachau) from 1933 to 1939; arrested again in February 1942; sentenced to death by People's Court in June 1944 and executed in September 1944. *22, 121, 240, 248–49.*

Rommel, Erwin (1891–1944) Career officer, held rank of field marshal; commander in chief of Afrika Korps in 1942–43; commander in chief of Army Group B in Italy in 1943 and then, as of November 1943, in France; died due to coerced suicide on October 14, 1944. *66.*

Rösch, Augustin (1893–1961) Jesuit priest; ordained in 1925; became Father Superior of Upper German Province of Jesuits in 1935;

went underground after July 20, 1944, assassination attempt on Hitler; arrested in January 1945 and detained until April 1945; director of Caritas Organization after 1945. *55, 195, 196, 227–29.*

Rosenfeld, Kurt (1877–1943) Politician, member of SPD, city councilman in Berlin from 1910 to 1920; cofounded USPD in 1917 and member of that party's executive committee; minister of justice in Prussia in 1918–19; member of Reichstag from 1920 to 1932; became member of executive committee of SAPD in 1931; fled to Paris in 1933; German citizenship revoked in 1934; emigrated to the United States in 1934; worked as attorney in New York. *171, 172.*

Rosenstock-Huessy, Eugen von (1888–1973) Historian, sociologist; professor in Breslau from 1923 to 1933; fled to the United States in 1933; taught at Harvard from 1933 to 1935 and at Dartmouth from 1935 to 1960; held guest professorships in Germany. *195.*

Rossaint, Joseph (1902–91) Catholic priest; became chaplain in Oberhausen and Düsseldorf in 1927; became member of Peace Alliance of German Catholics in 1928; became member of Center Party in 1929; had contacts with KJVD; arrested in February 1936 and sentenced to eleven years' imprisonment by People's Court in April 1937; chairman of Federation of Christian Socialists after 1945; became president of West Germany's Association of Victims of the Nazi Regime in 1961. *54, 69, 73.*

Rothe, Margaretha (Gretha) (1919–45) Medical student in Hamburg and in Berlin during 1939–40; arrested in November 1943; held in custody in prisons in Cottbus, Leipzig, and Meusdorf; died in custody in April 1945 a few days before liberation. *252.*

Rücker, Fritz Teacher in Berlin; participated in Russian campaign; returned to Germany (East) in 1945. *206.*

Rutha, Heinrich (1897–1937) Architect; became leader of Youth Movement and of Bohemian Movement after 1918; member of Sudeten German Party; vice president of German League of Nations and of European Congress of Minorities; indicted by National Socialists in 1937; committed suicide while in Czech custody. *134, 135.*

Sack, Karl (1896–1945) Lawyer; began working in army justice system in 1934; chief of army judicial system from 1942 to 1944; became judge in General Staff in May 1944; arrested in September 1944; murdered in Flossenbürg concentration camp in April 1945 after SS summary court proceeding. *144.*

Saefkow, Anton (1903–44) Machinist, truck driver; became member of Free Socialist Youth in 1918, of German Metal Workers' Union in

1920, and of KPD in 1924; served in various KPD regional administrations until 1933; first arrested in 1933; held in concentration camps and prisons until 1939; arrested again in July 1944; sentenced to death by People's Court in September 1944 and executed. *x, 23, 24, 126, 213, 232–33, 235.*

Samuel, Günther (1903–44) Businessman, cofounder of credit union "Grosser Einsatz" (Large Deposit) in Luckenwalde; deported to Theresienstadt concentration camp in 1943; died in Dachau. *139, 140.*

Sasse, Hermann (1895–1976) Protestant clergyman; pastoral work in Young Reformation Movement in 1920; became professor in Erlangen in 1933; left Bavarian State Church in 1948; became professor in Adelaid (Australia) in 1949. *47.*

Savigny, Friedrich Karl von (1906–70) Held Ph.D.; legation councilor. *150.*

Schairer, Erich (1887–1956) Journalist, private secretary to Friedrich Naumann and Erich Jäckh; editor in chief of *Neckar-Zeitung* (Neckar news) from 1912 to 1919; founded *Heilbronner Sonntags-Zeitung* (Heilbronn Sunday news) in 1920; forbidden to practice profession and to publish in 1937; commercial representative and railroad worker until 1945; copublisher of *Stuttgarter-Zeitung* (Stuttgart news) from 1946 to 1955. *8.*

Schapke, Richard (1897–1940) Politician; worked for youth movement; became editor of newspaper *Der Nationale Sozialist* in 1930; Hitler Youth leader and member of NSDAP; expelled from party after splintering of Otto Strasser group; arrested in 1933; imprisoned in Oranienburg concentration camp; fled to Copenhagen in 1934; drowned while fleeing to Sweden in 1940. *130.*

Scharff, Werner (1912–45) Electrician in Berlin; went underground in 1943; arrested in 1943 and deported to Theresienstadt; escaped in 1943; arrested again in 1944; murdered in Sachsenhausen concentration camp in 1945. *139, 140, 141.*

Schedlich, Reinhold (1909–50) Producer of bandages and artificial limbs; became member of KPD in 1931; expelled from party in 1932; member of Left Opposition of KPD (Bolshevists-Leninists); arrested in March 1934; sentenced to three years' imprisonment in January 1935; after serving prison sentence, imprisoned in Sachsenhausen concentration camp from 1937 to 1939. *247.*

Schehr, John (1896–1934) Locksmith; became member of SPD in 1912 and of KPD in 1919; KPD functionary in Hamburg; led KPD after

Thälmann's arrest; arrested in November 1933; murdered by Gestapo in Berlin in February 1934. *16.*

Schellheimer, Johann (1899–1945) Lathe operator; became member of KPD in Magdeburg in 1931; arrested in March 1933; held for three months in concentration camp; arrested again in November 1933; sentenced to two years' imprisonment; arrested in July 1944; sentenced to death by People's Court in November 1944 and executed in Brandenburg prison in February 1945. *146.*

Scherpenberg, Albert Hilger van (1899–1969) Legation councilor; worked in Bavarian Ministry of Economics from 1945 to 1949 and in Trade Policy Department of Foreign Office from 1953 to 1958; became director of that department in 1955; served as state secretary in Foreign Office from 1958 to 1961 and as FRG's ambassador to Vatican from 1961 to 1964. *239, 240.*

Schertling, Gisela (born 1922) Student in Munich; tried by People's Court in Munich in April 1943 and sentenced to one year's imprisonment. *249.*

Schindler, Oskar (1908–74) Businessman; became member of Sudeten German Party in 1938; began working for German intelligence in Poland in 1939; founded a factory in Kraków in 1939. *124.*

Schink, Bartholomäus (1927–44) Member of Hitler Youth; arrested in 1944; publicly executed in Cologne on November 10, 1944, without trial. *149.*

Schlabrendorff, Fabian von (1907–80) Attorney, staff officer of chief of staff of Second Army; arrested in August 1944; held in Flossenbürg and Dachau concentration camps; trial delayed due to death of Freisler; acquitted in March 1945; worked as attorney after 1945; served as judge on German Federal Constitutional Court from 1967 to 1975. *240.*

Schleiter, Franz Economist, journalist; member of KPD from 1918 to 1928 and worked in that party's Department of Information; became member of KPDO in 1929 and of SPD and ORG in 1930; worked for periodical *Gewerkschaftsarchiv* (Trade union archive) in Jena; fled to England probably in 1935, where he covered business as a journalist. *215.*

Schliestedt, Heinrich (1883–1938) Became member of executive committee of German Metal Workers' Union in 1910; cofounded Provisionary Reich Administration for Rebuilding of Trade Unions in Berlin in 1933; escaped being arrested by fleeing to Republic of Czechoslovakia in 1934; died in plane crash in 1938. *33.*

Schmedes, Brunhilde (married name Benecke as of 1941) (1912–86) Worked as editorial secretary at *Volkswillen* (The people's will) in Hannover until 1933; became member of SPD in 1932; arrested in 1936; sentenced to four years' imprisonment by People's Court in 1937. *238.*

Schmidt, Elli (1908–80) Politician; became member of KPD in 1927; attended Lenin School in Moscow from 1932 to 1934; fled to Prague, Paris, and the Soviet Union in 1936; worked for Radio Moscow; returned to Germany (East) in 1945; in central secretary's office and central committee of SED from 1946 to 1950; became chairwoman of Democratic Women's League in 1948; dismissed from all party posts in 1953; rehabilitated in 1956. *170.*

Schmidt, Kurt (1905–38) Locksmith, politician; member of SPD from 1927 to 1931; became member of KPD in 1931; became member of Prussian state parliament and city councilman in Dortmund in 1933; fled to France in 1936; member of coordination committee for volunteers for Spain; copublisher of *Information von Emigranten für Emigranten* (Information by emigrés for emigrés) in Paris in 1936–37; fought in Spanish Civil War in 1937, where he fell in March 1938. *170.*

Schmölders, Günter (1903–91) Economist; became assistant at Agricultural College in Berlin in 1924 and university lecturer in Berlin in 1931; became professor in Breslau in 1938 and in Cologne in 1940; member of academic advisory committee at Federal Ministry of Finance from 1950 to 1975; rector of University of Cologne from 1965 to 1966. *164, 165.*

Schmorell, Alexander (1917–43) Began study of medicine in Hamburg in 1939; became soldier in student company in Munich in 1940; soldier in Russia in 1942; arrested in February 1943; sentenced to death by People's Court in April 1943 and executed in June 1943. *249–53.*

Schneider, Paul (1897–1939) Protestant clergyman; transferred from Hesse to Rhineland in 1934; assistant clergyman in Essen; arrested numerous times in 1935–36; fought against being expelled from Rhineland in 1937; arrested in September 1937; sent to Buchenwald in July 1939 and murdered there. *54.*

Schneider, Reinhold (1903–58) Writer, Catholic; wrote for *Weisse Blätter* (White notes) and other publications; forbidden to publish in 1941; indicted for defeatism and high treason in 1945, but trial not opened due to end of war. *203.*

Schnibbe, Karl-Heinz (born 1924) Painter's apprentice, member of Hitler Youth; expelled from Hitler Youth due to insubordination in

1939; member of Mormon congregation in Hamburg; arrested in February 1942; sentenced by People's Court to five years' imprisonment in August 1942; released in 1945 and drafted into Wehrmacht; emigrated to the United States after 1945. *190.*

Schoettle, Erwin (1899–1976) Politician; became member of SPD in 1919 and of Württemberg state parliament in 1933; fled to Switzerland in 1933; worked in Sopade border secretariat for region of southwest Germany; in Prague and Paris from 1933 to 1938; moved to London in 1939; returned to Stuttgart in 1946; member of Bundestag from 1949 to 1972; vice president of German Bundestag from 1961 to 1969. *216.*

Scholl, Hans (1918–43) Became member of Hitler Youth in 1933, yet worked with the German Boys' Club; imprisoned for several weeks at end of 1937; began study of medicine in Munich in 1939; soldier in student company; soldier in Russia in 1942; arrested in Munich in February 1943; sentenced to death by People's Court and executed. *74, 249–51, 253.*

Scholl, Sophie (1921–43) Kindergarten teacher, student of biology and philosophy in Munich; arrested in Munich in February 1943; sentenced to death by People's Court and executed. *249–51.*

Schönfeld, Hans (1900–1954) Representative of Federation of German Evangelical Churches in Geneva in 1929; director of Ecumenical Council for Practical Christianity in Geneva from 1931 to 1946; head consistory adviser in ecclesiastical foreign office of German Evangelical Church from 1948 to 1950. *156, 158.*

Schottmüller, Oda (1905–43) Sculptor; became dancer at Volksbühne in Berlin in 1931; arrested in September 1942; sentenced to death by Reich Court-Martial in January 1943 and executed in Berlin-Plötzensee in August 1943. *224.*

Schröder, Johannes Participated in Russian campaign as Protestant clergyman in Wehrmacht. *207.*

Schröder, Karl (1884–1950) Educator; became member of SPD in 1911, of Spartacus League in 1918, of KAPD from 1920 to 1922, and of SPD in 1922; lecturer from 1926 to 1933; editor and writer; arrested in November 1936; sentenced to four years' imprisonment by People's Court in 1937; sent to concentration camp after serving prison sentence; began working in school system and as lecturer in Germany (East) in 1948. *32.*

Schubert, Hermann (1896–1938) Politician; became member of KPD in 1920; KPD and trade union functionary; attended Lenin School in Moscow; became member of Reichstag in 1924; member of Prussian state parliament from 1924 to 1933; in prison in 1924–25; fled to Prague in 1933; KPD representative at executive committee of Communist International in 1934; arrested in 1937; sentenced to death in course of Stalinist "cleansings" and shot. *16.*

Schüddekopf, Katharina (1916–93) Student in Munich; tried before People's Court in April 1943 and sentenced to one year's imprisonment; lived in Munich after war. *249.*

Schulenburg, Count Fritz-Dietlof von der (1902–44) Administrative lawyer; became member of NSDAP in 1932; deputy police chief of Berlin from 1937 to 1939; became deputy president of Upper and Lower Silesia in 1939, then officer in reserves on eastern front; arrested after July 20, 1944, assassination attempt on Hitler; sentenced to death by People's Court in August 1944 and executed. *38, 42, 121, 175, 176, 197, 225.*

Schulte, Fritz (1890–probably 1943) Politician; became member of KPD in 1920; became trade union secretary and KPD functionary in 1922; member of Prussian state parliament from 1928 to 1930; became member of politburo and central committee in 1929; member of Reichstag from 1930 to 1933; fled to Prague, Paris, and Moscow in 1933; arrested in the Soviet Union in 1937–38; is said to have died in 1943 as a result of "false accusations." *16.*

Schulze-Boysen, Harro (1909–42) First lieutenant; editor of national-revolutionary journal *gegner* (opponent) in 1932–33; arrested for first time in 1933; began working in news department of Reich Ministry of Air Travel in 1934; arrested in August 1942; sentenced to death by Reich Court-Martial in December 1942 and executed in Berlin-Plötzensee. *22, 23, 126, 223–26.*

Schulze-Boysen, Libertas (1913–42) Became press agent for Metro-Goldwyn-Mayer in Berlin in 1933; began volunteer work in 1935; imprisoned for short time in 1939; began working as film critic in 1940; began working in German Cultural Film Head Office of Reich Ministry of Propaganda in 1941; arrested in September 1942; sentenced to death by Reich Court-Martial in December 1942 and executed in Berlin-Plötzensee. *224.*

Schumacher, Elisabeth (1904–1942) Graphic artist; began living in Berlin in 1928; began working for Reich Office of Labor Protection on a freelance basis in 1933; arrested in September 1942; sentenced to death by Reich Court-Martial in December 1942 and executed in Berlin-Plötzensee. *224.*

Schumacher, Kurt (1895–1952) Politician; became member of SPD in 1918; member of Württemberg state parliament from 1924 to 1931; member of Reichstag from 1930 to 1933; in executive committee of SPD in Reichstag in 1932–33; held in various concentration camps from July 1933 until March 1943; arrested again in 1944 and held in Neuengamme concentration camp until September 1944; chairman of SPD from 1946 to 1952; member of Bundestag from 1949 to 1952 and chairman of SPD in Bundestag. *12.*

Schumacher, Kurt (1905–42) Sculptor; began living in Berlin in 1928; drafted into Wehrmacht in 1941; transferred to sentry duty in Berlin in July 1942; arrested in September 1942; sentenced to death by Reich Court-Martial in December 1942; executed in Berlin-Plötzensee. *224.*

Schumann, Edith (born 1886) Studied medicine and economics; member of SPD from 1911 to 1916; became member of KPD in 1919; worked in women's secretariat in central committee of KPD until 1924; secretary of Clara Zetkin in Moscow from 1924 to 1928; later distanced herself from KPD; in "protective custody" in 1933–34; became member of Leninist Organization in 1934; arrested in Cologne in September 1935; sentenced to long-term imprisonment. *213, 215.*

Schumann, Georg (1886–1945) Tool maker, politician, editor; became member of SPD and of German Metal Workers' Union in 1905; became member of KPD in 1919; in central committee of KPD from 1927 to 1929; became member of Reichstag in 1928; arrested for first time in June 1933; sentenced to three years' imprisonment in August 1934 and subsequently imprisoned in concentration camp until 1939; arrested again in July 1944; sentenced to death by People's Court in November 1944 and executed in Dresden in January 1945. *23, 145, 234–35.*

Schürmann-Horster, Wilhelm (1900–1943) Actor, dramatic producer; became member of KPD in 1923; cofounder of theater company Die junge Aktion (The young action); cofounded Die Truppe im Westen (Theater company in the West) in 1929; temporarily held under arrest in 1934 and 1935; dramatic producer in Constance, where he was arrested in October 1942; sentenced to death by People's Court in August 1943 and executed in Berlin-Plötzensee in September 1943. *225.*

Schwab, Alexander (1887–1943) Journalist; became member of USPD in 1917 and of Spartacus League in 1918; cofounded KAPD in 1920, which he left in 1922; press chief of Reich Institute for Employment and Unemployment Benefits from 1929 to 1933; held for six months in "protective custody" in 1933; arrested again in November 1936; sentenced to eight years' imprisonment by People's Court in 1937;

held in prison and concentration camp; died in Zwickau prison in 1943. *32, 223.*

Schwalbach, Johann (Hans) (born 1905) Journalist, editor of central organ of United Left Opposition in KPD; headed Funke Group prior to 1933; fled to France in 1933; German citizenship revoked in 1934. *246, 247.*

Schwantes, Martin (1904–45) Teacher; became member of KPD in 1928; middleman in Magdeburg regional directorate and central committee instructor until 1934; arrested in January 1934; sentenced to two and one-half years' imprisonment in August 1934; subsequently held in Sachsenhausen concentration camp; released in February 1941; arrested again in July 1944; sentenced to death by People's Court in November 1944 and executed in February 1945. *23, 145–46, 213.*

Schwarzschild, Leopold (1891–1950) Journalist; became copublisher of Frankfurt *Generalanzeiger* (General informer) in 1922; cofounded *Montag-Morgen* (Monday morning) in Berlin in 1923; became publisher of *Magazin der Wirtschaft* (Magazine of economics) in 1925; fled to Paris in 1933; publisher of *Neues Tagebuch* (New diary) until 1940; emigrated to the United States in 1940. *8.*

Schwersenz, Jizchak (born 1915) Teacher, member of Jewish Youth Movement; director of Youth Aliyah School in Berlin from 1939 to 1941; went underground in Berlin in August 1942; fled to Switzerland in February 1944; emigrated to Israel in 1953; has gone on lecture tours in FRG since 1979. *136.*

Seng, Willi (1909–44) Carpenter, politician; became member of KPD in 1932; arrested in 1933; held in Sachsenhausen concentration camp; became KPD functionary in Berlin, Halle and Ruhr region after release from concentration camp; fled to Amsterdam in 1935; attended Lenin School in Moscow from 1935 to 1937; returned to Amsterdam in 1937; returned to Ruhr region in 1941; arrested in Düsseldorf in January 1943; sentenced to death by People's Court in May 1944 and executed in July 1944 in Cologne. *194.*

Severing, Carl (1875–1952) Politician; became member of German Metal Workers' Union and of SPD in 1893; member of Reichstag from 1907 to 1911; editor of SPD organ *Volkswacht* (People's guard) from 1912 to 1919; member of Reichstag from 1920 to 1933; member of Prussian state parliament from 1921 to 1933; Reich minister of interior from 1928 to 1930; minister of interior in Prussia from 1920 to 1926 and from 1930 to 1932; retiree in Bielefeld after 1933; became member of North Rhine-Westphalian state parliament in 1947. *196.*

Seydewitz, Max (1892–1987) Politician; member of SPD from 1910 to 1931; member of Reichstag from 1924 to 1932; became cochairman of SAPD in 1931; fled to Prague in April 1933, to the Netherlands and Norway in 1938, and to Sweden in 1940; worked for Comintern newspaper *Die Welt* (The world) after his release; arrested in August 1942; after having been imprisoned in Stockholm, he was placed under police surveillance; returned to Germany (East) after 1945; in executive committee of SED from 1947 to 1949; prime minister of Saxony from 1947 to 1952. *171, 172.*

Seydlitz-Kurzbach, Walther von (1888–1976) Career officer; became artillery general in May 1942; taken as POW by Soviets in January 1943; sentenced to death in absentia by Reich Court-Martial in 1944; sentenced to death as war criminal in Moscow in May 1950; sentence commuted to twenty-five years' imprisonment; released in 1955; returned to FRG. *207, 211, 212.*

Sieg, John (1903–42) Journalist; became member of KPD in Berlin in 1929; worked at *Die Rote Fahne* (The red banner) from 1929 to 1933; arrested for first time in spring of 1933; began working for Reichsbahn (German railways) after his release in June 1933; arrested again in October 1942; committed suicide in Gestapo prison in Prinz-Albert-Strasse. *22, 23, 225.*

Siemer, Josef (Pater Laurentius) (1888–1956) Catholic priest; provincial of the German Dominican order from 1932 to 1946; taken into custody for questioning in April 1935 because of suspicion of violations involving foreign currency; sentenced to fifteen months' imprisonment in October 1936; acquitted after appeal in January 1937; began fleeing from Gestapo in September 1944 and went underground until end of war. *227.*

Sinz, Otto Construction worker; participated as soldier in Russian campaign; went to Soviet Occupation Zone in 1945; district magistrate in Saxony. *206.*

Smidt, Udo (1900–1978) Protestant clergyman; full-time maintenance worker for Alliance of German Bible Study Groups from 1930 to 1934; publisher of journal *Jungenwacht* (Boys' guard) until 1938; director of theological seminary in Elberfeld from 1951 to 1958; state superintendent of churches in Lippe from 1958 to 1970; member of council of German Evangelical Church from 1961 to 1971. *72.*

Sobottka, Gustav (1886–1953) Politician; became member of SPD in 1910, of USPD in 1918, and of KPD in 1920; member of Prussian state parliament from 1921 to 1932; fled to Saar region in 1933; fled to

France and the Soviet Union in 1935, where he did propaganda work in POW camps; returned to Pomerania in 1945. *206.*

Söhngen, Joseph (1894–1970) Bookseller; sentenced to six months' imprisonment by Special Court of Munich Regional Court in July 1943. *252.*

Solf, Johanna (Hanna) (née Dotti) (1887–1954) Widow of ambassador Wilhelm Solf; arrested in January 1944 after being denounced by Gestapo informers; imprisoned and liberated in 1945. *239–40.*

Sommer, Margarete (1893–1965) Studied philosophy and economics; dismissed as lecturer in 1933; began working in Episcopal Director's Office in Berlin in 1935; became diocese director for care of women in 1939; became director of relief organization for Catholic "non-Aryans" in Episcopal Director's Office in Berlin in 1941; worked with women under auspices of church in Berlin (East) after 1945; moved to Berlin (West) in 1946. *51.*

Spann, Othmar (1878–1950) Economist, philosopher and sociologist; held professorships in Brünn and Vienna; dismissed and arrested in March 1938; spent five months imprisoned in Munich; returned to Austria; lived in Austria after 1945. *135.*

Spengemann, Walter (1904–69) Journalist; became member of SPD in 1929; became head of Jungbanner (Young Banner) in Hannover in 1933; joined Socialist Front in 1933; arrested in 1936; sentenced to ten years' imprisonment by People's Court in 1937; journalist and municipal politician in Lower Saxony after 1945. *237, 238.*

Spengler, Oswald (1880–1936) Cultural philosopher, writer; considered to be "court philosopher" of influential antidemocratic circles; during initial years of Weimar Republic, he supported a dictatorship by the Reichswehr and clandestine military organizations; after Hitler's putsch in November 1923, he avoided making political statements; distanced himself from Third Reich, yet held individual representatives (such as Gregor Strasser) in high regard; turned down a professorship in Leipzig in 1933. *42, 203.*

Sperber, Manès (1905–84) Writer; teacher of individualist psychology in Berlin from 1927 to 1933; member of KPD in Berlin from 1927 to 1933; arrested in 1933; fled to Austria; fled to France via Yugoslavia in 1934; in French Army from 1939 to 1941; emigrated to Switzerland in 1942; interned in 1943; returned to France in 1945. *96.*

Sperr, Franz (1878–1945) Diplomat, monarchist; Bavarian envoy in Berlin from 1932 to 1934; resigned from all posts in 1934; afterward worked in Military Economic and Research Society; arrested in 1944;

sentenced to death by People's Court in January 1945 and executed. *198, 204, 228.*

Sproll, Johannes Baptista (1870–1949) Catholic clergyman; became suffragan in 1916 and bishop of Rottenburg in 1927; expelled from his diocese in August 1938 and lived in exile in Bavaria until his return in June 1945. *51.*

Stackelberg, Heinrich von (1905–46) Economist; became university lecturer in Cologne in 1935; associate professor in Berlin; received professorship in Bonn in 1941; became guest professor in Madrid in 1943. *165.*

Staehle, Wilhelm (1877–1945) Career officer; began working in Reich Ministry of Defense in 1923; worked in Supply Department of Office of Wehrmacht in Reich Ministry of Defense from 1935 to 1937; became military director of Berlin Home for War Invalids in 1937; first interrogated in 1944; arrested in June 1944; sentenced to two years' imprisonment by People's Court in March 1945 and murdered by SS commandos in Berlin in April 1945. *175, 176.*

Stamm, Robert (1900–1937) Technician; became member of Spartacus League in 1917 and of KPD in 1919; began working in journalism in 1926; member of Reichstag from 1932 to 1933; began working in administration of KPD northwestern region in 1933; became political secretary of Berlin-Brandenburg regional administration in 1934; arrested in March 1935; sentenced to death by People's Court in June 1937 and executed in November 1937. *18.*

Stampfer, Friedrich (1874–1957) Journalist, politician; member of Reichstag (SPD) from 1920 to 1933; editor in chief of *Vorwärts* (Forward) from 1916 to 1933; fled to Prague in 1933; became member of SPD executive committee in exile; published *Neues Vorwärts* (New forward) until 1935; in France from 1938 to 1940; editor of *Neue Volkszeitung* (New people's news) in New York from 1940 to 1948; teacher at Academy of Labor in Frankfurt am Main from 1948 to 1955. *219.*

Staritz, Katharina (1903–53) Protestant church worker; became director of Ecclesiastical Relief Station for Evangelical Non-Aryans in Breslau in 1938; evangelical consistory failed to protect her after she was attacked by *Das Schwarze Korps* (The black corps) in 1941; arrested in 1943; survived Ravensbrück concentration camp. *51.*

Stark, Oskar (1890–1970) Journalist, member of DDP; began working for *Frankfurter Zeitung* (Frankfurt times) in 1920; worked at *Berliner Tageblatt* (Berlin daily news) from 1931 to 1933; dismissed in 1933; chief of service at *Frankfurter Zeitung* from 1935 to 1943; founded Nordic Publishing Institute in 1943; editor in chief of *Badische Zeitung* (Baden news) after 1946. *241.*

Stauffenberg, Count Claus Schenk von (1907–44) Career officer; began working in Organizational Department of High Command of Army in 1940; returned from Africa after being badly wounded in 1943; became Chief-of-Staff of Reserve Army in Berlin in 1944; summarily executed in Berlin during night of July 20–21, 1944. *37, 38, 39, 62, 66, 67, 122, 145, 175, 187–89.*

Steber, Franz (1904–83) Youth Movement official; worked in Düsseldorf Youth House from 1927 to 1935; became first Reich leader of Catholic storm units in Düsseldorf in 1931; arrested in February 1936; sentenced to five years' imprisonment by People's Court in April 1936; released from Berlin-Moabit prison in May 1941; director of social welfare office of Alliance of German Catholic Youth in Düsseldorf from 1955 to 1965. *69.*

Stechert, Kurt (1906–58) Journalist; member of SAPD until 1932, when he became member of SPD; imprisoned in 1933; fled to Republic of Czechoslovakia; worked at *Neues Vorwärts* (New forward); emigrated to Sweden in 1936; in foreign delegation of German trade unions in Sweden in 1938; attempted in vain to return to Germany after 1945; worked as teacher and metal worker in Sweden until 1958. *223.*

Steidle, Luitpold (1898–1984) Farmer, politician; became member of NSDAP in 1933; achieved rank of colonel in 1942; taken as POW by Soviets in 1943; vice president of German Authority for Farming and Forestry in Soviet Occupation Zone from 1945 to 1948; in head executive committee of CDU; minister of labor and health of GDR from 1949 to 1958; sat in Volkskammer from 1950 to 1971; mayor of Weimar from 1960 to 1969. *207.*

Steltzer, Theodor (1885–1967) Politician; district magistrate in Rendsburg (Schleswig-Holstein) from 1920 to 1923; in Norway during war; arrested in August 1944; sentenced to death by People's Court in January 1945, but sentence not carried out due to intervention by Swedish friends; cofounded Berlin CDU in 1945; prime minister of Schleswig-Holstein in 1946–47. *157, 196, 198.*

Steurich, Heinrich (Heinz, also known as "Jonny"). *130.*

Stösslein, Herbert (born 1909) Engineer; became member of NSDAP in 1937; participated as major in Russian campaign; worked as journalist and functionary of NDPD in Soviet Occupation Zone after 1945. *206.*

Strasser, Gregor (1892–1934) Politician; became member of NSDAP in 1921; organizer of SA in Lower Bavaria; sentenced to but as Landtag deputy didn't have to serve eighteen months in prison after Hitler's putsch; founded Kampf Publishing House in 1926; became Reich director of propaganda in 1926; broke with Hitler in 1932; murdered after Röhm Putsch in 1934. *129.*

Strasser, Otto (1897–1974) Politician; became member of NSDAP in 1925; forced out of party by Hitler in 1930; editor at his brother Gregor's Kampf Publishing House; fled in 1933; began living in Canada in 1940; returned to FRG in 1955; founder of German Social Union and functionary in it from 1956 to 1961. *75, 93, 120, 129, 130, 132.*

Strassmann, Ernst (1897–1958) Lawyer; member of DDP from 1918 to 1930; afterward without party affiliation; became regional court judge in Berlin in 1930; member of executive committee of Reich Alliance of Democratic Youth Organizations; arrested in August 1942 and held in "protective custody" until April 1945; on executive committee of Electric and Water Company in Berlin (West) after 1945; member of SPD. *9, 10, 241–43.*

Strelow, Heinz (1915–43) Journalist; became member of KJVD in Hamburg in 1932; held in "protective custody" in Hamburg-Fuhlsbüttel in October/November 1935; entered military service in Hamburg in 1940; began living in Berlin in 1941; arrested in October 1942; sentenced to death by Reich Court-Martial in January 1943 and executed in Berlin-Plötzensee in May 1943. *225.*

Strünck, Theodor (1885–1945) Lawyer; became captain in reserves at Counterintelligence Office in 1937; arrested in 1944; murdered in Flossenbürg concentration camp in April 1945. *145.*

Stülpnagel, Karl-Heinrich von (1886–1944) Career officer, general of infantry; first quartermaster in General Staff of Army from 1938 to 1940; became commander in chief of Seventeenth Army in 1941; commander in chief in France from 1942 to 1944; arrested after July 20, 1944, assassination attempt on Hitler; sentenced to death by People's Court in August 1944 and executed. *63–64, 65.*

Sylten, Werner (1893–1942) Protestant social worker; Religious Socialist; dismissed as "half-Jew" in 1936; arrested in February 1941; imprisoned in Dachau after having been held for three months in detention for questioning; murdered in Hartheim in August 1942. *51.*

Thadden, Elisabeth von (1890–1944) Educator; founded Wieblingen Castle evangelical educational home near Heidelberg in 1929; arrested in France in January 1944; sentenced to death by People's Court in July 1944 and executed in Berlin-Plötzensee in September 1944. *239, 240.*

Thalheimer, August (1884–1948) Politician; became member of SPD in 1904; became editor in chief of *Freie Volkszeitung* (Free people's news) in 1909; became member of Spartacus League and of KPD in 1919; in central office of KPD until 1924; in Moscow from 1923 to 1928; expelled from KPD in 1928 and cofounded KPDO; fled to France in 1933 and to Cuba in 1941; Allies refused to allow him to return to Germany. *167, 169.*

Thälmann, Ernst (1886–1944) Politician; became member of SPD in 1903, of USPD in 1917, and of KPD in 1920; became KPD chairman in Hamburg in 1921; on Hamburg city council from 1919 to 1933; chairman of KPD from 1925 to 1933; member of Reichstag from 1924 to 1933; arrested in March 1933 and murdered in Buchenwald. *15, 169.*

Thiede, Richard Installer of electrical equipment; member of FAUD in Leipzig and leader of FAUD in Saxony; arrested in February 1937. *118.*

Thiel, Fritz (1916–43) Calibrator, watchmaker; became member of KJVD in 1932; volunteered for Luftwaffe in 1935; trained to be radio operator; imprisoned in 1936–37; drafted into Wehrmacht in 1939; radio operator in Poland; studied economics in Berlin in 1941–42; arrested in September 1942; sentenced to death by Reich Court-Martial in January 1943 and executed in Berlin-Plötzensee in May 1943. *225.*

Thiessies, Irene Secretary of Protestant theologian Heinrich Held; survived war without being persecuted; began working again for Protestant church after 1945. *108.*

Thomas, Georg (1890–1946) Career officer; became general of infantry in 1940; director of Office of Military Economics and Armaments at High Command of Armed Forces from 1939 until beginning of 1943; arrested in October 1944; imprisoned in Flossenbürg and Dachau beginning in February 1945; died after liberation in American POW camp. *164, 174, 175.*

Thurmann, Horst (born 1911) Protestant clergyman; assumed various curacies after being ordained in 1937; denounced in February 1940; sentenced to six months' imprisonment in Bonn in December 1940; in Dachau from spring of 1941 until liberation. *54.*

Tillich, Paul (1886–1965) Protestant theologian, philosopher, theoretician of religious socialism; became professor in Marburg in 1924 and in Frankfurt am Main in 1929; dismissed in 1933; fled to the United States; became chairman of Council for a Democratic Germany in 1944. *195.*

Tittel, Hans (1894–1983) Journalist; became member of SPD in 1912; switched to KPD; became director of press office of KPD in 1926; member of Thuringian state parliament from 1927 to 1930; expelled from party in 1928; member of KPDO until 1939; became political director of domestic administration of KPDO; fled to Republic of Czechoslovakia in 1933 and to France in 1938; interned in 1939; began living in the United States in 1941; returned to FRG in 1961; member of SPD. *168.*

Toller, Ernst (1893–1939) Writer, politician; became leading member of USPD in 1919; participated in formation of Munich soviet republic; sentenced to five years' confinement in a fortress in 1919; withdrew from politics in 1925; fled to the United States in 1936; committed suicide in exile. *5, 138.*

Tresckow, Henning von (1901–44) Career officer; became major in Army Group A in 1939; became first lieutenant and first general staff officer of Army Group B (later called Army Group Middle) in 1940; promoted to colonel in 1942 and to brigadier general in 1944; committed suicide after Stauffenberg's failed assassination attempt on Hitler. *38, 55, 65, 66, 67, 121, 174, 175, 188, 240.*

Trotha, Carl Dietrich von (1907–52) Economist; at Frankfurt School of Social Research from 1931 to 1933; became expert adviser at Reich Ministry of Economics in 1936; became director of Department of Energy Policy in Berlin magistrate's office after May 1945, then professor at College of Politics in Berlin (West). *73, 195, 225.*

Trott zu Solz, Adam von (1909–44) Lawyer; received scholarships to study at Oxford in 1932–33 and in China in 1937–38; became member of NSDAP in 1940; began working in Department of Information at Counterintelligence Office in spring of 1940; made several trips abroad; arrested in July 1944; sentenced to death by People's Court in August 1944 and executed in Berlin-Plötzensee. *38, 42, 55, 157, 158, 160, 175, 195–98, 225.*

Tschirschky und Boegendorff, Fritz-Günther von (1900–1980) Diplomat, founder of Youth Conservative Circle and of Silesian Gentlemen's Society; became von Papen's confidence man in Prussian State Ministry in 1933; personal adviser to vice-chancellor; arrested in June 1934 and held in Lichtenburg concentration camp; transferred to embassy in Vienna; dismissed in 1935; fled to England; interned from 1941 to 1944; returned to FRG in 1952; reentered diplomatic service. *150.*

Tucholsky, Kurt (1890–1935) Writer, journalist; began working for *Schaubühne* (The stage) in 1907, for *Vorwärts* (Forward) in 1918, and as foreign correspondent in Paris in 1924; became publisher of *Weltbühne* (The world stage) in 1926; emigrated to Sweden in 1929;

German citizenship revoked in 1933; committed suicide in exile in 1935. *4, 8.*

Uhrig, Robert (1903–44) Toolmaker; became member of KPD in 1920 and director of Communist cell at Osram lightbulb factory in Berlin in 1929; first arrested in 1934; sentenced to twenty-one months' imprisonment in November 1934; arrested again in February 1942; held for two years in Sachsenhausen concentration camp; sentenced to death by People's Court in June 1944 and executed in Brandenburg prison in August 1944. *22, 126, 225, 232, 247–49.*

Ulbricht, Walter (1893–1973) Politician; became member of SPD in 1912; cofounded KPD in Saxony in 1919; member of central committee of KPD in 1923 and from 1927 onward; in Moscow in 1924–25; member of Saxon state parliament from 1926 to 1928 and of Reichstag from 1928 to 1933; fled to Prague in 1933 and to Paris in 1935; fought in Spanish Civil War from 1936 to 1938; in the Soviet Union from 1938 until April 1945; became secretary general of SED in 1950; first secretary of central committee of SED from 1953 to 1971; chairman of State Council of GDR from 1960 to 1973. *16, 20, 138, 139, 169, 170, 206, 211.*

Unger, Joachim (born 1910) Served apprenticeship in advertising agency; member of KPD; switched to Left Opposition of KPD in 1932 and became its leading member in Berlin in 1933; editor of *Permanente Revolution;* switched to SAPD in 1935; fled to Copenhagen and Sweden in 1937; in Frankfurt am Main in 1948–49; became businessman in Berlin (West) in 1960. *246.*

Urbahns, Hugo (1890–1946) Politician; member of USPD; became member of Spartacus League in 1918 and of KPD in 1919; member of Reichstag from 1924 to 1928; elected to central committee of KPD in 1925; became member of Left Opposition of KPD in 1926; cofounded Lenin League; fled via Republic of Czechoslovakia to Sweden in 1933, where he worked as journalist and typographer. *246.*

Üxküll-Gyllenband, Count Nikolaus von (1877–1944) Career officer of imperial and royal monarchy until end of World War I, later businessman in Germany; entered Reich Commission for Price Control in 1936; drafted into Wehrmacht in 1941; arrested in 1944; sentenced to death by People's Court and executed in September 1944. *67.*

Wachter, Maria (born 1910) Worker; became member of KPD in 1930; attended Lenin School in Moscow in 1935 and afterward lived for a while in France; arrested in 1942; sentenced to five years' imprisonment by Court of Appeal; became member of KPD after 1945 and later of DKP; lives in Düsseldorf. *111.*

Wager, Josef (Bebo) (1905–43) Electrical engineer in Augsburg; became member of SAJ in 1922; member of SPD; cofounded Revolutionary Socialists; arrested in November 1942; sentenced to death by People's Court in May 1943 and executed in Munich-Stadelheim in August 1943. *33.*

Wagner, Eduard (1894–1944) Career officer, general of artillery; chief of Sixth Unit in General Staff of Army from 1936 to 1940; became general quartermaster in the General Staff of the Army in 1941; avoided arrest by committing suicide on July 23, 1944. *63.*

Wagner, Karl (1909–83) Stone-cutter; member of KPD; first arrested in March 1933; held for three months in Heuberg concentration camp and subsequently fled to Switzerland; returned to Germany in March 1935; arrested again in April 1935; sentenced to eighteen months' imprisonment in January 1936; sent to Dachau in December 1936; imprisoned in Buchenwald from July 1944 to May 1945. *88.*

Walcher, Jacob (1887–1970) Politician; became member of SPD in 1906; member of KPD from 1918 to 1928; cofounded KPDO in 1928; became member of SAPD in 1932; fled to France in 1933; interned in 1939; fled to the United States in 1941; member of Council for a Democratic Germany; returned to Germany (East) in 1946. *31, 171.*

Waldburg-Zeil, Prince Erich von (1899–1953) Financed monarchistic resistance organizations in Bavaria and *Der Freie Weg* (The free way). *204.*

Wangenheim, Gustav von (1895–1975) Writer, actor, theater director; member of USPD from 1918 to 1922; became member of KPD in 1922; entered Collective of Red Actors in 1931; fled to Paris in 1933; director of German Theater Column Left in Moscow from 1933 to 1935; returned to Germany (East) in 1945, where he worked at German Theater of Berlin. *206, 210.*

Wartenberg, Gerhard (1904–42) Editor in Leipzig; Reich director of FAUD until May 1933; in "protective custody" from August until December 1933; arrested again in May 1937 and subsequently held in concentration camp. *118.*

Wehner, Herbert (1906–90) Politician; member of KPD from 1927 to 1944; member of Saxon state parliament in 1930–31; in central committee and politburo of KPD from 1935 to 1944; fled to the Soviet Union in 1933 and to Sweden in 1941; interned in Sweden from 1942 to 1944; became member of SPD in 1946; editor in Hamburg from 1946 to 1949; member of Bundestag from 1949 to 1983; became member of executive committee of SPD in 1952; deputy party chairman from 1958 to 1973;

chairman of SPD opposition in Bundestag from 1969 to 1983. *ix, 21, 22, 138, 193.*

Weidt, Otto (1883–1947) Owner of brush workshop for the blind in Berlin; worked together with Swedish church; helped Jewess Alice Licht escape from Auschwitz; lived in Berlin (West) until his death. *123.*

Weinert, Erich (1890–1953) Writer, journalist; began working at *Die Rote Fahne* (The red banner) and *Weltbühne* (The world stage) in 1924; cofounded Alliance of Proletarian-Revolutionary Writers in 1928; became member of KPD in 1929; fled to Switzerland and France in 1933; fought in Spanish Civil War from 1937 to 1939; emigrated to the Soviet Union in 1939; returned to Germany (East) in 1946; member of SED; cofounded German Academy of Arts in 1950. *206, 207, 211.*

Weinmann, Franz (born 1909) Catholic priest, chaplain in Mannheim; charged and interrogated several times after 1933; arrested in March 1942; forbidden to teach; in detention for questioning until June 1942 and afterward in Dachau until April 1945. *54.*

Weisenborn, Günther (1902–62) Writer, dramatic producer; lived in Argentina from 1930 to 1933; fled to the United States in 1935; returned to Germany in 1937; chief dramatic producer of Berlin Schiller Theater; worked for Großdeutscher Runkfunk (Greater German radio) in 1941–42; imprisoned from 1942 to 1945; cofounded Hebbel Theater in Berlin (West) after 1945; publisher of *Ulenspiegel* (The rogue) from 1945 to 1947; became chief dramatic producer of Hamburg Chamber Theaters in 1951. *224.*

Weizsäcker, Ernst von (1882–1951) State secretary in Counterintelligence Office from 1938 to 1943; ambassador at Vatican from 1943 to 1945; sentenced to seven years' imprisonment by American court-martial in Nuremberg in 1948. *159–60, 240.*

Wels, Otto (1873–1939) Politician; became member of SPD in 1891 and of its executive committee in 1913; member of Reichstag from 1920 to 1933; chairman of SPD from 1931 to 1933; fled to Prague; German citizenship revoked in 1933; member of Sopade's executive committee in exile; fled to Paris in 1938. *169.*

Wendt, Willy (1906–67) Worker; became member of SPD in 1930; arrested in 1935 and sentenced by court of appeals in Hamm to five years' imprisonment. *236, 237, 238.*

Wenzel-Teutschenthal, Karl (1875–1944) Owner of estate, sugar producer; arrested after July 20, 1944, assassination attempt on Hitler; sentenced to death by People's Court in November 1944 and executed in December 1944. *175.*

Werfel, Franz (1890–1945) Writer; publisher's reader in Leipzig in 1910; became playwright and novelist in Vienna in 1919; fled to Switzerland, France, and Portugal in 1938 and to the United States in 1940. *92.*

Wessels, Theodor (1902–72) Economist; became university lecturer in Bonn in 1936 and professor in Cologne in 1940; became member of Academic Advisory Council in administration of the Bizone and in Federal Ministry of Economics in 1948; rector of University of Cologne from 1951 to 1954. *165.*

Wieland, Heinrich (1877–1957) Biochemist; director of Institute of Chemistry at University of Munich; professor in Freiburg im Breisgau; received Nobel Prize for chemistry in 1927; escaped arrest in 1936. *252.*

Wiest, Fritz (1895–1983) Politician; member of KPD from 1920 to 1929; began doing trade union work at KPD central office in Berlin in 1923; became member of KPDO in 1929 and, after 1933, member of KPDO's domestic administration (Berlin Committee); fled to Republic of Czechoslovakia in 1936, to Norway in 1938, to Canada in 1940, and later to England; returned to FRG at beginning of 1960s. *168.*

Winkler, Hans (1906–87) Justice system employee at county court in Luckenwalde; arrested in 1944; charged with making preparations for high treason; in detention for questioning until end of war; became senior police adviser in domestic administration of Soviet Occupation Zone in 1947/48; fled to Berlin (West) in 1948. *139–40, 141.*

Winter, Friedrich. *51.*

Wirmer, Josef (1901–44) Attorney in Berlin; legal representative of cartel consisting of Catholic student organizations during Weimar Republic; member of left wing of Center Party; arrested in August 1944; held in Ravensbrück concentration camp; sentenced to death by People's Court in September 1944 and executed in Berlin-Plötzensee. *55.*

Wiskow, Eberhard Member of USPD, KPD, and later of SPD; fled to Prague in 1935, where he committed suicide. *215.*

Wiskow, Wolfgang Member of KPD; became KPD functionary in Hamburg after 1945. *215.*

Witzleben, Erwin von (1881–1944) Career officer; became commander in chief of Third Military District in Berlin in 1934; became field marshal and commander in chief of Army Group D in France in 1940; became commander in chief in the West in 1941; dismissed from service for health reasons in March 1942; arrested on July 21, 1944;

sentenced to death by People's Court in August 1944 and executed in Berlin-Plötzensee. *37, 38, 61, 62, 121, 174, 175, 176, 188.*

Wobbe, Rudolf (born 1926) Locksmith's apprentice, member of Hitler Youth and of Mormon community in Hamburg; arrested in February 1942; sentenced to ten years' imprisonment by People's Court in August 1942; released in 1945 and drafted into Wehrmacht; taken as POW by British. *190.*

Wolf, Friedrich (1888–1953) Writer; became member of KPD and of Alliance of Proletarian-Revolutionary Writers in 1928; fled to France in 1933; interned in 1939; went to the Soviet Union in 1941; returned to Berlin (East) in 1945; cultural politician and writer; GDR's ambassador to Poland in 1950–51. *206.*

Wolff, Edith (Ewo) (born 1904) Daughter of a "privileged mixed marriage," student of philosophy; became clerk in 1941; arrested in June 1943; held in Ravensbrück concentration camp; sentenced to two years' imprisonment in January 1944; liberated from Lippstadt prison in 1945 and then emigrated to Palestine. *136, 192.*

Wolff, Theodor (1868–1943) Journalist; became Paris correspondent of *Berliner Tageblatt* (Berlin daily news) in 1894 and its editor in chief in 1906; cofounded DDP, which he left in 1926; fled to France in 1933; turned over to Gestapo in 1943; prison and concentration camp incarceration; died in Jewish Hospital in Berlin. *7–8.*

Wolker, Ludwig (1887–1955) Catholic clergyman, prelate, director of KJMV; became state and diocese president in 1925; became general president of KJMV in 1926; director of German Youth Strength; held in custody for several months in 1936; disbanded KJMV in 1939 and afterward performed ministerial duties with Fraternity of John. *71.*

Wurm, Theophil (1868–1953) Protestant clergyman; became prison clergyman for Evangelical Society in 1899; became member of Württemberg state parliament in 1920 (German National People's Party) and church president in Heilbronn in 1929; state bishop in Württemberg from 1933 to 1949; placed under house arrest; forbidden to publish and to speak publicly in 1944; first chairman of Council of German Evangelical Churches from 1945 to 1949. *52, 143, 196.*

Yorck von Wartenburg, Count Peter (1904–44) Lawyer; began career in administration with president in Breslau in 1934; became adviser in Reich Commission for Price Control in 1936; called up as reserve officer in 1939; began working in Economic Staff East at High Command of Armed Forces in 1942; arrested during night of July 20–21, 1944;

sentenced to death by People's Court in August 1944 and executed in Berlin-Plötzensee. *37, 38, 160, 164, 195, 196, 197, 198, 220.*

Zarden, Irmgard (born 1922) Arrested in 1943 or beginning of 1944 and detained from January to July 1944 (including in Ravensbrück concentration camp); acquitted by People's Court in July 1944; emigrated to the United States after 1945. *239, 240.*

Zehner, Emil Locksmith, member of FAUD in Erfurt; began working in outlawed Reich administration of FAUD in May 1933; charged in 1937. *118.*

Zehrer, Hans (1899–1966) Journalist, editor of *Vossische Zeitung;* supported a national socialism and believed that this was represented by left wing of NSDAP; began doing important work for antidemocratic journal *Tat* (The deed) in 1929 and resigned as its editor in 1933; publisher's reader until 1939; contributor and editor in chief of *Die Welt* (The world) after 1945; worked for *Bild-Zeitung* (Picture news) until 1961. *225.*

Zeigner, Erich (1886–1949) Politician; became member of SPD in 1919; Saxon minister of justice from 1921 to 1923; member of Saxon state parliament in 1922–23; worked for Social Democratic newspapers from 1928 to 1933; arrested several times after 1933; sent to Buchenwald in August 1944; mayor of Leipzig from 1945 to 1949. *169.*

Zimmet, Karl (born 1895) Locksmith, member of KPD and of Soldiers' Council in Munich soviet republic; confined in fortress for eighteen months; became publisher of *Volksruf* (The people's call) in 1929; was front man of SAPD and KPD after 1933; arrested in January 1944; indicted before People's Court in September 1944, yet was declared unfit for trial and avoided conviction. *119, 120, 161.*

Zippel, Hans Employee in a business firm; participated as lance corporal in Russian campaign; went to Soviet Occupation Zone after 1945. *206.*

Zott, Josef (1901–45) Gardener, city construction supervisor in Munich, monarchist; arrested in August 1939; sentenced to death in October 1944 and executed in January 1945. *203, 204.*

Zuckmayer, Carl (1896–1977) Writer, dramatic producer at various German theaters; fled to Switzerland in 1938 and to the United States in 1939; returned to Germany as civil service agent of U.S. government in 1945; moved to Switzerland in 1958. *221.*

Zühlke, Johannes Began working in outlawed Reich administration of FAUD in May 1933. *118.*

Zweig, Arnold (1887–1968) Writer and later editor of *Jüdische Rund-schau* (The Jewish review) and *Weltbühne* (The world stage); became member of PEN Club in 1926; fled to Palestine in 1933; returned to Germany (East) in 1948; became representative in Volkskammer in 1949 and president of German Academy of Arts (GDR) in 1950. *138, 170.*

List of Abbreviations

ADV	Anti-Nazi German People's Front (Antinazistische Deutsche Volksfront)
BDO	Alliance of German Officers (Bund Deutscher Offiziere)
BSW	Fraternal Cooperation of Prisoners of War (Bratskoje Sotrudnitschestvo Voyennoplennych)
CDU	Christian Democratic Union (Christlich Demokratische Union)
Comintern	Communist International
CSU	Christian Social Union (Christlich Soziale Union)
DAF	German Workers' Front (Deutsche Arbeitsfront)
DDJ	German Democratic Youth (Deutsche Demokratische Jugend)
DDP	German Democratic Party (Deutsche Demokratische Partei)
DKP	German Communist Party (Deutsche Kommunistische Partei)
DSP	German State Party (Deutsche Staatspartei)
DVP	German People's Party (Deutsche Volkspartei)
FAB	Freedom Action of Bavaria (Freiheits-Aktion Bayern)
FAUD	Free Workers' Union of Germany (Freie Arbeiterunion Deutschlands)
FDJ	Free German Youth (of the GDR) (Freie Deutsche Jugend)
FDP	Free Democratic Party (Freie Demokratische Partei)
FRG	Federal Republic of Germany
GDR	German Democratic Republic
IBV	International Bible Students' Association (Internationale Bibelforscher-Vereinigung)

IJB	International Youth Alliance (Internationaler Jugendbund)
ISK	International Socialist Combat League (Internationaler Sozialistischer Kampfbund)
ITF	International Transport Workers' Federation (Internationale Transportarbeiter-Föderation)
KAPD	German Communist Workers' Party (Kommunistische Arbeiterpartei Deutschlands)
Kapo	concentration camp inmate who led a work detail
KJMV	Catholic Young Men's Association (Katholischer Jungmännerverband)
KJVD	German Communist Youth Organization (Kommunistischer Jugendverband Deutschland)
KPD	German Communist Party (Kommunistische Partei Deutschlands)
KPDO	German Communist Party/Opposition (Kommunistische Partei Deutschland/Opposition)
KPO	German Communist Party/Opposition (Kommunistische Partei Deutschland/Opposition)
LO	Leninist Organization (Leninistische Organisation)
NDPD	German National Democratic Party (National-Demokratische Partei Deutschlands)
NKFD	National Committee "Free Germany" (Nationalkomitee Freies Deutschland)
NSDAP	National Socialist German Workers' Party (Nationalsozialistische Deutsche Arbeiterpartei)
OKH	Army High Command (Oberkommando des Heeres)
ORG	Leninist Organization (Leninistische Organisation)
SA	Storm Unit (Sturm-Abteilung)
SAJ	Socialist Workers' Youth (Sozialistische Arbeiterjugend)
SAP	Socialist Workers' Party (Sozialistische Arbeiterpartei)
SAPD	German Socialist Workers' Party (Sozialistische Arbeiterpartei Deutschlands)
Schufo	Defensive Formations (Schutzformation)

SED	German Socialist Unity Party (Sozialistische Einheitspartei Deutschlands)
SF	Socialist Front (Sozialistische Front)
Sopade	executive committee of the SPD in exile
SPD	German Social Democratic Party (Sozialdemokratische Partei Deutschlands)
SS	defense squad (Schutz-Staffel)
USPD	German Independent Social Democratic Party (Unabhängige Sozialdemokratische Partei Deutschlands)

Cross-Reference System

Items in bold are entries in parts 1 or 2.

Academic Legion. *See* Resistance against National Socialism before 1933

The Action (*Die Aktion*). *See* Resistance against National Socialism before 1933

Against the Current (*Gegen den Strom*). *See* German Communist Party/Opposition (KPDO or KPO)

Die Aktion (The Action). *See* Resistance against National Socialism before 1933

Alliance of German Officers. *See* National Committee "Free Germany"

Anarcho-Syndicalists, 117

Das andere Deutschland (The Other Germany). *See* Resistance against National Socialism before 1933

Das andere Deutschland (The Other Germany) (group). *See* Exile and Resistance

Antifascist Committees. *See* National Committee "Free Germany"

Anti-Nazi German People's Front (ADV), 119

Arbeiter-Illustrierte-Zeitung (Workers' Illustrated News). *See* Resistance against National Socialism before 1933

Assassination Attempts against Hitler, 120

Assistance and Solidarity, 122

"Aufbruch" ("New Beginining") *See* Uhrig-Römer Group

Bästlein Group, 125

Battle Group Auschwitz. *See* Resistance by the Persecuted

Bavarian Federation for Fatherland and King. *See* Monarchist Resistance in Bavaria

Beacon (*Fanal*). *See* Anarcho-Syndicalists

Danz-Schwantes Group (Magdeburg), 145

Das andere Deutschland (The Other Germany). *See* Resistance against National Socialism before 1933

Das andere Deutschland (The Other Germany) (group). *See* Exile and Resistance.

Das freie Wort (The Free Word). *See* Hanno-Günther Group/Rütli Group; National Committee "Free Germany"

Das Tage-Buch (The Diary). *See* Resistance against National Socialism before 1933

"Das Ziel." *See* "The Goal" ("Das Ziel")

Defensive Formations (Schufo). *See* Resistance against National Socialism before 1933; Socialist Front

Delp Circle. *See* Rösch Circle

Der Friedenskämpfer (The Fighter for Peace). *See* Communist Resistance; Knöchel Organization

Der Gerade Weg (The Straight Path). *See* Resistance against National Socialism before 1933

Der Vorbote (The Herald). *See* Lechleiter Group

Desertion. *See* Everyday Acts of Dissent and Disobedience; Military Subversion and Desertion; Parole Units

Desertion and Refusal of Military Duty. *See* Military Subversion and Desertion; Jehovah's Witnesses

Deutsche Freiheit (German Freedom). *See* Saar Battle (Status Quo Movement)

Deutsche Informationen (German Information). *See* Committee for the Preparation of a German People's Front

Deutsche Revolution (German Revolution). *See* Black Front

Deutschland-Berichte (Reports on Germany). *See* Foreign Contacts; Exile and Resistance; Socialist Resistance

The Diary (*Das Tage-Buch*). *See* Resistance against National Socialism before 1933

Die Aktion (The Action). *See* Resistance against National Socialism before 1933

Free Germany Movement. *See* Exile and Resistance; National Committee "Free Germany"

The Free Word (*Das freie Wort*). *See* Hanno-Günther Group/Rütli Group; National Committee "Free Germany"

Free Workers' Union of Germany (FAUD). *See* Anarcho-Syndicalists

Freiburg Circles, 164

Freiburg Council. *See* Freiburg Circles

Das freie Wort (The Free Word). *See* Hanno-Günther Group/Rütli Group; National Committee "Free Germany"

Freies Deutschland (Free Germany). *See* National Committee "Free Germany"

Freiheit (Freedom). *See* Knöchel Organization

Der Friedenskämpfer (The Fighter for Peace). *See* Communist Resistance; Knöchel Organization

Friends of Children (SPD). *See* Leipzig Hound Packs; Socialist Resistance; Youth Opposition

Fritz List Sporting and Hiking Goods Store. *See* Youth Opposition

Front Nationale de le Libération (FNL). *See* Exile and Resistance

Gegen den Strom (Against the Current). *See* German Communist Party/Opposition (KPDO or KPO)

Gegner (Opponent). *See* Red Orchestra

Der Gerade Weg (The Straight Path). *See* Resistance against National Socialism before 1933

German Boys' Club (d.j. 1.11). *See* Youth Opposition

German Communist Party/Opposition (KPDO or KPO), 167

German Communist Youth Organization (KJVD). *See* Youth Opposition

German Freedom (*Deutsche Freiheit*). *See* Saar Battle (Status Quo Movement)

German Freedom Radio. *See* Committee for the Preparation of a German People's Front

German Information (*Deutsche Informationen*). *See* Committee for the Preparation of a German People's Front

Contributors

ARETIN, BARON KARL OTMAR VON. Born in 1923; studied history, art history, and Bavarian history in Munich; received his Dr. Phil. in 1954; *Habilitation* in 1963; received honorary doctorate from Poznan in 1986; professor emeritus, director of Institute for European History in Mainz. Publications include: *Vom deutschen Reich zum Deutschen Bund* (1993); *Friedrich der Große* (1985); *Das Alte Reich,* vol. 1: *Föderalistische oder hierarchische Ordnung: 1648–1684* (1993).

AUERBACH, HELLMUTH. Born in 1930; studied history, sociology, and philosophy in Munich; academic assistant at Institute for Contemporary History since 1962; editor in chief of *Vierteljahrshefte für Zeitgeschichte* from 1968 to 1977; director of library from 1978 to 1984; has since been working in institute's department of research and consultation. Publications: bibliographic works and essays on contemporary history, especially on the early history of the NSDAP and German-French relations.

BLEISTEIN, ROMAN, S.J. Born in 1928; entered the Jesuit order in 1948; ordained in 1960; holds a Dr. Phil.; professor of pedagogy at College of Philosophy in Munich. Publications include: as editor, *Alfred Delp: Gesammelte Schriften,* 5 vols. (1985); *Alfred Delp: Geschichte eines Zeugen* (1989).

BRAUN, GÜNTER. Born in 1953; studied political science and German philology in Mannheim; received his Dr. Phil. in 1991; academic assistant at the Center for European Social Research of the University of Mannheim. Publications: as coeditor, *Widerstand gegen den Nationalsozialismus in Mannheim* (1984); as coauthor, *Widerstand der Sozialdemokraten und Kommunisten in der Pfalz* (1993).

COPPI, HANS. Born 1942; historian; received his Dr. Phil. in 1992; associate of the German Resistance Memorial in Berlin.

DISTEL, BARBARA. Born 1943; originally a librarian; cofounded Dachau Memorial in 1963 and has been its director since 1975; pursues journalistic activities. Coeditor of *Dachauer Hefte* since 1985.

DROBISCH, KLAUS. Born 1931; studied history in Leipzig; holds a Dr. Sc. Phil.; academic assistant at the Institute for History at the Academy of Sciences in East Berlin from 1968 to 1991 and subsequently at the German Resistance Memorial in Berlin; teaches at the Free University of Berlin in the Department of Political Science. Publications include: *Wir schweigen nicht! Eine Dokumentation über den antifaschistischen Widerstand Münchner Studenten 1942–43* (1984); *Das System der NS-Konzentrationslager 1933–1939* (1993).

FISCHER, ALEXANDER. Born 1933; holds a Dr. Phil.; professor of eastern European history at the University of Bonn. Publications include: as editor, *Teheran — Jalta — Potsdam: Die sowjetischen Protokolle von den Kriegskonferenzen der "Großen Drei"* (1968); *Sowjetische Deutschlandpolitik im Zweiten Weltkrieg 1941–1945* (1975); together with A. Karger, *Politische Weltkunde: Die Sowjetunion* (1985).

FOITZIK, JAN. Born 1948; academic assistant at the Institute for Contemporary History (Berlin Branch). Publications include: as coauthor, *Bibliographisches Handbuch der deutschsprachigen Emigration nach 1933* (1980–1983); *Zwischen den Fronten: Zur Politik, Organisation und Funktion linker politischer Kleinorganisationen im Widerstand 1933 bis 1939/40* (1986).

GARBE, DETLEF. Born 1956; studied Protestant theology, pedagogy, and history; received his Dr. Phil. in 1989; director of Neuengamme Memorial. Publications include: together with Brigitte Drescher, *Es begann in Hiroshima* (1982); *Die vergessenen KZs? Gedenkstätten für die Opfer des NS-Terrors in der Bundesrepublik* (1983); *"In jedem Einzelfall...bis zur Todesstrafe": Der Militärstrafrechtler Erich Schwinge: Ein deutsches Juristenleben* (1989).

GRAML, HERMANN. Born 1928; historian; academic assistant at the Institute of Modern History in Munich and editor in chief of the *Vierteljahrshefte für Zeitgeschichte* until 1993. Publications include: *Der 9. November 1939: "Reichskristallnacht"* (1956); *Widerstand im Dritten Reich: Probleme, Ereignisse, Gestalten* (1984 [reprint 1994]); *Die Alliierten und die Teilung Deutschlands* (1985); *Europa nach dem Zweiten Weltkrieg* (1983; Fischer's Weltgeschichte series, vol. 35, coeditor with W. Benz); *Weltprobleme zwischen den Machtblöcken* (1981; Fischer's Weltgeschichte series, vol. 36, coeditor with W. Benz).

GRUNER, WOLF. Born 1960; studied history in East Berlin; received his M.A. in history in 1989; presently a doctoral candidate.

HAASE, NORBERT. Born 1960; historian; holds an M.A.; received his Dr. Phil. in 1993; academic assistant at the Office of Research of the History of the Resistance at the Free University of Berlin in cooperation with the German Resistance Memorial in Berlin. Publications include: *Deutsche Deserteure* (1987); *Das Reichskriegsgericht und der Widerstand gegen die nationalsozialistische Herrschaft* (1993); as coeditor with Brigitte Oleschinski, *Das Torgau-Tabu: Wehrstrafsystem: NKWD-Speziallager: DDR-Strafvollzug* (1993).

HERLEMANN, BEATRIX. Born 1942; studied history and art history in Berlin, Constance, and Bochum; received her M.A. in 1972 and Dr. Phil. in 1976; historian. Publications: *Auf verlorenem Posten: Kommunistischer Widerstand im 2. Weltkrieg: Die Knöchel-Organisation* (1986); *Der Bauer klebt am Hergebrachten: Bäuerliche Verhaltensweisen unterm Nationalsozialismus auf dem Gebiet des heutigen Landes Niedersachsen* (1993).

HOFFMANN, VOLKER. Born in 1943; studied in Berlin and in Michigan to become a teacher; holds an M.A. and a Dr. Phil.; teacher and academic assistant at the former Pedagogic College of Berlin; lecturer at College of Arts since 1976. Publications include: *Die Rütlischule: Entwicklung und Auflösung eines staatlichen Schulversuchs im proletarischen Milieu.*

HUMMEL, KARL-JOSEPH. Born in 1950; holds a Dr. Phil.; director of the Research Office of the Commission for Modern History in Bonn. Publications include: *München in der Revolution von 1848/49* (1987).

KWIET, KONRAD. Born in 1941; studied history and political science at the Free University of Berlin and in Amsterdam; received his Dr. Phil. in 1967; *Habilitation* in 1973; professor at Macquarie University in Sydney. Publications include: together with Helmut Schwege, *Selbstbehauptung und Widerstand: Deutsche Juden im Kampf um Existenz und Menschenwürde 1933–1945* (1986); as editor, *From Emancipation to the Holocaust: Essays on Jewish History and Literature in Central Europe* (1987).

MAYR, MONIKA. Born in 1966; received an M.A. in library science in 1988; expert in the archives of the Institute of Modern History in Munich.

MEHRINGER, HARTMUT. Born in 1944; studied eastern European history, modern history, and political science in Erlangen, Paris, and Amsterdam; received his Dr. Phil. in 1977; *Habilitation* in 1987; academic assistant at the Institute of Modern History in Munich. Publications include: *Waldemar von Knoeringen: Eine politische Biographie* (1989).

MOMMSEN, HANS. Born in 1930; studied history, German studies, philosophy, and political science in Marburg and Tübingen; received his Dr. Phil. in 1959; *Habilitation* in 1967; has been professor of modern history at the Ruhr University in Bochum since 1968; has held guest professorships in the United States and Israel; fellow of the Institute for Advanced Study in Princeton, N.J., and of the Academic College of

Berlin; corresponding member of the British Academy. Publications include: *Beamtentum im Dritten Reich* (1966); *Die verspielte Freiheit: Der Weg der Republik von Weimar in den Untergang 1918–1933* (1989); *Der Nationalsozialismus und die deutsche Gesellschaft; From Weimar to Auschwitz* (1991).

MÜHLEN, PATRIK VON ZUR. Born in 1942; studied history, political science, and philosophy in Berlin and Bonn; received his M.A. in 1967 and Dr. Phil. in 1971; historian; academic adviser for Friedrich Ebert Foundation in Bonn. Publications include: *Spanien war ihre Hoffnung: Die deutsche Linke im Spanischen Bürgerkrieg 1936–1939* (1985); *Fluchtziel Lateinamerika: Die deutsche Emigration 1933–1945: Politische Aktivitäten und soziokulturelle Integration* (1988); *Fluchtweg Spanien-Portugal: Die deutsche Emigration und der Exodus aus Europa 1933–1945* (1992).

NEISS, MARION. Born in 1953; studied history and Jewish studies in Berlin and Tel Aviv; received her M.A. in 1992; historian; assistant at the Center for the Study of Anti-Semitism at the Technical University of Berlin.

NICOLAISEN, CARSTEN. Born in 1934; studied Protestant theology and German studies in Göttingen and Hamburg; received his D.D. in 1966; academic director in Munich. Publications include: as editor, *Dokumente zur Kirchenpolitik des Dritten Reiches* (1971ff.); *Der Weg nach Barmen* (1985); as editor, *Verantwortung für die Kirche* (1985ff.).

NORDEN, GÜNTHER VAN. Born in 1928; studied history, German studies, and philosophy in Cologne; received his Dr. Phil. in 1955; professor at the University of Wuppertal. Publications include: as editor, *Zwischen Bekenntnis und Anpassung* (1985); as coeditor with B. Klappert, *"Tut um Gottes willen etwas Tapferes!" Karl Immer im Kirchenkampf* (1989); as coeditor with V. Wittmütz, *Evangelische Kirche im 2. Weltkrieg* (1991).

OVERESCH, MANFRED. Born in 1939; studied history, Greek, and philosophy in Münster, Tübingen, and Vienna; received his Dr. Phil. in 1973; *Habilitation* in 1978; professor of history at the University of Hildesheim. Publications include: *Chronik deutscher Zeitgeschichte: Politik, Wissenschaft, Kultur* (5 vols., 1992ff.); *Hermann Brill in Thüringen 1895–1946: Ein Kämpfer gegen Hitler und Ulbricht* (1992); *Machtergreifung von links: Thüringen 1945/46* (1993).

PAUL, GERHARD. Born in 1951; holds a Dr. Phil.; political scientist; professor of history and the teaching of history at the Pedagogic College of Flensburg. Publications include: *"Deutsche Mutter — heim zu Dir!" Warum es mißlang, Hitler an der Saar zu schlagen: Der Saarkampf*

1933–1935 (1984); *Aufstand der Bilder: Die NS-Propaganda vor 1933* (1990); together with K. M. Mallmann, *Herrschaft und Alltag: Ein Industrierevier im Dritten Reich* (1991).

RÜTHER-ZIMMERMANN, DANIELA. Born in 1963; studied history, German studies, and political science in Bochum; received her M.A. in 1989; currently a doctoral candidate under Hans Mommsen.

SASSIN, HORST R. Born in 1953; studied history, German studies, philosophy, and pedagogy in Cologne; has been a teacher in a gymnasium (secondary school that prepares students for university) since 1981; received his Dr. Phil. in 1991. Publications include: as coeditor, *Ausstellung "Widerstand, Verfolgung und Emigration Liberaler 1933–1945" mit Katalog; Dokumente zur Geschichte des Liberalismus in Deutschland 1930–1945* (1989); *Liberale im Widerstand: Die Robinsohn-Strassmann-Gruppe 1934–1942* (1993) (awarded the Wolf Erich Kellner Prize in 1991 and the Carl von Ossietzky Prize in 1992).

SCHIEB-SAMIZADEH, BARBARA. Born in 1958; studied history and German studies in Freiburg im Breisgau and Berlin; passed civil service examination in 1986; historian. Publications: "Die Gemeinschaft für Frieden und Aufbau" and afterword in Eugen Herman-Friede, *Für Freudensprünge keine Zeit* (1991).

SCHILDE, KURT. Born in 1947; studied economics and social science; historian; doctoral candidate. Publications include: *Jugendorganisationen und Jugendopposition in Berlin-Kreuzberg 1933–1936: Eine Dokumentation* (1983); together with Johannes Tuchel, *Columbia-Haus: Berliner Konzentrationslager 1933–1945* (1990); as editor, *Eva-Maria Buch und die "Rote Kapelle": Erinnerungen an den Widerstand gegen den Nationalsozialismus* (1992).

SCHMID, HANS-DIETER. Born in 1941; studied history, political science, and English in Tübingen; holds a Dr. Phil.; historian and didactician of history; sits on the academic council at the Historical Institute of the University of Hannover. Publications include: together with G. Schneider and W. Sommer, *Juden unterm Hakenkreuz*, 2 vols. (1983); copublisher of the *Hannoverian Journals of Regional and Local History* (6 vols. published thus far).

SCHNEIDER, MICHAEL. Born in 1944; holds a Dr. Phil.; *Habilitation* in 1982; academic assistant at the Research Institute of the Friedrich Ebert Foundation in Bonn and teacher at the Institute for Political Science at the University of Bonn. Publications include: *Demokratie in Gefahr? Der Konflikt um die Notstandsgesetze: Sozialdemokratie, Gewerkschaften und intellektueller Protest 1958–1968* (1986); *Kleine*

Geschichte der Gewerkschaften: Ihre Entwicklung in Deutschland von den Anfängen bis heute (1989; translated into English and Chinese).

SELIG, WOLFRAM. Born in 1936; studied history, French, and philosophy in Tübingen, Munich, and Besançon; received her Dr. Phil. in 1965; chronicler of the city of Munich. Publications: as editor, *Richard Seligmann: Ein jüdisches Schicksal* (1983); *Synagogen und jüdische Friedhöfe in München* (1988).

UEBERSCHÄR, GERD R. Born in 1943; studied history, political science, and geography in Frankfurt am Main; passed state civil service exam in 1972; received his Dr. Phil. in 1976; historian at the Research Department of Military History in Freiburg im Breisgau; teacher at the University of Freiburg im Breisgau. Publications include: *Generaloberst Franz Halder* (1991); as coeditor, *Der deutsche Überfall auf die Sowjetunion: "Unternehmen Barbarossa" 1941* (1991); as coeditor, *Stalingrad: Mythos und Wirklichkeit einer Schlacht* (1992).

WEISS, HERMANN. Born in 1932; studied history, German, and English studies in Munich and Tübingen; archivist in the Institute of Modern History in Munich. Publication: as coeditor with Paul Hoser, *Die Deutschnationalen und die Zerstörung der Weimarer Republik: Aus dem Tagebuch von Reinhold Quaatz 1928–1933* (1989).

WETZEL, JULIANE. Born in 1957; studied history and art history in Munich; received her Dr. Phil. in 1987; historian at the Center for the Study of Anti-Semitism at the Technical University of Berlin. Publication: together with Angelika Königseder, *Lebensmut im Wartesaal: Die jüdischen DPs im Nachkriegsdeutschlcnd* (1994).

WICKERT, CHRISTL. Born in 1953; studied history, German studies and political science in Trier and Göttingen; holds a Dr. Disc. Pol.; historian in Berlin. Publications: *Unsere Gewählten: Sozialdemokratische Frauen im Reichstag und im Preußischen Landtag 1919–1933* (1986); *Helene Stöcker: Frauenrechtlerin, Sozialreformerin und Pazifistin: Eine Biographie* (1991).

ZARUSKY, JÜRGEN. Born in 1958; holds a Dr. Phil.; academic assistant at the Institute of Modern History in Munich. Publications: *Die deutschen Sozialdemokraten und das sowjetische Modell: Ideologische Auseinandersetzungen und außenpolitische Konzeptionen 1917–1933* (1992); " '...nur eine Wachstumskrankheit?' Jugendwiderstand in Hamburg und München," *Dachauer Hefte* 7 (1991).